The British Aircraft Industry and American-led Globalisation

Sakade challenges the narrative that the focus of British manufacturing went "from Empire to Europe" and argues rather that, following the Second World War, the key relationship was in fact transatlantic.

There is a commonly accepted belief that, during the twentieth century, British manufacturing declined irreparably, that Britain lost its industrial hegemony. But this is too simplistic. In fact, in the decades after 1945, Britain staked out a new role for itself as a key participant in a US-led process of globalisation. Far from becoming merely a European player, Britain actually managed to preserve a key share in a global market, and the British defence industry was, to a large extent, successfully rehabilitated. Sakade returns to the original scholarly parameters of the decline controversy, and especially questions around post-war decline in the fields of high technology and the national defence industrial base. Using the case of the strategically critical military and civil aircraft industry, he argues that British industry remained relatively robust.

This book is a valuable read for historians of British aviation and more widely of twentieth-century British industry.

Takeshi Sakade is Associate Professor in the Graduate School of Economics at Kyoto University, Japan.

Routledge Studies in Modern British History

The Casino and Society in Britain
Seamus Murphy

Great Britain, the Dominions and the Transformation of the British Empire, 1907–1931
The Road to the Statute of Westminster
Jaroslav Valkoun

The Discourse of Repatriation in Britain, 1845–2016
A Political and Social History
Daniel Renshaw

The Devil and the Victorians
Supernatural Evil in Nineteenth-Century English Culture
Sarah Bartels

Lord Dufferin, Ireland and the British Empire, c. 1820–1900
Rule by the Best?
Annie Tindley

Provincial Police Reform in Early Victorian England
Cambridge, 1835–1856
Roger Swift

Diplomatic Identity in Postwar Britain
The Deconstruction of the Foreign Office "Type", 1945–1997
James Southern

The Development of British Naval Aviation, 1914–1918
Alexander Howlett

Britain and the Puzzle of European Union
Andrew Duff

The British Aircraft Industry and American-led Globalisation
1943–1982
Takeshi Sakade

For more information about this series, please visit: https://www.routledge.com/history/series/RSMBH.

The British Aircraft Industry and American-led Globalisation
1943–1982

Takeshi Sakade

LONDON AND NEW YORK

First published 2022
by Routledge
2 Park Square, Milton Park, Abingdon, Oxon OX14 4RN

and by Routledge
605 Third Avenue, New York, NY 10158

Routledge is an imprint of the Taylor & Francis Group, an Informa business

© 2022 Takeshi Sakade

The right of Takeshi Sakade to be identified as author of this work has been asserted in accordance with sections 77 and 78 of the Copyright, Designs and Patents Act 1988.

All rights reserved. No part of this book may be reprinted or reproduced or utilised in any form or by any electronic, mechanical, or other means, now known or hereafter invented, including photocopying and recording, or in any information storage or retrieval system, without permission in writing from the publishers.

Trademark notice: Product or corporate names may be trademarks or registered trademarks and are used only for identification and explanation without intent to infringe.

British Library Cataloguing in Publication Data
A catalogue record for this book is available from the British Library

Library of Congress Cataloging-in-Publication Data
Names: Sakade, Takeshi, author.
Title: The British aircraft industry and American-led globalisation : 1943-1982 / Takeshi Sakade.
Description: Abingdon, Oxon ; New York, NY : Routledge, 2022. | Series: Routledge studies in modern British history | Includes bibliographical references and index.
Identifiers: LCCN 2021032272 (print) | LCCN 2021032273 (ebook) | ISBN 9780367651206 (hardback) | ISBN 9780367651213 (paperback) | ISBN 9781003127901 (ebook)
Subjects: LCSH: Aircraft industry–Great Britain–History–20th century. | Industrial policy–Great Britain–History–20th century. | United States–Foreign economic relations. | Great Britain–Foreign economic relations.
Classification: LCC HD9711.G72 S25 2022 (print) | LCC HD9711.G72 (ebook) | DDC 338.4/7629133340941–dc23
LC record available at https://lccn.loc.gov/2021032272
LC ebook record available at https://lccn.loc.gov/2021032273

ISBN: 9780367651206 (hbk)
ISBN: 9780367651213 (pbk)
ISBN: 9781003127901 (ebk)

DOI: 10.4324/9781003127901

Typeset in Galliard
by Taylor & Francis Books

For Professor Akio Sakai

Contents

List of illustrations	xii
List of abbreviations	xiii
Foreword	xv
Preface	xx
Britain's "new role" between Europe and the United States after 1945	xxiii

PART I
The post-war British aircraft industry, 1943–1964 — 1

1 The origins of Anglo–American production collaboration in the first jet-age, 1943–1956 — 3

Introduction 3
The Arnold-Towers-Slessor agreement of 22nd June 1942 4
The Brabazon programme 5
British and American transport aircraft compared 6
The "Fly British" policy (1945–1950) 7
Plan K aid and the US OSP 9
The success of Comet and Viscount jet airliners 10
The tragedy of Comet and choice of technologies 11
Cancellation of V-1000 pure jet transport and Pan Am order for 707 and DC-8 12
US congressional reactions to British success 13
The rush to jet engines 15
The end of the OSP 16
The BOAC purchase of 707-420 with Rolls-Royce Conway 17
Conclusion 19

viii *Contents*

2 Sandys White Paper and the rationalisation of the British aircraft
   industry, 1957–1960   23

   Introduction 23
   *The Sandys White Paper and the crisis of the British aircraft
      industry 24*
   A problem with the BEA new medium-range jet order 26
   The TSR-2 (OR339) contract 27
   Approval of the report by the Aircraft Industry Working Party 28
   Crisis in the civil sector 29
   Vickers' possible retreat from the civil air business problem 31
   Sandys and the reorganisation of the British aircraft industry 31
   "No More Boeings" 33
   Conclusion 36

3 BOAC's financial crisis and the end of the "Fly British" policy,
   1963–1966   39

   Introduction 39
   British-American battles over the North Atlantic route 40
   BOAC's financial problems 42
   Guthrie vs Amery 44
   The cancellation of the remaining ten Super VC10s 47
   Waking up from the "neo-Edwardian dream"? 49
   Conclusion 51

PART II
The British dilemma, 1964–1969   55

4 The cancellation of Britain's top projects, 1963–1965   57

   Introduction 57
   The TSR-2 as a nuclear umbrella East of Suez 58
   The American balance of payments 60
   The Hitch–McKean analysis of the NATO defence economy 62
   The European collaboration argument 63
   The Zuckerman system 65
   Commonwealth turf wars, Part I: India 66
   Commonwealth turf wars, Part II: Australia 67
   "White heat" 68
   The Chequers meeting in November 1964 69
   TSR-3? The Washington summit in December 1964 71

Contents ix

The US–UK Co-operative Logistic Agreement 72
London between Paris and Washington 74
Time runs out for the TSR-2 76
British domestic adjustments leading to the cancellation
  of TSR-2 78
Wilson meets de Gaulle 79
Conclusion 80

5 The politics behind the Plowden doctrine: European and American
   alternatives for the British aircraft industry   86

Introduction 86
The Plowden Committee's visit to Paris, April 1965 87
The Anglo–American co-development of a V/STOL engine 89
Discussions between the Plowden Committee and the US Department
  of Defense, May 1965 90
The Anglo–French defence package of 17th May 1965 92
Paris or Washington? 94
The position of British industry 95
The German factor in American–European collaboration 97
The Spey–Mirage affair 98
Agreement on developing the US–UK joint V/STOL engine 100
The Saudi Arabian aircraft deal 102
The "corner-stone" of British defence policy? 104
Britain seals the F-111 deal 105
Conclusion 107

6 The "European Technological Community" and the Anglo–German
   MRCA project, 1966–1969   113

Introduction 113
"Perfidious Albion" and the Atlantic alliance in the 1960s 114
"White Heat" vs financial and diplomatic realities 115
The NATO crisis of 1966 117
Anglo–French discussions on the crisis of the AFVG project 119
A possible German purchase of the Jaguar and the AFVG 121
Cancellation of the AFVG 122
Anglo–German offsetting and the MRCA 123
The Roberts Report of July 1967 124
Wilson's "European Technological Community" 128
Retreat from East of Suez and cancellation of F-111 129
Conclusion 129

x *Contents*

PART III

European co-operative airliner projects and Anglo–American industrial collaboration, 1968–1982   135

7 The second jet age and the bankruptcy of Rolls-Royce, 1967–1971   137

Introduction 137
Wide-body airliners 138
Anglo–French negotiations over the Airbus engine 139
The Lockheed/Rolls-Royce deal 143
The project definition stage of the European Airbus 146
The Airbus shrinks 147
British withdrawal from the European Airbus 148
The TriStar's European failure 150
The Anglo–German offset fund proposal 151
Rolls-Royce's first liquidity crisis in October 1970 153
A £60 million relief package 156
*Rolls-Royce between Cooper Brothers investigation and second
  liquidity crisis 157*
The Lockheed/Rolls-Royce showdown 159
The British government reinvestigates the RB211 161
Guaranteed problems 165
Hurdles in Washington 166
Conclusion 168

8 Trapped in a loveless marriage: The Anglo–French Concorde crisis
   of 1974   176

Introduction 176
The 1962 Treaty 177
The international politics of SST 179
The Benn/Chamant correspondence of 27th September 1968 183
Concorde, A300B/BAC3-11 and the MRCA 185
Continuing Concorde 187
The build up to the 1974 crisis 190
The French say "oui" 193
Conclusion 195

9 Playing a double game: The British aircraft industry in the third
   jet age   200

Introduction 200
Britain between Boeing and Airbus 201

Boeing's dual programme 201
The British response to the Boeing 757 offer 202
Callaghan in Washington 205
BA places its order 209
Conclusion 212

Conclusion   215

Appendix I: Types of jet aircrafts from the 1950s to the 1970s   219
Appendix II: UK balance of payments, 1946–1970   221
Bibliography   223
Index   232

Illustrations

Figures

I.1	The world's first jet services Comet 1 routes, 1953	xxviii
I.2	Pan American Airways jet network, October 1960 (two years after first service)	xxviii
4.1	Learning curve	62
4.2	Geographical coverage of the F-111	77

Tables

1.1	Comparison of US and UK airliners	7
1.2	Orders of Boeing 707s	18
3.1	BOAC's record of financial results (£ millions)	40
3.2	BOAC vs Pan Am on the North Atlantic route jet services	41
3.3	Operating results of BOAC and Pan Am (£ millions)	41
3.4	VC10 order	43
3.5	Various BOAC fleet plans	47
7.1	Comparison of wide-body (two-aisle) airliners and engines for airliners	141
AI.1	Types of jet aircrafts from the 1950s to the 1970s	219
AII.1	UK balance of payments, 1946–1970	221

List of abbreviations

ADO12	Advanced Development Objective No. 12
AFVG	Anglo–French Variable Geometry
ATLAS	Air France, Lufthansa, Alitalia and Sabena
ATMR	advanced technology medium range
AW	*Aviation Week*
AWST	*Aviation Week & Space Technology*
BA	British Airways
BAC	British Aircraft Corporation
BAe	British Aerospace
BAOR	British Army of the Rhine
BEA	British European Airways Corporation
BOAC	British Overseas Airways Corporation
BSE	Bristol Siddeley Engines
CAB	Cabinet
CC	Cabinet Conclusions
CLASB	Citizens' League Against the Sonic Boom
CM	Cabinet Minute
Cmd., Cmnd.	Command paper
CP	Cabinet Paper
CPRS	Central Policy Review Staff
DDR&E	Director of Defense Research and Engineering
EC	European Communities
EEC	European Economic Community
EU	European Union
FAA	Federal Aviation Administration
FCO	Foreign and Commonwealth Office
FRUS	*Foreign Relations of the United States*
GE	General Electric
GEN130	Ministerial Group of Aircraft Policy
HC Deb.	House of Commons Debates
HSA	Hawker Siddeley Aviation
ILN	International Logistics Negotiations
IPE	international political economy

xiv *List of abbreviations*

KUSS	KLM, UTA, Swissair and SAS
McDD	McDonnell-Douglas
MLF	Multilateral Force (NATO)
MoU	Memorandum of Understanding
MP	Member of Parliament
MRCA	Multi Role Combat Aircraft (Tornado)
MSA	Mutual Security Agency (London)
NARA	National Archives and Records Administration, College Park
NATO	North Atlantic Treaty Organization
NSAM	National Security Action Memorandum
OPD	Defence and Overseas Policy Committee
OSP	Offshore Procurement Program
P&W	Pratt & Whitney
Pan Am	Pan American World Airways
PREM	Prime Minister's Office File
R&D	research and development
RAAF	Royal Australian Air Force
RAF	Royal Air Force
RG	Record Group
SACEUR	Supreme Allied Commander Europe, NATO
SST	supersonic transport
TCA	Trans-Canada Air Lines
TNA	The National Archives, Kew, London
TSR-2	Tactical, Strike and Reconnaissance aircraft-2
TWA	Trans World Airlines
UK	United Kingdom
US	United States
USAF	United States Air Force
USOM	United States Mutual Security Agency
VG	Variable Geometry
V/STOL	Vertical & Short Take Off
VTOL	Vertical Take Off and Landing

Foreword

"Take back control!" – this was the battle cry of the Brexiteers in their ultimately successful campaign to end Britain's membership of the European Union (EU). Their objective was to regain the (largely illusionary) autonomy and capacity for self-determination which had supposedly been lost upon Britain's entry to the European Communities (EC) in 1972. Nonetheless, Brexit's more reasonable proponents were not blind to the fact that such a momentous step would massively disrupt the United Kingdom's (UK's) trade and investment relationships with its most important economic partners. Indeed, the consequences of Brexit threaten many sectors of the British economy, but they present a particular danger to those areas that most depend on international connections. These include the British aviation industry. New regulatory regimes, travel restrictions compounded by the impact of COVID-19, and the uncertain availability of vital parts for manufacturing are among the many challenges that British aviation will have to navigate in a post-Brexit environment.

Even before the referendum, many of the problematic repercussions of Brexit for the British economy and those branches exposed to international competition were abundantly apparent. Despite this, proponents of the Leave movement believed that readily available alternatives would compensate for the resulting losses. In particular, hopes were placed on relations with the United States. Despite the "America First" attitude of the Trump administration, many Brexit campaigners invoked a largely mythical past in which Britain had joined the United States in a "special relationship" that elevated the island nation to America's most important partner in managing global affairs. Such reminiscences harked back to the supposed golden era of the Cold War, during which the United Kingdom had skilfully managed and juggled the "three circles" of its core alliances – the United States, Europe and the Commonwealth.

But this narrative conveniently skipped over the decades after 1945, in which Britain seemed to be on the path towards irreversible decline. In the 1950s and 1960s, Europe re-emerged as an economic superpower, boasting growth rates that the United Kingdom seemed incapable of matching. Indeed, Britain had ignominiously left the negotiations for a European Economic Community at the 1956 Messina Conference which jump-started European integration. At the same time, the remnants of the British Empire were disintegrating. The Suez crisis of

xvi *Foreword*

1956 shattered the belief in a supposedly natural community of interest with the Americans, while the so-called withdrawal from "East of Suez" in 1968 effectively ended Britain's pretensions to a major role in Asia. British disillusionment was to be reconfirmed numerous times over the next decades, as the United States struggled with the effects of the Vietnam War, the costs of the Cold War and successive economic crises. The UK's comparatively sluggish economy and the persistent troubles of its currency, the pound, underlined the apparent fact that something was fundamentally wrong with the erstwhile superpower.

The three British applications for membership of the EC during the 1960s were a consequence of this feeling. These applications were twice humiliatingly rejected by the French president Charles de Gaulle. To be sure, Britain was finally admitted to the EC in 1973. And yet large parts of its political establishment, its media, and its population could never shake the feeling that membership of the EU was just an unwelcome stop-gap measure, born out of temporary desperation. Britain thus continued to sit uneasily between its many chairs, until a razor-thin majority decided that the way into the future was to go back to the past. However, once some of the harsher realities of isolation have become clear, and when the dust of Brexit and the exceptional situation created by COVID-19 have settled, it seems fair to expect that the UK's search for a role will continue.

This rather grim reading of post-war British history from the 1950s to the 1970s has given rise to a large literature by journalists and academics which purports to deal with the many facets of Britain's apparent "decline". A significant impact was made by titles such as Correlli Barnett's *The Audit of War: The Illusion & Reality of Britain as a Great Nation* (Macmillan, 1986). Margaret Thatcher's conservative revolution and Tony Blair's Third Way took their cue from this declinist narrative, with both leaders vowing that their policies would reverse the dismal trajectory of post-war Britain. Scholars such as David Edgerton,[1] however, have argued against these determinist histories of British decline, claiming that such a broad sweep obscures the many sectors in which Britain's society and economy were indeed modernising and remained competitive.

Professor Takeshi Sakade's detailed study of the British aircraft industry after 1945 speaks to this broader discussion. The study is based on a largely unexplored wealth of primary documents from British and American archives. Professor Sakade traces in detail the development of the civil and military sectors of the British aerospace sector. He shows how successive British governments tried to negotiate the survival and continued competitiveness of British aviation in an era which was characterised by rapid technological innovation and overwhelming American economic superiority.

After the Second World War, Britain boasted a large aircraft industry with about 70 manufacturers whose survival depended on both access to and success on global markets. However, many of these firms soon struggled to achieve sufficient sales, and the crumbling Commonwealth deprived the British aircraft industry of the one market to which it still had preferential access. In addition, advanced British developments such as De Havilland Comet, the world's first jet-airliner, suffered from construction problems. This led to a series of accidents which detrimentally impacted the reputation of the British aviation industry dearly. When these technological problems were solved, Britain had lost its advantage on the commercial airliner market to American giants, such as Boeing and McDonnell-Douglas. Promising new aircraft developments struggled to generate sufficient orders to be commercially viable.[2] Attempts were made to convince Britain's national airline, the state-owned British Overseas Airways Corporation, to exclusively "buy British" – but this failed. Numerous programme cancellations sapped the energy of the British aircraft sector. For many regions that depended on the jobs provided by British aircraft manufacturers, the resulting cuts only exacerbated an already dire economic situation.

The famous 1957 defence White Paper[3] issued by the government of Harold Macmillan constituted a reaction to these travails. The Conservative government and its defence minister Duncan Sandys attempted to force both the civilian and military branches of the aircraft industry to merge into larger, more profitable conglomerates. Over time, only two principal manufacturers emerged: British Aircraft Corporation and Hawker Siddeley Aviation. Moreover, the Sandys White Paper argued that the previous focus on military aircraft should make way for an emphasis on rocket technology. And yet, despite these efforts at reform, Britain was forced to abandon other headline projects in the years to follow. These included the TSR-2[4] fighter, an advanced strike and reconnaissance aircraft. Only one prototype of this model ever took to the air. The rather depressing overall picture was captured in a quote by Solly Zuckerman, one of the protagonists of this book and a core scientific adviser of Her Majesty's government at that time. After surveying the TSR-2 situation, he allegedly quipped that: "There is more technology in the little finger of one Professor from MIT than in the whole of British Industry".[5]

The TSR-2 disaster set in motion a pattern that characterised British policy in this area. The UK was now faced with the choice of aligning itself as junior partner with the Americans or trying its luck with the emerging European alternatives. Developments such as Concorde, Airbus or the MRCA Tornado posed a clear challenge to American dominance. Concorde was never profitable, but it stood out as a symbol of European technological progress. Airbus, meanwhile, developed into a formidable competitor to the American giants – although Britain, typically, left the Airbus Consortium early.

Sakade's book vividly illustrates persistent American attempts to undermine competition from across the Atlantic. US officials played the different challengers against each other, often skilfully. In 1964, London set up the Plowden committee to consider the future of the British aircraft industry. The resulting report recommended that the government embrace co-operation with both Europe and the United States. In fact, this was the line that London had been pursuing for some time. And, thus, it continued to "ride two horses" by participating in the American-led globalisation of the aircraft industry, while at the same time selectively joining common projects with the Europeans. Some of these were highly successful, such as Airbus after British re-entry in 1979, the Panavia Tornado or the French–British Jaguar fighter ventures.

xviii *Foreword*

Sakade's book traces this tortured and complicated history. It closely follows the debates in the British government and the intense discussions of government officials with their foreign counterparts and representatives of British industry. Sakade demonstrates how the British navigated a multitude of diverse problems and dilemmas and how they carved out niches for themselves which allowed some firms to thrive. A notable example is Rolls-Royce. After it merged with Bristol Siddeley in 1966, Rolls managed to capture a substantial part of the global market for aircraft engines.

This study therefore demonstrates that history rarely conforms to the dichotomous black-and-white image painted by journalists and historians, with their (often quite obvious) political agendas. Instead, it is necessary to plunge into the gritty detail of administrative battles, commercial ups and downs, and technological advances and dead-ends to understand how countries navigate the future of their industries and their economic sectors. There are many paths between, on the one hand, a strictly nationalist focus on supposed self-sufficiency and the superiority of all things British and, on the other hand, an all-out adaptation to the forces of economic globalization. The correct way ahead is often unclear. British politicians in the post-war period had to navigate these contradicting impulses and, in order to understand their choices, we must carefully examine the diplomatic records. This is precisely what Professor Sakade has done in this book.

Such an in-depth look inoculates observers against quick and easy judgments on the decisions of policymakers who are faced with huge uncertainty and often unpalatable alternatives. It also holds important lessons for current politics. Feasible policies rarely result from clinging to exclusive ideologies, be it the propaganda of British exceptionalism, the whole-hearted embrace of a purely market-driven economic policy, or the vision of a pan-European community of interests which should trump all other considerations. In fact, the best results frequently seem to be yielded by muddling through with an open mind towards a wide array of political alternatives that lead to acceptable outcomes.

With respect to its aviation industry, British policymakers had to learn this lesson the hard way. A glance at current British politics and a mediascape dominated by blaring headlines and populist blustering suggests that many of these lessons will soon have to be re-learned. After all, challenges such as the rise of China and the environmental impact of the aviation sector are as grave as anything that confronted the historical actors that are the subject of this book.

Hubert Zimmermann
Philipps-University, Marburg
11 May 2021

Notes

1 See, for example, his recent *The Rise and Fall of the British Nation: A Twentieth Century History* (London, Allen Lane, 2018).

2 Devereux, D.R. (2021), 'Jets across the Atlantic?: Britain and its civil aviation industry, 1945–63', *Journal of Transatlantic Studies*, 19, pp. 99–113.
3 Ministry of Defence, *Defence: Outline of Future Policy*, Cmnd. 124 (London, HMSO, 1957) (Sandys White Paper).
4 Tactical, Strike and Reconnaissance aircraft-2.
5 Wood, D., *Project Cancelled. The Disaster of Britain's Abandoned Aircraft Projects*, 2nd ed. (HIS Global Inc., 1987), p. 185.

Preface

This is a military history. In this story, a former hegemon does battle with an emerging hegemon behind the scenes of an apparently close alliance called the "special relationship". The primary focus lies on the crucial defence-industrial sector, and specifically, on aircraft manufacturing. In the end, as everyone knows, it cannot be said that Britain won the battle. But maybe it did, in the end, emerge with something profitable to show for its long and exhausting rear-guard action. Perhaps the gains and experiences obtained by Britain during this struggle have sowed the seeds for certain post-Brexit advantages. But that is another story that goes beyond the period examined in this book.

Why is a Japanese researcher interested in Anglo–American aerospace entanglements? The answer to this question lies in my personal experiences as a teenager. One of my earlies political memories is of the Lockheed bribery scandals of 1976. Kakuei Tanaka, who served as Prime Minister of Japan between 1972 and 1974, was arrested on suspicion of receiving bribes in order to influence a Japanese purchase of the Lockheed TriStar/Rolls-Royce RB211. When I was collecting British government documents in Kew for this book, I came across a most compelling conversation between Prime Minister Edward Heath and Tanaka. Heath pushed for a Japanese purchase of the TriStar by saying that; "the Japanese would be able to drink Scotch whisky as cheaply as Bourbon".[6] Of course, by Whiskey he meant the TriStar: the inferior Bourbon was the McDonnell Douglas DC-10. Then and now, I was impressed that the highest power in Japan was seemingly under the sway of a collaborative union between an American airframe maker and a British aeroengine maker, which also enjoyed the support of senior British and American politicians. I remain fascinated by these shadowy post-war entanglements.

A second key development, from my point of view, was the 1980 US–Japan FS-X fighter crisis. This was a crisis of US–Japanese technology. Japan had high hopes for an independent national project, and yet it was pressed to procure an American co-developed fighter (later named the F2). Japanese journalists fearfully remarked that, if Japan chose to go it alone, then Tokyo was in danger of treading on a tiger's tail. Even as a young man, I sensed that fighter development and production are more than merely military endeavours; they are key aspects of national pride.

Preface xxi

As a graduate, researching British aerospace, I learned that Britain had a not-dissimilar experience to the FS-X. This came in 1965 with the cancellation of the TSR-2. Indeed, the TSR-2's cancellation became the topic of my MA thesis, as well as the focus of Chapter 4 of this book. My sense that fighter production touches deeply on matters of national pride was further reinforced during the writing of this book when my copy-editor, a young British historian called Alex Burkhardt, told me a story from his own youth. Alex grew up near Preston, where his friend's brother worked for British aerospace, at the very same plant where the TSR-2 was to be built before its cancellation by a Labour government under Harold Wilson. After the axe fell, Alex's friend's father – a staunch Labour supporter – never voted for the party again. This story confirmed what I already suspected – that such developments can transcend economic interests and reshape political identities. The FS-X crisis also showed this – it was a matter of national pride. Indeed, it was a matter of community pride for the people of Nagoya, and especially for those working at the Mitsubishi Heavy Industry plant in Meiko. This same plant had developed and produced the Zero-fighter, which had fought American pilots over the Pacific during the Second World War. These are complicated histories indeed.

But what did Britain get, *quid pro quo*, for the cancellation of the TSR-2? Here we have a clue to the vitality of British manufacturing in the 1970s. Many Japanese saw – and continue to see – this period in British history as one of decline and destitution, of "the British disease". According to this reading, only with Thatcher's accession to power in 1979 was the ailing hegemon resuscitated. My book, however, tells a different story of these apparently dark decades, a story of resilience, diplomatic guile and, ultimately, of success. Perhaps the contemporary Japanese aerospace industry, reeling from the commercial failure of the MRJ airliner and anticipating the development of the F3 fighter, could learn a thing or two from the tough British aircraft industry of the post-war period.

The list of people I need to thank for their help with this book is very extensive. Hubert Zimmermann made trenchant comments on the whole draft. Alex Burkhardt's copy-editing made my manuscript readable and sophisticated. Without these two collaborators and critics, I could not have completed this project. David Edgerton made some crucial suggestions on modern British history. By translating his excellent book *Warfare State: Britain, 1920–1970* into Japanese, I received my introduction to the British "decline" controversy. Nobuki Kawasaki was one of the most pointed critics of my research – and its most irreplaceable supporter. Takeyasu Fujiki and Kenichi Shinohara's reviews of the Japanese version of this book were guiding lights for the English version. The encouraging recommendation to publish the book in English came from Tian-Kang Go. Asli M. Colpan's reading of Chapter 7 enabled me to include a hugely enriching business history angle. Junko Nishikawa and colleagues at the American Economic History Association of Japan offered me a frank and challenging venue for a presentation of the book's findings. Nobuo Take, the late Yoshiharu Ozaki, Hisashi Watanabe and Sachio Imakubo have always watched over and supported my progress. Lastly, my family (Yoko, Tsuna and Shin) and my mother Kiyoko have been the indispensable supporters of my study.

xxii *Preface*

My deep thanks also go to librarians at the Faculty of Economics, Faculty of Law, and Faculty of Letters at Kyoto University. I am also grateful to those professors who have been cultivating collections of books in these libraries. Archivists at the National Archives, Kew, the National Archives, College Park and Churchill College Archives Centre were most helpful for a foreign researcher with little experience in European archives.

This book was supported by Kyoto University funds and JSPS (Japan Society for the Promotion of Science) funds. The John Mung Program of Kyoto University provided me an opportunity to conduct one year of research in London. The JSPS Grant-in-Aid for Young Scientists (B) (18730231: 2006–2007), Grant-in-Aid for Scientific Research (C) (23530316: 2011–2013) (17K03835:2017–2019) and Kyoto University Research Development Program Ishizue (2016) provided the infrastructure for my research. KURA (Kyoto University Research Administration Office) including Yu Sasaki always helped me to obtain these funds.

I would like to dedicate this book to Professor Akio Sakai, who taught me everything I know about international political economy (IPE) and encouraged my study on military economics, which is a minor area in Japan. He once commented to me that budgetary and financial factors explain over 80 per cent of IPE. By concentrating on industrial factors, I suppose I ended up focusing on the remaining 20 per cent. Nonetheless, I hope my work on the British aircraft industry after the Second World War can contribute to an understanding not only of this historical era, but also to the combination of budgetary, financial and industrial dimensions that comprise the heart of IPE.

Takeshi Sakade
Yoshida, Kyoto
1 May 2021

Note

6 TNA PREM15/1052, Second Talk Between the Prime Minister and Mr. Tanaka – At 3.45 p.m. on 19th September 1972.

Britain's "new role" between Europe and the United States after 1945

How can we best characterise Britain's overall historical predicament and direction in the decades after the Second World War? What roles did burgeoning American hegemony, European integration, and the disintegration of the British Empire play during this period? So-called "declinists", as the term suggests, view British post-war history as a story of gradual and irreversible decline. They might respond to the questions posed above by pointing to several factors which seriously harmed British recovery, especially in the economic realm. Such factors might include Britain's reluctance to fully embrace the emerging European Common Market, its futile and self-injurious determination to preserve the Empire, its dogged but not always rewarding cultivation of a "special relationship" with the United States, and continued heavy defence expenditures.

This book looks afresh at some of these questions. It offers a contribution to scholarship on post-war British economic and business history, industrial policy, international relations and security studies by focusing specifically on the British aircraft industry in the decades after the Second World War. The book presents a very different portrayal of Britain's historical trajectory in the years after 1945 to the one sketched out in the previous paragraph. Its central, anti-declinist theme and contention are as follows: after the Second World War, Britain successfully conceived and created a "new role" for itself as a junior partner of the United States. The post-war British aircraft industry enjoyed considerable success through full-throated participation in an American-led process of globalisation (and not primarily through European collaboration).

To this end, the book traces the policy decisions and commercial operations of successive British governments, key figures from British industry and public life, and a range of non-British actors. As we shall see, a key theme of the book is that British officials were constantly caught between Europe and America in their loyalties and interests. The pressure to steer a course between these two poles in the realm of aerospace preoccupied British policymakers for the entire period covered in this book.

Indeed, the commercial struggle between US and European aerospace industries became increasingly intense from the 1950s onwards. This book shows how, at exactly this time, Rolls-Royce, a British aero-engine manufacturer, came to supply aero-engines to US airframe manufacturers, while British Aerospace (BAe),

xxiv *Britain's "new role" between Europe and the United States after 1945*

a British airframe manufacturer, was integrated into the European Airbus conglomerate, and British Airways (BA), Britain's most important airline, became a launch customer for American Boeing. Can all of this be taken as further historical evidence of *Perfidious Albion's* lack of good faith towards continental Europe, and a British determination to play both sides? With Brexit currently very much in the minds of policymakers on both sides of the English Channel, this is a tempting question to ask.

This book first traces the competitive process for domination of international markets between US and British aircraft industries which played out largely during the 30-year period from the end of the Second World War to the 1970s. Above all, the book focuses on both competitive and co-operative dynamics at the corporate level. These three decades saw the transition from reciprocal to jet engine propulsion for both military and commercial aircraft, as well as other dramatic technological innovations. Against the backdrop of this technological revolution, this book will show how the rivalry between the US and British aircraft industries played out in the areas of both commercial and military aircraft. Initially, this occurred in an overall context of British superiority with respect to jet engine technology. Indeed, the Americans "did not *invent* the jet engine".[7] To all intents and purposes, towards the end of the Second World War, the United States copied models that had been developed by the British. The ultimate aim of this book is to explain how and why this initially intensely competitive relationship resulted in Anglo–American production collaboration at the expense of close co-operation with Europe.

British "decline"

By assessing the intricate relationship between Britain, the United States and continental Europe in the decades after the Second World War, this book searches for new insights into the debate on British decline. Since the 1970s, the controversy over whether Britain's twentieth-century economic history can be better characterised as declinist or anti-declinist has been hotly contested. Well-known books which articulate the declinist view include *The Essential Anatomy of Britain: Democracy in Crisis* (1992) by Anthony Sampson, *The Lost Victory: British Dreams, British Realities, 1945–1950* (1995) by Correlli Barnett, and *English Culture and the Decline of the Industrial Spirit, 1850–1980* (1981) by Martin J. Wiener and others.[8]

Taken together, these books offer a damning portrait of British industrial decline during the twentieth century. Barnett makes a scathing indictment of the culture of the British elite and its role in this decline, while Wiener similarly points to a gathering decay in Britain's industrial spirit.[9] Meanwhile, Tomlinson's interpretation of "the Barnett-Wiener thesis"[10] focuses specifically on the weakness of British aircraft industry, especially in comparison with that of its mortal enemy, Nazi Germany.[11]

These works make a key contribution to our understanding of post-war Britain. The basic position arising from them is that, by clinging to its Empire and

Britain's "new role" between Europe and the United States after 1945 xxv

separating itself from the burgeoning movement towards European integration gathering pace across the channel, Britain's economy stagnated in the period after the Second World War. It has been argued that Britain's attempt in the post-war period to hold onto an independent aircraft industry constituted a massive over-stretch of national resources. Paul Kennedy, for example, has stated that, after 1945:

> Britain continued to rely upon captive colonial markets, struggled in vain to preserve the old parity for sterling, maintained extensive overseas garrisons (a great drain on the currency), declined to join the early moves toward European unity, and spent more on defense than any other NATO powers apart from the United States[12]

The putative contrast here is with West Germany and Japan, which concentrated their national resources onto the economy with only minimal defence burdens. Declinists paint a picture of Britain's post-war economy as characterised by domestic economic stagnation and decolonisation. According to this narrative, Britain's aircraft industry takes on a great symbolic significance. In *The Lost Victory* (1995), Correlli Barnett states that the ability of Britain to retain its aircraft industry was nothing but a "the neo-Edwardian dream"[13] bound to the politics and economy of the straggling Commonwealth.

On the other hand, scholars such as Cain and Hopkins have attempted to relativise the declinist narrative by pointing to a revival of the British financial sector during this historical period.[14] They have analysed this in order to emphasise Britain's "role" in a process of post-colonial, US-led globalisation as a "host and agent".[15] Similarly, William Rubinstein's *Capitalism, Culture, and Decline in Britain, 1750–1990* (1993) argues that the British economy did not actually decline as such, but that it did come to rely on finance and service sectors.[16] Rubinstein contends that "Britain's economy was *always, even during the period 1815–70*, primarily a commercial/financial-oriented economy whose comparative advantage always lay in these areas and increasingly so after 1870 ..."[17]

On the whole, however, both sides in the declinist debate acknowledge that a decline of British *manufacturing* occurred, even if they disagree about the overall impact of this on the British economy and Britain's place in the world. As the above cited scholarship indicates, there is a commonly accepted belief that, during the twentieth century, British manufacturing declined irreparably, that Britain lost its industrial hegemony. This constitutes a broad consensus that manufacturing sectors did indeed decline during this period.

This book returns to the original scholarly parameters of the decline controversy, and especially questions around post-1945 British decline in the fields of high technology and the national defence industrial base (i.e. the military aircraft industry). It aims to address the original point of the declinist controversy as to whether the British manufacturing sector can really be said to have "declined" at all, and it ultimately concludes that this picture is much more complicated than a straightforward declinist narrative might indicate.

xxvi *Britain's "new role" between Europe and the United States after 1945*

A comparable point has been made here by David Edgerton in his book *Warfare State: Britain, 1920–1970* (2006),[18] which shows that post-war Britain was not merely a *welfare state* but also a *warfare state*. According to this reading, the military sector (mainly aircraft and nuclear industries) was not a burdensome source of post-war British "decline", but rather the engine of post-war British vitality.[19] Edgerton argued this point through a focus on domestic institutions and society, whereas my book aims to place this story in a more international context. The present book thus extends the argument of Edgerton but from a more global perspective.

Broadly speaking, the book rejects the straightforward, and commonly accepted, narrative that, since the nineteenth century, Britain has been embroiled in an uncomplicated process of industrial decline. Certainly, Britain intended to maintain regional hegemony in the form of the British Empire, even after the Second World War, but it could not keep pace with the United States in the 1960s for budgetary and technological reasons. And yet Britain was able to carve out a key niche for itself in this new, American world order, preserving a crucial share of the global market and rehabilitating its defence industry. On the whole, this was a success story.

American triumph, British defeat?

Much like the shipbuilding industry that supported British imperial hegemony in the eighteenth and nineteenth centuries, primary manufacturing and the defence industrial base of the aircraft industry supported hegemony in the twentieth century *from masters of the seas to masters of the skies*. Pax-Britannica was based on naval power and shipbuilding industry. Since the Second World War, Pax-America has been based on airpower and aircraft industry.

As Patrick O'Brien has observed, British naval hegemony lasted broadly from 1805 to 1914.[20] The foundations of this "Empire of the Sea"[21] were first lain by the Whig oligarchy of the eighteenth century. In the nineteenth century, in order to maintain its dominance, Britain adopted the so-called "two-power ratio".[22] This stipulated that national naval strength should be equivalent to that of the combined force of the next two biggest navies (France and Russia) in the world. Even in the first half of the twentieth century, when Britain increasingly "could not provide the leadership"[23] on a global scale, it nonetheless remained "without doubt a great naval power".[24] This naval supremacy rested on Britain's defence industrial base: the capacity of its shipbuilding industry to provide the Royal Navy with ships, and the capacity of its munitions industry to produce ordnance and artillery. From the latter half of the nineteenth century to the First World War, Britain's shipbuilding industry, merchant marine fleet and navy were unsurpassed.

Geoffrey Owen has pointed out two significant advantages possessed by Britain's shipbuilding industry over its competitors during the nineteenth century. First, from the beginning of the Industrial Revolution, Britain accumulated considerable knowledge of steel making and steam engines; and second, Britain had a

Britain's "new role" between Europe and the United States after 1945   xxvii

large domestic market thanks to its maritime industry and navy. This owed substantially to the English Navigation Acts of 1651, which held that English trade should be carried in English ships, thereby eliminating Dutch vessels as serious rivals. With its robust domestic markets providing a base, Britain's manufacturers also ventured into international markets.[25]

During the twentieth century, however, air supremacy gradually supplanted maritime supremacy as the key determinant of a nation's military prowess. There followed a fierce rivalry to determine who would inherit the mantle of hegemony. This first became apparent during the First World War, which revealed the aeroplane as a revolutionary new instrument of war. During the inter-war years, major powers moved to establish national airlines linking home countries to the colonies. British Imperial Airways, Air France, Pan American, and German Lufthansa competed across the world for access to air routes and customers.[26]

Hot on the heels of the shipbuilding industry in the nineteenth century, the aircraft industry fully emerged after the Second World War as a critical sector which determined a nation's relative military and economic supremacy. A 1948 US Congressional Paper, *National Aviation Policy*, stated that:

> To defend ourselves in the age of atomic bombs, of radioactive dust, of bacteriological contamination and guided missiles – to mention some of the new and terrible weapons – we must have air power that is *supreme*.
>
> (emphasis added)[27]

Jeffrey Engel has suggested that, in the early years of the Cold War era, the former hegemon Britain and the emerging hegemon America fought for leadership of global air transport under the deceptively congenial auspices of an apparent "special relationship".[28] This book narrows Engel's focus on the Anglo–American struggle for air supremacy during the Cold War with a targeted look at the aircraft manufacturing industry, which is the technical basis of air supremacy (and, arguably, of a country's ability to project power globally). We can see some of these dynamics represented in Figures I.1 and I.2. Figure I.1 shows British Overseas Airways Corporation's (BOAC's) global jet services after the company began to fly the Comet 1s, the first commercial jet airliner. Figure I.2 shows Pan American's jet services with Boeing 707s and Douglas DC-8s.

This book pays particular attention to the transition to jet engines from the end of the Second World War until the 1970s. This period involved a technological switch from reciprocal propulsion to jet propulsion, a generational shift of jet technology, and a changing relationship between airframe makers and engine makers. Successive British governments (both Conservative and Labour) expected that Britain's aircraft industry would eventually bring economic prosperity and foreign currency through exports. Duncan Sandys, the second Churchill government's Minister of Supply, felt able to declare that, "[e]conomically, aircraft are a most attractive export".[29] As he argued in his policy paper to the Cabinet Economic Policy Committee, aircraft manufacturing was especially

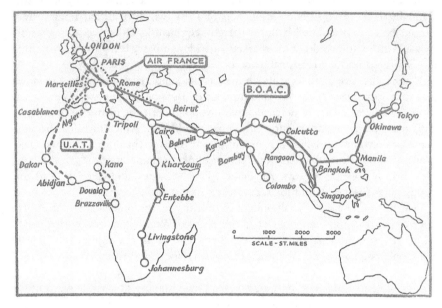

Figure I.1 The world's first jet services Comet 1 routes, 1953
Source: Davies ([1964] 1967, p. 453).

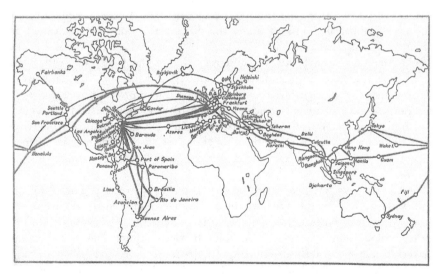

Figure I.2 Pan American Airways jet network, October 1960 (two years after first service)
Source: Davies ([1964] 1967, p. 482).

Britain's "new role" between Europe and the United States after 1945 xxix

attractive when compared with ships or automobiles from the point of view of finished product per pound's worth of materials.[30] He based this reading partly on Britain's very high level of technical capability, as evidenced by its development of the world's first commercial jet airliner Comet.

The present book challenges the conventional interpretation of the twentieth century's core hegemonic transition as a straightforward case of "US victory and British defeat". Such an assumption is widespread in the literature. John B. Rae's *Climb to Greatness: The American Aircraft Industry, 1920–1960* (1968), characterises the US aircraft industry in the post-Second World War era as "a success story, or rather a series of success stories, in the best American tradition",[31] which played out largely at British expense. Barnett regards the British post-war attempt to "obtain supremacy over Douglas, Lockheed and Boeing"[32] as little more than a dream. Clearly, then, the supposed decline of the British aircraft industry is regarded as a significant triumph of US aircraft manufacturers over their most formidable rival in the immediate post-war period, and a tremendous industrial success story for the US economy in terms of industrial output, exports and employment.

But this is too simplistic. In fact, in the decades after 1945, Britain staked out a new role for itself as a key participant in a US-led process of globalisation. Far from becoming merely a European player, Britain actually managed to preserve a key share in a global market, and the British defence industry was, to a large extent, successfully rehabilitated. If we accept this simplistic narrative of US "success" and British "failure", we are left incapable of explaining, for example, the apparent peculiarity of the continued strong competitiveness of Rolls-Royce, the preeminent British aero-engine maker, in the decades after 1945. Indeed, it would not be stretching the argument too much to suggest that British companies were indispensable to the rapid rise of the US aircraft industry after the Second World War.

In December 1962, just before the Anglo–American Nassau conference, Dean Acheson, a former US Secretary of State, observed that "Great Britain has lost an Empire and has not yet found a role".[33] With the end of the Empire, and in seeking such a "new role", the British aircraft industry did not ultimately elect for the certain but limited market that was available through enhanced European integration. Instead, through collaboration with Anglo–American aircraft engine manufacturers, it forayed into the global market dominated by the United States. Even in the sphere of manufacturing, and especially in the defence industry, Britain remained relatively robust. The reorientation of British manufacturing occurred largely due to its full-throated participation in a gathering process of American-led globalisation.

Britain between the United States and Europe

In the post-war era, Britain was faced with three alternatives that would determine its fundamental trajectory. These alternatives were famously articulated by Winston Churchill as the "three circles":

xxx *Britain's "new role" between Europe and the United States after 1945*

> The first circle for us is naturally the British Commonwealth and Empire, with all that that comprises. Then there is also the English-speaking world in which we, Canada, and the other British Dominions and the United States play so important a part. And finally, there is United Europe.[34]

First, Britain could try to maintain regional hegemony through a focus on the British Empire and Commonwealth; second, it could pursue the position of leader of European integration ("Taking the lead in Europe", as Alan Milward put it[35]); or third, it could become more closely connected to (and perhaps dependent upon) the United States. In the first years after the war, Britain largely pursued the first alternative. However, with the Empire in irretrievable dissolution by the mid-1960s, and with the budgetary situation becoming increasingly critical, Britain was compelled to choose one of the remaining two options.

This, however, embroiled Britain in a burgeoning commercial conflict between nominal NATO allies. During this period, high-technology, especially aerospace, was the focus of competition in transatlantic relations. A particularly colourful indication of this was the publication in 1967 of Jean Jacques Servan-Schreiber's best-seller *Le Defi Americain* (1968) – or, *The American Challenge*.[36] To overcome the "Technology Gap" between the United States and Europe, European leaders believed that technological cooperation – including British aerospace technology – was necessary. The unique position and strong bargaining power of the British in the Western Alliance were to a great extent (though not solely) based on the excellence of the British aircraft industry, especially the aero-engine sector, together with intimate sterling–dollar diplomacy around the control of global monetary policy, and general British support for the US Vietnam War.

The Americans, however, feared a combined European block, and especially French designs on limiting US dominance over Western Europe because of de Gaulle's challenge to the United States and the UK. Ellison in particular has raised the issue of de Gaulle's challenge from 1963 to 1968. This entailed a rejection of both "US hegemony in the West and British leadership of Western Europe".[37] In order to understand this complex political relationship between France and the Anglo–American tie, this book takes a particular interest in technological and economic conflicts between the Anglo–French direction and the Anglo–American direction in international aerospace co-operation. As we shall see, British policymakers were increasingly caught between this transatlantic rift – and they demonstrated not inconsiderable skill in navigating it.

Owen's *From Empire to Europe* devotes an entire chapter to the aircraft industry and posits the aircraft industry as "one of Britain's most successful industries throughout the post-war period".[38] However, Owen also argues that the British government expended too much on "a vain attempt to keep up with the Americans in the 1950s and 1960s", which "could have been used more constructively in other ways"[39] (possibly on European co-operation). This book, however, shows that Britain increasingly shied away from competition with the United States and opted instead for a mutually beneficial partnership, despite the powerful emergence of the second, European option. Indeed, in April 1969,

Britain's "new role" between Europe and the United States after 1945   xxxi

Britain withdrew from the European Airbus project, which up until that point it had championed.[40] Thereafter, Airbus was run primarily as a joint French–German initiative and, though Britain later returned to the project in 1978, it was unable to negotiate a favourable share of new Airbus development work.[41]

Some scholars have indicated that this "missed the opportunity"[42] for Britain. Indeed, this book looks very closely at Britain's tendency after the breakup of the Empire to waver between loyalty to the European integration and its special relationship with the United States. Overall, however, this book emphasises the considerable success of the British aviation industry in assuming an active role as a global aero-engine supplier, rather than choosing a guaranteed but limited market as a potential leader of a European cooperative Project. This can be taken as symbolic of British survival and even flourishing within the framework of American-led globalisation, not only in the financial sector but also in high-technology manufacturing sectors.

Structure and sources

This book addresses itself to the historiography sketched out above in nine empirical, chronologically organised chapters. Each chapter deals with a particular, and particularly significant, development in the post-war history of the British aircraft industry. The nine chapters are organised into three parts, each of which deals with a distinct phase in this history. At all times, the emphasis is on the painful ambivalences experienced by British policymakers and economic actors in the field of aviation during the post-war period. These uncertainties were legion – from dilemmas over whether to maintain an independent British aircraft industry or opt for international co-operation, to the choice of partner for international co-operation, to which sectors of the domestic aircraft industry to privilege and which to neglect.

Part I offers an analysis of the British aircraft industry from 1943 to 1964, which encompasses the period between Winston Churchill's wartime Cabinet up to the Conservative Cabinet of Harold Macmillan. Chapter 1 focuses on the wartime Brabazon civil airliners project, as well as the relative success of British civil and military jet aircrafts. Chapter 2 analyses the policies of Aubrey Jones, Minister of Supply, and Duncan Sandys, Minister of Aviation. These political actors attempted to rationalise British industry in order to match up with the United States, which entailed the development of the military aircraft TSR-2 and civil airliner VC10. Chapter 3 lays bare BOAC's financial difficulty with the VC10, which had its roots in the increasingly expensive "Fly British" policy, as well as Chairman Guthrie's attempts to improve BOAC's management.

Part II of the book picks up the story in the mid-1960s, with the advent of a Labour government under Harold Wilson. The main theme of this part comprises Britain's gradual transition from an independent military aerospace policy and towards international collaboration – as well as the considerable uncertainty around exactly which nations Britain would predominantly co-operate with. Chapter 4 traces government decision making around the cancellation of the

xxxii *Britain's "new role" between Europe and the United States after 1945*

TSR-2 – a watershed moment in the post-war history of British aviation. Chapter 5 analyses British ambivalence with respect to the choice of a new partner for international aviation development after the cancellation of the TSR-2, with France and the United States both in contention. Chapter 6 analyses Wilson's concept of a "European Technological Community", which added West Germany to the mix and ultimately produced the Anglo–German MRCA Tornado fighter.

Part III of this book focuses mainly on three civil airliners, showing how some of the dilemmas and uncertainties which arose in Part II were ultimately resolved. Chapter 7 takes wide-body airlines as its topic, laying bare Britain's uncomfortable position between the European Airbus and the US Lockheed TriStar – an ambivalence which ultimately resulted in the bankruptcy of Rolls-Royce in 1971. Chapter 8 traces the evolution of the Anglo–French supersonic transport Concorde, and the impact of this project's failure on the British aircraft industry's international position. Chapter 9 returns to the conflict between US and European manufacturers, analysing the role of three British aerospace players – BAe, Rolls-Royce and BA – in their attempts to negotiate between the European Airbus A310 or the US Boeing 757 during the 1980s.

The book makes extensive use of unpublished British governmental documents from the Prime Ministerial Office, the Cabinet, the Treasury and the Foreign Office, as well as a range of other aviation related-organisations. It also draws on unpublished US governmental documents at the State and Treasury Departments. A full and comprehensive list of these sources can be found in the extensive notes to each chapter, the Bibliography and Appendix Tables AI.1 and AII.1.

Notes

7 Giffard (2016, p. 235).
8 Sampson (1992); Barnett (1995); Wiener (1981).
9 Wiener (1981, p. 154).
10 Tomlinson ([2000] 2001, p. 60).
11 Tomlinson ([2000] 2001, pp. 58–61).
12 Kennedy (1987, pp. 423–24); Holland (1991, p. 10).
13 Barnett (1995, p. 228).
14 Cain and Hopkins (2002).
15 Cain and Hopkins (2002, p. 678).
16 Rubinstein (1993).
17 Rubinstein (1993, p. 25).
18 Edgerton ([2006] 2008).
19 Edgerton ([2006] 2008, pp. 2–3).
20 O'Brien (2002, pp. 99–100).
21 Lichtheim (1971, p. 42).
22 O'Brien (2002, p. 99).
23 Kindleberger (1973, p. 296).
24 Edgerton ([2006] 2008, p. 26).
25 Owen (1999, pp. 91–93).
26 Davies ([1964] 1967, pp. 141–86); Bender and Altschul (1982, p. 339).
27 U.S. Congress (1948, p. 3).

28 Engel (2009).
29 TNA AVIA63/25, EA (52)69th, Expansion of Aircraft Exports, 23rd May 1952.
30 TNA AVIA63/25, EA (52)69th, Expansion of Aircraft Exports, 23rd May 1952.
31 Rae (1968, p. vii).
32 Barnett (1995, p. 246).
33 Ashton (2002, p. 170).
34 Churchill (1950, p. 417).
35 Milward ([1992] 2000, p. 424).
36 Servan-Schreiber (1968).
37 Ellison (2007, p. 189).
38 Owen (1999, p. 295).
39 Owen (1999, pp. 326–27).
40 Johnman and Lynch (2006, p. 139).
41 Aris (2002, p. 115).
42 Camps (1964, p. 507).

Part I

The post-war British aircraft industry, 1943–1964

The conventional narrative of British history during the immediate post-war period is one of unmistakeable and ineluctable decline. Part I of the book re-examines this narrative through an analysis of the British aircraft industry during the two decades after the Second World War. To be sure, and in keeping with the conventional narrative, the British aircraft industry did, indeed, seem to be suffering reverses on every front during this period. And yet, a single British aero-engine maker (Rolls-Royce) was quietly making a case for itself as the principal supplier to American airliners. Ultimately, Part I shows how the seeds of Britain's future role as a key player in an American-led process of globalisation were sown during the two, apparently bleak, decades after the Second World War.

DOI: 10.4324/9781003127901-1

1 The origins of Anglo–American production collaboration in the first jet-age, 1943–1956

Introduction

An examination of the US–European order in the post-war era must begin from the premise that evolving European integration was profoundly connected to the Atlantic Alliance. This was, to some extent, an inevitable result of the disintegration of the British Empire. Up until the end of the Second World War, the Americans anticipated the post-war breakup of the British Empire. After the war, however, they belatedly came to appreciate the Empire's strategic value in a burgeoning confrontation with the Soviets. This was to some extent complementary to the guiding principles of British foreign policy at the time, as based on Winston Churchill's famous "three circles".[1] According to Churchill, "the three circles" encompassed the three roles that Britain was obliged to embody after the war if it hoped to preserve its great power status – as leader of the British Empire, as a close ally with special ties to the United States, and as a dominant power in Western Europe. This elaborate foreign policy framework was taken up by successive administrations.

Did US aid play a significant role in British post-war recovery? This question lies at the centre of a significant scholarly controversy. According to Michael J. Hogan, the Marshal Plan was critical to West European recovery, whereas Alan S. Milward has argued that, even without Marshal Aid, Western Europe would still have recovered.[2] This chapter touches on this controversy through an exploration of US aid and British post-war reconstruction. It offers a close analysis of US Plan K aid and the Offshore Procurement Program (the OSP), both of which have been afforded rather less attention in the scholarly literature.

US aid and British military production were intimately connected because the United States made continued aid conditional on the nature of British rearmament. At the centre of this rearmament programme lay the aircraft industry. The military historian Correlli Barnett has argued that Britain essentially wasted its portion of Marshal Aid on a doomed attempt to maintain and even extend its military aircraft industry. This was a "neo-Edwardian dream",[3] and competition with the United States a clear case of "technological overstretch".[4] Indeed, stiff competition against BOAC's route network came from the other side of the Atlantic in the form of Pan American World Airways (Pan Am), the flagship

DOI: 10.4324/9781003127901-2

4   *The post-war challenge, 1943–64*

international airline of the United States. Although a private company, Pan Am had emerged against the backdrop of the Second World War and was regarded as a "chosen instrument" of American foreign policy. For Barnett, Britain hoped to maintain its aircraft industry for the purely irrational reason of "[p]restige".[5]

This chapter offers a different assessment of Britain's post-war pursuit of airpower. This encompassed the wartime manufacturing of airliners from the Brabazon programme, the attempted production of interim airliners converted from military bombers, an initial British superiority via jet airliners, and the survival of Britain's aero-engine sector despite the rise of US airliners after 1955. As mentioned, many historians consider these programmes to have been profligate and pointless. Alongside Barnet, Keith Hayward has stated that, "[s]adly, most of the others in the [Brabazon] programme were disappointing, and some were quite disastrous, commercially and technically".[6] And yet, as this chapter shows, the wartime British attempt to establish an independent aircraft industry later provided the basis for the renaissance of this same industry.

The Arnold-Towers-Slessor agreement of 22nd June 1942

The Battle of Midway on 4th–7th June 1942 changed the war in the Pacific – not just for, but also among, the Allied Powers. The Royal Air Force (RAF) Coastal Command called on the United States to build Consolidated B-24 Liberators and Boeing B-17 Fortresses.[7] Anglo–American discussions on this question began at the end of May. At this time, H.H. Arnold, the Commanding General of the US Army Air Forces, and J.H. Towers, US Chief of the Bureau of Aeronautics, Navy Department, visited London. On 21st June 1942, Arnold, Towers and J.G. Slessor, Air Vice Marshal of the RAF, signed the so-called Arnold-Towers-Slessor agreement in Washington DC. According to this agreement, the United States would allocate aircraft to Britain. Notably, this agreement stipulated that allocations of transport aircraft to Britain for 1943 would remain open to discussion and revision.[8]

After the Arnold-Towers-Slessor agreement, British dependence on US aircraft – and especially transport aircraft – remained evident. In *The Central Blue*, his autobiography, Slessor wrote that:

> We [British] were unable to shake Arnold on the subject of transport aircraft, for supply of which we were depending entirely on U.S. production. We were in no position to embark on the production of any class in the U.K. at this advanced stage, and it was agreed that we should in the main have to rely upon American air transport units to lift British airborne troops when required.[9]

Before US officials finalised their production programme for 1943, Oliver Lyttelton, Minister of Production, visited Washington in an attempt to organise the integration of British and American aircraft production. He frankly assumed Britain's "nearly 100 per cent" dependence in the area of transport aircraft.[10]

This effectively entailed a virtual US monopoly over the post-war airliner market (4 engine reciprocal). As John Wilmot, Minister of Supply, and Lord Winster, Minister of Civil Aviation, would later state in a Cabinet memorandum, "[t]the war time concentration of production of transport aircraft in American hands" would pay "handsome dividends"[11] to the United States after the war.

The Churchill War Cabinet was understandably rattled by the prospect of an exclusive British concentration on fighters and bombers, and thus a prospective loss of transport technology. Indeed, in early 1943, the Cabinet recognised that supremacy in post-war "control of the construction, use, servicing and piloting of the air transport"[12] was essential to post-war reconstruction and the preservation of the Empire. This prompted the British government to summon an advisory committee – the Brabazon Committee, chaired by Lord Brabazon of Tara – to select specifications for domestic and commercial airliners after the war. The first meeting of this Committee was held on 23rd December 1942.[13]

The Brabazon programme

In 1943, the Churchill Cabinet began to engage more intensively with the question of post-war reconstruction. On 22nd February 1943, the Subcommittee on Civil Aviation in the Committee on Reconstruction Problems concluded that "British air transport after the war shall be on a scale and quality in keeping with our world position, and that work on the design of new types of civil aircraft and on the conversion of existing military types should proceed".[14]

In keeping with this principle, the Brabazon Committee made a recommendation to the Secretary of State for Air and Minister of Aircraft Production to design five new types of aircraft. These were as follows:

Type 1 Multi-engined landplane for North Atlantic (later Bristol Brabazon).
Type 2 Medium-size, twin-engined landplane for European and feeder service (Douglas DC-3 type, later Vickers Viscount).
Type 3 Four-engined landplane for Empire trunk route (York replacement).
Type 4 Jet-propelled mail-plane for North Atlantic (later de Havilland Comet).
Type 5 Small twin-engined landplane for internal service.[15]

It was envisioned that these new designs would go into service after the end of the war. Consequently, the Brabazon Committee also recommended the development of "interim types" to fill the gap until new models were in service. In addition to these new models, the Brabazon Committee recommended that the York Bomber be adapted for civil use.[16] True to its name, the Committee initially attached the most importance to the Brabazon I aircraft, which was selected for development by the Bristol Aeroplane Company. This would be a pressured long-range airliner capable of flying non-stop from London to New York.[17] It was expected that, after the war, this aircraft would compete with the American Douglas DC-4, Lockheed Constellation and Boeing 377 Stratocruiser.

6 *The post-war challenge, 1943–64*

Ultimately, the British government effectively resuscitated the Bristol Brabazon and Saunders-Roe SR.45 Princess (Flying Boat) in an effort to take the initiative. The Brabazon Committee urged that these developments should begin immediately, in order to ensure that Britain would play a respectable role after the war. Following the recommendations of the Subcommittee on Civil Aviation, Sir Archibald Sinclair, Secretary of State for Air, and Sir Stafford Cripps, Minister of Aircraft Production, asked the Cabinet to allocate sufficient financing to supply the minimum number of types of aircraft in the immediate post-war period.[18]

British and American transport aircraft compared

At the end of 1943, before the Brabazon models materialised, the British government faced the necessity of introducing the Douglas C-54A and C-54B (the civilian version is the DC-4) on the Atlantic and Empire routes. The York would be inadequate for this purpose, and the only available British type was the Tudor (a civil version of the Lancaster IV bomber). Lord Beaverbrook, the Lord Privy Seal, expressed considerable alarm that, "if we fail to provide British aircraft and British engines for the Dominion at the end of the War, then the leadership of air routes in the Empire must pass to the United States".[19] Essentially, Beaverbrook was admitting that action was needed for aircraft to come into service quickly and that the key model in this endeavour was the Tudor.

Further concerns over the developmental status of Britain's civil aviation for the post-war era were expressed in a Cabinet meeting held on 1st September 1944. Lord Beaverbrook voiced his opinion that the York was of no value for civil use, that the Tudor was of very little value, and that the real need was for Brabazon types, particularly the Brabazon type 1. Members of the Cabinet underlined the significance of civil aviation development, but they also expressed their dissatisfaction with the Brabazon aircraft, and touched on the possibility of acquiring proven US aircraft types. At the end of this discussion, the War Cabinet requested that Sinclair and Cripps submit a comparative report on British and US transport aircraft. The report was commissioned to accurately answer the question of whether Britain's aircraft design was adequate, and its authors were asked to include BOAC's views on Brabazon aircrafts.[20]

Sinclair and Cripps submitted their comparative report on 1st September 1944. The report concluded that British airlines could match up with their US equivalents (Table 1.1). The report can be summarised as follows. First, the Brabazon aircraft were on par with the types of aircraft being developed in the US. Second, however, American airliners were certain to advance more quickly than British aircraft. Therefore, the development of the Brabazon aircraft needed to be accelerated at a maximum pace, within the obvious confines of the demands of the British war effort.[21]

The Brabazon aircraft were already being developed, but they were nonetheless not due to go into service until after 1950. Thus, the only available aircraft prior

The origins of US–UK collaboration, 1943–56 7

Table 1.1 Comparison of US and UK airliners

US airliners				UK airliners			
Model	Weight (lb)	Engines	Prototype fly	Model	Weight (lb)	Engines	Prototype fly
Douglas DC-7	162,000	4	Early 1945	Brabazon 1	250,000	8	1948
Boeing Strato-cruiser	120,000	4	1944	Brabazon 3A	120,000	4	Early 1948
Lockheed Constella-tion	82,000	4	Flying	Avro Tudor	70,000	4	1945
Douglas DC-6	80,000	4	March 1945	Avro York	68,000	4	Flying
Douglas DC-4 (C-54)	78,000	4	Flying	Brabazon 4 (Comet)	?	Jet	Flying
Douglas DC-3	25,200	2	Flying	Brabazon 2	45,000	2	Early 1947

Source: TNA CAB66/57, WP(44)611, Appendix A, 1st November 1944.

to 1950 were interim models such as the York and the Tudor. In contrast to British interim airliners, the United States would soon offer comfortable airliners such as Douglas DC-4, DC-6, Lockheed Constellation and Boeing Stratocruiser. The Attlee government would inevitably be confronted by BOAC's demand for superior US aircraft over British interim aircraft. BOAC added that the jet-powered Brabazon Type 4 (later named the Comet) should be developed as quickly as possible to establish initiative in new areas "as a matter of prestige, and to establish a lead in this new field of development".[22]

The "Fly British" policy (1945–1950)

In 1945, Churchill was succeeded as Prime Minister by Clement Attlee, who headed a new Labour government. Attlee inherited the civil transport aircraft development policy adopted by the War Cabinet and continued to pursue the "Fly British" principle. This effectively forced BOAC and the British European Airways Corporation (BEA) to purchase British airliners. The 1945 aviation White Paper articulated this in some detail:

It will be the general policy of His Majesty's Government to require the Corporations [BOAC and BEA] to use British aircraft types. As a result of wartime policies agreed with our Allies, transport aircraft were not produced in this country during the war, and the development of British civil aircraft has been interrupted since 1938. At the moment we are, on this account, placed at a grave disadvantage.[23]

8 *The post-war challenge, 1943–64*

Contrary to this principle, however, the British government was compelled to accept BOAC's purchase of American aircraft immediately after the end of the war. Initially, the Brabazon models were scheduled to fly after 1950. In February 1946, however, BOAC purchased five Lockheed Constellations from the United States for the North Atlantic service to compete with foreign airlines, most of which were, by this point, also using American models. Even on the Empire route (Sydney–London), Australian officials were seriously weighing a purchase American aircraft. This jeopardised the British–Australian "partnership operation, based on the use of common types of aircraft".[24]

On 23rd July 1946, the Interdepartmental Committee on Civil Aircraft Requirements issued its First Interim Report. This report reiterated the fact that, between 1948 and 1950, no British airliner capable of competing with American models on the North Atlantic Servicer and Empire trunk routes would be available. The Committee thus recommended that priority should be given to de Havilland Comet (Brabazon Type 4), pure jet and Vickers VC2 (later named as Viscount, Brabazon Type 2), with possible delays attaching themselves to the Bristol Brabazon. The Committee expected that the Comet would fly both the North Atlantic and the Empire routes, would have strong passenger appeal, and perhaps even offer export possibilities on the US market.[25]

In summer of 1946, John Wilmot, the Minister of Supply, and Lord Winster, Minister of Civil Aviation, proposed the purchase of American aircraft, the Boeing Stratocruisers or the Republic XF-12 Rainbow. It seemed likely that, by late 1947, various American, Swedish, Dutch and French airlines would have brought the new Boeing Stratocruiser into service. This would completely outclass BOAC's Tudors and Constellations.[26]

In the view of the ministers, this situation was a clear "legacy of the war". The British had concentrated on bombers and fighters while the Americans had developed their military transport models. This enabled the Americans to easily convert their military types to civil Constellation, Stratocruiser and DC-6. "During the next 10 years",[27] the ministers pointed out, it was essential that Britain "must explore the full commercial possibilities of jet propulsion".[28] They nonetheless proposed a British purchase of six Stratocruisers to compete on the North Atlantic route "before our own designs are in production".[29]

The delicate question of a British purchase of American aircraft resurfaced in the form of a mooted acquisition of the Canadair DC-4M in July 1948. This issue turned into a debacle for the British government. BOAC had ordered 16 Tudor IV aircraft and 25 Handley Page Hermes. Christopher Addison, the Lord Privy Seal, proposed to the Cabinet that the development of the Brabazon 1 and Comet should be pursued, but that the Tudor II and its derivative model, the Tudor V, should not be commissioned. Instead, BOAC should be granted permission to purchase 22 Canadair DC-4M aircraft as an alternative. He insisted that such a purchase would in no way prejudice the introduction of new types of British aircrafts.[30]

Addison's argument met heavy resistance from within the Cabinet. In a memorandum dated 10th July 1948, Minister of Supply George Strauss opposed

Addison's proposal to purchase 22 DC-4M aircraft instead of the Tudor IV for the North Atlantic and Empire routes. Strauss argued that, although the Rolls-Royce Merlin engine was used on the DC-4M, almost every other component of the aircraft was made in the United States. BOAC's abandonment of the Tudor operation and introduction of American aircraft would thus constitute a wholesale departure from the "Fly British" policy. According to Strauss, this would have a serious impact. Negative consequences could be expected for the technological advancement of the British aircraft industry, for British exports, and even for Britain's potential war readiness.[31]

The basic question was whether the interim needs of BOAC could better be met by DC-4Ms or Tudor IVs. After the discussion, the Cabinet approved the section in Addison's memorandum which requested permission to purchase the DC-4M aircraft.[32] This signalled that, before the Brabazon types went into service after 1950, BOAC openly hoped to purchase US aircraft, such as the Constellation, Stratocruiser and DC-4M. Only in this way could BOAC hope to compete with foreign airlines and jointly operate Commonwealth routes already traversed by American aircraft.

Clearly, then, the Attlee administration experienced considerable difficulties in maintaining the "Fly British" Policy from a relatively early stage. Certainly, and as Barnett argues, the policy faced severe and repeated challenges from American civil airliners.[33] And yet, in this critical period, Britain still pinned its hopes on the two forthcoming Brabazon jet propulsion civil airliners – the de Havilland Comet and Vickers Viscount.

Plan K aid and the US OSP

In 1951, Churchill returned to Number 10 Downing Street and a Conservative government resumed office. This government soon realised that Atlee's 3-year rearmament plan was based on the totally unrealistic assumption that all necessary resources – labour, materials, machine tools and so on – would be available in the necessary quantities. On 20th November 1951, Duncan Sandys, Minister of Supply, suggested that an approach be made to the United States to secure an extension of "end-item aid".[34]

Churchill visited Washington from the 5th to the 9th January 1952, and then again from the 16th to the 18th of the same month. He discussed Anglo–American co-operation with President Truman. The main outcome of these talks was the establishment of "Operation Dovetail", which envisioned a merger of the US–UK military programme according to the principle of more closely aligned military production.[35] The precise contours of this agreement were fleshed out in more detail on 10th January 1952, at a meeting between US and British officials. This occurred in the offices of C.E. Wilson, the Head of General Motors and later Secretary of Defence. Those in attendance included Wilson (presiding), Averell Harriman, William H. Draper and Lord Cherwell, a close friend of Churchill. In effect, "Operation Dovetail" entailed two key principals. First, US military procurement on the UK market would be extended in order to bolster the

10 The post-war challenge, 1943–64

declining British dollar reserve. Second, an attempt would be made to obtain "military end items" for US dollars, instead of simply supplying dollars in the form of economic aid.[36]

On 23rd May 1952, Sandys and William Sidney, Secretary of State for Air, submitted a paper entitled "Expansion of Aircraft Export" to the Cabinet Economic Policy Committee. This report indicated that, over the coming years, the UK would have the opportunity to develop its aircraft industry as a key export sector. The report also namechecked a range of forthcoming British civil and military jet aircraft: the Comet, the Viscount and the Britannia airliners, the Canberra and the Valiant bomber, and the Hunter fighter.[37] Sandys also recommend that the Cabinet allocate more steel to the engineering industry (including the aircraft industry) and make more effort to support armament exports to non-sterling countries.[38]

On 23rd April 1953, another US/UK summit occurred in Paris at the George V Hotel. This meeting was attended by Sandys, Sir Edwin Plowden, Chief Planning Officer, Harold Stassen, the US Director for Mutual Security, and Lincoln Gordon, Mutual Security Agency (MSA), London. The attendees discussed a possible $400 million-allocation of US military aid to the UK in the form of the OSP. According to the OSP, the UK would be able to export aircraft to European North Atlantic Treaty Organization (NATO) countries. In the discussion, Stassen showed interest in the British Javelin all weather fighter as an OSP item.[39]

This US commitment to British industrial recovery was enhanced at a meeting of the NATO Council in Paris in 1953. US representatives informally agreed to support the overall British defence budget and the RAF modernisation programme (Plan K) to the tune of $210 million of the OSP, $275 million of economic aid and $43.1 million of other supporting materials.[40]

The success of Comet and Viscount jet airliners

The Brabazon Committee initially emphasised the importance of the Bristol Brabazon I (type 1). In fact, however, it was the small-scale, jet propulsion-based aeroplane Comet that showed the most initial promise. The development of the large-scale aircraft Bristol Brabazon I and Saunders-Roe SR.45 Princess (Flying Boat) was much slower. These programmes would cost a projected £14 million, despite the fact that BOAC had no apparent interest in operating either.[41] In the meantime, the Brabazon airliner showed many instances of fatigue failures in the areas around the propellers and mounts, and as a result, no certificate of airworthiness was issued. The ignominious end of this project came on 17th July, when the Minister of Supply, Duncan Sandys, announced the abandonment of the Bristol Brabazon project in the House of Commons.[42]

In contrast, British jet aircraft development was more advanced than equivalent efforts from the American aviation industry. Indeed, Britain succeeded in placing into service the world's first jet airliner, the Comet, while American airlines, such as Capital and Continental, purchased the British-made turboprop-engine Viscount (Brabazon Type 3).[43] On 2nd May 1952, BOAC put into commission

The origins of US–UK collaboration, 1943–56 11

Britain's de Havilland Comet, the world's first commercial jet airliner, for the London–Johannesburg route.[44] Subsequently, BOAC placed the Comet into service for the Far East routes and built up airline networks with jet aircraft that covered the entire Commonwealth.

In October 1952, Pan Am agreed on a sales contract on the de Havilland Comet jet airliner.[45] Juan Trippe, the President of Pan Am, ordered Comets in the autumn of 1952.[46] This was the first foreign aircraft imported by American airlines after the Second World War. American aviation experts uneasily noted Britain's headway on international markets. Indeed, the launch of the pure-jet Comet 1 in 1952 had a significant impact on US airlines and manufacturers, because jet services could dramatically shorten flight times between New York and London.

The success of the Comet was followed by the turboprop airliner Vickers Viscount. This model was a turboprop airliner that offered lower operation costs and a purchase price as its strengths and eventually became the most significant success for the post-war British aviation industry on export markets. The Viscount was successfully sold to BEA, Air France, Trans-Canada Air Lines (TCA) and Trans Australia Airlines.[47] In June 1954, Capital Airlines purchased a large number of the Vickers Viscount turboprop commercial transports.[48]

Demand for military aircraft was also on the rise, owing partly to Western rearmament after the outbreak of the Korean War. With the American offshore procurement policy, Britain enjoyed steady exports of military aircraft, mainly to NATO countries. These included the Hunter fighter (636 Hunters were exported of a total 1,525 built) and the Canberra light bomber (197 Canberra were exported of a total 935 built).[49]

In other words, it was during this period when Britain established a certain status in international markets in the area of private demand through the development of jet airliners. This signified an advancement of British airliners into American markets for the first time since the end of the war. Britain's jet technologies constituted a significant competitive advantage and a striking example of British industrial prowess in the realm of aircraft production.

The tragedy of Comet and choice of technologies

The auspicious start for Britain's international ambitions with respect to jet technologies soon came to an abrupt halt. Between 1953 and 1954, de Havilland Comets operated by BOAC were involved in various crashes, and the competitive advantage against the United States began to recede. The reason for the accidents involving the Comet was determined to originate from fuselage ruptures caused by metal fatigue.[50] As a result, BOAC and other airlines suspended operations of the aircraft. Not only did these incidents lead to deteriorations in BOAC's and de Havilland's business performances; they also caused a loss of technological credibility in pure-jet airliners and a significant shift in the BOAC fleet plan toward turboprop Bristol Britannia and away from pure-jet Vickers V-1000.

12   *The post-war challenge, 1943–64*

After the launch of the pure-jet Comet 1, US airlines and manufacturers were profoundly divided over whether to further develop the revolutionary pure-jet technology, or to more gradually pursue turboprop technology. Pan Am, the flag carrier of the United States, had to compete with BOAC, which meant that more jets carrying more passengers were needed. Boeing was working on the development of a pure jet on the basis of the jet technology acquired from its experience with bombers, military transport aircraft. The production of B-47 and B-52 jet bombers afforded Boeing considerable background experience with jet technology. On 21st April 1952, not long before the first Comet flight, the board of Boeing decided to develop a prototype pure-jet 707 under the secret code name of 367-80.[51]

Douglas had originally announced the development of a DC-8 pure-jetliner in 1952, whereas BOAC commenced commercial flight of the pure-jet Comet 1 in May of the same year. However, it soon became apparent that US domestic airlines had no interest in either the 707 or the DC-8 pure-jet, which potentially caused excess transport capacity and further cost increases. Instead, they sought to avoid introducing pure-jet passenger aircraft that would rapidly bring about the obsolescence of existing machines. In 1953, on the fiftieth anniversary of powered flight, Donald Douglas, the President of Douglas, announced that work on the DC-8 would cease. Instead, the future of the company would be staked on the turbo-compound DC-7. Lockheed, meanwhile, had amassed some experience with turboprop aircraft development through the military transport aircraft Lockheed C-130 Hercules. It thus decided to develop a civil version of the C-130, the L-188 Electra.[52]

Cancellation of V-1000 pure jet transport and Pan Am order for 707 and DC-8

From late 1940, Rolls-Royce began to develop the world's first turbofan engine, the Conway. The Handley Page Victor V-bomber and the Vickers V-1000 transport aircraft had been arranged as carrier aircraft for the engine. The Vickers V-1000 was based on Vickers' Valiant V-bomber wings and powered by the Rolls-Royce Conway.[53] The V-1000s were developed as a long-range transport aircraft for the RAF. However, in November 1955, the Ministry of Supply cancelled its order of the V-1000 due to delayed deliveries and changes in the military necessity and defence budget. As a result, the possibility of the V-1000 development depended on whether it could be converted into a commercial aircraft.[54]

Unfortunately, demand for civilian aircraft at this time was powered mainly by BOAC, which did not need the V-1000. BOAC's equipment plans could be met with the Comet 4 and the Britannia, which were considered sufficient to cover the North Atlantic and Empire routes. Initially, the V-1000s were mooted for conversion to commercial aircraft. After 1954, however, BOAC began to fear that introducing pure-jet airliners may have been premature, owing to the repeated crashes involving the Comet. It was for this reason that BOAC cancelled the purchase of Vickers' pure-jet V-1000 airliner with the Rolls-Royce Conway turbofan engine and opted instead for Bristol's Britannia turboprop-engine airliner as the main fleet on long-range routes.[55]

BOAC's change of course had a significant impact on the aircraft manufacturers' development policies. Vickers began to focus on the Vanguard, increasing the size of the Viscount, while Bristol pursued the development of a larger-sized Britannia. Both companies were thus primarily pursuing turboprop-engine airliners.[56] Because of the limited number of Victor bombers procured, Rolls-Royce could not secure an adequate number of these aircraft for sales to recover development investments, even though the Conway had a competitive advantage.

The US transition in propulsion technology from reciprocating engine to jet engine was obviously oriented to the needs of the military. Pratt & Whitney's (P&W's) JT3D and JT4D jet engines for Boeing 707 and DC-8 were basically civil conversions of the J57 and J75, which were both military aircraft engines. The airframe had a similar history. The fuselage and wing design of Boeing 707 was based on the experience of the B-47 and B-52 bombers, while the prototype of the Boeing 707 (367-80) was used for the United States Air Force (USAF) Boeing KC-135 military Stratotanker. After placing their orders for 707s and DC-8s, many US airliners ran into significant financing difficulties. This prompted Washington to step in with the CRAF (Civil Reserve Air Fleet) Program. This compensated domestic airliners for the delay of introducing jet transport in USAF MATS (Military Air Transport Services).[57]

All of this underlines the fact that the US transition from reciprocating to jet engine technology was rooted in the needs of the military, and in technical developments in the military sphere. The British aircraft industry, however, lacked this background in military procurement – as well as the massive government funds associated with it. Consequently, the RAF's cancellation of the Vickers V-1000 transport aircraft endangered the development of its civil variant, the VC7. This was one of the chief reasons for the VC10's launch delay, and it severely dented the aircraft's competitiveness on the world market. Moreover, BOAC's decision to concentrate turboprop development around the Britannia model was directly instantiated by the RAF's lack of interest in pure jet in contrast with the USAF.

By the mid-1950s, at the latest, the dramatic differences in the respective sizes of US and British internal markets and capacities for state financing were starting to become plain. The long-term prospects of bridging this gap through Britain's legacy of technical superiority in certain aspects of aircraft production were slim indeed.

US congressional reactions to British success

On 1st and 2nd March 1954, Senators Bridge and Symington (the Appropriation Committee) visited the UK and conducted a survey of the British aircraft industry. Capital Airlines' purchase of the Vickers Viscount turboprop airliner in June

14 *The post-war challenge, 1943–64*

1954 had sparked a sense of crisis in the US Congress over the British aircraft industry.[58] This was closely connected to the issue of the following year's fiscal budget deliberations. The prospect of continued financial aid to the British aircraft industry hung in the balance.

On 2nd July 1954, the *United States Aid to the British Aircraft Program* (known as the Bridge-Symington Report) was submitted to Congress. This document heavily criticized the US government's financial support for the British aircraft programme over three key issues. First, US taxpayers' money was being used both directly and indirectly to support the British aircraft industry, which also enjoyed the protection of British government subsidies. Indeed, US resources were still being invested despite wide-ranging British spending cuts and the continued subsidisation of Britain's domestic aviation industry. Second, the report alleged that the partly US-funded RAF modernisation programme posed a serious threat to the entire US aviation industry, including engine manufacturers, aircraft manufacturers and airlines. It was unconscionable, the report argued, that US aid was being used to strengthen the industrial base of other countries, and that a highly strategic US industry was thereby being endangered. Third, the report suggested that financial support provided to the RAF had allowed the UK to amply fund private jet airliner development. Overall, the report was damning of US policy in this area.[59]

On 3rd September 1954, W.G. Brown of the United States Mutual Security Agency (USOM) sent a long telegram to the British representative at the Foreign Operations Administration in Washington. This telegram demanded a response to the Bridge-Symington report, which was quickly forthcoming. The British attempted to argue that there was in fact no relationship between, on the one hand, US financial support for the RAF modernisation programme (Plan K) and, on the other hand, the allocation of large amounts from the British budget to subsidising the development of commercial jet airliners.[60] On 29th September 1954, Lincoln Gordon, MSA, UK representative, also dismissed the claim that "U.S. aid is being used to subsidize the development of British civilian jet aircraft".[61]

The Bridge-Symington report had also alleged that US aid to Britain had impacted the military OSP, especially the development and sale of the Gloster Javelin supersonic all-weather fighter. Certain European countries, such as Belgium and Italy, had shown an interest in the Javelin. Italy, however, had received substantial dollar aid and decided to buy the North American F-86 Sabre. Belgium was interested in the Javelin on the assurance that the RAF would adopt the aircraft through the OSP.[62]

Needless to say, the success of British military and civil jet aircrafts was highly unsettling to the US aircraft industry. Congress and the Hoover Commission pressed the Eisenhower administration to reduce foreign military aid. Indeed, it is no exaggeration to state that criticisms of the Senate Appropriation Committee triggered a shift in the US government's RAF support policy. A subsequent US Congressional budget review resulted in $35 million in final expenditures, reduced from $75 million in initial aircraft special plan requests.[63] The American purse was slowly closing.

The rush to jet engines

On 15th December 1954, Lord Hives, Chairman of Rolls-Royce, and Denning Pearson, Managing Director of Aero Engine Division Rolls-Royce and an official at the Ministry of Supply, met to discuss possible uses of the Conway engine for the Boeing 707. Lord Hives commented that Boeing were "extremely interested in the Conway for a civil version of the 707".[64] Indeed, Boeing had already obtained a sizeable order for 80 models of the Stratotanker version (KC-135) from the USAF. In contrast, there would be only eight orders for the eight V-1000s. Pearson said that "collaboration had already gone a long way"[65] with respect to the Conway-fitted civil version of the Boeing 707.

Before long, the unstable situation surrounding the technological choices of these next-generation passenger aircraft would be transformed. When this occurred, it triggered a large order of jet passenger aircraft from Pan Am. In June 1955, Douglas again presented the pure-jet DC-8. At this point, however, the DC-8 existed only as a blueprint – in contrast with the operational Boeing 707. Juan Trippe, Pan Am's chairman, was not satisfied with the versions of the 707 and DC-8 which were fitted with a P&W J57 engine. These models could not fly the North Atlantic route non-stop. Instead, he wanted the P&W J75 version – a truly intercontinental airliner.[66]

Boeing, however, proved hesitant over the additional developmental costs of the J75 version of the 707. At this point, Trippe showed himself to be a cunning operator. He dealt separately and secretly with Boeing and Douglas. On 13th October 1955, Pan Am announced an order of 25 Douglas DC-8 aircraft and 20 Boeing 707 aircraft. The DC-8s were either J57 for domestic versions or J75 international versions, while the 20 Boeing 707s were J57 versions.[67] When he learned of this news in *The Wall Street Journal*, "[President of Boeing] Allen felt like an earthquake victim".[68] Boeing quickly realised that European airliners only wanted the J75 version of the 707. Boeing was thus forced to develop the 707-320 International equipped with the J75.

It was this substantial investment that spurred US airliners in their "rush to jet". European airline companies were also racing to place orders for the Boeing 707 and Douglas DC-8 in order to compete against Pan Am. Air France (France) and Sabena (Belgium) ordered Boeing 707s as the primary aircraft for long-range routes, while KLM (the Netherlands), Swissair (Switzerland) and SAS (three Scandinavian nations) placed an order for the Douglas DC-8. This avalanche of orders helped to shift the technological and commercial dominance in the aviation industry from Britain to the United States.[69] The commanding position of the long-range airliner markets achieved by the Boeing 707 and Douglas DC-8 had far-reaching implications for the "Fly British" policy, the very foundation of British aviation policy.

On 17th December 1955, Pearson discussed European airlines' purchase of 707 and DC-8 with British government officials. He reported that KLM, SAS and Air France had all decided to use American jets, and that both Sabena and Swissair would follow them. A silver lining lay in the fact that these airlines were interested in purchasing Rolls-Royce Conway for their American airframes.[70]

16 *The post-war challenge, 1943–64*

The end of the OSP

The MSA fiscal debates over the 1955 and 1956 budgets were grim indeed from the perspective of the UK. Congress further tightened restrictions with a view to protecting its own industry. The Hoover Commission, which existed in order to investigate government activity, had begun an intensive review of British fighters in the out-of-bounds procurement agreement. This review concluded that US military requirements were not well served by this deal, and that payment for British-made Javelin fighters should be cancelled.[71] On 30th August 1956, Martin Tank at the US Embassy officially outlined this position in a letter to Sir Richard Powell at the Ministry of Defence. The letter merely stated that the US Department of Defense had recommended cancellation of the OSP Javelin contract because "the aircraft has failed to meet performance and contract specifications".[72]

On 30th October 1956, Harold Macmillan, the Chancellor of the Exchequer, informed Prime Minister Sir Antony Eden that the US government was considering suspending the remaining $108 million (£39 million) of Plan K aid (including $64 million in Javelin fighters and $44 million pending). He outlined two reasons for this reversal. First, there were apparent doubts from the US side that Javelin fighters could meet their military requirements; second, the UK was expected to cut military spending to a degree where US aid would no longer be justified. Moreover, the UK apparently had other customers (such as Belgium) for the Javelin fighter.[73]

The implications of US financial aid for the British economy and rearmament programme were considerable. The $108 million (£39 million) Plan K aid cut may have seemed small based on the UK's £1.5 billion military budget, but it still constituted one-twentieth of the UK's £2.3 billion gold reserves. Without military aid, the balance of payments would be a £160 million surplus in 1954 and a £133 million deficit in 1955.[74]

In fact, Plan K aid underpinned one of the three fundamental weaknesses of Britain's economy. The first of these was an inflationary tendency due mainly to government expenditure. The second lay in insufficient production investment and competition between defence, exports and investment. The third element was the insecure balance of payments. In effect, Plan K aid switched the commercial basis of engineering industries from government orders to exports. The lack of aid would reduce the demand on British foreign exchange resources. This balance was in constant need of central supplementation. The $108 million of US aid had three components. The budget for the purchase of Javelin IV was $64 million; for the purchase of Corporal missiles, $28 million; and for the purchase of the Canberra light-bombers, $16 million.[75]

The wind was blowing in only one direction. In the mid-1950s, US military aid policy shifted from generous support to the British aircraft industry to forceful selling of US fighters to European NATO countries. The most striking example of this policy change were Lockheed F-104G Starfighter sales to West Germany, Italy, Holland and Belgium. In effect, the British were gradually deprived of their foothold in the West European military market through the OSP.

The BOAC purchase of 707-420 with Rolls-Royce Conway

As mentioned previously, BOAC was sceptical about a wholesale implementation of pure-jet airliners. This scepticism owed mainly to the accidents with the Comet, and the cancelled orders of Vickers' V-1000 pure-jets. Unfortunately for BOAC, this meant that, when the company's US and European competitors decided to put American jet airliners into commission after 1958, it did not have any appropriate British-made models to rival them. This prompted BOAC to request permission from the British government to order 17 Boeing 707s on 26th July 1956.[76]

Boeing and Douglas expressed interest in equipping their aircraft with the Rolls-Royce Conway engine. In May 1956, Minister of Supply Reginald Mauling held a meeting with Pearson to discuss the choice of engine for the Victor and Vulcan. At this meeting, Pearson raised the question of equipping US airframes with Rolls-Royce engines. He observed that US manufacturers were evidently impressed with the Dart engine equipped on the Viscount, and with its parts service. They were thus eager for an opportunity to equip their aircraft with the Conway. Pearson also mentioned TCA's plans to purchase a Conway-equipped DC-8.[77]

In a statement to Minister of Supply Maudling on 27th July 1956, Rolls-Royce offered support to BOAC's decision to order American aircraft. Rolls argued that, in the absence of such an order, TCA might switch its choice of engines to P&W's J75. Air India would most likely submit an order for the Conway, but if the number of Conway sold for commercial use did not reach 100, then even that airline would probably switch to P&W engines. Lufthansa was also rumoured to be weighing a selection of the P&W engine instead of the Conway in the absence of a BOAC order. Overall, the production plans for the Conway would collapse if BOAC did not place an order for American aircraft.[78]

On the other hand, if BOAC did submit an order, follow-up orders from Cathay Pacific Airlines, Qantas Airways and South African Airways could be expected. Moreover, both Sabena and Air France would reconsider their engine selection if BOAC and Lufthansa ordered American aircraft equipped with the Conway.[79] The British government was apparently convinced by this argument. On 24th October 1956, BOAC was given permission to purchase 15 Rolls-Royce Conway-engined Boeing 707-420. However, the Board of BOAC had already been informed on 20th October that this purchase was conditional on BOAC buying 20 British airliners.[80]

On 24th October, Harold Watkinson, Minister of Civil Aviation, made this purchasing decision public. He stated that its objective was to maintain BOAC's competitiveness against foreign airlines using the Boeing 707 in the North Atlantic routes from 1958 to 1960. These were stop-gap years in which no comparable British aircraft would be available. Watkinson stressed that the BOAC purchase of American aircraft was an "exceptional measure"[81] to bridge the gap until new British aircraft could be developed.

But this exceptional measure nonetheless faced stiff opposition from the British Parliament. Their approval was contingent upon Rolls-Royce engines being equipped in the Boeing 707. The British government apparently hoped that the

18 *The post-war challenge, 1943–64*

image of the Boeing 707 as a purely American aircraft would be mitigated through the use of the Conway engine.[82] Clearly, it was necessary to extract some kind of patriotic payoff from this eminently rational but rather sobering – not to say demoralising – development.

Still, the decision did enable Boeing to gain ground with important clients of the British aviation industry who were located in the former British Commonwealth, including BOAC, Air India and El Al Israel. Table 1.2 shows the worldwide orders of Boeing 707s by engine types, which appeared in Boeing's *Annual Report* in 1960. It is evident from Table 1.2 that 31 Rolls-Royce Conway equipped 707-420s were ordered (about 20 per cent of all 707s). The Americans were able to build a market for the Conway-equipped 707-420 aircraft in collaboration with the British engine sector.

Ultimately, then, Britain's Rolls-Royce Conway engine made it possible for Boeing to advance into the former British Commonwealth countries. Yet promoting such sales was a necessary measure for Rolls-Royce to recover the massive development investments against the background of the cancellation of the Vickers V-1000 project, which had been designed to accommodate the Conway.

Table 1.2 Orders of Boeing 707s

	707-120/220 (P&W JT3(J57))	707-320 (P&W JT4(J75))	707-420 (Rolls-Royce Conway)
Air France		20	
Air India			4
American	26		
BOAC			15
Braniff	5		
Continental	5		
Cubana	2		
El Al			3
Ghana			2
Lufthansa			5
Pan American	6	31	
Qantas	10		
Sabena		5	
South American		3	
TWA	15	12	
Varig			2
Total	69	71	31

Source: Boeing Airplane Company, *Annual Report*, 1960, p. 14.

The origins of US–UK collaboration, 1943–56   19

A British aero-engine manufacturer (Rolls-Royce) thus retained a competitive technological advantage over American manufacturers in the engine field due to the development of the turbofan engine, which represented second-generation jet engines. This collaboration between Britain's engine sector and America's airframe sector was the only means by which the survival of the former could be secured. The necessary background was an ineluctable decline in international competitiveness in an area where, at the start of the 1950s, British expectations had been high.

Conclusion

In the immediate aftermath of the Second World War, Britain struggled to preserve not only its Empire, but also its declining air supremacy. Even at this point, Britain was still endeavouring to leverage its competitive edge in jet technology to become the pre-eminent world leader in aviation.

Churchill's War Cabinet established the Brabazon programmes, which foresaw the development of several civil airliners. The Atlee government continued these programmes under the policy moniker "Fly British", whereby BOAC bought domestically produced airliners rather than American models. Moreover, British manufacturing in military production and exports was in full-swing, partly due to the US OSP and Plan K (the RAF modernisation programme) aid. During this period, Britain essentially used American money in an attempt to go toe to toe with American airliners, mainly through the production of the jet-powered Comet and Viscount. However, Britain's jet-powered airliners became victims of their own success on the US market. Congress increasingly perceived the British aviation industry as a threat. Plan K aid to Britain was abruptly discontinued. After 1955, US airliners (such as the Boeing 707 and Douglas DC-8) regained competitive superiority.

These developments seemed to indicate to British aero-engine manufacturers such as Rolls-Royce that they were now participating in a global jet airliner market dominated by US airframe manufacturers. For the latter, however, production collaboration with the British aircraft engine sector appeared promising. The US airframe sector sold aircraft to BOAC and other airways, which were customers of British aircraft engine manufacturers. For British aero-engine manufacturers, powering US airframes was of vital interest; being obliged to power only British aircraft would have been commercial suicide. In order to gain access to the world market, British aero-engine manufacturers needed US aircraft.

It is in this context that the origins of Anglo–American airframe-engine production collaboration can be found. The leading scholar of the British aircraft industry, Keith Hayward, dismissed all Brabazon airliners except the Comet as failures. However, compensated with interim airliners, British airliners competed with US aircraft, and Vickers Viscount was a commercial success. Barnett dismissed the British effort to build its own aircraft industry as a "dream" and "technological overstretch". And yet the British aircraft industry

20 *The post-war challenge, 1943–64*

made itself virtually indispensable to American airliners with the jet-powered Comet and Viscount. Even after US airliners regained superiority in 1955, the British aero-engine manufacturer Rolls-Royce continued to hold technological supremacy over US aero-engine manufacturers and powered American jet airliners.

Notes

1 Churchill (1950, p. 417).
2 Kawasaki and Sakade (2001, p. 3); Hogan ([1987] 1989); Milward ([1984] 1992, p. 465).
3 Barnett (1995, p. 228).
4 Barnett (1995, p. 229).
5 Barnett (1995, p. 228).
6 Hayward (1983, p. 17).
7 Buckley (1995, pp. 180–82).
8 TNA AIR8/1360, Memorandum of Agreement between Lt. Gen. Arnold, Rear Admiral Towers and Air Chief Marshal Portal; *FRUS, The Conferences at Washington, 1941–1942, and Casablanca, 1943*, Document 299; Buckley (1995, p. 180–81). As for the controversy over the Arnold-Towers-Slessor agreement on transport aircraft allocation, see Engel's (2009) footnote 28 for Chapter 1 (Engel (2009, pp. 308–9)).
9 Slessor (1957, p. 410); Arnold did not mention about this agreement in his autobiography *Global Mission* (Arnold (1951)).
10 TNA CAB66/30, WP (42)486[th](Revised), Visit of the Minister of Production to America, 29th October 1942.
11 TNA CAB129/12, CP (46)317th, Civil Aircraft Requirement, 2nd August 1946.
12 TNA CAB87/104, Committee on Reconstruction Problems, Sub-Committee on Civil Aviation, 3rd March 1943.
13 Hayward (1989, pp. 39–40); Phipp (2007, p. 15).
14 TNA CAB66/34, WP (43)83rd, Civil Air Transport, 24th February 1943.
15 Phipp (2007, p. 17).
16 Phipp (2007, p. 17).
17 Simons (2012a, p. 13).
18 TNA CAB66/34, WP (43)83rd, Civil Air Transport, 24th February 1943.
19 TNA CAB66/43, WP (43)537th, Post-War Civil Aviation, 3rd December 1943.
20 TNA CAB65/43, WM (44)114th, 1st September 1944.
21 TNA CAB66/57, WP (44)611th, Comparative Performances of British and American Civil Transport Aircraft, 1st November 1944.
22 TNA CAB66/57, WP (44)611th, Comparative Performances of British and American Civil Transport Aircraft, 1st November 1944.
23 Ministry of Civil Aviation, *British Air Services*, Cmd. 6712 (London, HMSO, 1945).
24 TNA CAB129/12, CP (46)317th, Civil Aircraft Requirement, 2nd August 1946.
25 TNA CAB129/12, Annex B to CP (46)317th, Interdepartmental Committee on Civil Aircraft Requirements, First Interim Report, 23rd July 1946.
26 TNA CAB129/12, CP (46)317th, Civil Aircraft Requirement, 2nd August 1946.
27 TNA CAB129/12, CP (46)317th, Civil Aircraft Requirement, 2nd August 1946.
28 TNA CAB129/12, CP (46)317th, Civil Aircraft Requirement, 2nd August 1946.
29 TNA CAB129/12, CP (46)317th, Civil Aircraft Requirement, 2nd August 1946.
30 TNA CAB129/28, CP (48)179th, The Civil Aircraft Programme, 9th July 1948.
31 TNA CAB129/28, CP (48)182nd, Future of the Tudor Aircraft and of the "Fly British Policy", 10th July 1948.
32 TNA CAB128/13, CM (48)51st, 15th July 1948.

The origins of US–UK collaboration, 1943–56 21

33 Barnett (1995, pp. 241–44).
34 NARA RG59/E1548/Box 3, Super Priority; TNA CAB129/48, C (51)27th, Progress of Rearmament Production, 26th November 1951.
35 *FRUS, 1952–1954, National Security Affairs, Volume II*, Part 2, Document 2; NARA RG59, E1548, Box 2, Lovett-Ismay Agreement (Operation Dovetail), Military Production Program of the United States and United Kingdom, 12th January 1952.
36 NARA RG59/E5148/Box2, Meeting 5:00 pm, 10th January 1952 in Mr. C.E. Wilson's office with U.K. Representatives to Discuss Operation Dovetail.
37 TNA AVIA63/25, EA (52)69th, 23rd May 1952.
38 TNA CAB129/52, C (52)181st, Expansion of Engineering Exports, 28th May 1952.
39 NARA RG56, Office of the Assistant Secretary for International Affairs/UK9/11, Agreed Minutes of a Meeting held at Georges V Hotel Paris on 23rd April 1953.
40 U.S. Congress (1954, p. 14).
41 TNA CAB129/50, C (52)58th, Brabazon and Princess Aircraft, 3rd March 1952.
42 Simons (2012a, p. 121).
43 Phipp (2007, p. 86).
44 Simons (2013, p. 101).
45 *Aviation Week (AW)*, 27th October 1952, pp. 13–14.
46 Verhovek (2010, p. 8).
47 *AW*, 2nd March 1953, p. 251; 13th September 1954, pp. 99–101; Hayward (1989, p. 54).
48 USNA RG59/E1548/Box 2, Capital Airlines $45 Million Purchase of British Commercial Transports.
49 Minister of Aviation, *Report of the Committee of Inquiry into the Aircraft Industry*, Cmnd. 2853 (London, HMSO, 1965), Appendix E. Canberra light bomber was exported to Australia, as the name itself (*AW*, 2nd March, p. 251); Sampson (1977, p. 107).
50 Simons (2013, pp. 125–31).
51 Rodgers (1996, pp. 164–67).
52 Eddy et al. (1976, p. 42).
53 Phipp (2007, p. 134).
54 *AW*, 22nd June 1953, pp. 91–92; Hayward (1983, pp. 22–23); Phipp (2007, pp. 134–35).
55 Hayward (1983, p. 23).
56 TNA AVIA65/745, Note by the Minister of Supply, 13th October 1955; Higham (2013, p. 134).
57 U.S. Congress (1959, p. 15).
58 NARA RG59/E1548/Box 2, Capital Airlines $45 Million Purchase of British Commercial Transports.
59 U.S. Congress (1954, p. 30).
60 NARA RG59/E1548/Box 3, Mission Comments on Senate Appropriations Committee Staff Report, 3rd September 1954; US Congress (1954).
61 NARA RG59/E1548/Box 3, USOM/UK Comment on Senate Committee Report on Aid to UK Aircraft Industry, 29th September 1954.
62 TNA AIR2/14568, Brief in Support of Efforts to Obtain a Revision of the American Decision to Cancel the Offshore Javelin Contract.
63 TNA T225/1566, U.S. Aid.
64 TNA AVIA65/745, Notes of a meeting held on 15th December 1954.
65 TNA AVIA65/745, Notes of a meeting held on 15th December 1954.
66 Bender and Altschul (1982, p. 473).
67 Bender and Altschul (1982, pp. 474–75).
68 Bender and Altschul (1982, p. 475).
69 *AW*, 4th November 1957, p. 41; Hayward (1983, p. 21).
70 TNA AVIA65/745, Conway: Discussion on 17th December 1955.
71 NARA RG59/E1548/Box 2, James Hay Stevens to Eric Bradley, 29th August 1955.

22 *The post-war challenge, 1943–64*

72 TNA AIR2/14568, Brief in Support of Efforts to Obtain a Revision of the American Decision to Cancel the Offshore Javelin Contract, November 1956.
73 TNA PREM11/1276, Harold Macmillan to Prime Minister, 30th October 1956.
74 TNA AIR2/12871, Aide-Memoire on Plan K Aid.
75 USNA RG56/UK9/14, American Embassy, London to the Department of State, Washington, 25th October 1956.
76 Higham (2013, p. 209).
77 TNA AVIA65/745, Note of the Minister's meeting with Rolls Royce Ltd. on 2nd May 1956.
78 TNA AVIA65/745, Rolls Royce Limited to Reginald Maudling, 27th July 1956.
79 TNA AVIA65/745, Rolls Royce Limited to Reginald Maudling, 27th July 1956.
80 As for the purchase of 20 British machines, as de Havilland was interested in the Comet 5 for BEA, BOAC was compelled to buy Vickers airliners (Higham (2013, p. 210)).
81 TNA PREM11/3680, Statement by the Minister of Transport and Civil Aviation, 24th October 1956.
82 Hayward (1983, pp. 23–24).

2 Sandys White Paper and the rationalisation of the British aircraft industry, 1957–1960

Introduction

As Chapter 1 showed, in the decade or so after 1945, British foreign policy was founded on Winston Churchill's famous "three circles". According to Churchill, these "three circles" encompassed the roles that Britain was required to embody after the war if it hoped to preserve its great power status. These were: leader of the British Empire; the closest ally of the United States; and a dominant power in Western Europe. However, the Suez Crisis and the Sputnik shock offered two traumatic indications of Britain's diminished place in the world. It became increasingly apparent that Britain had no choice but to drop the pretence that it was a global power on par with the United States and the Soviet Union. The logic of the dismantling of the British Empire after the Suez Crisis ultimately pushed Britain in the direction of membership of the EU. However, this entailed a challenging balancing act between the United States and the Europeans, and especially with France, the self-styed leader of Western Europe.

Many scholars have seen in these developments a narrative of inexorable British decline, a linear process of decolonisation, defeat and belated European integration. This process encompassed retreat from East of Suez,[1] a second depreciation of the pound sterling in 1967, and late membership of the EC in 1973. Kyle and Sasaki, for example, have described the Suez Crisis as a watershed moment in this history that marked the end of British global power.[2] Similarly, John W. Young has divided these processes into three periods: 1945–1956 saw Britain as a "Third force" between Europe and the United States; 1957–1972 saw Britain gradually "Without a role": while post-1973 saw it as a "Reluctant European".[3]

The first of these periods is said to have been particularly catastrophic. As Britain clung to the Empire and the "special relationship" with America, it was required to bear massive defence and research and development (R&D) expenditures that scuppered participation in European integration. Consequently, Britain suffered from a chronically low growth rate, and only belatedly joined the EC as a fully-fledged member after the collapse of the Empire and out of a pressing need to facilitate a post-war economic recovery.

Needless to say, an overlooked aspect of this narrative is that Anglo–French forces successfully overcame Nasser in military operations. In fact, it was the US–Soviet

DOI: 10.4324/9781003127901-3

24 The post-war challenge, 1943–64

intervention that induced the British withdrawal. That said, my argument in this chapter does not rest on the implications of the Suez Crisis. I show here that the overarching narrative of British decline is put into doubt by a close examination of the post-war British aircraft industry. Indeed, it was precisely during the second half of the 1950s – i.e. the half-decade of "catastrophic" decline – that the industrial and commercial foundations were laid for the retrenchment and resurgence of British air-engine manufacturing. The results of this became much more visible in the last third of the twentieth century.

Chapters 2 and 3 focus on attempts by conservative politicians to reorganise the British aircraft industry in the late 1950s. Chapter 3 concentrates on Julian Amery, the son-in-law of Harold Macmillan. Amery was a key member of the anti-Nasser "Suez Group" during the Suez Crisis. As Minister of Aviation (1962–1964), he tried to recover air supremacy from the United States through the development of a long-haul airliner and supersonic transport (SST) (Chapter 3).[4] The second conservative politician, and the main focus of this chapter, was Duncan Sandys, the son-in-law of Winston Churchill. Sandys maintained that "the Suez crisis ha[d] altered nothing".[5] He refused to accept that Britain had become "a 'second class power'".[6] As Minister of Defence (January 1957–October 1959) and Minister of Aviation (October 1959–July 1960) in the Macmillan administration, Sandys initiated a programme of British nuclear deterrence and air power.

This chapter focuses on two key politicians – Aubrey Jones, the Minister of Supply from 1957 until 1959, and Duncan Sandys, the Minister of Aviation from 1959 until 1960. The chapter aims to show how these two politicians in particular attempted to master the crisis that faced the British aircraft industry towards the end of the 1950s. This was a harrowing period for the industry and for British policymakers. American aid had dried up and the Suez Crisis seemed to point towards an inglorious future. Sandy's and Amery's ambitious reforms seemed to be doomed to failure, and, indeed, they had some near-ruinous ramifications in the 1960s. However, as later chapters in this book will show, they formed the basis for a rationalised British aircraft industry which would enjoy a resurgence in the last third of the twentieth century.

The Sandys White Paper and the crisis of the British aircraft industry

Soon after the Suez Crisis, the Sputnik shock occurred, triggering a new phase in the competition for the development of advanced missiles. The immediate aftermath of the crisis saw Harold Macmillan's Conservative government come to power in Britain. Macmillan faced the urgent need for missile development in the context of a continuing drain on Britain's gold and dollar reserves.[7] Moreover, if the United States ceased or even reduced its military aid, it was expected that Britain would not be able to continue its current military strategy beyond 1958.[8]

Nevertheless, Macmillan was determined to maintain Britain's independent military-industrial base, even under the condition that US military aid dried up completely. To this end, Duncan Sandys, Minister of Defence, published a

Sandys White Paper and rationalisation, 1957–60 25

famous defence White Paper, *Defence: Outline of Future Policy* (the so-called "Sandys White Paper") in March 1957.[9] The Sandys White Paper envisioned a reliance on the Blue Streak rocket missile as a method of nuclear delivery.[10]

Overall, Sandys adopted two concepts for British defence: first, nuclear deterrence by ballistic missile; and, second, "the substitution of missiles for aircraft for the air defence".[11] The Sandys White Paper stated that "[t]he means of delivering these [nuclear] weapons is provided by medium bombers of the V-class. These will in due course be supplemented and later replaced by ballistic rockets".[12] Sandys evidently believed that Britain would not be in a position to develop other long-range bombers after the existing V-bombers, or to develop sophisticated fighters after the Lightning.[13] Under the condition of limited defence budgets, the British Cabinet had to cut back on development projects under the manned aircraft budget. This forced British aircraft firms into severe difficulties. Jones and Sandys, the Ministers of Supply in the Macmillan government, were faced with the task of rebuilding British aircraft firms through industrial reorganisation.

Aubrey Jones, the British Minister of Supply, made strenuous attempts to overcome the British aircraft industry's difficulties. These comprised a reduction of military orders and a decline in civil exports. His main approach was to stipulate that contracts would be awarded by the government only to a small number of rationalised aircraft manufacturers. Against the background of the Sandys White Paper, Jones presented a memorandum dated 1st July 1957 to the British Cabinet. In this memo, Jones argued that the implications outlined in the Sandys White Paper would become fully apparent only over the next two to three years. He predicted that many firms would disappear, and that total employment in the aircraft industry would decrease from around 266,000 to some 100,000 over a period of four or five years. The volume of military aircraft production would thus be limited, and the aircraft industry would have to sustain itself principally on civil work and exports.[14]

For these reasons, Jones first recommend that the government should use its power to award contracts to shrink the aircraft industry into fewer firms, with the remaining firms larger in size. Second, he suggested that the government should induce a manufacturer to develop a new civil aircraft as a private venture through an initial domestic order (BOAC, BEA and the RAF Transport Command).[15] However, Harold Watkinson, the Minister of Transport and Civil Aviation responsible for express national airways BOAC and BEA, was opposed to Jones' position. Neither of the firms attached to his ministry had any interest in buying a new airliner nor had any individual specifications. In his response to Jones, Watkinson stated that neither the BOAC nor the BEA were likely to make large orders.[16]

At a Cabinet meeting on 9th July 1957, the aircraft industry problem was again discussed, and Jones' and Watkinson's memos were examined. Jones insisted that some continuing Exchequer assistance appeared to be essential. The industry would collapse without it, which necessitated a substantial initial order and a coordination of the aircraft requirements of the RAF Transport Command with

26 The post-war challenge, 1943–64

BOAC and BEA. For the British aircraft industry, and ruling out any unexpected foreign customers, the only possible customer for British airliners were the BOAC, BEA and the RAF Transport Command.[17]

In his reply to this argument, Watkinson stated that the Bristol Britannia was already ordered for Transport Command, while BOAC and BEA had also placed orders for the main aircraft. They were likely to need these during the next five years. As a result, no major orders could be foreseen in the immediate future. Jones needed the BOAC and BEA to order the same transport aircraft alongside the order of RAF Transport Command so as to reach a particular number of transport aircraft orders. He believed that the combined RAF/BOAC/BEA order could provide leverage for a thoroughgoing rationalisation of the aircraft industry.[18]

Watkinson, however, maintained that there would not be a substantial order from BOAC and BEA. The burgeoning conflict between the two ministers remained unsolved in the Cabinet meeting. Prime Minister Harold Macmillan indicated that Peter Thorneycroft, the Chancellor of the Exchequer, should make an enquiry into the future of the aircraft industry in order to seek a solution to this problem. Thorneycroft thus took on the chair of the Aircraft Industry Working Party.[19]

A problem with the BEA new medium-range jet order

In late 1957, BEA planned to order aircraft with 70–80 seats. These were scheduled to go into operation from 1963 to 1965.[20] In December 1957, Jones suggested to Hawker Siddeley and Bristol to merge and form a Consortium in order to acquire the BEA order. However, this placed the government in a difficult position. BEA preferred the de Havilland airliner, the DH.121 (Trident). De Havilland was prepared to offer its project as a private venture. And yet Jones continued to insist that the winner of the BEA jet order should merge with another major unit in the airframe industry.[21] Subsequently, de Havilland established the Consortium, known as Airco on 30 January 1958. This Consortium consisted of de Havilland, Fairey Aviation and Hunting Aircraft Companies. Each of the individual partners would lose their separate identity and independence.[22] The Hawker/Bristol Consortium contended with Airco for the BEA order. Both sides prepared for the development of aircraft through private ventures.

In early 1958, BEA pointed to several reasons for favouring the de Havilland project. It was the only British firm with experience of civil jet aircraft, and Trident, it was felt, would be a natural successor to the Comet.[23] Initially, Jones tried to persuade BEA to abandon its preference for the de Havilland design in favour of the joint Hawker Siddeley/Bristol project, because this was in accordance with the policy of reducing the number of aircraft firms. Jones feared that de Havilland was "a weaker firm financially and desirous of financial support from the Ministry of Supply".[24] He was convinced that the Hawker–Bristol combination had more potential to compete on the world market. He also considered BEA's 24-item order to be uneconomical. Indeed, substantial export sales to Pan Am would be necessary in order to guarantee a reasonable profit.[25]

On 4th February 1958, Jones presented a paper on the BEA jet order to the Cabinet. He advanced two main arguments: first, that the British aircraft industry had to be strengthened in order to compete with US industry; and, second, that the heavy dependence on Exchequer finance had to be curtailed. He made this second point despite the fact that, in the military field, there were no new contracts in the pipeline, while in the civil field, there was only one – the new BEA order for jet aircraft.[26]

Jones also related the results of his attempted rationalisation of British aircraft firms ahead of the BEA order. He suggested that, while Bristol and Hawker Siddeley did not need government money, de Havilland quite obviously did. He further recommended that BEA's order should be placed with the Hawker–Bristol team so as to promote industrial rationalisation. Once again, he was opposed by Watkinson, who insisted that BEA should be allowed to place its order with the de Havilland group.[27]

At a Cabinet meeting on 12th February 1958, Reginald Manningham-Buller, the Attorney-General, argued that BEA was under no statutory obligation to seek consent for its purchase or non-purchase of aircraft. If BEA was able to finance the purchase of aircraft from the de Havilland group from its own resources, then it was free to do so. Moreover, the de Havilland group had made it clear that the Trident project had been undertaken as a private venture. Ultimately, then, both Hawker Siddeley/Bristol and de Havilland framed their impending BEA order as a private venture policy. Furthermore, de Havilland's announcement of the establishment of Airco was in accordance with the government's industrial rationalisation policy. Consequently, the Cabinet authorised Watkinson to inform BEA that it might enter into negotiations with the de Havilland group over the production of a new jet aircraft.[28]

To sum up: in the wake of the Trident affair, Jones attempted to rationalise industry by merging numerous smaller manufacturing firms with larger ones. He induced this by stipulating that contracts would be awarded by the government only to a small number of rationalised aircraft manufacturers. But despite his efforts, prestigious manufacturers such as de Havilland resisted the government's rationalisation policy out of a determination to maintain managerial independence. British aircraft industrialisation policy in the aftermath of the Suez Crisis was anything but plain sailing.

The TSR-2 (OR339) contract

In the field of military production, neither Sandys nor the Air Ministry considered that they had any need of further manned aircraft.[29] A significant role in Jones' industrial rationalisation policy was played by the OR339. This was considered to be the successor to the light bomber Canberra, later known as the Tactical, Strike and Reconnaissance aircraft-2 (TSR-2) fighter-bomber contract, which was in turn the successor to the English Electric Canberra light-bomber.

On 16th September 1957, at a meeting between the Ministry of Supply and nine airframe firms, Jones made four key announcements. First, he stated that

28 *The post-war challenge, 1943–64*

publication of the Sandys White Paper had made the future government demand for military aircraft unmistakeably clear. Second, he observed that only a small number of projects remained in the hands of the Ministry of Supply, and that, of these, the OR339 was by far the most important. Third, he made a strong case for a measure of reorganisation to reduce the number of small units of which the aircraft industry was comprised. Fourth, he stressed that, in placing a contract for the OR339, the Ministry of Supply had to be satisfied that the winner of the contract had the resources necessary to undertake the project.[30]

The Services favoured the Vickers' design proposals for the OR339. However, the government policy of rationalisation and the "ideal standard" for an aircraft firm were a potential spanner in the works. It was decided that no single firm alone had the technical and financial resources to accomplish the project in the given time scale. Thus, on 1st January 1959, the main contract was placed with Vickers-Armstrong, with the work to be shared with English Electric Aviation on a 50–50 basis. This is the only case where it appears that the government compelled the establishment of a joint company with the partners being selected by the Ministry.[31]

Approval of the report by the Aircraft Industry Working Party

On 14th April 1958, the Aircraft Industry Working Party, chaired by Peter Thorneycroft, the Chancellor of the Exchequer, submitted a report entitled *The Future of the Aircraft Industry: Aeronautical Research and Development* to the Cabinet. The Working Party had been asked to consider a series of questions in preparation of their report. First, what reduction in the size of the aircraft industry was implied by the Sandys White Paper, and what was the time scale of this reduction? Second, should this reduced industry be re-organised into a smaller number of units? If so, how could this best be brought about, and which of the existing units should be retained? Third, was it in the national interest that the government should continue to provide financial support to the aircraft industry, and, if so, on what scale?[32]

The Working Party's report was amply summarised, and responded to, in a memorandum by Heathcoat Amory, the new Chancellor of the Exchequer, on 2nd May 1958. The Amory memorandum reported the following two main recommendations of the Working Party: first, the government should maintain the present level of support for R&D in both the military and civil sectors, on condition that the aircraft industry reorganise and strengthen itself in order to better contend with international competition. Second, substantial government assistance might be necessary in the field of civil development. Such assistance might prove particularly important for a future generation of aircraft, such as SST or Vertical Take Off and Landing (VTOL).[33]

The Cabinet Economic Policy Committee generally agreed with the Aircraft Industry Working Party. The former explicitly recommended that the government concentrate on fewer and stronger units in the difficult transitional period of reduced military orders and severe international competition[34]

The Cabinet meeting of 6th May 1958 centred on Amory's memorandum. According to the Chancellor, it was necessary to press the aircraft industry to reorganise and become more efficient if it wanted to guarantee financial support from the government. The Cabinet agreed that the government should continue to provide financial support for the R&D on the lines proposed by the Working Party of officials. There was also a consensus that the large airliner should be developed for export.[35] Increasingly, however, the focus in the Cabinet was on the nature of the government's policy towards the aircraft industry under the Sandys White Paper. Of particular concern was the continuation of governmental financial aid to the aircraft industry. On 13th May, Jones explained in the House of Commons that government aid would be provided for the development of civil airliners, and he outlined the conditions under which this would be offered.[36]

Ultimately, then, the British aircraft industry continued to face severe difficulties in both the military and civil sphere during the first half of 1958. In the former, the Sandys White Paper reduced military procurement. In the latter, American jet airliners had come to dominate the global market. Jones thus established the criteria for what he considered an ideal standard for an aircraft firm. This would be "a firm which was engaged in both military and civil aircraft and industrial, non-industrial activities, so that it could raise its capital on the basis of its entire diversified structure".[37] The priority, it seems, was to close the government purse.

Crisis in the civil sector

In January 1958, BOAC made a contract with Vickers to purchase 35 VC10s with an option for a further 20.[38] However, Vickers expressed its inability to absorb a further prospective loss of £8–10 million. It insisted that such a loss would accrue if sales of the VC10 were limited to the existing BOAC order of 35, and if BOAC had no other potentially successful projects in hand. Such projects included smaller versions of the VC10, which it hoped to develop as a Viscount replacement. The VC10 was technically superior to the existing versions of the comparable American types – Boeing 707 and Douglas DC-8 – but its production process was less advanced than the American models, and the prospects for its success on the world market were uncertain.[39]

Government help for the VC10 could have taken various forms. Certain conditions needed to be in place in order for Vickers to avoid severe losses on this model, and perhaps even to gain export orders for it. These conditions included a willingness on the part of BOAC to convert its existing option for 20 additional aircraft into a firm order, and perhaps also an RAF order of 20 VC10s. However, even if BOAC were to order additional VC10s, it would probably not need them until its Britannia and Comets began to go out of service in the mid-1960s. Moreover, any possible RAF requirements for VC10s in order to replace the Britannia were not likely to materialise until around 1967 or later.[40]

In fact, by July 1959, the British aircraft industry had reached a critical stage. Vickers, the main British manufacturer, was planning to close its civil aircraft

30 The post-war challenge, 1943–64

business due to losses incurred on the failed Vanguard civil airliner project, and also due to the bleak future of the VC10 long-range airliner project. This would surely mean that BOAC would fly the Atlantic in the Boeing 707. Moreover, de Havilland had access only to slender monetary resources. The company had made no profit from the Comet, and no prospective sales for the 24 Trident for BEA were on the horizon. If de Havilland completed this contract, it would cost the company a lot of money. The government had to take control of this situation. Alternative courses would either entail Britain entirely giving up its aircraft industry, or put irresistible pressure on Britain to nationalise this industry completely.[41]

In his Cabinet paper of 18th December 1958, Jones stated that the decline in employment in the aircraft manufacturing sector over the previous five months had been approximately 10,000 jobs, and that another decline of 25,000 was envisioned for the immediate future. He further pointed out that, owing to cuts in the defence budget, crises of management were envisioned for the Hawker Siddeley Group, the Bristol Aircraft Company, and perhaps even companies such as Vickers and de Havilland. There were further signs that Vickers' forthcoming civil project, the Vanguard, would not be a commercial success, with catastrophic consequences for the finances of the company. Jones concluded that the British aircraft industry was suffering not only in the military field, but it also faced severe difficulties on the civil side. Indeed, he predicted a possible withdrawal from the civil field and the virtual disappearance of an important industry over the following decade.[42] At the Cabinet meeting on 23rd December 1958, Jones called for significant governmental support for the development of civil airliners.[43]

On 3rd July 1959, Prime Minister Harold Macmillan chaired a meeting of concerned ministers in an attempt to solve these problems in the civil sector. At this meeting, Jones reiterated the Cabinet's approval in 1958 for the de Havilland Trident to be developed as a private venture for BEA. BEA had decided that it wanted a smaller aircraft than was initially envisaged, while Rolls-Royce had asked for a financial contribution of up to £7 million towards the new engine Spey.[44]

Jones argued that the government should not support the Trident-Spey, on the grounds that Trident would not obtain the export orders needed to make it a commercial success. Alternatively, he recommended Vickers' new airliner, because TCA had shown some interest in it. If a Canadian order for up to 50 aircraft of this design materialised, then TCA's order could be combined with an order by BEA. In this way, a foundation might be laid for the commercial success of this model.[45]

Jones asked that the Minister of Transport should endeavour to persuade BEA to cooperate in these arrangements. Harold Watkinson, the Minister of Transport and Civil Aviation, was opposed to this position. Watkinson argued that Trident was virtually a Viscount replacement aircraft. He insisted that care be taken to avoid any commitment to support two types of aircraft. The best solution would be some form of joint operation by Vickers and the de Havilland Group in the

Sandys White Paper and rationalisation, 1957–60 31

development and production of a Viscount replacement. Macmillan concluded that only one type of each of the main categories of future civil aircraft could be developed by the British aircraft industry.[46]

Vickers' possible retreat from the civil air business problem

The prospective abandonment of the development and production of VC10 presented a severe problem. It meant the possible retreat of the British aircraft industry from the long-range airliner market.[47] A ministerial meeting was held on 9th July 1959 to deal with the twin problems of Viscount replacement and the long-range VC10. With respect to the former issue, ministers agreed that a Vickers project would offer the best prospects for British industry to compete on world markets for a Viscount replacement. To launch a Vickers project, it would be desirable that Vickers should be associated with BEA requirements. At this time, these requirements were being negotiated between BEA and de Havilland's Airco group.[48]

At this meeting, Jones also remarked on the trickiness of the VC10 problem. The VC10 project required £21 million of investment in order to be viable. Jones called on the accountant Henry Benson, a senior partner of Cooper Brothers, to speak at the meeting. Benson reported that the prospective loss on VC10 was £15 million and that BOAC had to buy 35 VC10s. Jones recommended a merger of Vickers with English Electric and, if possible, de Havilland.[49]

Jones' aim continued to be the rationalisation of the British aircraft industry, mainly through the use of government military contracts (for the TSR-2) and national airline (BEA) orders. But he continued to clash with Watkinson, Minister of Transport and Civil Aircraft, who represented the preferences of national airlines. In the view of these aircraft manufacturers, Jones' made an unfortunate impression which combined "ignorance of markets, laxity of costs, and greed for public money".[50]

Sandys and the reorganisation of the British aircraft industry

The Ministry of Supply was the government's aircraft procurement authority. As such, it was in close contact with the aircraft manufacturing industry. The latter also had close links to civil aviation. Such a division of responsibilities could obviously lead to conflicting views between the two ministers, one tending to represent supply and the other representing the demand side of civil procurement. In this situation, Duncan Sandys became Minister of Aviation, thereby combining his roles of Ministry of Supply and Ministry of Transport and Civil Aircraft. It was from this position that Sandys attempted to complete the rationalisation of the aircraft industry.

As the author of the 1957 defence White Paper, Sandys' position and ambitions were already clear. Rationalisation was his agenda. And indeed, the formation of the Ministry of Aviation in 1959 resulted in the virtual elimination of conflict between the aircraft industry and airlines.[51] The Ministry of Aviation planned both the military and civil projects that were intended to contest US

32 The post-war challenge, 1943–64

manufacturers for market control during the 1960s. The new ministry set the conditions for cooperation over the winning of project contracts.[52]

As already noted, in October 1956, the British government allowed BOAC to buy the Boeing 707 as a "stop-gap" until British-made models were complete. But the government also insisted that this purchase was conditional on BOAC buying 20 British airliners.[53] By early 1957, the British government had decided to endorse BOAC's order of a large, four-engined British long-range airliner. In fact, BOAC was still hoping for a British version of Boeing 707, or perhaps even a British-built, licensed version of the Boeing model. However, BOAC's paymasters in government insisted on a British-designed airliner. The possible contenders included the DH.118 (de Havilland), the HP.97 (Handley Page), the Bristol 200 and the Vickers VC10. Ultimately, BOAC elected to buy 25 Vickers VC10s. This was closely tailored to BOAC's needs – the VC10 could be used in the kind of "hot and high" conditions, and on short runway airports, that were typical of the Empire routes that BOAC flew. The Boeing 707 and Douglas DC-8, by contrast, were built to meet more global requirements.[54]

In November 1959, Sandys met senior representatives of the aircraft industry to discuss his plans for rationalisation. He attempted to introduce the government launch aid programme to civil projects and established core initiatives in both the military (the TSR-2) and the civilian sector (the VC10).[55] He also proposed the introduction of government financial aid for the development of civil airliners and, by this measure, to complete the industrial rationalisation.[56]

Above all, Sandys made clear to the gathered representatives of the aircraft industry that it was necessary to merge several companies into no more than two main airframe and two main aero-engine groups.[57] He expressed the hope that one group would be based upon Hawker Siddeley, perhaps in association with de Havilland, and that the other would be based upon Vickers and English Electric. On the aero-engine side, two major groups already existed, namely Rolls-Royce and Bristol Siddeley. Sandys estimated that, in order to help the industry, additional government assistance on civil aircraft and aero-engine projects would be necessary. In light of the difficulties facing the aircraft industry, he pegged this figure at £15 million a year.[58]

Sandys secured the consent of representatives of the aircraft industry for his rationalisation plans. With this in the bag, he then turned to the Chancellor of the Exchequer for a guarantee of government aid. In the Cabinet meeting of 17th December 1959, Heathcoat Amory, the Chancellor of the Exchequer, stated that, if additional government assistance were provided for these purposes, it was likely to exceed the average rate of £15 million. Prime Minister Harold Macmillan agreed with Sandys and concluded that the aircraft industry should be maintained and reorganised on the basis of two main airframe and two aero-engine groups. However, it did not seem possible to determine what the scale of long-term government assistance should be. Projections could only be made for current and likely future projects and, in particular, the projects over which Vickers found itself in considerable difficulty.[59]

A ministerial meeting was held on 21st December 1959 and chaired by Amory, with Sandys also in attendance. The key topic was governmental launch aid.

Amory stated that the long-term aircraft development and production costs were notoriously hard to predict. However, they usually exceeded initial estimates considerably. Overall, the sales prospects for the British aircraft industry were uncertain. In his reply, Sandys insisted that the government's drive to rationalise the aircraft industry into two main airframe groups and two main aero-engine groups was proceeding well. The Hawker Aircraft company had already made certain amalgamations. Moreover, Vickers, English Electric and Bristol were now prepared to form a group, subject to a satisfactory assurance of government support. Sandys recommended government support for the VC series – long-range VC10 and medium-range VC11. Amory stated that the proposed government offer of £20 million for the development of VC aircraft would be acceptable if it led to the merger of Vickers, English Electric and Bristol.[60]

On 22nd December 1959, Amory and Sandys reached the following agreement. First, the government would offer £20 million for development of the VC series (VC10 and VC11) on the condition that Vickers, English Electric and Bristol merged. Second, the government was prepared to underwrite 50 per cent of the cost of production of up to 20 Super VC10s and up to 20 VC11s beyond any initial orders placed by operators. Third, over the following five years, the government agreed to spend, on average, about £15 million a year for the support of promising civil airframes and aero-engines.[61]

Now Sandys needed industry backing for his agreement with Amory. On the afternoon of 22nd December, he met with representatives of Vickers, English Electric and Bristol. With the approval of the Chancellor of the Exchequer, Sandys was able to inform the relevant manufactures of the nature and extent of the financial assistance which they might now expect from the government. The prospective recipients of such support included the following: Vickers Group – VC10 and Super VC10 (Transatlantic version of VC10) and VC11 (medium-range airliner).[62] In an ensuing memorandum, Sandys reported to the Cabinet that the reorganisation of the British aircraft industry was nearing completion.

British aircraft firms, it seemed, were ready to toe the line. In airframe manufacturing, a new private company – the British Aircraft Corporation (BAC) – was formed by Vickers, English Electric, Bristol and Hunting. The new BAC board quickly cancelled the Vickers VC11 airliner and launched the Hunting-designed BAC1-11. The new company also took charge of the military TSR-2 (the OR339 contract), the long-range airliner VC10 and the medium-range BAC1-11. A second airframe manufacturer – Hawker Siddeley Aviation (HSA) – was formed out of Hawker, Gloster, A.V. Roe and Armstrong Whitworth, de Havilland, Blackburn and Folland. Aero-engine manufacturing, meanwhile, would be structured around Rolls-Royce, plus a new company – Bristol Siddeley Engines (BSE) – comprised of Bristol, Hawker Siddeley, Blackburn and de Havilland.[63]

"No More Boeings"

Sandys' grand plan of rationalising the British aircraft industry into four core companies was anything but a *fait accompli*. In January 1960, BOAC was

34   *The post-war challenge, 1943–64*

informed that the entire VC10 programme was in danger of cancellation because Vickers had incurred significant losses in civil business. Even though Vickers was about to become part of BAC, the company still had to carry the cost of the VC10. To ease Vickers' cash-flow difficulties, BOAC was asked by the government to change its ten options to order. Unfortunately, BOAC had its own problems. Its re-equipment programme was already a heavy commitment. Similarly, new airlines in the emerging nations of the Third World were competing on routes where BOAC had once exercised a virtual monopoly. BOAC also suspected that a larger aircraft such as the standard VC10 would lack the necessary flexibility. In any case, BOAC planned to restrict itself to the use of Boeing 707s on its North Atlantic services. Sandys also informed BOAC that he was concerned about the financial health and welfare of both the airline and aircraft industries. However, he added that, in this instance, a larger order for the VC10 would help to secure the formation of BAC. The "Fly British" policy was alive and kicking.[64]

On 15th February 1960, Sandys made a statement in the House of Commons. He first revealed a sharp reduction in government orders for military aircraft – i.e. in a large proportion of the industry's business. This, he contended, had made it urgently necessary to expand sales of civil aircraft at home and overseas. He added that the government had been considering ways of helping manufacturers adjust themselves to this changed situation. Sandys pointed out the importance of the development of civil airliners and proposed the necessity of reorganising the British aircraft industry into four major groups, plus a helicopter company, based on the principle of industrial rationalisation.[65]

Significantly, Sandys further commented that, given the growing importance of the civil market, the government had decided to provide increased support for promising civil aircraft and aero-engines. Sandys also clarified the nature of governmental financial aid for the development of a civil airliner. This financial aid would entail a government offer of direct budgetary support to civil airliners and aero-engines.[66] This represented a significant departure from Jones's private venture policy. Sandys even explicitly named the four projects for which the government would provide launch aid: the long-range airliner VC10, the medium-range airliner BAC1-11, Trident and Spey engine for BAC1-11 and Trident.[67]

In June 1960, BOAC placed a revised order for 30 Super and 15 Standard VC10s. Due to the order by BOAC and RAF, the number of VC10 orders rose to almost 60. This meant that the VC10 project was already approaching a breakeven point that would recover the costs of development. BOAC Chairman Sir Matthew Slattery admitted that the decision to order more VC10s was "a bit of gamble"[68] given the fact that traffic was failing. But Sandy's grand design was clearly bearing fruit. Development aid from the Ministry of Aviation was consolidating the rationalisation of the British aircraft industry and accelerating the merger of firms.[69]

Ultimately, the Ministry of Aviation hoped that the British aircraft industry would grow into a rival for the US aircraft industry. The key to achieving this seemed to consist in both rationalising and supporting this slimmed-down sector.

The Ministry funded the VC10 project of BAC by compelling the RAF and BOAC to order this model as part of the "Fly British" policy. These activities were designed to help the British aircraft industry to regain its competitiveness in the long-haul market.

The Sandys White Paper had made ambitious demands. It had called for Britain to maintain the same capability in military operations, especially East of Suez, but with fewer forces and more restricted defence budgets. In the field of weapons and equipment, the solution to this requirement seemed to lie in the development of Vertical & Short Take Off (V/STOL) capabilities in fighter and transport developments under the concept of "Strategic Mobility".[70] Consequently, in the early 1960s, requirements were issued for an advanced jet fighter and a tactical transport. Both of these would be based on revolutionary V/STOL concepts which had been financed mainly by HSA, with some support from the NATO Mutual Weapons Development Programme. However, after two inconclusive NATO competitions held in 1962 for VTOL projects, the British government decided unilaterally to go ahead with two HSA designs. These were the P.1154, a supersonic VTOL strike-fighter, and the AW681 (later named HS.681), a complementary VTOL military transport.[71]

In fact, a series of purchasing decision in the early 1960s clearly indicated that the British government was expecting to fund significant aircraft projects for the duration of the 1960s. In early 1963, it was decided to develop the HS.681 transports as a replacement for the Beverleys and Hastings.[72] Then, in October 1963, the Ministers of Aviation and Defence agreed to develop a Supersonic P.1154 V/STOL fighter from HSA, as well as engines for the P.1154 from BSE.[73] These new models would have V/STOL capability, as well as Rolls-Royce engines. According to Darby and Dockrill, the TSR-2, the P.1154 and the HS.681 were all "East of Suez" weapons.[74] The TSR-2 was intended to provide a "nuclear umbrella" East of Suez. The TSR-2 had broadly similar specifications to the American General Dynamics F-111 Aardvark, while the HS.681 transport was superior to the American Lockheed C-130 Hercules in V/STOL technology.[75] The supersonic P.1154 V/STOL fighter was a revolutionary innovative machine, while the American McDonnell Douglas F-4 Phantom was "a less sophisticated, more flexible, combined offensive/defensive tactical weapon".[76]

Clearly, then, the British government intended to put its money where its mouth was. This was also reflected in the civil sector. Here, Sandys' main aim was to pressure BOAC to purchase the VC10 long-haul airliner and to compete with the Boeing 707. Indeed, the Macmillan government's rivalry with the United States was apparent in its frank hostility to purchasing the Boeing 707. In June 1962, BOAC asked the government for additional purchases of the Boeing 707-320 Intercontinental, powered by P&W J75. The company wanted to operate this model on the London–Los Angeles non-stop route, in much the same way as Pan Am, TWA and Air France intended. But the government flatly refused this request because it implied a possible cancellation of VC10 and damage to the British aircraft industry.[77] Macmillan sent a note to Peter Thorneycroft, Minister of Aviation, which simply read; "No More Boeings, I hope".[78]

36 The post-war challenge, 1943–64

Conclusion

The loss of American aid in the late 1950s triggered a crisis in the British aircraft industry and propelled a reorganisation of government policy. The new policy consisted, first, of industrial rationalisation; second, new development projects for the 1960s; and, third, the establishment of the Ministry of Aviation. The overall aim of the government's aircraft industrial policy was to achieve independence from the US aircraft industry in both military and civil fields in the 1960s. This was an ambitious aim because, due to the US aircraft industry's domination of the world market by the mid-1950s, and defence order cuts in the wake of the Sandys White Paper, the British aircraft industry faced a managerial crisis.

In the first stage of industrial rationalisation, Aubrey Jones, the Minister of Supply, tried to consolidate manufacturers using the OR339 contract (the TSR-2) and a jet airliner order for BEA through a private venture policy. The government was largely successful in this endeavour, despite some recalcitrance from companies such as de Havilland, which were determined to maintain managerial independence. In the second stage of industrial rationalisation, the Macmillan government established the Ministry of Aviation in 1959. Its head, Duncan Sandys, attempted to consolidate the rationalisation programme by introducing governmental launch aid to the new companies. The Ministry planned the "1960s development programme", which consisted of the VC10 in the civil sector and the TSR-2 in the military sector in competition with the US aircraft industry.

In effect, these reforms constituted a concerted attempt to maintain an independent defence industrial base for the British Empire, even in the wake of the Suez Crisis. Such an approach was, of course, rife with danger. The new willingness of the British state to fund the aircraft industry would have some dire ramifications in the 1960s, as several key aircraft projects ran into financial difficulties and became a significant drain on the public purse. On the other hand, however, the later resurgence of British aircraft manufacturing in the 1970s and 1980s would not have been possible without the ambitious reforms of the late 1950s.[79]

Notes

1 Saki Dockrill regarded "East of Suez" as the Persian Gulf and the Far East (Dockrill 2002, p. 2). This book follows that definition.
2 Kyle (1991); Sasaki (1997).
3 Young (1997, p. ii).
4 Onslow (2008, pp. 67–68).
5 Brooke (2018, p. 25).
6 Brooke (2018, p. 25).
7 Jones (1985, p. 71).
8 TNA AIR2/12871, The R.A.F. Programme in relation to American Aid, 13th January 1956.
9 Minister of Defence, *Defence: Outline of Future Policy*, Cmnd. 124 (London, HMSO, 1957) (Sandys White Paper).

Sandys White Paper and rationalisation, 1957–60 37

10 TNA CAB129/86, C (57)69th, Statement of Defence, 1957, Note by the Minister of Defence, 15th March 1957.
11 Jones (1985, p. 72).
12 TNA CAB129/86, C (57)69th, Statement of Defence, 1957, Note by the Minister of Defence, 15th March 1957.
13 Minister of Aviation, *Report of the Committee of Inquiry into the Aircraft Industry,* Cmnd. 2853 (London, HMSO, 1965), para. 92; TNA CAB129/86, CC (57)17th, Statement of Defence, 1957, Note by the Minister of Defence, 15th March 1957.
14 TNA CAB129/88, C (57)154th, The Aircraft Industry, 1st July 1957.
15 TNA CAB129/88, C (57)154th, The Aircraft Industry, 1st July 1957.
16 TNA CAB129/88, C (57)159th, The Aircraft Industry, 5th July 1957.
17 TNA CAB128/31, CC (57)50th, 9th July 1957.
18 TNA CAB128/31, CC (57)50th, 9th July 1957.
19 TNA CAB128/31, CC (57)50th, 9th July 1957.
20 TNA CAB129/91, C (58)19th, Aircraft for British European Airways, 23rd January 1958.
21 TNA CAB129/92, C (58)94th, Aircraft Industry, 2nd May 1958.
22 Hartley (1965, p. 849).
23 TNA CAB129/91, C (58)31st, British European Airways, 31st January 1958.
24 Jones (1985, p. 76).
25 TNA CAB129/91, C (58)19th, Aircraft for British European Airways, 23rd January 1958.
26 TNA CAB129/91, C (58)32nd, The Aircraft Industry and the British European Airways, 1st February 1958; TNA CAB128/32, CC (58)14th, 4th February 1958.
27 TNA CAB129/91, C (58)31st, British European Airways, Memorandum by the Minister of Transport and Civil Aviation, 31st January 1958; TNA CAB129/91, C (58)32nd, The Aircraft Industry and the British European Airways, Memorandum by the Minister of Supply, 1st February 1958; TNA CAB128/32, CC (58)14th, 4th February 1958.
28 TNA CAB128/32, CC (58)16th, 12th February 1958; TNA PREM11/2597, Viscount Replacement, 2nd July 1959.
29 Jones (1985, p. 74).
30 TNA AVIA65/1276, Size and shape of the aircraft industry and G.O.R.339, 13th September 1957; TNA AVIA65/1276, G.O.R.339, Note of a meeting held in Shell Mex House on 16th September 1957; Hayward (1989, pp. 72–73).
31 Hartley (1965, p. 849).
32 TNA CAB129/92, Appendix B to C (58)94th, The Future of the Aircraft Industry: Aeronautical Research and Development, First Report by the Aircraft Industry Working Party.
33 TNA CAB129/92, C (58)94th, Aircraft Industry, 2nd May 1958.
34 TNA CAB129/92, C (58)94th, Aircraft Industry, 2nd May 1958.
35 TNA CC (58)38th, 6th May 1958.
36 588 HC Deb., 13th May 1958, cols. 228–29.
37 Hartley (1965, p. 848).
38 "Option" means the right of an airline to order additional airliners.
39 TNA PREM11/2597, The Aircraft Industry, Record of a Meeting held at 10, Downing Street, S.W.1., on Thursday, 9th July 1959 at 6.30 p.m.
40 TNA PREM11/2597, The Aircraft Industry, Record of a Meeting held at 10, Downing Street, S.W.1., on Thursday, 9th July 1959 at 6.30 p.m.
41 TNA PREM11/2597, Note for Talk with the Chancellor of the Exchequer, 14th July 1959.
42 TNA C (58)257th, The Aircraft Industry, 18th December 1958.
43 TNA CC (58)87th, 23rd December 1958.
44 TNA PREM11/2597, The Aircraft Industry, Record of a Meeting Held at 10, Downing Street, S.W.1., on Friday, 3rd July 1959 at 10 a.m.

38 *The post-war challenge, 1943–64*

45 TNA PREM11/2597, The Aircraft Industry, Record of a Meeting Held at 10, Downing Street, S.W.1., on Friday, 3rd July 1959 at 10 a.m.
46 TNA PREM11/2597, The Aircraft Industry, Record of a Meeting Held at 10, Downing Street, S.W.1., on Friday, 3rd July 1959 at 10 a.m.
47 TNA PREM11/2597, The Aircraft Industry, Record of a Meeting Held at 10, Downing Street, S.W.1., on Thursday, 9th July 1959 at 10 a.m.
48 TNA PREM11/2597, The Aircraft Industry, Record of a Meeting Held at 10, Downing Street, S.W.1., on Thursday, 9th July 1959 at 10 a.m.
49 Jones (1985, p. 79).
50 Jones (1985, pp. 77–80, 83–84).
51 Hartley (1965, p. 846).
52 Hayward (1989, p. 74).
53 As for the purchase of 20 British machines, as de Havilland was interested in the Comet 5 for BEA, BOAC was compelled to buy Vickers airliners (Higham (2013, p. 210)).
54 Cole (2017, pp. 95, 97).
55 Hayward (1989, pp. 74–75).
56 TNA CAB129/99, C(59)185th, The Aircraft Industry, 16th December 1959.
57 Hayward (1983, p. 41); Hayward (1989, pp. 74–75).
58 TNA CAB129/99, C (59)185th, The Aircraft Industry, 16th December 1959.
59 TNA CAB128/33, CC (59)64th, 17th December 1959.
60 TNA CAB130/170, GEN701/1st, Aircraft Industry, 21st December 1959.
61 TNA PREM11/3637, to Prime Minister, 22nd December 1959. Sandys pressed Vickers, English Electric and Bristol to form BAC through his "marriage bureau" (Hayward (2012)).
62 TNA CAB129/100, C (60)21st, The Aircraft Industry, 9th February 1960; TNA PREM11/3637, to Prime Minister, 22nd December 1959.
63 Hayward (1989, p. 78).
64 Hayward (1983, pp. 47–48).
65 617 HC Deb., 15th February 1960, col. 958.
66 617 HC Deb., 15th February 1960, col. 958.
67 Minister of Aviation, *Report of the Committee of Inquiry into the Aircraft Industry*, Cmnd. 2853 (London, HMSO, 1965), para. 111.
68 Hayward (1983, p. 48).
69 Hayward (1983, p. 48).
70 Darby (1973, p. 166).
71 Hayward (1989, p. 85).
72 Darby (1973, pp. 259–60).
73 Wood (1986, pp. 204–6).
74 Darby (1973, p. 266); Dockrill (2002, p. 81).
75 Dockrill (2002, p. 78).
76 Wood (1986, p. 191).
77 TNA PREM11/3680, Prime Minister to Minister of Aviation, 14th June 1962; TNA PREM11/3680, Minister of Aviation to Prime Minister, 15th June 1962.
78 TNA PREM11/3680, Prime Minister to Minister of Aviation, 23rd June 1962.
79 Hayward (1989, pp. 63–82).

3 BOAC's financial crisis and the end of the "Fly British" policy, 1963–1966

Introduction

As outlined in previous chapters, the "Fly British" policy obliged the UK's national airlines to purchase domestically produced aircraft. This chapter examines why and how this policy came to a conclusive end. It shows how, from 1962 to 1963, BOAC sustained heavy losses on the North Atlantic route due to stiff competition from Pan Am. This was immensely concerning to the British government. However, the official response was ambivalent. On the one hand, ministers continued to urge BOAC to purchase domestically produced aircraft. On the other hand, however, the government also hinted at a possible British purchase of American Airliners (Boeing 707 or Douglas DC-8) at some point in the future.

Overall, this chapter shows how a severe conflict arose between the requirement to use British aircraft (which were inferior to American aircraft) and the necessity to compete with foreign operators (which did use US models). This conflict went to the very heart of BOAC's management structure. As one historian has observed, "the years 1956 to 1963 can now be regarded as one of the troughs into which BOAC slid from time to time".[1] BOAC attempted to simultaneously "do what was best for BOAC and at the same time what was best for the nation".[2] However, these two objectives "were not always compatible in the eyes of the responsible Minister of the day, and divergent views arose".[3]

A key conflict here was between Sir Giles Guthrie, the new Chairman of BOAC, and Julian Amery, the Minister of Aviation. Guthrie represented the interests of British airlines; he consistently pushed for the use of cheaper American aircraft. Amery, meanwhile, represented the British aircraft industry, which aimed to preserve long-haul airliner manufacturing under the "Fly British" policy. As Table 3.1 indicates, Guthrie had no compunction about prioritising operational profit over the putative "national interest". In an interview with the aviation journal *Intervia*, Guthrie was asked; "Do you consider it a part of the function of BOAC to support the British aircraft industry by buying and operating British aircraft?" His answer:

> "No. We must buy the aircraft best suited to our needs. Otherwise, we will again lose money. We would serve neither our own interests nor those of the

DOI: 10.4324/9781003127901-4

40 *The post-war challenge, 1943–64*

Table 3.1 BOAC's record of financial results (£ millions)

	1961–62	1962–63	1963–64	1964–65	1965–66
Traffic revenue of BOAC	92.7	92.3	103.82	114.3	124.7
Operating surplus (deficit) of BOAC	-10.5	4.7	8.7	16.8	20.7
Group profit (loss) before interest on borrowing and taxation	-43.2	-6.2	-2.7	17.9	11.8
Group profit (loss) after interest on borrowing and taxation	-50.0	-13.1	-9.8	9.9	9.4
Group profit (loss) attributable to BOAC after interest on borrowing and taxation	-50.0	-12.9	-10.4	8.9	8.1
Dividend on Exchequer dividend capital	–	–	–	–	3.5

British aircraft industry if we bought their products merely because they were British. Of course, we are delighted when the best aircraft available is British, but our main function is to operate profitably, not to support the British aircraft industry at all costs".[4]

Guthrie's record as a cost-cutter speaks for itself. In 1961–62, BOAC was operating with a deficit of £10.5 million. By 1965–66, this had been transformed into a surplus of £20.7 million. This seems to provide an apparent vindication of his insistence on obtaining US aircraft. But the political and economic costs for the British aircraft industry, and for the "Fly British" policy in particular, were severe indeed.[5]

British-American battles over the North Atlantic route

In 1946, Britain and the United States signed the Bermuda Agreement, which aimed to regulate civil air transport in the post-war period. In the years after the conclusion of this agreement, BOAC and Pan Am had been vying for hegemonic control of international air transport. For the British government, BOAC had two main responsibilities with respect to British national interests after the Second World War. First, BOAC was responsible for the operation of the Empire routes; and, second, it was supposed to support the development of airliners by the British aircraft industry under the "Fly British" policy.

The "Fly British" policy was explicitly articulated in the 1945 civil aviation White Paper.[6] As already outlined in previous chapters, this policy obligated BOAC to use British-built models during the post-war period. BOAC thus supported the development of British aircraft as a launch customer for models such as the de Havilland Comet 1 and the Bristol Britannia. This inevitably embroiled BOAC, the flag carrier of the UK, in a competition with Pan Am, the "chosen

The end of the "Fly British" policy, 1963–66 41

Table 3.2 BOAC vs Pan Am on the North Atlantic route jet services

Start date	Airline	Airframe	Engine	Passengers	Speed (mph)	Cruise distance (miles)
4th October 1958	BOAC	Comet 4	Rolls-Royce Avon	72	505	3,250
26th October 1958	Pan Am	Boeing 707-120	P&W JT3 (J57)	132	570	3,250
26th August 1959	Pan Am	Boeing 707-320 Intercontinental	P&W JT4 (J75)	144	545	5,000

Source: Davies ([1964] 1967, pp. 482, 486, Tables 46 and 51).

instrument"[7] of US national interests in the aviation sector in the years after the Second World War. Pan Am was sponsored by the US government for international transport on the North Atlantic route, the world's most profitable air channel.

Table 3.2 shows the date of the first jet service of BOAC and Pan Am on the North Atlantic route. As we can see, BOAC's date of service – 4th October 1958 – was actually earlier than its US rival's on 26th October 1958. The passenger capacity of the Comet 4, however, was only 72, compared to the 132 of the Boeing 707-120. Moreover, on 26th August 1959, Pan Am flew the 707-320 Intercontinental with a cruise distance of 5,000 miles and also began non-stop services on the North Atlantic route. The gap between BOAC and Pan Am began to widen. Soon after, major airlines such as TWA (the United States), Sabena (Belgium), Air France (France) and Lufthansa (West Germany) started services using the Boeing 707 on the North Atlantic route. Once again, this adversely affected BOAC's bottom line.

Table 3.3 compares the operating revenues of BOAC and Pan Am. The latter made a considerable profit operating half of all the Boeing 707-320 Intercontinental, which enabled Pan Am to serve the North Atlantic route service non-stop. In contrast, BOAC's business performance was worse because the Comet 4 was inferior to the Boeing 707 in passenger capacity and cruise speed.

Table 3.3 Operating results of BOAC and Pan Am (£ millions)

Year	BOAC	Pan Am
1958	-2.3	3.1
1959	3.2	6.6
1960	2.2	8.2
1961	-13.9	8.1
1962	-5.8	15.3

Source: Ministry of Aviation, *The Financial Problems of the British Overseas Airways Corporation* (London: HMSO, 1963), p. 18.

42 The post-war challenge, 1943–64

In response, on 27th May 1960, BOAC launched a London–New York route and used the Boeing 707-420 (Rolls-Royce Conway engine version) as a stopgap.[8] However, BOAC could not buy more Boeing 707s because it was already scheduled to buy BAC's VC10s under the "Fly British" policy. As we saw in Chapter 2, Prime Minister Harold Macmillan ruled out any further BOAC purchases of the Boeing 707.

BOAC's financial problems

In 1961 and 1962, BOAC ran up considerable deficits. By mid-1962, the company had fallen into a severe management crisis. This proved highly discomfiting to the British government. On 2nd August 1962, the Cabinet Economic Policy Committee accepted Minister of Aviation Julian Amery's proposal to inquire into the causes of BOAC's financial problems. On 1st October 1963, Amery presented his analysis of the finances of BOAC to the Cabinet Economic Policy committee in a paper entitled "The Financial Problems of the British Overseas Airways Corporation".[9]

This paper pegged BOAC's projected gross accumulated deficits at a staggering £100 million and called for a parliamentary inquiry into this problem. The paper traced the origins of these deficits to 1956; the same year when various international airlines began to place orders for American jet aircraft. The report pointed out that BOAC had incurred heavy losses on the Comet 1 and the Britannia. The company's long-term planning for the 1950s had been based on these two models, with each aircraft costing around £1 million. However, the Comet 1 programme was disrupted by the series of accidents and catastrophes outlined in Chapter 2, while the Britannia was delayed by various technical troubles. Moreover, the introduction of big American jets such as the Boeing 707 and the DC-8 on long-haul routes had noticeably impacted the usefulness of British aircraft. To compete on long-haul routes, BOAC sought to buy 15 Boeing 707s in October 1956 as a stopgap until more promising British models were ready. The government supported this move.[10]

As we saw in Chapter 1, BOAC's purchase of the 707s was conditional on a purchase of 20 British models. In April 1957, BOAC decided that the Vickers VC10 was the model best suited to its requirements. The company sought government approval for the purchase of 35 aircraft, as shown in Table 3.4. The Ministry of Aviation also considered the Vickers model to be a potential rival to the Boeing 707 and Douglas DC-8. To be sure, VC10s were more expensive than the mass-produced 707s. That said, VC10s had a rear-engine configuration which allowed it to run exceptionally quietly, lending it an obvious passenger appeal, especially on long-haul flights. Moreover, it was better suited for landing in the kind of tropical regions where some Commonwealth airlines operated. However, this also implied that the VC10 was perhaps overly customised to BOAC and Commonwealth routes, rendering it less competitive on the highly lucrative North Atlantic route than its American rivals.[11]

Table 3.4 VC10 order

Date	BOAC VC10		Super VC10		Vickers wanted
	Firm	Option	Firm	Option	
October 1956, Ministry required BOAC to buy 20 British aircraft					
23rd April 1957	25	10			45
25th April 1957	35	20			
January 1958	35				
June 1960			10		
August 1960	15		30		
June 1961	12 (and penalties paid on 3 cancelled)				
April, September 1963	(BOAC wished to cancel 13)				Vickers agreed to suspend 10
22nd May 1964	(BOAC wished to cancel all 30)				
20th July 1964			17 (with 10 more in suspense)		(and 3 to RAF with penalty)
19th March 1965	(BOAC wished to cancel the last 17)				
18th June 1965	(BOAC wanted to cancel the last 10)				
7th February 1966	(BOAC cancelled the 10 held in suspense with Vickers' (now BAC) approval)				

Source: Higham (2013, p. 213).

In early 1960, Vickers came into severe financial difficulties, which suddenly plunged the VC10 programme into jeopardy. To save it, the Ministry of Aviation asked BOAC to buy ten more VC10s.[12] In June 1960, BOAC obligingly revised its order and opted for 30 Super VC10s and 15 Standard VC10s. *Flight* pointed quizzically to the fact that BOAC was increasing capacity at the very time when traffic was falling. Sir Basil Smallpiece, BOAC's Managing Director, also admitted that BOAC's decision was "a bit of gamble".[13] As subsequent events would show, this comment was very much in the best traditions of British understatement.

Indeed, from 1960, the rate of air traffic growth had fallen, and BOAC's competitive position had worsened noticeably. If BOAC took the full order of 42 VC10s then, by 1966/67, its existing order of eight VC10s and 20 Boeing 707s would leave it with a total fleet of 70 aircraft. This would be excessive, to say the least. As a result, BOAC's board began to intensively examine the economic merits of either cancelling or postponing some VC10s, or of eliminating some of its Boeings. These were difficult matters.[14]

44 The post-war challenge, 1943–64

At a Cabinet meeting on 14th November 1963, Amery insisted on the publication of a White Paper that would provide an official analysis of BOAC's deficit. He cited the Government's responsibility for holding a national company's management to account. Second, Amery proposed to make a statement in Parliament that would coincide with the publication of the White Paper. This statement would describe the changes in the management of BOAC which the Government had proposed. It would also suggest the retirement of Sir Matthew Slattery from the post of Chairman, thereby saddling him with the blame for BOAC's deficit. The replacement for the unfortunate Slattery would be Sir Giles Guthrie, a merchant banker at Prudential Assurance Company. Moreover, Amery proposed to announce that, over the course of 1964, the new management of BOAC would be required to prepare a plan for making the company financially sound. This might involve turning management of the company over to private investors.[15]

After the publication of this highly critical White Paper,[16] Sir Giles Guthrie took over the chair of BOAC in January 1964. Guthrie assumed personal responsibility for refashioning the management of BOAC along the lines set down in the White Paper. In a governmental directive dated 1st January – the "Magna Carta" of the BOAC[17] – Amery informed Guthrie that the immediate task for BOAC was:

> to achieve the break even point after meeting interest and depreciation. How this can be done is a matter for you [Guthrie], but for my part, I am also much concerned in view of my responsibility for financing the accumulated and continuing deficit [...] If the national interest should appear, whether to the Corporations or to the Government, to require some departure from the strict commercial interests of the Corporation, this should be done only with the express agreement or at the express request of the Minister.[18]

The directive laid out the principles that had to be adhered to if BOAC were to overcome its management crisis. Chief among these principles was that BOAC should prioritise making an operational profit. However, this principle was in direct contradiction with two putative national interests which BOAC had been serving up to this point: providing a market for British airliners under the "Fly British" policy, and connecting the Commonwealth. These interests were now cast into uncertainty.

Guthrie vs Amery

Amery's directive asked for a plan that would enable BOAC to break even. In order to meet this demand, Guthrie attached greater importance to the size and composition of BOAC's fleets. He outlined this in a review of the existing VC10 purchase plan. Guthrie concluded that, through higher utilisation of existing aircraft, it would be possible to maintain BOAC's service with about 40 fewer aircraft than the existing fleet of 62. This would also entail the cancellation of the 30 Super VC10s and the purchase of six new Boeing 707-320s.[19]

The end of the "Fly British" policy, 1963–66   45

Guthrie favoured the 707 over the VC10, for two key reasons. First, the American models had already been amortised, and the estimated running costs were around £2 million cheaper than a fleet of 30 Super VC10s. Second, the 707 could be serviced for decades to come, whereas Vickers promised only to provide parts for the VC10 for ten years after the delivery of the last aircraft. Indeed, new Boeing aircraft and Boeing spare parts would surely be readily available for many years to come. Guthrie estimated that the cost of cancelling the VC10s would be £65–£70 million, but this seemed a small price to pay in order to acquire cheaper aircraft with better prospects.[20]

Nonetheless, Guthrie's plan for changing the vehicular basis of BOAC from British to American was a tremendous shock to the ministers. It basically entailed releasing BOAC from its existing role of supporting the development of British airliners. BOAC's order for Super VC10s was by far the largest of all Super VC10 orders; its cancellation would mean the collapse of the entire project. Prime Minister Sir Alec Douglas-Home organised a small group of ministers to specifically examine BOAC's order for Super VC10s. Amery, Minister of Aviation, and Reginald Maudling, Chancellor of Exchequer, produced two memorandums on this topic.[21]

According to Amery, Guthrie had come to accept that it was too late to cancel the 12 Standard VC10s. In his report, Amery stressed the industrial implications of the Guthrie Plan. First, BOAC's cancellation of VC10s would damage sales of VC10s abroad; it would damage the reputation of BAC; and it would do severe harm to the prospects of BAC's other airliners, such as the BAC1-11 and Concorde. Second, there would be an immediate loss of 2,500 jobs at BAC.[22]

The political implications of the Guthrie Plan were sketched in similarly dour terms: it would entail the spending of £90–100 million of taxpayers' money on a predominantly American fleet. Moreover, the VC10 contract was one of the foundations upon which the Government had persuaded Vickers and other firms to join in setting up the BAC. If the Government allowed this contract to be cancelled, it would shatter the confidence of the aircraft industry in the Government's aviation policy.[23]

At this point, Amery stepped in to propose an alternative plan that would see BOAC sell off its 20 Boeing 707s as soon as the VC10 fleet became available.[24] In this way, the "Fly British" policy might be preserved. But the basic conflict at the heart of British aviation policy was now unmistakeable. P.R. Baldwin at the Cabinet Office described this burgeoning crisis to Prime Minister Sir Alec Douglas-Home as "a clash between Government policies".[25] BOAC, a nationalised industry, should be commercially efficient, but Britain should maintain an independent aircraft industry. Guthrie's plan would be "a very hard blow to our aircraft manufacturers, namely, cancellation of the whole order for thirty Super VC10s".[26] If BOAC bought six new Boeing 707s instead of 30 Super VC10s, BOAC would be accepting "a predominantly American fleet".[27] On the other hand, Amery's all-VC10 plan seemed to point to "the opposite extreme"[28] – a rejection of economic logic in pursuit of the distant vision of a British-produced fleet.

46 The post-war challenge, 1943–64

Maudling's report made the case for an intermediate position between the extremes represented by Guthrie and Avery. He proposed a VC10/Boeing 707 mixed fleet. Under this plan, BOAC would reduce its order of Super VC10s from 15 to 12. The RAF would take three Super VC10s. The remaining 20 Boeing 707s would be retained. This would be a cheap solution, costing some £20–30 million less than keeping all the VC10s.[29] Maudling pointed out that if BOAC operated a purely VC10 fleet, then it would face difficulties if further aircraft were required when the VC10 production line ended. A mixed VC10/Boeing 707 fleet plan would keep both options open. This would be advantageous if the VC10 proved more of a commercial hit than seemed likely, especially compared with the runaway success of the Boeing.[30]

On 7th July, the VC10 problem occupied centre stage at a senior ministerial meeting chaired by Sir Alec Douglas-Home. The consensus at this meeting was that a complete cancellation of the whole order for 30 VC10s in favour of an all-Boeing fleet was unrealistic. However, there was also an acceptance that BOAC had ordered around 20 long-haul aircraft too many. Douglas-Home drew on the Guthrie, Amery and Maudling memoranda to conclude that there were three possible courses of action. The first was an all-VC10 fleet, which entailed no cancellation of the Super VC10s. The second and third alternatives were a cancellation of ten or 15 of the Super VC10s, which would dispose prematurely of ten to five Boeings, respectively.[31]

In short, British ministers were haggling over the balance between British and American aircraft in the future civil airliner fleet. After this Cabinet meeting, Amery, Maudling and Guthrie met to discuss BOAC's projected requirements. These were now pegged at around 39 aircraft by 1968, and possibly eight more after that year (for a total of 47). Amery assumed that, in any case, the RAF would take three of the 30 Super VC10s originally ordered by BOAC.[32]

On 13th July, Amery put his case at another ministerial meeting. His argument was based on projected BOAC fleet plans (see Table 3.5). Guthrie had apparently decided that he would need a total of 47 passenger aircraft after 1968, and he now accepted that his original proposal of cancelling all the VC10 orders was unrealistic. Instead, he suggested that he should be allowed to cancel no fewer than 12 VC10s in order to keep his entire Boeing fleet of 20. This meant the cancellation of 20 VC10s.[33]

The continued haggling over the precise makeup of the British fleet was once again the order of the day at a senior ministerial committee meeting chaired by Selwyn Lloyd, the Lord Privy Seal, on 15th July. Amery continued to voice his opposition to cancelling the Super VC10 from the standpoint of the "Fly British" policy. Maudling distanced himself from Amery's position and put his case for cancellation of the 12 Super VC10s, implying that BOAC would operate 12 standard VC10s, 20 Boeing 707s and 15 Super VC10s. The Maudling Plan would leave Guthrie free to pin his hopes on either British or American aircraft, and opened the door for BOAC to choose a jetliner from the American fleet.[34]

The following day, on 16th July, the Cabinet discussed the VC10 problem yet again. Selwyn Lloyd probably expressed the weariness of everyone in the room by

Table 3.5 Various BOAC fleet plans

	Super VC10s	Standard VC10s	Boeing 707s	Total
June 1960 revised order	30	15	20	65
Guthrie Plan (all-Boeing fleet plan)	0 (Cancel 30, RAF takes 3)	About 12	26 (Buy 6 new 707s)	About 40
Amery Plan (all-VC10 plan)	27 (RAF takes 3)	12	0 (Sell 20 707s)	About 40
Maudling Plan (mixed VC10/707 plan)	12 (Cancel 15, RAF takes 3)	12	15 (phasing out 5 707s)	About 40
Cabinet decision on 16th July 1965	17 (RAF takes 3, postpone decision on 10)	12	18 to 20	47

Source: TNA CAB130/200, GEN. 870/1st, 30th June 1964; TNA PREM11/4676, to Prime Minister, 3rd July 1964; TNA CAB130/200, GEN. 870/1st, 7th July 1964; *Aviation Week (AWST)*, 27th July 1964, p. 26; 699 HC Deb., 20th July 1964, cols. 39–40.

suggesting that a decision on the remaining ten Super VC10s be postponed. Sure enough, ministerial opinion for this course of action was generally supportive: first, because it would offer further opportunities for technical discussions; and, second, because some uncertainty still remained about the future fleet requirements of BOAC. The Cabinet proceeded to allocate the already ordered 30 Super VC10s, with BOAC taking 17 and the RAF taking three. A decision over the ten remaining Super VC10s remained in the balance.[35]

What did this postponement of a decision over the remaining ten Super VC10s mean from the standpoint of the "Fly British" policy? For Guthrie, the option of flying an (at least partly) American fleet remained open, though his radical proposal for an immediate all-American fleet had been defeated. Amery, meanwhile, had avoided the doomsday scenario of a massive cancellation of Super VC10s. And yet it was clear to everyone at this meeting that not even the British flag-carrier was prepared to operate a purely British fleet. None of the ministers in attendance openly said so, but this decision effectively negated the VC10 as a viable competitor to the Boeing 707 and Douglas DC-8.

The cancellation of the remaining ten Super VC10s

Guthrie never renounced his intention to cancel the remaining ten Super VC10s. In 1964, power in Britain was assumed by a Labour government under Harold Wilson which notably harboured less enthusiasm for the VC10 and other such "prestige" aircraft projects. On 8th February 1966, Fred Mulley, the new Minister of Aviation, submitted an extensive report to Wilson on the problems between BOAC and BAC (Vickers) surrounding the cancellation of the remaining ten Super VC10s.[36]

Mulley reported that Vickers, which was wholly responsible for financing the production of the Super VC10, had begun to press BOAC for a decision.

48 *The post-war challenge, 1943–64*

Extensive correspondence had been exchanged between Guthrie and Sir Charles Dunphie, chairman of Vickers. On 27th January, Guthrie wrote to Mulley to the effect that the board of BOAC had come to the conclusion that there existed no foreseeable requirement for ten Super VC10s. BOAC had thus decided to cancel this order, and to pay Vickers cancellation charge of £750,000 per aircraft. Guthrie stated that he would make this payment on 8th February.[37]

These conclusions were reiterated at a meeting between Guthrie and Mulley. Guthrie confirmed that, after making full allowance for the foreseeable growth in traffic between now and 1970, BOAC would have no requirement for any of the last ten Super VC10s. The Super VC10s were wholly surplus to requirements. BOAC would need further capacity after 1970 but this would have to be met by a new generation of altogether larger aircraft. Guthrie emphasised that many of BOAC's past misfortunes and much of the criticism levelled at the company had been due to ordering too many aircraft for the future. Guthrie had no intention of repeating the mistakes of his predecessors. Vickers had already agreed to accept the cancellation of these ten aircraft on the terms stated.[38]

On the morning of 8th February, Mulley met with Sir Charles Dunphie. Dunphie stressed that, for years, Vickers had been embarrassed by the obligation to finance work in progress on the Super VC10, and by the uncertainty surrounding the last ten models. Vickers desperately needed the money which BOAC had agreed to pay it in respect of the cancellation. Both Dunphie and Guthrie assured Mulley that the amount of £750,000 per aircraft had been carefully calculated to put Vickers in the same financial position as would have obtained if the Super VC10s had been built. Dunphie emphasised that this was essentially a commercial decision between Vickers and BOAC, and that he was counting on immediately receiving the sum which had been agreed.[39]

Mulley maintained that the government had no contractual or legal standing in this matter. Both Vickers and BOAC were justified in taking and standing by their own decisions. In a discussion with Wilson, Mulley observed that the cancellation of the last ten Super VC10s would sound "the death knell"[40] of the VC10 and eliminate any chance of further sales either abroad or at home.

Guthrie's wide-ranging savings programme did not stop at changes to the fleet plan, however. He also tackled the various problems with BOAC's route structure, especially with respect to the East Coast of South America route. In December 1963, this route was operating at a loss of £60,000 – a significant portion of BOAC's total deficit for the year. Once again, the problem partly lay in "national prestige", because the route flew VC10 large jets, rather than the cheaper Comet 4. Indeed, the route had lost £5.3 million between 1946 and 1965, mainly because of air disasters with the Tudors and the Comets. On 21st July 1965, Guthrie decided that, without government subsidies, BOAC would close the route by 1st November. This was refused. Consequently, on 1st September, BOAC ceased to fly the East Coast of South America route. In effect, BOAC was sending a message that its route structure would be determined by the company's commercial interests, rather than the diplomatic needs of the British government.[41]

Soon after this decision, BOAC's former Chairman, Slattery, wrote scathingly in *Aeroplane* magazine that none of these actions would benefit the British aircraft industry.[42] And yet Guthrie's ambitious programme of restructuring BOAC's fleet plan and route structure dramatically saved money for the company. The financial year 1964–1965 proved to be a successful one; BOAC's group profit before interest was £17.8 million. On 31st March 1965, BOAC wrote off the deficit of £81 million.[43] The company was back on a firm financial footing. However, the implications for the British aircraft industry, and Britain's broader place in the world, were inauspicious indeed.

Waking up from the "neo-Edwardian dream"?

On 11th February 1966, James Callaghan, Chancellor of the Exchequer, advised Prime Minister Harold Wilson to accept the Minister of Aviation's proposal that the government cancel BOAC's ten remaining Super VC10s. This, he suggested, was the only way to re-establish BOAC as an economically efficient enterprise. According to Callaghan, "I think we must accept with regret that the Super VC10 has no further export prospect. It is technically a very good aircraft but too costly and too late".[44]

This mooted change of policy was fully realised when BOAC, in ordering a fleet of next-generation long-haul wide-body airliners, chose the Boeing 747. This effectively sounded the death knell of British-manufactured long-haul aircraft. Through the use of American airliners and the liquidation of traditional "imperial obligations", such as operating Empire routes and the "Fly British" policy, BOAC undoubtedly improved its management position. However, this came at a high cost to British manufacturing.

The choice of Britain's next generation aircraft fleets essentially completed Guthrie's victory over Amery. The success of the Boeing 707 and Douglas DC-8 underscored the need for fleets that could carry more than 100–150 passengers (although the latter's success was to be relatively short-lived).[45] Based on this market forecast, in mid-1965, Guthrie approached airframe manufacturers about the prospect of building a long-haul jet airliner. Possible contenders were the BAC's Superb (a stretched version of the Super VC10), the Boeing 747, and Douglas's stretched version of the DC-8.

On 14th February 1966, Fred Mulley made a report to Wilson on the successor to the Super VC10. He stated that, in the summer of 1965, BAC had advanced a proposal for a stretched version of the Super VC10 (the Superb). The Superb was based on the design philosophy of the VC10, but it would be a double-decker aircraft capable of carrying 265 passengers. BAC estimated the launch costs of the airframe at £40 million. In addition, BAC planned to fit the aircraft with a Rolls-Royce RB178s, a high by-pass ratio 30,000 lb thrust successor to Conway.[46] This would be a powerful aircraft.

The possibility that it would ever be made, however, was slim. As Mulley observed, if Britain were to cease producing long-haul jet airliners, then the prospects for British medium- and short-haul aircraft were also bleak. Mulley

50 *The post-war challenge, 1943–64*

suggested that BAC should be informed of the non-existent prospect of any government support for the launching of a successor to the Super VC10 for the long-haul market – even though the Superb constituted a possible "British solution"[47] to BOAC's problems.

The fact remained that most international airlines were, at this time, operating Boeing 707s or Douglas DC-8s, and so they would naturally prefer stretched versions of these aircraft. Douglas had indicated its intention to stretch the DC-8, while Boeing planned to develop the very large 747 aircraft. The chances of Britain selling enough Superb models were thus limited from the very start. In any case, the Superb was never really a serious proposition. The cost of developing the model (£40 million on the airframe alone, along with additional engine costs) would have fallen on the Exchequer, and the market prospects held out no hope of recovering this expenditure.[48] On 11th May, Mulley announced in the House of Commons that the government did not support the development of the Superb.[49]

In May 1966, an alternative to the Boeing emerged which would at least have offered some consolation to those who still clung to the "Fly British" policy. US manufacturer Douglas proposed the DC8-84, a much smaller aircraft than the very large 747, which would meet BOAC's requirements. The great merit of this proposal was that it would incorporate a British engine, a scaled-down version of the Rolls-Royce RB178. BOAC was due to make a decision between the 747 and Douglas' proposed airliner on 17th June 1966. However, the latter decided to withdraw its proposal due to a lack of interest from other airlines.[50]

This left only one viable option: the Boeing 747. Boeing wanted 50 pre-orders before embarking on the manufacture of the aircraft. By mid-April, Pan Am had ordered 25, while Lufthansa and Qantas were weighing their options. A British purchase of the model seemed inevitable. Mulley tried to "ensure the maximum content of British equipment in the Boeing, not only for BOAC's order, but for the whole production run".[51] He initially hoped that the Boeing might be powered by a Rolls-Royce engine, the RB178. However, on 26th April, Boeing informed BOAC that such a prospect was off the table. The US company proved unwilling to contemplate the setting up of separate production lines for the same aircraft model based purely on engine differences. In a bitter blow to the British aircraft industry, and to Rolls-Royce especially, the P&W JT9D got the nod.[52]

On 19th August, the Board of BOAC resolved to order six 747s, and 80 per cent of the financing for this purchase would come from the US Export–Import Bank. On 18th November, the Treasury approved this proposal. Ultimately, 72 per cent of the money came from the Export–Import Bank, 8 per cent was financed by Boeing, and BOAC put up 20 per cent from its dollar earnings.[53] This was a significant development. During the immediate post-war period, BOAC's purchase of American airliners had been restricted not only for reasons of "national prestige", but also because it would have entailed a considerable dollar outlay. The BOAC purchase of the 747 basically entailed the British national airliner acquiring financial help from an American source because the British government, which was at this time embroiled in a financial crisis, was unable to stump up the cash. This move also effectively allowed BOAC to lower its seat/mile cost on the North Atlantic and positioned the British firm as one of the 747's principal launch customers. Insult had been added to injury.

Barnett has suggested that all of these developments can lead to only one conclusion; that BOAC, at least, had awoken from "the neo-Edwardian dream".[54] Wilson's approval of BOAC's purchase of the 747, after many years of bitter wrangling, was a blow to the British aircraft industry. The fact that this purchase was made largely with American funds due to the dire financial straits of the British exchequer was the proverbial salt in the wound. The "Fly British" policy was effectively dead in the water (or, perhaps, dead in the air).

Conclusion

Sir Giles Guthrie's appointment as Chairman of BOAC marked the beginning of the end of the "Fly British" policy. At first, the radical proposals he put forward under the Guthrie Plan evidently spooked the Conservative government about the possible damage that might be caused to the British aircraft industry. However, though the government continued to urge BOAC to purchase domestically produced aircraft, ministers were not totally blind to economic reality. The door remained open for a future purchase of American models. This mooted policy change was fully realised in 1966 when BOAC, in ordering a fleet of next-generation long-haul wide-body airliners, chose the Boeing 747. British airframe makers had no launch customers other than BOAC, and so this indicated Britain's effective withdrawal from the manufacture of long-haul aircraft.

To be sure, BOAC improved its management through the use of American airliners and the liquidation of traditional "imperial obligations", such as operating Empire routes. But this change in direction also signalled the effective end of the "Fly British" policy – the political and financial basis for Britain's post-war civil aircraft development. British aircraft manufacturers had good reason to feel profoundly unsettled by these developments – and, indeed, to ask anxiously about the prospects for their continued existence in a world dominated by American industry.

Notes

1 Higham (2013, p. 242).
2 Higham (2013, p. 242).
3 Higham (2013, p. 242).
4 *Interavia*, February 1967, p. 190.
5 *Interavia*, February 1967, p. 193.
6 Ministry of Civil Aviation, *British Air Services*, Cmd. 6712 (London, HMSO, 1945).
7 Bender and Altschul (1982).
8 Davies ([1964] 1967, p. 486); Higham (2013, p. 215).
9 TNA CAB134/1703, EA (63)159th, Financial Problems of the British Overseas Airways Corporation, 1st October 1963.
10 TNA CAB134/1703, EA (63)159th, Financial Problems of the British Overseas Airways Corporation, 1st October 1963.

52 *The post-war challenge, 1943–64*

11 TNA CAB134/1703, EA (63)159th, Financial Problems of the British Overseas Airways Corporation, 1st October 1963.
12 Hayward (1983, p. 47).
13 Hayward (1983, p. 48).
14 TNA CAB134/1703, EA (63)159th, Financial Problems of the British Overseas Airways Corporation, 1st October 1963.
15 TNA CAB129/115, CP (63)14th, Financial Problem of the British Overseas Airways Corporation, 12th November 1963; TNA CAB128/38, CM (63)5th, 14th November 1963.
16 Ministry of Aviation, *The Financial Problems of the British Overseas Airways Corporation*, Cmnd. 5 (London, HMSO, 1963).
17 Higham (2013, p. 245).
18 688 HC Deb., 5th February 1964, cols. 1141–42.
19 TNA CAB130/200, GEN870/1st, The V.C. 10, Memorandum by the Minister of Aviation, 30th June 1964; TNA PREM11/4676, Draft Cabinet Paper.
20 TNA CAB130/200, GEN870/1st, The V.C. 10, 30th June 1964; TNA CAB129/118, CP (64)141st, The Super VC.10, 15th July 1964.
21 TNA PREM11/4676, T.J. Bligh to Burke Trend, 25th June 1964.
22 TNA CAB130/200, GEN870/1st, The V.C. 10, Memorandum by the Minister of Aviation, 30th June 1964.
23 TNA CAB130/200, GEN870/1st, The V.C. 10, Memorandum by the Minister of Aviation, 30th June 1964.
24 TNA CAB130/200, GEN870/1st, The V.C. 10, Memorandum by the Minister of Aviation, 30th June 1964; TNA PREM11/4676, Draft Cabinet Paper.
25 TNA PREM11/4676, P.R. Baldwin to Prime Minister, The VC-10, GEN. 870/1 and 2, 6th July 1964.
26 TNA PREM11/4676, P.R. Baldwin to Prime Minister, The VC-10, GEN. 870/1 and 2, 6th July 1964.
27 TNA PREM11/4676, P.R. Baldwin to Prime Minister, The VC-10, GEN. 870/1 and 2, 6th July 1964.
28 TNA PREM11/4676, P.R. Baldwin to Prime Minister, The VC-10, GEN. 870/1 and 2, 6th July 1964.
29 TNA CAB130/200, GEN870/1st, The V.C. 10, Memorandum by the Minister of Aviation, 30th June 1964.
30 TNA CAB130/200, GEN870/2nd, The VC.10s: Cost of Alternative Proposals, 1st July 1964.
31 TNA CAB130/200, GEN870/1st, 7th July 1964.
32 TNA PREM11/4676, P.R. Baldwin to Prime Minister, The VC-10, GEN. 870/3 and 4, 14th July 1964.
33 TNA CAB130/200, GEN870/3rd, The V.C.10, The Super V.C.10, 13th July 1964; TNA CAB130/200, GEN870/4th, The V.C.10, The Super V.C.10, 14th July 1964.
34 TNA CAB130/200, GEN870/2nd Meeting, 15th July 1964.
35 TNA CAB128/38, CM (64)38th, 16th July 1964.
36 TNA PREM13/1355, Super V.C.10 aircraft for B.O.A.C., the Minister of Aviation to Prime Minister, 8th February 1966.
37 TNA PREM13/1355, Super V.C.10 aircraft for B.O.A.C., the Minister of Aviation to Prime Minister, 8th February 1966.
38 TNA PREM13/1355, Super V.C.10 aircraft for B.O.A.C., the Minister of Aviation to Prime Minister, 8th February 1966.
39 TNA PREM13/1355, Super V.C.10 aircraft for B.O.A.C., the Minister of Aviation to Prime Minister, 8th February 1966.
40 TNA PREM13/1355, Super V.C.10 aircraft for B.O.A.C., the Minister of Aviation to Prime Minister, 8th February 1966.
41 Higham (2013, pp. 260–62).

42 Higham (2013, p. 262).

43 Higham (2013, pp. 263–64).

44 TNA PREM13/1355, Chancellor of the Exchequer to Prime Minister, 11th February 1966.

45 Boeing was able to make a profit from the 707 on the US market because the airliner had already completed production batches for the 707 based on a contract with the USAF for the KC-135 (the military version of the 707). The small 737 and the medium 727 also became best-sellers. In contrast, Douglas had no military contract for the DC-8. Nor did Douglas benefit from the learning curve effects of military manufacturing. Furthermore, the DC-9 missed the boom-period of short-range airliners, whereas the BAC1-11 benefited greatly from this. In the end, Douglas lost competitiveness, falling into a management crisis in 1959. This resulted in a merger with McDonnell on 28th April 1967. See Eddy et al. (1976, pp. 42–46).

46 TNA PREM13/762, Successor to the Super VC.10, 14th February 1966.

47 TNA PREM13/1355, The Minister of Aviation to Chancellor of the Exchequer, 4th July 1966.

48 TNA PREM13/762, Successor to the Super VC.10, 14th February 1966.

49 728 HC Deb., 11th May 1966, col. 373.

50 TNA PREM13/1355, The Minister of Aviation to Chancellor of the Exchequer, 4th July 1966.

51 TNA PREM13/1355, The Minister of Aviation to Chancellor of the Exchequer, 4th July 1966.

52 Higham (2013, p. 314); TNA PREM13/1355, The Minister of Aviation to Chancellor of the Exchequer, 4th July 1966.

53 Higham (2013, p. 314).

54 Barnett (1995, p. 228).

Part II

The British dilemma, 1964–1969

By the mid-1960s, British officials – including key figures in the aircraft industry – had largely awoken from the "neo-Edwardian dream" of independence and continued world-power status that had, to some extent, underpinned the policies of the 1950s. The British aircraft industry, it seemed, could not go it alone – it needed partners. But to which side of the Atlantic should London look? Part II of the book shows how the mid-1960s constituted a period of crisis and uncertainty for the British aircraft industry. As the dream of independence melted away, British officials of this period were confronted with an existential question. Would the domestic aircraft industry be fully integrated into a burgeoning European aerospace sector in competition with the United States? Or would Britain come to function as a junior – but favoured and indispensable – partner of the Americans?

DOI: 10.4324/9781003127901-5

4 The cancellation of Britain's top projects, 1963–1965

Introduction

A decisive turning point in the post-war history of the British aircraft industry came between February and April 1965. During this two-month period, Harold Wilson's Labour government cancelled three key military programmes – the TSR-2 fighter-bomber, the P.1154 V/STOL fighter, and the HS.681 V/STOL transport. These cancellations, as well as the subsequent purchase of US aircraft, derived from purely financial considerations. But the British public and media were shocked. Through these measures, the Wilson government effectively discontinued Britain's most prominent program for the development of a sophisticated fighter jet. This was also somewhat incongruous with the concept of "white heat", which had been central to the Labour Party's plan for technical modernisation, as articulated by Wilson himself in 1963.[1]

David Edgerton has attempted to explain these cancellations as emblematic of a broader aversion to technological innovation on the part of Wilson's government. They constituted "an ending rather than the beginning of an overweening enthusiasm for national technology".[2] As Edgerton observes, the Labour party terminated "many large-scale techno-national projects and was hostile to many that survived".[3] But whether we agree with Edgerton or not, it seems clear that Wilson's decision symbolised Britain's retreat from the dream of autonomy and a critical step toward enhanced international co-operation. Soon after the Wilson government cancelled the project, the Conservative MP Stephan Hastings published a book entitled *The Murder of TSR-2* (1966). Hastings expressed the prevailing sentiment that the government's decision had damaged both national prestige and the British aircraft industry. It was evident that Britain could no longer rely on its own initiatives and undertakings to meet its defence needs.[4]

However, recent studies based on newly available government documents and the biographies of key decision-makers generally support the view that the Wilson government's dramatic measures were justified. Straw and Young, for example, have described the decisions as rational, courageous and above all necessary in order to achieve budget cuts. As Saki Dockrill has argued, the scrapping of such "prestige projects"[5] was essential to shoring up Britain's fiscal position for the defence of East of Suez.[6] Indeed, this connection was constantly made at

DOI: 10.4324/9781003127901-6

58 *The British dilemma in military field, 1964–69*

ministers' meetings, from Chequers in November 1964 to the Cabinet decision to cancel TSR-2 on 1st April 1965.[7]

Keith Hayward has depicted the project cancellations as an overture towards "the growth of an international infrastructure linking the companies of Europe".[8] To be sure, it was precisely these cancellations which constituted an initial first step in a long-term collaboration with France. However, of crucial importance here was the Wilson government's attempt at a *quid pro quo* with the United States. For instead of advancing the British aircraft projects, the Wilson government decided to purchase American-produced F-4 fighters, C-130 transports, and the F-111 fighter-bomber. During intensive US–UK military logistics negotiations from December 1964 to March 1965, the British delegation aimed to secure a contract for the US procurement of British military equipment, in order to offset the massive foreign exchange costs induced by the purchase of the US aircraft.

The TSR-2 as a nuclear umbrella East of Suez

As Chapter 2 showed, Duncan Sandys, then Minister of Aviation, introduced government launch aid to the aircraft industry as leverage to force the industry to rationalise. However, Sandys' measure allocated an excessive amount of national resources to the aircraft industry as a proportion of the national economy. Airframe and engine makers were rationalised, BAC was established, and considerable resources were dedicated to next-generation aircraft such as the TSR-2.

Ultimately, Macmillan's government aimed at a far-reaching reorganisation of British national defence. However, the Conservative "prestige" programmes TSR-2, P.1154 and HS.681 became heavy burdens for a British economy characterised by stagnation and "stop-go" cycles. From the 1950s onwards, government spending on such projects briefly led to domestic economic booms, but a worsening balance of payments, a fall in the value of the pound and thus deflationary measures, such as monetary tightening, public expenditure cuts and frozen wages. At such moments of crisis, British trade unions opposed government policy. This tended to trigger a government swing from "stop" to "go", and another round of inflationary measures.[9]

To overcome this highly unstable economic pattern, key government figures came to the conclusion that a permanent reduction of budgets and a durable improvement in the balance of payments were necessary. The primary targets for such cuts included the defence budget and foreign exchange costs. This could encapsulate defence R&D for aerospace, the East of Suez commitment and the British Army of the Rhine (BAOR). A more radical option might encompass a total retreat from East of Suez.[10]

The TSR-2 programme was the core of the Macmillan government's military industrial policy. Macmillan's approach entailed both continued co-operation with the United States and the development of an independent nuclear capability. This culminated in the February 1958 Anglo–American Intermediate-Range Ballistic Missile Agreement.[11] Furthermore, on 24th February 1962, the

The cancellation of top projects, 1963–65   59

Macmillan government abandoned the Blue Streak nuclear missile project, and instead positioned the TSR-2 as a substitute for the strategic nuclear role played by the V-force (Vulcan, Victor and Valiant aircraft squadrons).[12]

The Kennedy administration adopted the Flexible Response strategy based on NSAM40 (the Acheson Report).[13] This strategy rejected an exclusive concentration on nuclear deterrence in favour of sustained support for every form and level of warfare, including (and perhaps especially) conventional forces. The flexible response strategy certainly aimed at a concentration of western nuclear power in the United States. The UK and France were thus placed under considerable pressure to abandon their national nuclear arsenals. NSAM40 directed that "[o]ver the long run, it would be desirable if the British decided to phase out of the nuclear deterrent business. If the development of Skybolt is not warranted for U. S. purposes alone, the U.S. should not prolong the life of the V-Bomber force by this or other means".[14] At a NATO meeting in Athens in May 1961, Robert McNamara criticised "independent, small" nuclear forces because they increased the likelihood of a nuclear war breaking out.[15]

Despite the new US policy, Macmillan's government tried hard to preserve an independent British nuclear deterrent. Indeed, Macmillan apparently had designs on a purchase of Skybolt missiles from the United States. On 7th November 1962, however, this project was cancelled by the Kennedy administration, mainly due to budgetary concerns. Partial compensation for this inconvenient development came at the Nassau talks in December 1962, when Macmillan's government was able to obtain Polaris ballistic missiles which could be launched from a submarine.[16]

Crucially, however, Kennedy stipulated that the Polaris force provided to Britain would be assigned to the NATO Multilateral Force (MLF), which ultimately fell under the control of the Supreme Allied Commander Europe (SACEUR). Only under emergency circumstances would this force revert to British national jurisdiction.[17] The question of whether or not this could really be considered an "independent nuclear deterrent" was thus very much on the minds of British policymakers after Nassau.

Moreover, though Britain nominally gained an independent nuclear arsenal from the Nassau agreement, it also lost the promise of a "nuclear umbrella" in East of Suez – the kind of nuclear umbrella that V-bombers with the Skybolt were expected to provide. At the Nassau meeting of 20th December, 1962, Macmillan asked Kennedy whether Britain could use the Polaris submarines against Iraqi Prime Minister Abd al-Karim Qasim, who was at this time threatening Kuwait. Kennedy replied rather dismissively that he assumed Britain "did not have the intention of using nuclear weapons against Qassim".[18]

Did Britain's acquisition of the Polaris fleet really constitute an "independent nuclear deterrent"? This question obviously troubled British policymakers of the 1960s. However, it has proven equally vexing to scholars of nuclear history. Judging the true extent of British control over its nuclear weapons depends partly on how we interpret the idea of Britain's "supreme national interest". This was the crucial legal criteria that Britain had to invoke in order to use the Polaris fleet

60 *The British dilemma in military field, 1964–69*

outside the confines of the MLF. John Baylis places significant emphasis on Britain's room for manoeuvre within the confines of the MLF, whereas Andrew Pierre stresses that "the Polaris force could only be used within a NATO context, not for the unilateral defence of Kuwait or Singapore".[19]

Just after the Nassau agreement, Kennedy (apparently with Macmillan's backing) also offered the use of the Polaris submarine force to de Gaulle, though again under the auspices of the MLF. De Gaulle refused this offer on the grounds that the MLF was controlled by the United States. He then pressed on with his concept of a *force de frappe*, the primary instrument of which would be Mirage fighters. After the Nassau meeting, British politicians started to regard the TSR-2 as "Britain's replacement for the other aborted nuclear weapons system, such as *Blue Streak, Blue Water* and *Skybolt*",[20] as well as for "'East of Suez weapons".[21] These included TSR-2 (later F-111) and the new aircraft carriers such as the CVA-01.[22]

It was for precisely this reason that the Macmillan government placed greater emphasis on the strategic nuclear role of the TSR-2, which was expected to assume the function of Britain's "Nuclear Umbrella" East of Suez.[23] The TSR-2 was initially pencilled in as a replacement for the Canberra bomber. It was designed to have both conventional and nuclear tactical strike capabilities in the Indo–Pacific Area.[24]

Macmillan regarded the TSR-2 as a "useful back-up"[25] with "a secondary deterrent role",[26] one designed to complement the UK's Polaris missiles. The TSR-2, which was very similar to the American F-111, thus became emblematic for British technological equality with the United States, for the Conservative government's East of Suez policy, and for the state of British advanced technology more generally. It was the core element of the Macmillan government's principal military aircraft development programme, but its symbolic meaning extended beyond that of a mere aeronautical project.

The American balance of payments

Britain was not the only state that ran into balance of payments problems during this period. In the United States, Secretary of Defense Robert McNamara spent much of the mid-60s making concerted attempts to rationalise US military spending through a cost-effectiveness approach. This entailed significant cuts to inefficient programmes such as the XB-70 bomber. In order to reduce the financial burden of these programmes, McNamara merged the USAF and US Navy fighter-bomber in the form of the F-111. This move was based partly on the positive experience of the US Navy F-4 Phantom, which had performed well in the USAF operation. Then, procurement of the F-105 was discontinued.[27]

The military economy, and especially foreign military sales, represented crucial problems for the Kennedy administration. From 1958, the US balance of payments fell into the red and thereafter showed a continued annual deficit of approximately $3 billion. This inevitably resulted in a significant drain on the US's gold reserves. Indeed, this became so severe that the very existence of the Bretton-Woods system[28] was threatened.[29]

Military equipment sales to West European NATO countries and the Middle East offered a tantalising possibility for improving the parlous state of the US balance of payments. McNamara also attempted to rationalise NATO military R&D in order to avoid developmental duplication. This entailed a possible sale of the F-111 to Britain and Australia. Such a prospect represented not only an obviously favourable option for the US aircraft industry, but also a possible boost to the British defence budget. It might even facilitate a heightened British commitment in the Far East and possible participation in the Vietnam War.

McNamara's drive to settle the US balance of payments problem through foreign military sales was partly delegated to International Logistics Negotiations (ILN), a subsection of the US Department of Defense established in the autumn of 1961. McNamara's chief lieutenants in this undertaking were Henry J. Kuss Jr., Deputy Assistant Secretary of Defense for international security affairs, and Charles J. Hitch, Assistant Secretary of Defense. Kennedy also appointed Henry J. Kuss as the ILN's head.[30]

The main brief of the ILN was to sell US military products to European countries that wanted to be self-sufficient in the area of military production. Its task was made difficult because the United States had to shift from providing arms to NATO without charge to actually selling them. From the mid-1950s, US foreign military aid policy proceeded under the generous auspices of "Marshall Plan psychology".[31] The United States offered military aid to European NATO countries and Canada under the Mutual Assistance Program and offered North American F-86 fighters without charge. Moreover, under the offshore procurement program, the US procured British jet fighters such as the Hunter and jet bombers such as the Canberra.[32] In terms of West European fighter procurement, the Lockheed F-104G was a licenced product in West Germany, Belgium, Canada, the Netherlands and Italy.[33] Ultimately, under the licensed production of the F-104G, the US government economised military aid. Moreover, however, US aircraft manufacturers essentially invaded the European market – and thereby displaced their British rivals.

Kuss's promotional strategy was to present foreign military sales as part and parcel of improved logistics co-operation between the United States and Europe. West Germany would provide the primary target market.[34] Indeed, soon after its founding, the ILN was applying pressure to the German government to buy American military goods as a means of offsetting the cost of US troops stationed in Germany. McNamara took steps to promote NATO standardisation and to establish a NATO Common Market, thereby exporting his rationalisation programme to other NATO countries.[35]

The American F-111, then, would be procured by both the USAF and the US Navy. By contrast, the success of the TSR-2 project was heavily dependent on projected sales to European and ex-Commonwealth countries, especially Australia, which was the main customer for the British Canberra light bomber. The developmental costs of this project were significant. Indeed, these costs were rising considerably due to the continued incorporation of new technologies. Unfortunately for Britain, McNamara was determined to sell the F-111 to

Australia; partly because a foreign contract for this model would render cancellation difficult. From McNamara's point of view, production of the model needed to be preserved in order to support his policy of USAF/US Navy standardisation (which was opposed by some congressmen and navy personnel).[36] United States/UK competition in arms sales to Australia thus became a key commercial battleground.

The Hitch–McKean analysis of the NATO defence economy

There have been many scholarly attempts to explain the dynamics of competition in the military market with reference to military alliance economic theory. A key debate here has pitted the Hitch–McKean analysis against European collaboration theory. In a study first published in 1960, the US economists Charles Hitch and Roland McKean drew on Ricardo's comparative advantage principle to argue for the benefits of material specialisation. Hitch and McKean claimed that the potential mutual gain through arms specialisation would be considerable. This was because, first, individual countries would be able to pursue manufacturing areas in which they enjoyed a comparative advantage; and, second, profits could be maximised by reducing the per unit cost as output increased (economies of scale and learning curve effects). This principal is illustrated in Figure 4.1, which shows the learning curve effects in aircraft production from the Elstub report. In short, by concentrating manufacturing in one country, nations could pursue their comparative advantage in arms production.[37]

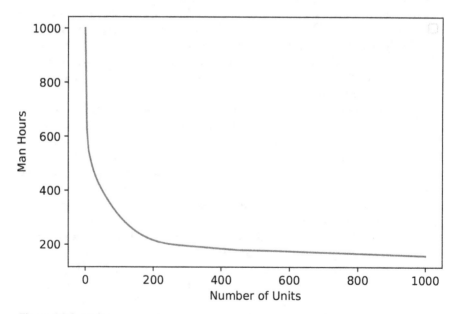

Figure 4.1 Learning curve

It is precisely here, in price competitiveness, that US manufacturers enjoyed a considerable advantage. They were able to produce a large number of products, whereas European manufacturers were at an obvious disadvantage due to their much more restricted production potential. Economies of scale and learning curve effects are highly characteristic of the aircraft industry. In 1969, this was pointed out by the Elstub Committee, the official British committee tasked with these questions. One report from this committed observed that "fixed capital per employee in the US was three times higher than in Britain",[38] despite relatively low British labour costs.

Economies of scale and learning curve effects ultimately depend on the amount of national defence budget spending. Consequently, any cost-effectiveness analysis of the US and European aircraft industries would have soon revealed that the latter had little choice but to forfeit sectors of their markets to the superior price competitiveness of American manufacturers. The Europeans would be compelled to look for other specialised areas in which they enjoyed a comparative advantage.

If we accept Hitch and McKean's application of Ricardo's comparative advantage concept to defence economics, then we can assume that a certain degree of collective profit should be generated among allies.[39] The question lies over the distribution of this collective profit. In the context of 1960s military aircraft sales, US makers enjoyed an obviously privileged share, given the cost-effectiveness and sheer scale of US domestic production. The US could thus readily benefit from the "transformation of public goods to private goods".[40]

At the same time, US manufacturers effectively closed the domestic military market to foreign producers. The Kennedy administration, with its ongoing balance of payments problem, provided this development with a legal underpinning through an amendment to the Buy American Act. This act had originally been enacted in 1933; it included a clause restricting US governmental procurement to domestic manufacturers. In 1962, the Kennedy administration added a 50 per cent price differential regulation for military procurement to improve the balance of payments. Under this regulation, foreign manufacturers could not participate in bids for US military procurement contracts without quoting prices 50 per cent lower than those of US manufacturers.[41] Any foreign company that managed to bypass this stipulation and gain unfettered access to the US military market could expect a most lucrative payday.

The European collaboration argument

During the Cold War, many European nations (including Britain) initially resisted their obvious and growing dependence on American weapons. European collaboration seemed to offer a viable alternative to this dependence. The fundamental conflict between the West European desire for military independence, on the one hand, and the US desire to sell US military equipment to Europe, on the other hand, are reflected in the divergence between the Hitch–McKean theory and the European collaboration argument.

64 *The British dilemma in military field, 1964–69*

Some embryonic notion of extended European aerospace collaboration had first been born after the US licencing of Lockheed F-104G production in West Germany, Belgium, the Netherlands and Denmark. The first moves in this area were the French–German Transall C-160 transport, which offered a possible alternative to the Lockheed C-130. The idea of European aerospace collaboration was explicitly noted for the first time in an official document in December 1965, the *Report of the Committee of Inquiry into the Aircraft Industry* – otherwise known as the Plowden Report. This document outlined the prospects for international co-operation as follows:

> The national aircraft industries in Europe all suffer from the same basic problem that their home markets are too small. They are not strong enough singly to secure a reasonable share of world markets in the face of United States competition. None of them is likely to survive alone for many years as significant forces in world aviation. But the combined resources of the English and French industries marshalled in good time towards common objectives offer a basis, probably the only basis, for maintaining a major aircraft industry in Europe throughout the 1970s.[42]

According to the Plowden Report, the aim should be the promotion of a European aircraft industry consisting of British, French, German, Dutch and Italian industries, plus any other European countries that wanted to participate. Theoretically, if the European countries were to co-operate in the procurement of military aircraft, they could also achieve comparable economies of scale and scope in order to realise the lowest unit cost. The key to this model – and to predicting the broader evolution of the US–Europe relationship – remained the British position. Britain had the option of serving as leader of European aerospace collaboration, or as a parts supplier to US industry.[43]

The rest of this chapter is dedicated to examining some of these broader issues through a specific emphasis on a single, critical feature of the military aircraft industry: the interdependence and relative autonomy of airframe and engine divisions. Aircraft manufacturing comprises an assembly process in which various parts and components from many different manufacturing sectors are combined to produce an aircraft. In order to assemble a complete aircraft through this process, many manufacturers must work together and establish collaborative production alliances. Among these participants, the airframe and engine manufacturers typically assume a key role as the primary contractors who orchestrate the process and put together the many subsystems and parts.

In other words, different economic entities are involved in the production of the final product, most notably manufacturers of the airframe and manufacturers of the engine. While both types of manufacturers are indispensable in this cooperative enterprise, their technological competitiveness may be asymmetrical. A typical case discussed in this chapter is that of Rolls-Royce. This was a well-known, British aero-engine manufacturer that maintained its competitiveness even while the competitiveness of Britain's airframe manufacturers was in decline.

The cancellation of top projects, 1963–65   65

In fact, these contrasting approaches to inter-NATO arms sales played a tangible role in the thinking of European and American policymakers. On the one hand, the Hitch–McKean theory constituted an effective justification for the British purchase of American arms and a British concentration on relatively advantaged sectors such as aero-engine or avionics. On the other hand, however, the logic of the European defence industrial base theory seemed to compel Britain to an enhanced co-production with France, a (relatively) equal partner.

The Zuckerman system

In the early 1960s, the British concern with its declining Empire and the commonwealth began to fade. The remaining two of Churchill's "three circles" – the "special relationship" and Europe – became the source of considerable conflict. British aircraft makers naturally supported the second option, simply because US aircraft makers were too big, too dominant and had little apparent interest in cooperation with Britain. Key government figures, however, were strong advocates of US–UK cooperation (and of Hitch's theory). One of these was Sir Solly Zuckerman, the chief scientific adviser to the British Ministry of Defence.

In 1961, Zuckerman devised a system for reviewing the cost of arms development – the so-called Zuckerman system. According to this system, once defence research programmes had gotten underway, they could no longer be cancelled. The main conclusions of Zuckerman's report were "the need to invest heavily both in time and money during an extended technical cost evaluation at the outset of a programme", and the necessity "that the procurement process should also include break clauses if expensive mistakes were to be stopped".[44] He also emphasised the need for standardisation within NATO.[45] Ultimately, Zuckerman's system opened the door to a cancellation of British "prestige" projects through an enhancement of budgetary control over the escalation of costs. In fact, the TSR-2 was the first aircraft procured in accordance with the checklists of the Zuckerman system.

The Conservative government subsequently endeavoured to restrain the escalating developmental costs for military projects such as the TSR-2. But the Zuckerman system not only strengthened the authority of the Treasury in arms procurement – it also introduced the idea that any duplication of arms development among allies should be strenuously avoided. The logic underpinning the Zuckerman system held that under no circumstances should Britain find itself in competition with the United States in highly advanced technology development. Instead, British industry should concentrate on those areas where it already enjoyed an advantage.

To be sure, Zuckerman was broadly pessimistic about British prospects for vying with the United States in the spheres of research, development and production. This pessimism resulted partly from his visit to the McDonnell-Douglas F-4 Phantom factory in the United States. Zuckerman personally witnessed 20 F-4 production lines operating at full capacity. He later described this in his autobiography as "a dramatic indication of the difference between British and

66 *The British dilemma in military field, 1964–69*

American production methods".[46] What it really represented was an uncomfortable first-hand glimpse into the productivity gap that existed between the two countries.[47]

Zuckerman was also opposed to European co-operation. In a discussion with Denning Pearson of Rolls-Royce, Zuckerman was informed of Rolls' ambition for enhanced involvement with the French aero-engine maker Snecma. But Zuckerman was opposed to this idea, opining instead that "No – Rolls had to get into the American market on its own".[48]

Commonwealth turf wars, Part I: India

Behind the scenes of the Western Alliance, Anglo–American competition for aircraft sales continued. As the United States strengthened foreign arms sales, Britain, the number two aircraft producer in the West, increasingly emerged as a potential competitor. Britain's three major military programmes for the 1960s – the TSR-2, P.1154 and HS.681 – used technologies similar to those used in comparable American programmes. British manufacturers were thus capable of producing the same type of products. Indeed, in developmental terms, the TSR-2 fighter-bomber was more advanced than its American rival, the F-111. Similarly, the P.1154 fighter and HS.681 transport enjoyed technological superiority in V/STOL ability when compared with the American F-4 fighter and C-130 transport.

The key markets in this gathering commercial struggle between the two leading NATO members were frequently members of the Commonwealth, such as Australia, India and Canada. Indeed, the transition from Empire to Commonwealth had not deterred Britain from trying to maintain its influence in the Asia–Pacific region (i.e. India, Australia and so on). One of the primary vehicles for accomplishing this was the Colombo plan (the British international aid strategy), as well as the attempted restoration of pound sterling/dollar parity after the Suez Crisis.

India presented a potentially tantalising prize for any aircraft industry looking to expand its commercial remit. By 1957, India had used up the sterling reserves accumulated during the Second World War, and was on the lookout for a new aid scheme – and, indeed, aimed at the creation of an independent aircraft industry.[49] There was market potential here.

The first shots were fired in the late 1950s. Hawker Siddeley made some attempt to sell the Avro 748 military transport to the Indian Air Force. Lockheed, however, pushed for a scheme whereby India would purchase much-needed US wheat, with the resulting charge used to build an aircraft factory that would produce a competitor to the Avro 748 – free of charge. This unmistakeably constituted an American "gift of an aircraft plant to India"[50] in order to secure a US hold over a possible Indian aircraft industry. Reginald Maudling, President of the Board of Trade, explained to Prime Minister Harold Macmillan that "American aid [was] to provide commodity against payment in local currencies and then to allow the recipient to use those local currencies to build up their own home industries".[51] In fact, this was a fairly generous interpretation of US commercial incursions on Britain's supposed "turf".

Maudling also warned Macmillan that if, the United States supplied wheat to India as part of an aircraft deal, then this would potentially deprive Australia of a traditional market.[52] Britain was losing control of the Commonwealth. It seemed that the Eisenhower administration, hand in hand with US aircraft industry, was penetrating into the historically "British dominated" Pacific region and dismantling London's traditional trade networks. The next critical target was the Royal Australian Air Force's (RAAF's) Canberra light-bomber replacement: British TSR-2 or American F-111?

Commonwealth turf wars, Part II: Australia

India was not the only scene of United States/British commercial competition for aircraft manufacturing supremacy. Australia in particular was a traditional customer of the British aircraft industry. In 1953, the RAAF introduced the British Canberra as its main bomber. By the mid-1960s, however, this model was nearing obsolescence. A burgeoning confrontation between Australia and Indonesia lay on the horizon, and so the question of replacing the Canberra inevitably arose.[53] Would Australia opt for the British TSR-2 or the American F-111?

Within the British defence community itself, there were two key opponents to the continued development of the TSR-2. Zuckerman was one of them; the other was Lord Louis Mountbatten, who from July 1959 served as Chief of the Defence Staff. As already mentioned, Zuckerman was convinced of an insurmountable US supremacy in any competition with British technology. Conversely, Mountbatten's outlook was heavily informed by his time as First Sea Lord of the British Admiralty. From his distinctly "pro-naval" perspective and his hope to allocate defence budgets to more aircraft carriers instead of TSR-2s, Mountbatten consistently argued that the RAF should aim to procure a land version of the Buccaneer (Navy fighter). In November 1963, the *Sunday Times* printed an article by Mountbatten in which the Chief of the Defence Staff commented on five photographs of the Buccaneer and one of the TSR-2 with the somewhat derisive statement, "Five of one or one of the other at the same cost".[54]

On 28th August 1960, the Commonwealth Chiefs of Staff – including the Australians – met at Camberley. At this meeting, British officials made a secret presentation for the TSR-2. Thereafter, the British government and BAC continued in their efforts to sell the TSR-2 to Commonwealth countries. At the same time, however, Australia was also becoming an increasingly important market for the United States, partly due to domestic factors.[55] If Australia agreed to buy the F-111 then, US Secretary of Defense Robert McNamara reasoned, domestic US opposition to the project would be significantly weakened.

The competition between the United States and Britain for the Australian contract to replace the Canberra bombers reached its zenith during the autumn of 1963. In intensive negotiations, leaders from the United States, Britain and

68 *The British dilemma in military field, 1964–69*

Australia discussed prices, delivery dates and offers of substitute bombers before delivery. Initially, Britain tried to sell 24 TSR-2s to the RAAF at a cost of £100 million. But the RAF's planned procurement of 138 TSR-2 against approximately 1,700 F-111s proved highly problematic for the British. Due to economies of scale, Britain had severe difficulty in managing the TSR-2's developmental costs of £175–200 million, with each TSR-2 costing a likely £2.5 million. On 24th October 1963, the RAAF decided to purchase 24 F-111s at US $224 million (£79 million). In the end, the United States was simply able to quote a lower price.[56]

Britain's loss of the Australian market to the United States dramatically decreased the scheduled production quantity of TSR-2 and escalated the model's per unit cost.[57] Under the Zuckerman system, this implied that the very existence of the project was threatened. The prospects for nationally independent projects began to look bleaker by the day. In this context, two doors to an escape from Britain's impasse were opened by the Hitch–McKean theory and the European collaboration argument. London would have to pick one.

"White heat"

In the party's 1964 manifesto, Labour fleshed out its vision of "white heat" with the following policy indicators. First, Britain would establish new industries through a partnership between the public and private sectors. Second, there would be an extension of R&D contracts from military to civil projects. Third, Britain would set up a Ministry of Technology to promote advanced technology.[58] The second proposal had particularly radical implications. It pointed to a wholesale reassessment of the British military aircraft industry. Up to this point, this industry had lain at the heart of British R&D activities, both in terms of its position in the national economy and with respect to international collaboration.

It was in his speech to the Labour Party conference in 1963 that Harold Wilson, then leader of the opposition, first referred to the "white heat of the technological revolution" which would allow Britain to match up with the United States and the Soviets. The emphasis of this speech was that national resources would be "mobilised" and "redeployed". What this meant in practice was the cancellation of the TSR-2, the Conservative government's "prestige" programme, and a shifting of government money from the military to the civil sector through the development of Concorde.[59]

Indeed, the status of the "prestige" aerospace projects – the TSR-2, the P.1154 and the HS.681 – was one of the most controversial political issues dividing the Conservative from the Labour party. Britain was essentially faced with three alternatives: to continue nationally independent programmes, to collaborate with the United States, or to take the "European route" and throw in its lot with, above all, France.

The possible cancellation of the TSR-2 project became an exceedingly prominent issue during the General Election campaign of 1964. The Labour Party was heavily critical of the project. This criticism was sharpened by the fact that, in the wake of the loss of the Australian market, a dwindling number of advanced orders for the TSR-2 entailed a dramatic increase in per unit cost. The discussion flared up on many occasions in the run-up to the elections. In a House debate in 1963, for example, Labour MP Denis Healey attacked Minister of Aviation Julian Amery for ensuring that BAC factories would be located in Amery's constituency of Preston. Healey accused Amery of "confusing national and sectional interests".[60]

Wilson's stance with respect to the TSR-2 was less clear. In March 1964, during a discussion with McNamara in the Pentagon, Wilson used some rather cryptic words to broach a possible purchase of US aircraft. He stated that Britain "would be happy to have a smaller set of golf clubs" if the United States had "in its bag the mashie for getting out of the bunker".[61] In June 1965, however, Wilson made a speech in Preston, the site of the BAC factory tasked with producing the TSR-2. The Prime Minister denied the rumour that his Party would cancel the project if it won the upcoming General Election.[62] Then, in a television interview given that same month, he also indicated that the TSR-2 "would not have suited the changing needs"[63] of Britain's national security interests.

On 15th October 1964, the Labour Party did indeed win the General Election. After taking office, the Wilson government immediately began a review of the outgoing Conservative government's aircraft programmes. This was publicly announced on 26th October by George Brown, Minister of Economic Affairs. Brown stated in Parliament that the new Labour government would:

> carry out a strict review of all government expenditure. Their object will be to relieve the strain on the balance of payments and release funds for more productive purposes by cutting out expenditure on items of low economic priority, such as 'prestige projects.'[64]

Roy Jenkins was appointed as Minister of Aviation. His first task was to undertake "a survey of all problems facing British aviation".[65] To implement the task, Jenkins soon established a small independent committee of Inquiry into the industry. He appointed Sir Edwin Plowden as Chairman. Plowden was a former chief planner at the Treasury, and head of the Atomic Energy Authority. He was joined by Monnet and Harriman, who constituted the three "wise men" tasked with directing the committee. Jenkins also asked Aubrey Jones, who had rationalised the aircraft industry as Minister of Supply under the Macmillan government, to become a member of the committee. This soon became known as the Plowden Committee.[66]

The Chequers meeting in November 1964

Just after taking office as Minister of Defence, Denis Healey proposed that the TSR-2, P.1154 and HS.681 projects should be cancelled. This was music to the ears of Harold Wilson. Upon assuming office, Wilson fully grasped the scale of the British state's balance of payment problems. On 21st and 22nd November, the

70 The British dilemma in military field, 1964–69

new Prime Minister met with crucial Cabinet members at Chequers to discuss the British defence policy, in preparation for discussions with US President Lyndon B. Johnson in December. Senior ministers agreed that British defence expenditure should be reduced from the current estimate of £2,400 million to £2,000 million – and, indeed, that this latter figure should be the absolute ceiling for military expenditure.[67]

A report previously prepared by the Treasury and Ministry of Economic Affairs pointed out that military spending had trended upwards over the previous five years. It predicted that this would continue to rise to £2.4 billion by 1969–1970. The Minister of Economic Affairs proposed a cap on this figure of £2 billion on the military budget in order to help address the economic difficulties that Britain had faced under the Conservative government.[68] Wilson approved the proposals and commented that Britain, "should not seek to maintain in the future our three roles on their present scale".[69] Churchill's "three circles" were, it seems, simply unrealisable.

Several possible cuts of major items of defence outlay were proposed, including: (1) defence R&D; (2) the BAOR; and (3) East of Suez deployments. With respect to defence R&D, Denis Healy, Minister of Defence, pointed out that replacing the TSR-2, P.1154 and HS.681 with the American F-111, F-4 and C-130 would result in savings of £600 million. As for the BAOR, this was the topic of the so-called "Equipment Paper", presented by Cabinet Secretary Burke Trend at the second Chequers debate on 13th June 1965.[70]

The most effective means of cutting military spending would have been a British retreat from East of Suez. This was the topic of a Ministry of Defence paper completed in July 1965. This paper proposed a reduction of commitments in Europe, the Mediterranean, the Middle East and the Far East for savings of £350 million.[71] However, most ministers supported the continuation of British involvement in this region. Consequently, a reduction of military research and development expenditures appeared as the most effective means of achieving the target of cutting £400 million from the military budget. In place of these projects, Healey advocated the purchase of equivalent American aircraft.[72]

Trend advocated for cutting the size of British forces in Germany in order to save £90 million (£83.5 million from BAOR and the rest from RAF Germany, which amounted to about half of overseas defence expenditures).[73] Indeed, Wilson initially proved highly amenable to the idea of withdrawing the BAOR. In 1963, British military personnel levels in Germany stood at 51,000, with the foreign exchange costs of British Troops totalling £73 million.[74] Any reductions to the British presence on the Rhine, however, represented a most unappealing prospect from the perspective of President Lyndon B. Johnson's government in Washington. Johnson was concerned to contain a Gaullist challenge and to preserve a flexible NATO response strategy.

The Labour government was determined to rationalise defence expenditures and minimise the balance of payments to stabilise the value of the pound sterling. But it seemed that there were no good options for accomplishing this.

The cancellation of top projects, 1963–65 71

TSR-3? The Washington summit in December 1964

The Washington summit took place from 7th to 9th December 1964. At this summit, the US Department of Defense produced a position paper entitled "TSR3". This paper pointed out that Britain faced significant problems in continuing the TSR-2. Instead, it proposed the joint US–UK production of a modified F-111 (dubbed TSR-3). The TSR-3 would be fitted with the British Rolls-Royce Spey engine, as well as the same British avionics equipment which had been pencilled in for the TSR-2. According to this joint production plan, the United States would manufacture most of the aircraft and Britain would manufacture more than 50 per cent of the total weapon system cost. For the UK, this held out the prospect of not only saving money, but also of retaining engine-building and electronics capabilities.[75]

Minister of Aviation Roy Jenkins informally indicated some interest in the "TSR3 proposal". However, he also opined that it did "not go to the heart of the British aviation problem".[76] He also saw that the fundamental objectives for the United States were, in addition to sales of the model, the accomplishment of a "closer defense relations with the British and perhaps other NATO nations, including Germany".[77]

The problems of British defence and foreign policy were again on the agenda at the crucial Anglo–American summit held in Washington, DC on 7th December 1964. At this time, McNamara was strenuously endeavouring to rationalise US and NATO defence expenditure from the standpoint of cost-effectiveness, mainly in order to cover the escalating costs of defence R&D and the Vietnam War.[78]

McNamara had some choice words for Wilson at this summit. He informed the British Prime Minister that, for Britain to achieve the defence budget goal, "hard decisions regarding equipment"[79] would be necessary. He offered US help under the auspices of a more collaborative R&D development programme, but he added that, "speaking frankly, the UK [was] financing certain projects which [made] no sense militarily and really represent a waste of money, in particular the TSR2".[80] He added that "it was necessary to destroy the myth that an arms industry is necessary for economic expansion".[81] With this body blow delivered, McNamara went on to tell Wilson that Britain and the United States would mutually benefit from the integration of weapons development, though he acknowledged that this would be a painful process for Britain in particular.[82]

Ultimately, then, McNamara believed that economic logic would (or should) compel Britain to liquidate its R&D costs for the TSR-2, and to replace this model through a mass-purchase of the American F-111. The US Secretary of Defense also apparently believed that such a step would enable Britain to maintain its commitment to global affairs, including in the Far East and perhaps in support of the escalating US engagement in Vietnam. Clearly, in the Cold War climate, a key priority for the United States was to secure a continued British commitment to international engagement, especially East of Suez.

McNamara's position had at least one supporter at the conference in the form of Denis Healey, Wilson's Defence Secretary. Healey outlined the difficulties of

72   The British dilemma in military field, 1964–69

cutting the defence budget through a mere reduction of manpower, and he reiterated McNamara's view that the only practical way to accomplish savings on such a scale was to economise on equipment. He also agreed with McNamara that Britain should buy "certain weapons"[83] (i.e. the F-111) from the United States rather than produce them domestically.

In essence, the American view was that Britain had no option but to rationalise its defence budget (i.e. switch its nuclear umbrella from the TSR-2 to the F-111) in order to afford the cost of a continued role East of Suez. This role was necessary from the perspective of continued US involvement in Vietnam.[84] It seemed that Britain would take the bait. The Washington summit was attended by Zuckerman and Healey, as well as Dr Harold Brown, the Director of Defense Research and Engineering in the Office of the US Secretary of Defense. These officials agreed to expand US–UK R&D co-operation. The stated objectives of the expansion were, first, for the UK to concentrate its R&D activities; second, to save R&D money in both countries; and, third, to achieve equipment standardisation.[85]

Barely a week after the conference, on 14th–18th December 1964, negotiations for a British purchase of American aircraft commenced. The main parties to these discussions were Henry Kuss, head of the ILN, and British Air Marshall Sir Christopher Hartley. The main obstacle to purchasing the F-111, the F-4, and the C-130 was the vast foreign exchange impact for Britain. If Britain bought 100 F-111s, 180 F-4s and 100 C-130s, then the likely foreign exchange cost to Britain was, according to the ILN's estimates, about £2 billion over ten years.[86]

The ILN recommended to Robert McNamara that he send a letter to Denis Healey expressing the willingness of the United States to discuss a possible means of easing the foreign exchange impact of a British purchase of US aircraft. This would likely entail an "offset by foreign exchange earnings directly or indirectly attributable to this program".[87] The ILN's offer to Britain through McNamara was that the US Department of Defense would purchase British military equipment in return for British purchases of the F-111, F-4 and C-130. This, it was hoped, would significantly ease British foreign exchange problems.

The US–UK Co-operative Logistic Agreement

On 11th–12th January 1965, US/UK military sales negotiations were held in London.[88] The US Department of Defense team proposed various arrangements to the British. The US position paper for the talks was prepared by a Mr Feigl from the US Department of Defense, International Security Affairs and ILN, and by the State Department. This document offered a clear (and unsurprising) solution to the British government's continuing problems in maintaining its domestic aircraft industry – the purchase of cheaper and superior American aircraft. It pointed out that key figures within the British government were already advocating such a policy, and further recommended that the UK concentrate on the production of items where it already enjoyed a competitive position, such as aircraft engines.[89]

The American position paper acknowledged that the TSR-2 was a particularly sensitive issue because it had become a matter of British national pride. There had already been substantial investment in the TSR-2; if the British government now purchased the American-produced F-111 in large quantities, then this would likely consume the entire budget for continued investment in the TSR-2. That the British government would deliberately decide to sound "the death knell for all or part of the British aircraft industry"[90] was, the report recognised, hard to imagine. The logic of such a decision from a financial and even technological perspective seemed to be of secondary importance. A significant purchase of American aircraft would likely give rise to a "political furor".[91]

Nonetheless, the US position paper maintained that the acquisition of a significant share of the UK market for the US military aircraft industry was highly likely. And with an American foot in the door, over time the British might come to "depend on us almost entirely for military aircraft". The paper did acknowledge, however, that this was "likely to be a gradual and lengthy process"[92] rather than a single, seismic shift.

At an OPD[93] meeting on 15th January, Healey recommended the cancellation of the TSR-2, P.1154 and HS.681 and their replacement through the purchase of the American produced F-111, F-4 and C-130. This, Healey claimed, would save the British government about £600 million and reduce defence expenditure to the £2 billion level stipulated in official spending plans.[94]

Some ministers were solidly opposed to Healey's plan. Jenkins proposed a compromise solution that would entail the purchase of 50 TSR-2s and 50 F-111s.[95] This occasioned a three-way split within the Cabinet. First were those who supported the cancellation of TSR-2 and purchase of the F-111; second, those who supported the continued development of TSR-2; and third, those who rejected both the TSR-2 *and* the substitute purchase of US aircraft. This third alternative would almost certainly have entailed an immediate British retreat from East of Suez.[96]

Healey's advocacy for the wholesale purchase of US aircraft was unsurprising. After all, since the Washington summit, he had maintained a close, co-operative relationship with Robert McNamara, and had fully introduced the cost-effectiveness analysis used by McNamara into the British military budget. He had become a "McNamara boy", as Richard Crossman, Minister of Housing and Local Government, somewhat derisively noted in his diary.[97] By contrast, Minister of Aviation Roy Jenkins leaned toward the second alternative because he feared the likely damage inflicted on the British aircraft industry by a wholesale cancellation of the TSR-2. That said, he also showed signs of favouring the third alternative, due to his private doubts about the British role East of Suez.[98]

The prospect of halting airframe development and concentrating instead on engine development was – to nobody's surprise – vehemently opposed by the British aircraft industry. On the night of 15th January 1965, Prime Minister Harold Wilson and Minister of Aviation Roy Jenkins met with representatives of this industry at Chequers to discuss a mooted cancellation of the British aircraft projects and the substitute purchase of American aircraft. Of particular concern

74 *The British dilemma in military field, 1964–69*

was the possible competitive position of the British engine sector if Britain did indeed cease airframe development. The industry representatives insisted that, if the British aircraft industry ceased production of completed planes, then Rolls-Royce would be unable to maintain its international position. They further argued that foreign buyers would not rely on British engines if they were not incorporated into British airframes.[99]

Aircraft industry heads even questioned the apparent financial advantages of a switch to American aircraft. In their view, the government overestimated the projected costs of the TSR-2 and P.1154 and underestimated the likely balance of payments problems that a massive purchase of American aircraft might entail. They also raised the possibility of "joint R. and D. projects with the French, the Germans, and possibly the Italians – though not with the Americans, who had in the past proven to be difficult partners".[100]

Ultimately, then, Healey's recommendations to purchase American aircraft were given a mixed reception by the British Cabinet. The cancellation of P.1154 and HS.681, and the purchase of the F-4 and C-130, were all approved with relative ease on 1st February. These projects were still in their formative stages, and few within the military services were prepared to give them a full-blooded backing.

But the government proved unable to take the plunge with respect to the TSR-2. This project was not cancelled, because Chancellor of the Exchequer James Callaghan proposed a postponement of any decision on its future.[101] It seems likely that an impression had been made by a glut of mass marches and union-sponsored meetings of aircraft workers who feared job losses if the aircraft projects were cancelled.[102]

This proved to be the source of a public debate. In some circles, "prestige" aircraft programmes such as the TSR-2 were regarded as a "kind of Tory toy and symbol of Tory extravagance".[103] Indeed, it soon became clear which way the wind was blowing. As Dockrill has shown, "[b]y the end of January, a consensus was reached among senior ministers (Wilson, Healey, Brown and Callaghan) that the TSR-2 would eventually have to be cancelled, mainly on economic grounds".[104]

On 18th January 1965, Healey communicated to Wilson that "obviously we must try to concentrate our efforts more than we have done in the past. More important, our aim must be to make our technical resources go further by collaborating over as wide a field as possible in joint R&D products, both with the Americans and with our European partners".[105] Healey, then, had apparently accepted the demise of an independent British aerospace industry. But his attitude with respect to Britain's choice of partner remained open and pragmatic.

London between Paris and Washington

On 9th February 1965, Healey made a statement to the British press on the US–UK Co-operative Logistics Agreement. Under this agreement, Britain would commit itself to the purchase of American aircraft. Initially, the agreement specified the F-4 rather than the P.1154, and the C-130 instead of HS.681. Britain and the United States further agreed that both countries would expand their co-operation in defence R&D, especially in the joint development of an advanced V/STOL engine.[106] The British, however, still wished to defer a decision on the F-111.

Clearly, taking the plunge and actually cancelling the TSR-2 remained an uncomfortable prospect for the British Cabinet.[107] And yet, as far as British ministers (especially Jenkins) were concerned, the real question was how British R&D capabilities might be maintained in the event of a cancellation. A document produced by the Foreign Office and prepared for the OPD pointed out that the UK would be at "the mercy politically of the American government and commercial of United States industry"[108] unless Britain could maintain first-class research, development and production capabilities. This would surely require international co-operation, either with the United States or France.

Co-operation with the United States had been the agreed-upon strategy since the Wilson–Johnson summit in December 1964. However, its actual implementation was expected to be difficult. "Many attempts have been made to do so [enhance US/UK co-operation] in the past, but none has had much success, mainly because of disproportion between the American and the British arms industries and the active opposition of American industry to anything that might prolong the existence of a competitor".[109] On the other hand, the Foreign Office paper suggested "horse-trading: if we buy certain weapons in the United States, they should buy certain weapons in the United Kingdom".[110] Clearly, the Foreign Office also recognised that there were significant obstacles around deeper collaboration with France, whose diplomatic policy was apparently opposed to that of Britain and America. The paper explicitly recommended that Britain should "be careful to avoid appearing to acquiesce in French policy".[111]

With the P.1154 and the HS.681 officially cancelled, Anglo–French negotiations on aerospace projects developed a new momentum. On 20th January, Jenkins formally announced that the Labour government would proceed with Concorde – in collaboration with France.[112] On 2nd February, Healey sent a message to Pierre Messmer, French Minister of the Armed Forces, confirming Britain's intention to embark on a joint study for an Anglo–French strike/trainer aircraft.[113] On 27th February, Healey and Jenkins met with Messmer in Paris in order to explore the possibility of deeper Anglo–French collaboration.[114]

France had two motivations for enhanced co-operation in this area. First, only the combined efforts of the French and British aircraft industries could conceivably match up with the powerful US aircraft industry. Second, deeper Anglo–French collaboration held out a renewed prospect for survival to the faltering French aero-engine sector.[115] However, because of his evident desire for deeper Anglo–French co-operation, Messmer also expressed certain reservations about the British decision to purchase US aircraft. Ultimately, both sides agreed to proceed with a joint Strike/Trainer project (later named Jaguar) to replace the Hunter and the Gnat. It was also envisaged that future Anglo–French co-operation would entail the development of a variable geometry (VG) aircraft (later

76   *The British dilemma in military field, 1964–69*

named Anglo–French variable geometry (AFVG)).[116] At an OPD meeting on 10th March, Healey advocated the advancement of these two Anglo–French aerospace projects (the Jaguar and the AFVG), and he was given Prime Ministerial approval.[117]

On 22nd March, British Foreign Secretary Michael Stewart pressed Denis Healey to talk to Robert McNamara immediately in order to establish a firm price for the F-111. This urgency, Stewart insisted, owed to substantial domestic political and industrial pressures against the cancellation of the TSR-2 within a budgetary timetable.[118] Indeed, TUC (Trade Union Congress) chiefs had already warned Jenkins of further mass marches and strikes of aircraft workers.[119] On the same day, a meeting of the US State Defense Coordinating Committee on Military Sales was held. This meeting, which took place every Monday afternoon, was known as the "Kuss-Kitchen [C]abinet"[120] after Henry Kuss and Jeffrey Kitchen, Deputy Assistant Secretaries of State for Politico–Military Affairs. Its goal was to coordinate State and Defense Departments.[121] On this particular Monday, Kuss reported that Healey had two weeks to decide whether or not to purchase the F-111. He also noted the UK's desire for "a dramatic selection by the US of some British produced item"[122] such as the V/STOL lift engine, as well as the UK's apparent hope of a French purchase of the TSR-2. An Anglo–French procurement of 300 TSR-2s would reduce the R&D costs per aircraft. The Americans, then, were well aware that London had misgivings about placing itself entirely at the mercy of the US aircraft industry.

Three days later, Denning Pearson, the chairman of Rolls-Royce, sent a letter to Wilson based on his discussions with the relevant French civil servants. In the letter, Pearson acknowledged that both the United States and France were possible partners for international collaboration. However, he added that a partnership with the United States would lead to an undesirable dependence on American technology. He thus argued that France was the only partner capable of guaranteeing independent British aviation technology in the long term. Pearson further expressed some alarm around the penetration of the French market by the US aircraft manufacturer P&W, which had recently acquired a 10.9 per cent stake in the French firm Snecma. Rolls-Royce's aim was to replace P&W.[123]

Time runs out for the TSR-2

On 25th March 1965, a meeting took place in the Pentagon between Robert McNamara and Lord Shackleton, British Minister of Defence for the RAF. McNamara informed Lord Shackleton that, although Zuckerman had been "virtually employed as his purchasing agent for a lengthy period, no suitable items of equipment had emerged".[124] He was also critical of the insufficient concentration of British R&D efforts. Britain, he argued, should concentrate on specific fields in aviation and cease attempts to compete unilaterally with the United States. For his part, Lord Shackleton pressed McNamara for concessions on the British purchase of the F-111, and he was successful, with McNamara offering to waive the

50 per cent preference rule which applied to any UK equipment bought for the USAF and the US Navy.[125]

In an OPD paper on 26th March, Healey outlined four proposals that he hoped would set the course of future British policy in military aircraft procurement. First, Britain needed to procure 110 units of a TSR-2/F-111-style aircraft. Second, Britain should purchase the F-111 and cancel the domestic TSR-2 project. Third, Britain should press the United States for a number of concessions in return for the purchase of the F-111 – including guaranteed American purchase of British hardware. Fourth, the British government should immediately inform the French that the cancellation of the TSR-2 would make Britain available for enhanced Anglo–French collaboration in the area of military aircraft production.[126]

Healey hoped that the purchase of the F-111 would allow Britain to maintain its role East of Suez. He also apparently believed that enhanced Anglo–French co-operation would help to absorb some of the British technological resources released by the cancellation of the TSR-2.[127] His view was not unwarranted. As we can see from Figure 4.2, in 1965/66, the F-111 had more or less the same coverage as the TSR-2, from the West Pacific to the South Atlantic and including regions of Soviet influence.

On the same day that Healey issued his OPD paper, however, Roy Jenkins outlined a different case in his own OPD paper. The Minister of Aviation argued

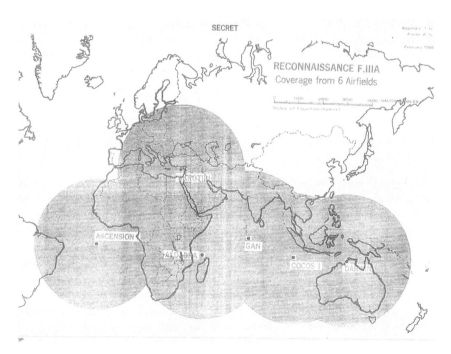

Figure 4.2 Geographical coverage of the F-111
Source: TNA CAB148/27, OPD (66)30th, 8th February 1966.

78 The British dilemma in military field, 1964–69

that, first, and irrespective of any budgetary advantages to buying the F-111, a mass purchase of American aircraft would inevitably result in a heavy balance of payments problem. Second, Jenkins warned that the switch from the TSR-2 to the F-111 placed Britain "further in the hands of the American aircraft industry".[128] Third, although the cancellation of TSR-2 would undoubtedly release resources for enhanced Anglo–French collaboration, the purchase of American aircraft would surely arouse French suspicions and significantly complicate, among other things, the Prime Minister's impending visit to Paris. Jenkins concluded that Britain should certainly cancel the TSR-2, but also that the decision to buy the F-111 should be postponed.[129]

At the OPD meeting on 29th March, ministers finally reached a general agreement on the need to cancel the TSR-2. Once again, however, a consensus remained elusive on the question of whether or not, and if so how many, F-111s should be procured to replace it.[130] The next day, British and French ministers met to discuss international aviation co-development. They focused particularly on attack-trainer and VG technologies. The attitude exhibited by the French at this meeting with respect to an immediate VG commitment gave rise to exasperation among British ministers.[131]

Nonetheless, in a letter to the Prime Minister on 31st March, Healey recommended that the government proceed with attack-trainer and VG co-development with France. He buttressed his argument with the point that the cancellation of the TSR-2 project had rendered such co-development eminently feasible because Britain could now shift resources allocated for this aircraft towards emerging Anglo–French projects.[132] The French, of course, were concerned to bind Britain as firmly as possible to the idea of Anglo–French co-operation, and to exclude the prospect of future Anglo–American co-operation. Britain, however, endeavoured to "retain as much freedom as we [Britain] can to collaborate as best suits us".[133]

British domestic adjustments leading to the cancellation of TSR-2

On 1st April 1965, two lengthy Cabinet sessions took place at which ministers intensively discussed the proposed cancellation of the TSR-2 project. The British Cabinet ministers were 12–10 in favour of cancellation. However, the majority was divided over whether Britain would purchase the American F-111s. The main issue was the balance of payments problem. The discussion began with a general agreement that cancelling the production of 110 TSR-2 units would result in £280 million in budgetary savings – but that purchasing the same number of F-111s would cost roughly £500 million.[134] Healey, the primary proponent of replacing the TSR-2 with the F-111, pointed out that US authorities had agreed in principle that, should Britain agree to the mass purchase of the F-111, then the United States would waive its usual 50 per cent preference rule in order to ease Britain's resulting balance of payments problem.[135]

Nonetheless, Prime Minister Harold Wilson and Roy Jenkins, Minister of Aviation, strongly opposed Healey's plan.[136] Wilson apparently had misgivings

The cancellation of top projects, 1963–65   79

about the impact on British manufacturing of cancelling the TSR-2. Jenkins, however, was not so much sceptical about cancelling the British model (which he supported), but rather about the prospect of buying the F-111 (which he did not).

Indeed, Jenkins was unconvinced about the viability of a continued British role East of Suez. He later explained that "My scepticism about a continuing British East of Suez role predisposed me in favour of doing without either [the TSR-2 or the F-111]. This divided me from Healey, who was determined to buy the American plane".[137] Budgetary costs, antipathy to purchasing the US machine instead of the British aircraft, and doubt about the British role East of Suez thus coalesced in Jenkins thinking and led him to reject both alternativeness.[138] As he observed, the savings made by cancelling the TSR-2 would be unlikely to offset the £500 million investment involved in purchasing the US aircraft.[139]

Sensationally, during the meeting itself, a new American proposal arrived with the Cabinet: Britain would be entitled to purchase an initial ten F-111s for training purposes, and then be given the rest of the year to decide whether or not to order an additional 70–100 F-111s. This would allow Britain to postpone the decision to mass purchase the F-111s until January 1966 – and, more importantly, to review at length British overseas defence policy.[140]

This 11th-hour American proposal ultimately proved decisive. At 12:30 a.m., after a full day of detailed and occasionally rancorous discussion, the British Cabinet decided to cancel the TSR-2 project and purchase ten F-111s, with an additional option to buy up to 100 F-111s the following January.[141] Despite the fact that the Cabinet had not come to a firm conclusion on the mass purchase of the F-111, the decision taken at this meeting constituted an effective abandonment of three major military programmes (the TSR-2, the P.1154 and the HS.681). The Americans had played their cards well – but a heavy blow had been dealt to the idea of an independent British aircraft industry.[142]

Wilson meets de Gaulle

On 2nd April, Prime Minister Harold Wilson and French President Charles de Gaulle held a two-day discussion at the Élysée Palace which focused, above all, on aircraft development. By this point, and as Wilson explicitly stated during the discussion, "the lesson [of TSR-2] was simple"[143] – Britain could not afford to unilaterally produce and procure a sophisticated military aircraft. The production of 150 such aircraft, Wilson conceded, would cost £750 million – or £5 million per unit. But the British had need of far fewer than the 150 units envisioned in these production figures, meaning an inevitable rise of unit cost to about £9 million.[144] This was simply unaffordable.

The obvious alternative, Wilson conceded, was the mass purchase of an equivalent aircraft "off the shelf" from the United States. America's vast production scale meant that it could easily absorb the huge R&D costs involved in the production of such an aircraft, and thus sell each unit at a much lower price. As Wilson pointed out, the brutal fact was that the cost of a TSR-2-equivalent

80 The British dilemma in military field, 1964–69

aircraft produced by the United States would be half the price of a British-produced TSR-2. Yet it was impossible for Britain to accept the prospect of total dependence on the US aircraft industry. This was precisely why Wilson hoped for immediate and even long-term Anglo–French collaboration in the area of military aircraft production.[145]

In his reply, de Gaulle agreed that neither Britain nor France could afford an independent civil and military programme. On the other hand, however, he did not believe that either country "was 'ready' to be absorbed by the US aviation industry".[146] If Britain was in favour of practical co-operation in this enormously important field, he concluded, then "France saw no disadvantage".[147]

Over the course of this discussion, Wilson also expanded on the implications of the TSR-2's cancellation for future Anglo–French collaboration. This development, he insisted, would have no impact on such collaboration in the field of aviation, including with respect to civilian projects such as Concorde. He added that the primary purpose of cancelling the TSR-2 was to release resources for an intended Anglo–French accord. The British government, he stated, had not conclusively decided to replace the TSR-2 with a comparable American aircraft.[148]

In his reply, de Gaulle emphasised the significant importance attached by France to the prospect of a broader collaboration between the industries of the two countries, especially in aviation. He described this as a question of survival for both countries, for otherwise they would be reduced to the status of American customers, submerged into and dependent on US industry.[149] At no point did de Gaulle explicitly bring up the subject of the possible replacement of the TSR-2 with the F-111, or voice his concerns that the British purchase of American models might undermine the prospect of Anglo–French collaboration.

In the first three days of April 1965, Harold Wilson thus made two fateful decisions – the cancellation of the TSR-2 and possible purchase of the F-111 on 1st April 1965, and AngloFrench co-operation in military aerospace on 2nd and 3rd April 1965. The first of Churchill's "three circles" had melted away, and two paths now apparently lay open before Britain; collaboration principally with the Americans or with the French. The options had narrowed from three to two, but the ultimate outcome remained uncertain.

Conclusion

With the decision to cancel the TSR-2, the British government effectively abandoned its independent aircraft development programme. Despite this decision, the two primary goals of British aviation technological development remained a VG aircraft and a V/STOL airframe and engine. But the erstwhile superpower was now forced into a new direction – international co-operation. This new direction actually comprised two distinct alternatives: co-operation with continental Europe, or co-operation with the United States.

The F-111 option agreement concluded in April 1965 came with a hugely significant stipulation. US and British officials agreed that the US Department of

The cancellation of top projects, 1963–65   81

Defense would no longer apply the "Buy American" policy in the case of British military products. This agreement enabled Rolls-Royce to compete on the same terms as US manufacturers in the world's biggest military market. As G.C. Peden states, US resources had effectively been harnessed in order to sustain British industry at a time when Britain's own economic base was inadequate to the task. And yet all of this entailed the effective abandonment of the idea of an independent military aircraft project, and a new susceptibility to US imports. In the mid-1960s, with memories of the British Empire as a world-bestriding imperium still widely shared, this seemed a heavy price to pay.[150]

Notes

1   Edgerton ([2006] 2008, p. 217).
2   Edgerton ([2006] 2008, p. 264).
3   Edgerton ([2006] 2008, pp. 264–65).
4   Hastings (1966). Also, Wood (1986). Both were mainly based on governmental statements and interviews. They formulated the view that emphasised the negative effect on the British aircraft industry.
5   Dockrill (2002, p. 58).
6   Dockrill (2002, p. 57).
7   Straw and Young (1997, pp. 22–24).
8   Hayward (1989, p. 132).
9   According to *The MIT Dictionary of Modern Economics*, 4th ed., "Stop-go" means that "[a]ction on the part of the government to curtail aggregate demand due to a balance of payment deficit, soon followed by action with opposite effect to ameliorate the rise in unemployment caused by the first policy intervention" (Pearce (1992, p. 412)).
10   Dockrill (2002, p. 51).
11   Baylis (1981, p. 65).
12   Baylis (1981, p. 67); Dockrill (2002, pp. 80–81).
13   *FRUS, 1961–1963, Volume XIII*, Document 100.
14   *FRUS, 1961–1963, Volume XIII*, Document 100.
15   Sakade (1996).
16   Sakade (1996).
17   Peden (2007, pp. 329–30).
18   *FRUS, 1961–1963, Volume XIII*, Document 406.
19   Pierre (1972, p. 237). Did Britain keep "independent nuclear deterrence" through the Nassau agreement? Baylis stated that by the Nassau agreement, "Macmillan had secured the independence as well as the continuation of the British deterrence which he considered so necessary" (Baylis (1981, p. 74)) and "Britain undoubtedly lost an important measure of its strategic independence" (Baylis (1995, p. 356)).
20   Dockrill (2002, p. 81).
21   Dockrill (2002, p. 81).
22   Dockrill (2002, p. 138).
23   According to Dockrill, the TSR-2 was expected to work either a replacement for the Canberra in Europe or supplement Britain's deterrent ability and "thus developed that the aircraft was intended for the 'East of Suez' role" (Dockrill (2002, p. 82)).
24   TNA CAB148/27, OPD (66)30th, 8th February 1966.
25   Dockrill (2002, p. 81).
26   Moore (2010, p. 225).
27   Kaufman (1964, pp. 245–47).

82 *The British dilemma in military field, 1964–69*

28 Zimmermann (2002, p. 24).

29 Zimmermann (2002, p. 247).

30 Kaufman (1964, p.172); Nardi (1995, pp. 3-61–3-62).

31 The Commission on International Trade and Investment Policy (1971, p. 2).

32 U.S. Congress (1954, pp. 21–24); Leigh-Phippard (1995, pp. 68–71).

33 Badrocke and Gunston (1998, p. 70).

34 NARA RG59, E5178, Box 1, Military Export Sales Program, Germany (Draft), 23rd November 1965; Thayer (1969, pp. 183–84).

35 NARA RG59, E5172, Box 21, Abortive Proposal for Munition Control Policy Council, 26th May 1965; NARA RG59, E5178, Box 1, Proposal for a NATO Expenditure Payments Union, 28th June 1965.

36 Shapley (1993, p. 220).

37 Hitch and McKean (1960, p. 292).

38 Hayward (1989, pp. 126); Department of Trade and Industry, *Productivity of the national aircraft effort: report of a committee appointed by the Minister of Technology and the President of the Society of British Aerospace Companies, under the chairmanship of St. John Elstub* (London, HMSO, 1969).

39 Hartley (1983, p. 43–48).

40 Sakai (1998, p. 98).

41 TNA PREM/13/2003, The Arrangement for Offsetting the Dollar Cost for the F111 Aircraft.

42 Minister of Aviation, *Report of the Committee of Inquiry into the Aircraft Industry*, Cmnd. 2853 (London, HMSO, 1965), para. 252.

43 Minister of Aviation, *Report of the Committee of Inquiry into the Aircraft Industry*, Cmnd. 2853 (London, HMSO, 1965).

44 Segell (1998, p. 129); Office of the Minister for Science, *Report of the Committee on the Management and Control of Research and Development* (London, HMSO, 1961), pp. 71–72; Hastings (1966, p. 129).

45 Zuckerman (1988, p. 163).

46 Zuckerman (1988, p. 204).

47 Hastings (1966, p. 129); Hayward (1989, pp. 87–88); Segell (1998, pp. 129–30).

48 Zuckerman (1988, p. 200).

49 Watanabe (2021, pp. 199–200).

50 TNA PREM 11/2898, Chancellor of Exchequer to Prime Minister, 15th July 1960; TNA PREM 11/2898, Extract from a letter of 16th June 1960 from Sir Roy Dobson of the Hawker Siddeley Group to the Minister of Aviation.

51 TNA PREM 1/2898, President of Board of Trade to Prime Minister, 24th June 1960.

52 TNA PREM 1/2898, President of Board of Trade to Prime Minister, 24th June 1960. In the fighter aircraft field, as the United States decided to provide the F-104 to Pakistan, India hoped to introduce the Soviet MiG-21. This was a potential major change to the power balance in South Asia, so the United States and Britain co-operatively tried to prevent the introduction of the MiG-21 into India in 1962 (Watanabe 2021).

53 TNA T225/3313, F.111 Termination Charges, 15th May 1969.

54 Wood (1986, p. 158); Zuckerman denied the "Zuckbatten Axis" in his biography (Zuckerman (1988, p. 214)).

55 McNamara tried to integrate USAF requirement and US Navy requirement by means of the F-111. The US Navy was opposed to the F-111 because of its heavy weight, and later cancelled the Navy version of the F-111 (the F-111B). In addition, US Congressmen, who supported the Boeing design for the F-111, were also opposed to the General Dynamics design (Shapley (1993, pp. 204–23); Prouty ([1996] 2011, pp. 143–47)).

56 TNA T225/2497, Sale of T.S.R.2 to the Australians, 17th October 1963; TNA T225/2497, Treasury Press Cutting Section, 25th October 1963; TNA T225/2497, Treasury Press Cutting Section, 28th October 1963.

The cancellation of top projects, 1963–65   83

57   Simultaneously, the Nassau agreement and purchase of Polaris meant Britain's chief nuclear deterrent role shifted from the RAF to the Royal Navy.
58   Edgerton ([2006] 2008, p. 240).
59   Edgerton ([2006] 2008, p. 239–40).
60   Hayward (1989, p. 90). It is hard to say whether or not Amery's self-serving gesture proved beneficial to him; in the 1964 General Election, the Conservative majority in his seat was reduced to a mere 14 votes against Labour hopeful Russell Kerr (20,566 votes against 20,552 votes). See https://en.wikipedia.org/wiki/Preston_North_ (UK_Parliament_constituency) [accessed 9.9.2020].
61   Dockrill (2002, p. 58).
62   Reed (1973, pp. 55–56).
63   Worcester (1966, p. 156).
64   Hastings (1966, p. 106).
65   NARA RG59/E5172/Box 16, American Embassy London to Department of State, 28th November 1964.
66   Jenkins (1991, pp. 166–67).
67   Dockrill (2002, pp. 56–57).
68   Dockrill (2002, pp. 56–57).
69   Dockrill (2002, p. 57).
70   Dockrill (2002, p. 96).
71   Dockrill (2002, p. 123).
72   Straw and Young (1997, p. 25); Wilson (1971, pp. 35–37); Zuckerman (1988, pp. 374–78).
73   Dockrill (2002, pp. 96–98, 162).
74   Zimmermann (2002, pp. 248–49).
75   NARA RG59/E5172/Box 16, Secretary McNamara/Wilson-Healey Visit Washington-Omaha 7th–9th December 1964.
76   NARA RG59/E5172/Box 16, Secretary McNamara/Wilson-Healey Visit Washington-Omaha 7th–9th December 1964.
77   NARA RG59/E5172/Box 16, Secretary McNamara/Wilson-Healey Visit Washington-Omaha 7th–9th December 1964.
78   *FRUS, 1964–1968, Volume XII*, Document 236.
79   *FRUS, 1964–1968, Volume XII*, Document 236.
80   *FRUS, 1964–1968, Volume XII*, Document 236.
81   *FRUS, 1964–1968, Volume XII*, Document 236.
82   *FRUS, 1964–1968, Volume XII*, Document 236. Hastings (1966, pp. 107–8).
83   *FRUS, 1964–1968, Volume XII*, Document 236.
84   Baylis (1981, pp. 93–94); Straw and Young (1997, p. 27); Dockrill (2002, pp. 91–92). For McNamara, the British order of the F-111 would provide an argument against US Congressional opposition to the F-111 program (Pincher (1978, p. 314)); Segell (1998, p. 30).
85   NARA RG59/E5172, Box 17, Expansion of Cooperation in Defense Research and Research Between the United Kingdom and the United States, 15th February 1965.
86   NARA RG59/E5172/Box 16, Report of United Kingdom Aircraft Survey and United States Proposal, 23rd December 1964.
87   NARA RG59/E5172/Box 16, Report of United Kingdom Aircraft Survey and United States Proposal, 23rd December 1964.
88   NARA RG59/E5172/Box 21, Jeffrey C. Kitchen to Rusk, 7th January 1965.
89   NARA RG59/E5172/Box 16, US/UK Military Sales Negotiations, January 1965, Background Data.
90   NARA RG59/E5172/Box 16, US/UK Military Sales Negotiations, January 1965, Background Data.
91   NARA RG59/E5172/Box 16, US/UK Military Sales Negotiations, January 1965, Background Data.

84 *The British dilemma in military field, 1964–69*

92 NARA RG59/E5172/Box 16, US/UK Military Sales Negotiations, January 1965, Background Data.

93 OPD is the abbreviation of the Cabinet Defence and Overseas Policy Committee, which was the British substantive decision-making body on foreign and military policy. The OPD consisted of senior ministers such as Defence Minister, Foreign Minister and so on, and was chaired by Prime Minister.

94 TNA CAB148/18, OPD(65)2nd, 15th January 1965.

95 Dockrill (2002, p. 84).

96 TNA CAB128/39, CC (65)6th, 1st February 1965; Jenkins (1991, p. 172).

97 Crossman ([1975] 1978, p. 191); Baylis (1981, pp. 92–93).

98 Jenkins (1991, p. 172).

99 TNA PREM13/121, Note of a Meeting at Chequers at 8.30 p.m. on Friday, 15th January 1965.

100 TNA PREM13/121, Note of a Meeting at Chequers at 8.30 p.m. on Friday, 15th January 1965.

101 TNA CAB128/39, CC (65)6th, 1st February 1965.

102 Pincher (1978, p. 313).

103 Pincher (1978, p. 311).

104 Dockrill (2002, p. 85).

105 TNA PREM13/716, The Political Implications of Dependence on America for Military Aircraft, March 1965.

106 NARA RG59/E5172/Box 21, UK Purchase of US Military Aircraft, 8th February 1965.

107 NARA RG59/E5172/Box 21, Jeffrey C. Kitchen to the Acting Secretary, 30th January 1965.

108 TNA PREM13/716, The Political Implications of Dependence on America for Military Aircraft, March 1965.

109 TNA PREM13/716, The Political Implications of Dependence on America for Military Aircraft, March 1965.

110 TNA PREM13/716, The Political Implications of Dependence on America for Military Aircraft, March 1965.

111 TNA PREM13/716, The Political Implications of Dependence on America for Military Aircraft, March 1965.

112 705 HC Deb., 20th January 1965, cols. 197–98.

113 TNA PREM13/714, Foreign Office to Paris, 2nd February 1965; TNA PREM13/714, Anglo–French Collaboration Projects, 2nd March 1965.

114 Segell (1998, p. 30).

115 Ichige (2016, p. 11).

116 TNA PREM13/714, Anglo–French Collaboration Projects, 2nd March 1965; Segell (1998, p. 30).

117 TNA CAB148/18, OPD(65)14th, 10th March 1965.

118 TNA PREM13/716, Foreign Office to Washington, 22nd March 1965.

119 Pincher (1978, p. 313).

120 Thayer (1969).

121 Thayer (1969, p. 191).

122 NARA RG59/E5179/Box 4, State Defense Coordinating Committee on Military Sales Meeting of 22nd March 1965.

123 TNA PREM13/363, Denning Pearson to Prime Minister, 25th March 1966.

124 TNA T225/2583, Note of the Meeting between Mr. McNamara, The Minister of Defence for the Royal Air Force and the Charge D'affaires at the Pentagon on 25th March 1965.

125 TNA T225/2583, Note of the Meeting between Mr. McNamara, The Minister of Defence for the Royal Air Force and the Charge D'affaires at the Pentagon on 25th March 1965; TNA CAB148/18, OPD (65) 18th, 29th March 1965.

The cancellation of top projects, 1963–65   85

126 TNA CAB148/20, OPD (65)57th, 26th March 1965.
127 TNA CAB148/20, OPD (65)57th, 26th March 1965.
128 TNA CAB148/20, OPD (65)59th, 26th March 1965.
129 TNA CAB148/20, OPD (65)59th, 26th March 1965.
130 TNA CAB148/18, OPD (65)18th, 29th March 1965.
131 TNA PREM13/714, Anglo/French Discussions, 30th March 1965: Agreed Summary.
132 TNA PREM13/714, Anglo–French Co-operation in Military Aircraft Development, 31st March 1965.
133 TNA PREM13/714, Anglo–French Aerospace Collaboration – Supplementary Brief.
134 TNA CAB128/39, CC (65)20th, 1st April 1965; TNA CAB128/39, CC (65)21st, 1st April 1965.
135 TNA CAB128/39, CC (65)20th, 1st April 1965.
136 Healey (1989, p. 273).
137 Jenkins (1991, p. 172).
138 NARA RG59, E5172, Box 21, Jeffrey C. Kitchen to the Acting Secretary, 9th April 1965.
139 TNA CAB128/39, CC (65)20th, 1st April 1965.
140 Dockrill (2002, pp. 89–90); Straw and Young (1997, pp. 35–36).
141 TNA CAB128/39, CC (65)21st, 1 April 1965; Wilson (1971, p. 90).
142 NARA RG59/E5172/Box 21, UK Purchase of F111: British Interest in Quid Pro Quo, 12th April 1965.
143 TNA PREM13/714, Record of a Conversation between the Prime Minister and the President of France at the Élysée Palace at 11 a.m. on Friday, 2nd April 1965.
144 TNA PREM13/714, Record of a Conversation between the Prime Minister and the President of France at the Élysée Palace at 11 a.m. on Friday, 2nd April 1965.
145 TNA PREM13/714, Record of a Conversation between the Prime Minister and the President of France at the Élysée Palace at 11 a.m. on Friday, 2nd April 1965.
146 TNA PREM13/714, Record of a Conversation between the Prime Minister and the President of France at the Élysée Palace at 11 a.m. on Friday, 2nd April 1965.
147 TNA PREM13/714, Record of a Conversation between the Prime Minister and the President of France at the Élysée Palace at 11 a.m. on Friday, 2nd April 1965.
148 TNA PREM13/714, Record of a Conversation between the Prime Minister and President de Gaulle at the Elysee Palace at 10 a.m. on Saturday, 3rd April 1965.
149 TNA PREM13/714, Record of a Conversation between the Prime Minister and President de Gaulle at the Elysee Palace at 10 a.m. on Saturday, 3rd April 1965.
150 Peden (2007, p. 344).

5 The politics behind the Plowden doctrine

European and American alternatives for the British aircraft industry

Introduction

In December 1964, Roy Jenkins, Britain's Minister of Aviation, appointed Lord Edwin Plowden to head a new committee which was charged with investigating the state of the British aircraft industry. The Plowden Committee was handed a range of tasks; to review the position of the aircraft industry in the national economy with respect to other industries, to assess the industry's future direction, and to recommend a course of action to maintain its strategic health.[1] The findings of this Committee were finally published in December 1965 as the Plowden Report. At the time of its publication, this report was regarded as a doctrinal statement of the British aircraft industry's move towards deeper European collaboration. This was buttressed by the fact that the report appeared in the wake of the cancellation of several independent British aerospace projects such as the TSR-2, the P.1154, and the HS.681 in February to April 1965.

More recent evaluations of the report and its context have generally concurred with this view. For Anthony Sampson, the Plowden Report constituted an explicit move towards "collaborating with other countries, particularly with Europe".[2] Saki Dockrill has also depicted the Plowden Committee as an official encouragement to the British aircraft industry to deepen continental co-operation.[3] Geoffrey Owen has suggested that the Wilson government basically accepted the Plowden Report's conclusion that the United States was not "an appropriate partner"[4] for British aircraft production. The scale and scope of the American aircraft industry, Owen observed, meant that only a partnership between the UK and France could provide "the basis for a viable European aircraft industry".[5] An article by Lewis Johnman and Frances Lynch on the European Airbus also styled the Plowden Report as a prerequisite to European co-operation.[6] That said, this view of the Plowden Report's significance has not found unequivocal support. David Edgerton, for example, has argued that, irrespective of the content of the report, the purchase of the F-111 in place of an independent British model necessarily entailed a dependence on US aircraft, at least for the foreseeable future.[7]

In the long run, it seemed that the British aircraft industry was still confronted with the basic dilemma of whether to choose further collaboration

DOI: 10.4324/9781003127901-7

with France and other European partners, or to acquiesce to dependence on the United States. The resolution of this dilemma would determine whether Britain, the second most significant airpower in the western alliance, would opt for enhanced European co-operation, or a deepening of the "special relationship".

Any scholarly attempt to understand this dilemma must grapple with the contents and significance of the Plowden Report. This is precisely what I aim to do in this chapter. I argue that, despite nominally being the principal advocate for greater European aircraft co-operation under the auspices of the Plowden Report, a close examination of British policy actually reveals a preference for Anglo–American rather than European co-operation. However, to depict this as mere "acquiescence" to "dependence" on the United States is to misrepresent the considerable success achieved by the British in this area during the 1960s. Britain played its hand well – and, in the end, made unprecedented inroads into the United States (and other) military markets *without* completely sacrificing the European option.

In order to support these claims, I draw on case studies of US–Europe collaboration on R&D of VG and V/STOL technologies. These were the two most crucial aeronautical innovations of the late 1960s.[8] I further substantiate my argument through an examination of the Wilson government's negotiations and decisions around the cancellation of the TSR-2 in April 1965. Particular attention is paid here to international collaboration between the British aero-engine sector and the US airframe sector.

Certainly, from the early 1960s, British aircraft companies naturally continued to participate in European aerospace projects such as the Anglo–French SST (Concorde), European Airbus, the Anglo–French Jaguar and AFVG. And yet, as we shall see, British officials such as Denis Healey, Minister of Defence, and Sir Solly Zuckerman, the government's Chief Scientific Advisor, tended to push for enhanced Anglo–American collaboration. In the end, it was their perspective which was to exert the most influence on the long-term direction of British aviation industrial policy.

The Plowden Committee's visit to Paris, April 1965

Immediately after its creation, the Plowden Committee found itself confronted by the basic existential questions at the heart of the British aircraft industry. What would be the future place and organisation of this industry within the overall structure of the British economy? And how would the answer to this question be shaped by persistent issues around British national defence and export possibilities, and the relationship between the industry and government?[9] Ultimately, the Plowden Committee came into existence in the context of the cancellation of a series of British military aircraft projects in February to April 1965. It is thus perhaps unsurprising that the committee increasingly focused on international co-operation as a survival strategy for the British aircraft industry. This reflected the thinking of the British government.

88 *The British dilemma in military field, 1964–69*

On 2nd and 3rd April, Prime Minister Harold Wilson and President Charles de Gaulle met in Paris to discuss co-operation between the British and French aircraft industries. The aftermath of these meetings saw an intensification of Anglo–French collaboration on a trainer/light strike aircraft (later named Jaguar) and a VG combat aircraft (later named AFVG).[10] On 6th April 1965, a Plowden Sub-Committee on International Co-operation met to discuss the ramifications of this visit. The Sub-Committee showed itself to be a convinced proponent of intensifying progress on the Jaguar and the AFVG according to British and French requirements. With respect to the Jaguar, members of the sub-committee expected that the French would express firm intentions for continued co-operation. This would surely be carried out on a 50/50 basis.[11]

The Wilson–de Gaulle talks proved highly stimulating for British–French co-operation in the sphere of aviation. This became apparent between the 7th and 9th April 1965, as Plowden Committee members Lord Plowden and Aubrey Jones, the former British Minister of Supply, visited Paris for discussions with senior French officials about the prospects for future international co-operation. The French team was led by Pierre Messmer, the Minister of the Army, and Rene Bloch, the Co-ordinator of International Activities at the Ministerial Delegation for Armaments.[12]

During the discussion in Paris, the French expressed their conviction that, in the placing of contracts for military aeronautic equipment, a joint military project should be in the hands of an Anglo/French committee. Moreover, French officials made yet another appeal for close collaboration between the French and British aircraft industries to ensure their mutual survival. The French officials informed Jones that, "without such collaboration, they believe that first the French and then the British industries would succumb and disappear within five to ten years".[13] They also feared that, if the British government bought the US-produced F-111 VG, then the Americans would attempt to sabotage full Anglo–French co-operation over the development of the VG aircraft. They might even insist that no such AFVG aircraft were needed.[14]

At a meeting of the OPD on 30th April, Healey and Jenkins reaffirmed Wilson and de Gaulle's mutually articulated hope for enhanced Anglo–French aerospace collaboration. They further stressed Messmer's desire for an immediate British commitment to AFVG, and raised the question of whether US- or UK-oriented technology would be adapted in the development of a French engine. The issue here was the fact that the Snecma engines fitted into French Mirage fighters were licensed to the US company P&W. For some time, Rolls-Royce had been trying to dislodge the US foothold in this area. The British company hoped that Snecma would replace the P&W components in its aircraft with Rolls-Royce equipment.[15]

Healey and Jenkins insisted that BAC was to be the British contractor for both Jaguar and AFVG, that Rolls-Royce would develop Jaguar's engine, and that BSE would develop AFVG's engine.[16] A French firm, Breguet, would lead on the development of the Jaguar's airframe, with BAC serving as a partner. Conversely, Rolls-Royce would lead on the engine, with Turbomeca as a partner. Finally,

Jenkins and Healey sought the OPD's approval for continued Anglo–French collaboration on the Jaguar and the AFVG. The two ministers authorised the signature of a Memorandum of Understanding (MoU) with a view to the forthcoming meeting with Messmer in London on 17th May.[17]

In a message to Wilson, Burke Trend, a Cabinet Secretary, pointed out that the possible cost of the Jaguar would be £50 million, while that of the AFVG would be £200 million. He also stressed that, by developing the F-111, the United States would likely gain a substantial lead in VG technology. By contrast, it was highly doubtful that Britain would be able to produce a VG aircraft until the late 1970s.[18]

An OPD meeting on 4th May focused on the Anglo–French MoU and Messmer's imminent visit to London some two weeks later. The French were hoping for a joint declaration that both countries intended to procure a minimum of 200 AFVGs each. British ministers, however, were keen to avoid such a firm commitment. Britain still had one eye on the American aircraft. Another view expressed at the meeting was that, although Anglo–French joint R&D could prove economical, Britain should nonetheless sound out other allies, in order to draw political benefits and seek further export sales for the proposed aircraft. In a further OPD paper, Wilson endorsed the Anglo–French collaboration – but he strictly stipulated Britain's entitlement to withdraw from the projects at any stage.[19]

The Anglo–American co-development of a V/STOL engine

In the mid-1960s, the American government negotiated the co-development of various aircraft projects with a range of European governments. Among these projects, the specific focus of Anglo–American negotiations increasingly focused on a V/STOL fighter and engine. This owed to the importance of V/STOL technology, which carried a symbolic significance beyond its actual value. In fact, Britain had shown itself superior to the United States in the development of this technology. Given the UK's lead in this area, the United States was understandably reluctant to see it tilt entirely towards Europe.

The beginning of negotiations came in October 1964. The US Department of Defense, mindful of Britain's leading role in developing the V/STOL engine, proposed the creation of an Anglo–American V/STOL engine based on the Rolls-Royce engine (RB162). An Anglo–American co-operative logistics agreement signed in February 1964 envisioned expanding co-operation in military research and development. At the same time, however, the United States also pursued a project with Germany to develop a V/STOL fighter (ADO12 (Advanced Development Objective No. 12)) and engine. Under the US–Germany V/STOL co-operation, the United States tried to control German V/STOL technology, and West German industry profited from the "Transfer of American Military Technology".[20] From October 1964, Dr Harold Brown, Director of Defense Research and Engineering (DDR&E), had been initiating discussions on an Anglo–American V/STOL engine co-operation for ADO12.[21]

90   The British dilemma in military field, 1964–69

In a letter to Robert McNamara dated 9th March 1965, Denis Healey asked if an engine developed co-operatively by Britain and the United States could be used to power the American–German ADO12 V/STOL fighter and thus transform the Anglo–American project into a trilateral American–British–German project. Britain's determination to participate in the American–German fighter project was underpinned by its need to maintain a V/STOL development capability in the wake of the cancellation of the P.1154 V/STOL fighter and HS.681 V/STOL transport projects.[22] This essentially meant that, with respect to the development of a VG/V/STOL fighter, Britain had two options in terms of engaging in an international co-operation program: the Anglo–French VG (AFVG), or the American–German–British V/STOL fighter, fitted with a Rolls-Royce engine. Needless to say, these two projects existed in conflict with each other. For their part, the Germans were growing increasingly tired of British involvement in the project, because "the British would be more apt to be a seller rather than a buyer of the ultimate aircraft".[23] This withering judgement was not wholly inaccurate, because the British were hedging their bets.

Discussions between the Plowden Committee and the US Department of Defense, May 1965

In mid-May, Lord Plowden and Aubrey Jones visited Washington. They met with Robert McNamara and Henry Kuss, Deputy Assistant Secretary of Defense for ILN, and Dr Harold Brown, DDR&E. At these meetings, the British contingent raised several essential questions on the future of three segments of the UK aircraft industry – airframe, engines and avionics. They also raised the topic of the survival of British engine and avionics companies.[24]

Dr Harold Brown insisted that Rolls-Royce would only be able to compete with US companies such as P&W and General Electric (GE) if the US government granted the British company equal consideration with US firms.[25] Brown added that, should the UK cease development of sophisticated airframes, then UK engine and avionics companies would be permitted access to US aircraft markets. According to Kuss, US/UK co-operation would bring mutual gains. An excellent example for such a mutually beneficial joint project already existed in the form of the V/STOL engine for the ADO12 fighter.[26]

In light of these statements, the British delegation asked for an assurance that their aircraft companies would be able to compete freely on the US market. In their response, the representatives of the US Defense Department pointed to "the waiving of the Buy American Act provisions for the UK"[27] as "a gesture of good faith",[28] though they manifestly declined to make guarantees for the policies of future administrations.

The Plowden Committee members proceeded to posit two possible defence scenarios to their American hosts. Should the UK focus on "free competition throughout the 'common market of defense'"?[29] Or should the UK collaborate almost exclusively with Europe and maintain "a smaller but more certain portion of the market in just Europe?"[30]

The politics behind the Plowden doctrine 91

In his response to this, Kuss articulated what he considered to be some compelling financial realities. For the period 1962–1971, he anticipated regional defence equipment markets to take shape as follows: the Scandinavian market would be worth £680 million ($1.9 billion); the European market, £20–22 billion ($56–61 billion); the Far Eastern market, £1.2–1.7 billion ($3.4–4.7 billion); for a total of £22–24 billion ($61–68 billion), the penetrable portion of which would be £3.6–5.4 billion ($10–15 billion, 16–23 per cent). During the same period, Kuss estimated that the US defence equipment market would total around £70 billion ($200 billion).[31]

In light of these forecasts, Kuss suggested that the answer to the UK's dilemma was obvious; she should compete in the US market. Indeed, he even made the ominous statement that, "if [the UK collaborates] with the French, recognise the threat of U.S. competition, like on the Concorde. We might still undersell you because the U.S. defense budget is five times that of the U.K. plus France".[32]

With this veiled threat still ringing in their ears, the members of the Plowden Committee asked whether or not the United States would continue to exchange intimate and sensitive technical information with the UK, if the UK continued to collaborate with Europe. The US Department of Defense replied that, if the UK's principal point of collaboration should develop with non-American partners, then the United States would have to "reexamine [their] policy of cooperation".[33]

At around the same time as these meetings were taking place, and as if on cue, de Gaulle's challenge to American "hegemony" became more acute. In February 1965, the French president opened his press conference with a proposal to reform the international monetary system and replace the dollar as the world's leading currency. He also continued to build up the *force de frappe*, France's independent nuclear power.[34] Thus, in both the monetary and the nuclear realms, de Gaulle was trying to break, or at least to limit, US domination of the West. This rendered aerospace collaboration between France and Britain extremely sensitive – not least because military aircraft was one delivery method for nuclear warheads.

On 14th May 1965, Plowden held a personal meeting with US Defense Secretary Robert McNamara in which he raised three alternatives and asked McNamara's opinion of them. These were: (1) outright British procurement of US military equipment; (2) manufacture of engines, equipment and possibly relatively modest aircraft types in open competition with US industry on both sides of the Atlantic; and (3) wholehearted industrial co-operation with France. McNamara replied that the best course for Britain would be to adopt the second alternative and that, although no US administration could answer for the decisions of its successor, the concept of open competition within the overall framework of the Western Alliance could become a standard and enduring feature of US policy. McNamara commented on the third alternative and argued that the proposal of a "root and branch" interlocking of British and French industry would be a mistake for Britain.[35]

92 *The British dilemma in military field, 1964–69*

The Plowden Committee brought its Washington visit to an end on 14th May. The conclusion they had reached was that Britain could not hope to match the United States' enormous technological and economic efforts in the area of sophisticated aircraft development. Two basic notions arose from this conclusion: first, that the demands of modern technology were such that Britain should concentrate on fewer objectives in greater depth; and, second, that the survival of British industry was dependent on international collaboration. There were, it seemed, two possible options: a subordinate relationship with the United States as an effective sub-contractor, or an industrial partnership with France (a combination of the two was not ruled out).[36]

The Committee saw some clear drawbacks to the possibility of association with the United States. First, Britain would give up its capacity to manufacture complete aircraft and weapons systems, at least of the sophisticated variety. Second, the partnership with the United States would place the British aircraft industry at "the mercy of any United States government",[37] although it would also entail "efficient British component firms [gaining] entry to the huge U.S. military market".[38]

On the other hand, the Committee assessed the drawbacks of deeper association with France as follows. First, an Anglo–French industrial union would be unlikely to stand up to American competition, unless it could be assured of hegemony in – at least – the other Common Market countries. The critical factor here would be German military procurement. However, it was almost certain that the United States would attempt to penetrate the German market. Second, if the UK did, indeed, opt to extend collaboration with the French, then the United States would taper or close the existing flow of valuable R&D information on defence matters between the UK and the United States. Third, British industry would face severe competition from the United States across a range of international markets, and would probably have to contend with tariffs and other protective barriers that the United States would surely establish around its domestic markets.[39]

The Anglo–French defence package of 17th May 1965

Despite the somewhat menacing sounds emanating from the US Department of Defense, Healey and Jenkins were determined to stick to their vision of Anglo–French collaboration. On 17th May 1965, both ministers met French Minister of Defence Pierre Messmer in London and signed an MoU. This document addressed the mooted Anglo–French development of the Jaguar, as well as the joint study of the possibility of the AFVG. A Foreign Office telegram from 18th May called the attention of British representatives to the fact that:

> Anglo–French collaboration is regarded as an essential foundation. But we want collaboration on the widest basis both from the point of view of scale economies in cost-sharing and sales to the widest possible market, and for political reasons in conformity with our policy of seeking to bridge the gap

The politics behind the Plowden doctrine 93

between EFTA and the E.E.C. and of achieving the wider working unity of Europe.[40]

On 24th May, Aubrey Jones, having recently returned from trips to Paris and Washington, sent a note to Plowden which stated that the primary question facing the British aircraft industry was "how best to widen the market".[41] Jones argued that "[t]he question is how does one thread one's way between two difficult courses".[42] This entailed an attempt to achieve the widest possible market share through collaboration with the United States and, should this prove unsuccessful, "then and then only"[43] should Britain focus on collaboration with France.

In other words, Anglo–French co-operation should be seen "not as an end in itself but as a means of bringing pressure on the US".[44] Jones recognised that the French would not be particularly amenable to this approach. But they could do nothing about it because they had no one else to co-operate with. Jones reached the rather optimistic conclusion that, among the United States, the UK and France, only Britain enjoyed something in the way of a "bargaining advantage",[45] even though "at the moment we are not using it".[46]

The Plowden Committee met again on 31st May. According to Lord Plowden, Britain's inability to maintain an independent aircraft industry left three courses of action open to the British government. These comprised: first, collaboration with France; second, collaboration with the United States; and, third, a compromise "in which we collaborated with the French on certain projects, tried to sell as much equipment as possible to U.S. industry, and bought the most sophisticated aircraft from the United States".[47]

The pragmatic Plowden was broadly in favour of the third alternative. He argued that the proposed association with France made sense on condition that France accepted British membership of the Common Market. He further recommended that Britain negotiate political agreements with the United States, "to enable our engine and equipment manufacturers to compete without political interference in the US market".[48] He also urged an acceptance of the fact that Britain would soon have to entirely abandon the production of airframes.[49]

The British–French defence package of 17th May 1965 caused some consternation among both the Americans and the Germans. Two days after its announcement, Robert McNamara drafted a recommendation for the future development of V/STOL. He drew some hard conclusions about further British participation in the American–German ADO12 V/STOL fighter programme. The possible future scenarios for this programme comprised: first, shared US/British development of the lift engine; and, second, shared US/German development of every other aspect of the aircraft.

McNamara was highly sceptical about Britain's motivation for participating in the programme. In his view, this was due to: first, the desire to sell British engines and avionics; second, to acquire as much advanced design technology as cheaply as possible, including VG, for use in the Anglo–French Jaguar and AFVG; third, to slow down the development of the American–German project,

94 *The British dilemma in military field, 1964–69*

which was a potential competitor to the Anglo–French fighters. Against this background, McNamara unsurprisingly concluded his draft by recommending that British participation in the American–German V/STOL programme should be minimised.[50]

In negotiations between the United States and UK, the latter insisted on a guaranteed share of any production order for the ADO12 fighter. According to this scheme, Rolls-Royce would be assured a certain share of the production of a V/STOL engine for the ADO12. McNamara, however, insisted on the principle of free competition between companies from both countries. This entailed a possible risk to Rolls-Royce, who would be in competition with US engine makers such as P&W or GE.[51]

At this stage, the British were ruling nothing out. British officials were trying to maximise their advantages in negotiations with the Americans, Germans and French – to keep their fingers in as many pies as possible, as Plowden himself had suggested. Against the background of growing tensions within the Atlantic alliance, however, the inherent risks and contradictions of such an approach were becoming increasingly apparently.

Paris or Washington?

On 25th May, Jeffrey C. Kitchen, Assistant Secretary of State for Politico–Military Affairs, submitted a report to US Secretary of State Dean Rusk which expressed considerable concern about the Plowden Committee and its activities. The Committee, Kitchen suggested, had apparently "concluded that it is virtually impossible to cooperate successfully in joint R&D projects with the US",[52] especially in V/STOL. He further suggested that "the US/UK lift engine project has assumed symbolic importance far beyond its actual value, as a test of whether or not the US would engage in cooperative R&D ventures with the UK".[53]

In his report, Kitchen also pointed to Britain's apparent recognition of its own inability to compete with the United States, as well as British satisfaction with the progress made by Anglo–French R&D co-operation. Kitchen recommended practical co-operation with the UK in the field of aircraft engines, where British and American engineering were roughly on par. This, he suggested, "would help strengthen the position of the British Government by demonstrating that the US considers the UK a worthy partner in a technically advanced field".[54]

Overall, it seemed that the State Department was inclined towards coming to some sort of agreement with Britain with respect to the advanced lift engine issue. On 29th May, US Defense Secretary Robert McNamara was due to meet Denis Healey. Ronald M. Murray, Assistant DDR&E at the US Department of Defense, was tasked with producing a position paper for McNamara on the joint V/STOL programme.[55]

In this document, Murray first explained the British attitude on international collaboration. He pointed to a growing belief at the Ministry of Aviation and Ministry of Defence that co-operation with the United States was simply impractical. Jenkins, the Minister of Aviation, was apparently convinced that "the

The politics behind the Plowden doctrine 95

future of the UK aircraft industry lies with the Continent and not with the US".[56] Healey, the Minister of Defence, had also expressed scepticism about US–UK co-operation. According to Murray, the British were increasingly convinced that "cooperation with the French Government and industry is easy and rewarding, and with the US it is difficult and unrewarding".[57]

By this time, the only high-placed British official who continued to support Anglo–American co-operation was Zuckerman, chief scientific adviser of the British government. Murray pointed out that, if the United States and the UK failed to collaborate over V/STOL, then it would be "very unlikely that we can get together on any major development program".[58] Pearson, chairman of Rolls-Royce, was redoubtably pro-European and considered merging Rolls-Royce with the French firm Snecma. But Zuckerman was opposed to this idea; he believed that Rolls-Royce, the symbol of British industrial competitiveness, should try to break into the American aircraft market.[59]

The position of British industry

The British dilemma was becoming more acute. Its resolution depended on three factors: the position of British domestic industry, the German question, and general British policy towards Europe.

With respect to the first of these factors, the opinion of British aerospace businesses was, at this time, organised mainly around the Society of British Aerospace Companies. Within this organisation, scepticism was rapidly arising with respect to the sincerity of the United States' stated desire to purchase British goods. With respect to the second factor, the most critical prospective target for aerospace collaboration at this time was, for all interested parties, the West German military market. West German participation in Anglo–French collaboration was the key element for transforming the Anglo–French bilateral programme into a wider project of European collaboration. However, the West German military market was already in the clutches of the United States, largely due to American–German offsetting agreements for American troops on German territory.

Despite this apparent US dominance, however, the Plowden Committee forged ahead in its attempts to establish a British foothold in the West German military market. From June 1965, the committee held hearings with two British airframe manufacturers and two British aero-engine manufacturers which, it was hoped, might be key to future overtures to Germany. These companies had been established during the process of industrial rationalisation which occurred between 1958 and 1960 (see Chapter 2 of this book). At the same time, delegates from the Plowden Committee also visited Bonn for talks with the West German government. The waters were being tested.

In June 1965, Rolls-Royce submitted a report to the Plowden Committee. This report stated that, in future, the UK aero-engine industry would rely predominantly on projects which had been initiated as part of a European Consortium. The report further insisted that future aero-engine export sales

96   *The British dilemma in military field, 1964–69*

would depend largely on building up collaboration with Europe – and especially with France – in the airframe sector. The report also outlined the primary aim of Rolls-Royce in France – to replace the P&W JTF30 engine for the Mirage series currently manufactured by Spey, and to eliminate P&W's influence on the nationalised company Snecma.[60]

On 13th July 1965, the Plowden Committee welcomed Lord Portal, representative of airframe manufacturer BAC. Portal made it clear to the Plowden Committee that collaboration with France was, indeed, possible. He acknowledged that co-operation with foreign countries in such projects often proved painful. But he also insisted on the importance of increasing the size of the guaranteed market for a given aircraft. BAC thus welcomed the opportunity of further joint ventures with France and other European countries. However, Portal regarded Anglo–American collaboration as impracticable.[61]

At an OPD meeting on 16th July, Roy Jenkins outlined the prospects and conclusions of Anglo–American advanced V/STOL engine development. The first possible disadvantage was the lack of a prospective civil or military application for this type of engine. The second disadvantage lay in Britain's hope that production of this engine could be shared – despite McNamara's insistence that price competition among producers was necessary in order to achieve efficiency.[62]

By contrast, the first possible argument in favour of production was that, although it had no immediate use, the need for a V/STOL engine was likely to become much more acute in the 1970s. A British failure to continue developing such an engine would surely result in Rolls-Royce losing its technical advantage in a crucial field. The second argument in favour of continued production was that the US government evidently regarded this project as "a test case". If Britain did not proceed, then Minister of Aviation Fred Mulley feared that the Americans might come to doubt British seriousness with respect to Anglo–American R&D. This might accelerate the gathering split within NATO between rival London/Paris and Washington/Bonn axes.[63]

On 26th July 1965, the Plowden Committee held a hearing with representatives of Rolls-Royce. The company looked to France as a natural partner, mainly because the aircraft industries of the two countries were more equally matched in size when compared with the vast American aviation sector. However, Rolls-Royce rejected the possibility of France taking sole responsibility for airframe development with Britain assuming control of aero-engine development on future projects. Rolls-Royce also indicated that, based on its experience of the joint development of advanced V/STOL engines with the United States, a collaboration of this kind was eminently possible, if highly challenging to implement in practice.[64]

Unsurprisingly, Rolls-Royce representatives also expressed great confidence in their own ability to compete with P&W in technology and capital. They recognised "no conflict between a desire to collaborate whenever possible with the Americans and to create a close relationship with the French industry".[65] After all, in the final resort, Rolls-Royce needed a domestic airframe industry because it was the airframe constructor who "determined the design of an aircraft".[66] According to one Rolls-Royce delegate, it "seemed undesirable"[67] that the company should "place [itself] entirely at the mercy of the French"[68] with respect to the production of the Anglo–French machine's airframe.

Ultimately, then, the position of British airframe and aero-engine companies seemed largely congruent with the Plowden Committee's view that France represented a more appropriate partner for international co-operation than the United States. Significantly, however, Rolls-Royce had also expressed considerable confidence with respect to the prospect of international co-operation with the United States.

The German factor in American–European collaboration

Germany's devastation in 1945 had left the country's military-industrial base severely damaged, but not irretrievably destroyed. After the war, West Germany rearmed swiftly. Thereafter, the Bonn government showed considerable levels of defence spending. Furthermore, and unlike its west European neighbours, West Germany did not have to pay for the defence of colonies. As a result of all of this, the West German military procurement market was enormous. This market was dominated by the United States, partly through co-operative logistics, but also through the offsetting agreement with respect to US troops stationed in West German territory, described in Chapter 4.[69]

On 14th September 1962, the West German government promised to purchase US military goods worth $14,000 million over the course of 1963 and 1964. This agreement was extended on 11th May 1964, as Bonn promised to purchase US military goods worth $13,500 million for a further two years.[70] West Germany was able to purchase the most advanced military goods on the market from the United States. These included guided-missile destroyers (DDGs) and F-104G fighters.[71] Indeed, as Minister of Defence Franz Josef Strauss openly claimed, one of the key aims of the arrangement was for West Germany to acquire advanced military technology.[72]

The UK viewed the Federal Republic of Germany as a possible sales target for the Jaguar and the AFVG. However, the United States was already involved in several joint projects with West Germany, including the ADO12 V/STOL fighter. Moreover, the Americans continued to push for European countries to develop arms under US leadership within the framework of NATO.

In the long-term, however, Anglo–French co-operation, independent from the United States, could potentially exclude the US aircraft industry from the European market. No doubt mindful of this eventuality, US Secretary of Defense Robert McNamara proposed a NATO-wide "Defence Common Market" at the NATO Defence Ministers' Meeting, which began on 31st May 1964. This would be based on recommendations made in the Kuss memorandum of 25th May. Such a common market would ensure that NATO countries could produce arms according to the principle of cost-effectiveness.[73] For obvious reasons, such an arrangement would favour the Americans.

98 *The British dilemma in military field, 1964–69*

From 21st to 23rd July 1965, a visit was paid to Germany by the Sub-Committee on International Co-operation of the Plowden Committee, which included Aubrey Jones. British officials held talks with West German Minister of Defence, Kai-Uwe von Hassel, in the West German Ministry of Economics. During these discussions, members of the Plowden Committee raised some fundamental questions. Most of the responses were provided by Dr Knieper, Deputy State Secretary of the West German Ministry of Defence.[74]

The Plowden Committee first inquired into the prospects for Anglo–German collaboration on aircraft, and into the viability of "a European aerospace industry",[75] as well as the extent to which the Germans would "wish to participate in it".[76] The German representatives replied that, though they did consider international collaboration and European aerospace industry to be "necessary",[77] they did not "see a black and white choice between association with America and collaboration within Europe".[78]

After the visit to Bonn, the Sub-Committee on International Co-operation drew the following conclusions about the West German stance towards international collaboration. First, West Germany was clearly heavily invested in its aviation association with the United States and would do nothing to damage this relationship. Second, West Germany was evidently militarily dependent on the United States and hoped to preserve joint R&D between the two countries for sophisticated weapons systems. Third, however, the Germans had shown some enthusiasm for the prospect of European collaboration in the field of R&D in both military and civilian projects.[79]

On the whole, it seemed that West Germany took a pragmatic view of European collaboration, rather than seeing this as "a doctrinaire policy".[80] The Germans apparently saw "no basic conflict between their links with America and the extension of cooperation within Europe".[81] As we have already seen in this chapter, several members of the Plowden Committee – including Plowden himself – were by no means unsympathetic to such an approach. Ultimately, German indifference to the choice between a European or an American option in aviation technology served to dampen the Plowden Committee's enthusiasm for European collaboration.

The Spey–Mirage affair

Broad segments of British industry were nonetheless still very much on board with the idea of extensive European collaboration. BAC, for example, attempted to undercut the mass-purchase of the American F-111 by proposing the adoption of the French Mirage IV fighter, and its equipping with a Rolls-Royce Spey engine. Rolls and French Dassault would act as partners in this venture.

On 9th August 1965, BAC made a presentation on the Spey–Mirage to the British government in London. BAC claimed that this aircraft would cost around £1.5 or £1.6 million – £1 million less than the F-111.[82] Indeed, a BAC spokesman explicitly stated that the Spey–Mirage would be "dramatically cheaper"[83] than the F-111. The company revealed concrete plans to redesign and produce a

The politics behind the Plowden doctrine 99

large number of Spey–Mirage aircraft. BAC hoped that the British government would adopt this proposal, and that sufficient quantities for production could be guaranteed. This, BAC representatives argued, would largely negate the job losses at the company's Weybridge and Preston factories caused by the cancellation of the TSR-2. Such a project would also mean that, in return for the RAF adopting a French airframe, the French Air Force would adopt the Rolls-Royce-powered Spey–Mirage.[84]

The Spey–Mirage was thus "exactly in accord with the announced government policy of Anglo–French collaboration".[85] Despite this, Healey unexpectedly lost his temper over the proposal. He complained that such a project would divert future work on the Jaguar and AFVG to Hawker Siddeley. He insisted that it ran contrary to the plan of purchasing the F-111.[86] Moreover, the Mirage IV was the core of the French independent nuclear deterrent, the *force de frappe*, to which the US government was strongly opposed. A British adoption of the Mirage IV instead of the F-111 thus had the potential to damage the Anglo–American relationship. This fear was pointed out on 11th August in FCO (Foreign and Commonwealth Office) guidance No. 338, which warned that "any idea of using a French rather than an American aircraft as our next generation nuclear strike"[87] would almost certainly lead to a worsening of relations with the United States.

The Spey–Mirage affair constituted a highly sensitive issue in an equally sensitive context. This context was defined by the development of the V/STOL engine, ongoing negotiations over an offsetting deal for purchasing the F-111, continued uncertainty over Britain's choice of partner in international co-operation, and widespread unease over the French role in the Western alliance. Even at this stage, however, British aircraft companies continued to support Anglo–French collaboration because they knew that they could establish an equal partnership with French companies. This was a welcome contrast to their previous experiences with more domineering US manufacturers.

At the Cabinet-level, Minister of Defence Denis Healey was the unreserved champion of purchasing the F-111, which he considered central to Britain's broader East of Suez policy. Zuckerman was also an enthusiastic supporter of Anglo–American collaboration. Jenkins, however, seemed to lean more towards European collaboration. He was sceptical about British ambitions East of Suez, and thus about the need for F-111s.

Healey was faced with the challenge of bringing pro-European ministers such as Jenkins around to his position. This meant that McNamara's promise – to help solve Britain's F-111-related foreign currency problems by purchasing British equipment – had to be realised. Moreover, Zuckerman needed to provide some proof that Anglo–American R&D co-operation really could be effective, and that the UK could show at least a degree of technological superiority over the United States in areas such as V/STOL technology.

Fortunately for these pro-American British officials, the Americans had already realised that the UK–US V/STOL engine project carried a "symbolic importance far beyond its actual value",[88] and that it constituted "a test of whether or not the United States would engage in a cooperative R&D venture with the UK".[89]

100 *The British dilemma in military field, 1964–69*

The US had a clear interest in ensuring that a successful agreement was reached with London over the V/STOL engine. The spectre of a united European aircraft sector could apparently still chill the blood in Washington.

Agreement on developing the US–UK joint V/STOL engine

Britain had some specific demands with respect to V/STOL co-operation with the United States. The British envisioned an arrangement whereby government contracts would be awarded to a formal partnership between Rolls-Royce and a selected US contractor.[90] McNamara, however, continued to insist on competition in this area. On 24th August, he put precisely this position in writing to Jenkins. He rejected the idea of guaranteed production sharing, and he insisted that a contractor be selected on a competitive basis. He concluded that, should the United States and the UK governments indeed reach an agreement, then the United States would start proceedings to select a contractor to work with Rolls-Royce.[91]

The V/STOL engine co-development project became a key test of how seriously the United States took the idea of co-operating with Britain, and of promoting British military hardware to the US domestic market. Distrust was growing steadily on both sides of the Atlantic. The British needed America to purchase high-technology products in return for the British purchase of the F-4, C-130 and F-111 aircraft. Moreover, Britain wanted to see concrete evidence that the United States could co-operate in the development of aero-engines, at least in cases where Britain had the same level of technology as the United States. This would prove the United States' high regard for the British ability to develop advanced aircraft technologies.[92]

A concrete example of this basic conflict came in the form of Robert McNamara's insistence that Rolls-Royce was obliged to compete with US manufacturers in powering the American–German V/STOL fighter. McNamara promised that, if Britain implemented the F-111 option agreement and procured additional F-111s, then Rolls-Royce would enjoy equally competitive conditions with US manufacturers (P&W and GE). Jenkins, however, considered McNamara's proposal to be unacceptable. Competition in production meant that the United States would offer no guarantees with respect to Rolls-Royce's contracts. It was at this point that, dramatically, Robert McNamara increased the pressure further. He informed his British counterparts that, if the two countries could not reach an agreement by mid-September, then the United States would proceed with V/STOL engine development alone.[93]

Such an outcome would have presented Britain with two substantial problems. First, if the United States proceeded independently with V/STOL engine development, then Rolls-Royce would almost certainly lose its superiority in V/STOL technology to US manufacturers. This would leave the firm lagging behind in an area of essential technological development. Second, the US government saw this proposal as a test case for Anglo–American co-development. If the British government did not accept the American ultimatum, then Washington would surely conclude that the British were not serious about Anglo–American technological co-operation. Such a conclusion was not only politically problematic from a British perspective, but it would also produce a deep division within NATO between a London–Paris axis and a Washington–Bonn axis.[94]

On 7th September 1965, Zuckerman sent Prime Minister Harold Wilson a memorandum which dealt explicitly with the critical question of V/STOL engine development. In his note, Zuckerman made it unmistakeably clear that the decision of the British government with respect to the American ultimatum depended on British self-confidence about Rolls-Royce. If Rolls really was worthy of its reputation then, Zuckerman argued, the British government should have no reservations about allowing the company to compete with US and European manufacturers in an open market. Rolls-Royce itself expressed great confidence in this area, provided that it enjoyed a level playing field with its competitors.[95]

Consequently, on 8th September, Jenkins wrote a letter to McNamara in which he accepted the American principle of opening the field of production to market competition. As he put it, "I am prepared to accept as the basis of our agreement full freedom and equality of competition between the British and American firms for U.S. and U.K. defence orders".[96]

At this point, however, Zuckerman increasingly appeared as "the only high-placed Britisher still actively pursuing cooperation with the US"[97] within Britain. To be sure, his was a *very* strong voice; he was the chief scientific adviser to the British government, and he was a key member of an international circle of scientists which included Harold Brown, the US DDR&E at the US Department of Defense. The consensus within this circle was that the United States enjoyed a significant technological superiority over all of its European allies, and that R&D duplication within the western alliance should be avoided.

Ronald Murray, Assistant DDR&E, also seemed to recognise Zuckerman's isolation. On 11th October, he submitted a report to Washington on the situation in London which was based on a record of a Plowden Committee meeting from the previous May. Murray expected that the Plowden Committee would recommend to the British government a more intensive pursuit of Anglo–French co-operation, and a general tilt towards the continent. He further pointed out that only positive production prospects would persuade the British Ministry of Defence to pursue enhanced co-operation with the United States. As he put it in his report, "the greatest attraction for the British in the R&D cooperation program will be the good entree it gives them into the US market" (e.g. the V/STOL engine).[98]

All of this showed that, even as late as 1965, the basic dilemma at the heart of Britain's aerospace policy was still no closer to being resolved. Nonetheless, the British government did accept McNamara's proposal – mainly out of a growing fear that failure to do so would torpedo Anglo–American co-operation. And so, in early October, the United States and Britain reached agreement on co-development of a V/STOL engine.[99] According to this agreement, the United States assured Rolls-Royce of equal terms in competing with US manufacturers when it came to powering the American–German V/STOL fighter.

102 *The British dilemma in military field, 1964–69*

However, there was a crucial prerequisite to this deal: Britain had to purchase the additional F-111s. This was despite ongoing British foreign currency problems related to this purchase. Indeed, negotiations following the signing of the April F-111 option agreement had manifestly failed to resolve the persistent difficulties regarding price and quantity. Nonetheless, the agreement over the V/STOL – as well as the series of conditions attached to it – undoubtedly bound London closer to Washington. The momentum had begun to shift, slowly but perceptibly, away from the continent.

The Saudi Arabian aircraft deal

From the British perspective, the Anglo–American agreement over the V/STOL engine effectively settled the symbolic problem of US–UK aerospace cooperation. However, the more material problem represented by Britain's foreign currency outlays remained unresolved. This had been the main obstacle to a British purchase of the F-111. It was further complicated by the question of possible compensation owing to BAC for the cancellation of the TSR-2. Britain had demanded that the US Department of Defense procure British goods as a *quid pro quo* for their F-111 purchase, but such purchases had not materialised.

McNamara and Healey hoped that the Saudi military market offered a possible route out of this impasse. In the autumn of 1965, both the American and British governments were looking to secure a Saudi Arabian aircraft order. Lockheed (the United States), BAC (Britain), as well as Dassault (France) were all vying for the order, with the Saudi government initially inclining towards Lockheed's F-104. In an attempt to try to win this lucrative contract, Minister of Defence Denis Healey appointed Sir Donald Stokes, a civilian, as a government adviser to liaise with the Americans over the selling of arms to the Saudis.[100]

On 23rd August, George S. Newman, Counsellor for Politico–Military Affairs, reported to Henry Kuss on growing British anxiety that a US purchase of British arms would not actually be forthcoming. Newman had spent August in London, where he had been involved in some uncomfortable conversations with representatives from the Ministry of Defence, including Healey and Stokes. Healey, Newman reported, did not expect "a large scale procurement",[101] but he did need "something to show"[102] to reassure the government. Newman quoted the words of his friends in "The Establishment"[103] of Britain to the following effect: "for heaven's sake, George, have the Pentagon give us an order soon!"[104]

In August, Stokes approached McNamara directly. His aim was to elicit US support for an impending British bid for the Saudi order.[105] McNamara immediately realised that Stoke's idea was intended as a solution to the F-111 purchase problem. Awarding the Saudi air defence order to a British company would clearly help to ease the British foreign currency problem. McNamara instructed Kuss to work out the details. Kuss met with Jeffrey Edwards, BAC's agent for the deal, in Rome, in an effort to learn more about British intentions. He discovered

The politics behind the Plowden doctrine   103

that BAC expected to sell 36 Lightning fighters, worth approximately \$100–110 million, to Saudi Arabia.[106]

In his report to McNamara, Kuss presented two alternatives. The first was to explicitly tell the Saudis that the United States would prefer them to buy British aircraft. This proposition was clearly unacceptable, both with respect to previous US commitments to the Saudis and to government relations with American aircraft manufacturers (Lockheed had already tried to sell the F-104 to precisely this market). The second option was to encourage the British to participate in a new US project – a joint programme to combine the British Lightning Mk.3 fighter, British radar and communications equipment, and US Hawk missiles.[107]

At this point in time, McNamara had to be mindful of certain diplomatic pressures being brought to bear on the administration. There was an obvious difficulty in the United States selling arms to Saudi Arabia while simultaneously restricting arms sales to Israel.[108] McNamara thus authorised Kuss to proceed with the second alternative. Kuss noted that a British purchase of the F-111 would depend on the UK's ability to sell its equipment for foreign currency.[109] The total cost of purchasing the Polaris, F-4, C-130 and F-111 amounted to \$725 million. The United States initially proposed that \$725 million should be covered by \$325 million for reciprocal purchase, plus \$300 million for US assistance to British sales to third countries, including Saudi Arabia. When the United States agreed to increase the latter figure to \$400 million, Britain accepted the proposal. The Saudi defence deal to the UK was pegged at around \$200 million.[110] An agreement was reached, and the United States and Britain submitted a joint bid to the Saudis. This not only compensated BAC for the cancellation of the TSR-2, but it also eased the British balance of payments problem.

However, the bid remained extremely sensitive because Lockheed was still promoting its F-104 to the Saudis. On October 11th, Christopher Everett at the British Embassy met with Kuss. Officially, the United States was continuing to recommend the Northrop F-5 to the Saudis. Kuss thus believed that he needed to send "a high level 'political'"[111] letter to the Lockheed Board Chairman, because "the subject was an extremely touchy one with our US aircraft producers".[112]

Despite these complications, however, the Saudi government ultimately selected the BAC Lightning and US Hawk missiles proposal. This entailed a rejection of bids not only from Dassault, but also from Lockheed. The order totalled about £125 million.[113] John Stonehouse, an official at the Ministry of Aviation, rather cynically remarked that the Saudi decision owed not least to the fact that King Faisal was said to be an "American protégé".[114]

The Saudi Arabian defence deal was crucial leverage in Britain's consent to the F-111 purchase. And yet, when Stonehouse announced the Saudi Arabia order in the House of Commons on 21st December 1965, he stated that "There is no question of the agreement with the Americans to cooperate in giving technical and political support in this proposed deal being in any way linked with a commitment concerning the F.111".[115] He was not being entirely truthful.

104 *The British dilemma in military field, 1964–69*

The "corner-stone" of British defence policy?

In the autumn of 1965, the Plowden Committee completed its discussions with Britain's prospective partners for international collaboration – the United States, France and Germany – as well as all hearings for domestic aircraft manufacturers. The Committee then began to compose its final report for submission to the British government.

On 23rd October, members of the committee gathered to review the draft of the report. At this meeting, Aubrey Jones objected to a line in the draft which described Anglo–French collaboration as "the cornerstone"[116] of Britain's future international collaboration on aviation defence. Such a "declared choice between Europe and the United States"[117] was, according to Jones, "unnecessary",[118] and might even damage Britain's political and economic interests. Jones' biggest fear was that such a declaration could lead to the loss of valuable technical information from the US. It might also disrupt key US–UK arrangements, such as those recently concluded on the RB189 V/STOL engine.[119]

Furthermore, if Britain were to take such an explicit stance, then she would be conclusively tied to France – a country that had been pursuing *force de frappe* in spite of US opposition – for years to come. According to Jones, Britain's "bargaining position vis-à-vis all possible partners"[120] would remain "a strong one"[121] provided she "was not openly committed to any particular direction of collaboration".[122] France, however, was not in a position to decline Anglo–French collaboration simply because such collaboration was not exclusive, while the US government was eager to continue selling US aircraft to the UK. The deal with the United States also carried obvious benefits for British industry.[123] In the end, at a meeting held on 25th October, the Plowden Committee decided to omit the phrase that described the Anglo–French collaboration as "the cornerstone of future interdependence policy"[124] from its Report. This was a significant symbolic gesture.

As for future international co-development, the Plowden Report insisted, first, on promoting Anglo–French co-operation and on the establishment of "a European aircraft industry" to sell equipment to the United States. The key advocate of such a policy was Aubrey Jones, who stated that:

> There may be scope, nevertheless, for selling more British engines and equipment for use in American aircraft [...]. Hitherto, a major difficulty has been that British products have had to compete against price discrimination both from the "Buy American" Act and from administrative decisions of the Department of Defence. [But] [t]here was a relaxation of this policy in the contract recently concluded for the joint development of the Rolls-Royce RB.189 advanced lift engine.[125]

These sentences reveal the ambivalent character of the Plowden Report. The vision of "a European aircraft industry" presupposed Anglo–French collaboration, and yet the Plowden Committee had demonstratively omitted the phrase

The politics behind the Plowden doctrine 105

about Anglo–French collaboration being "the cornerstone of future inter-dependence policy". All of this indicated the limited character of British involve-ment in European co-development at the time and, above all, Britain's determination to keep its options open.[126]

As Jones later stated, "[i]nternational co-operation should not stop at Europe. It should also extend to the United States, The Plowden Committee was sceptical of this possibility. I was more hopeful. And events proved me right. The classic example of such Anglo–American co-operation was the Harrier [V/STOL]".[127]

Britain seals the F-111 deal

It seemed clear that the adoption of the Mirage would inevitably push Britain into deeper co-operation with the French. And yet, as already noted, France's position within the western alliance had become increasingly uncertain due to their policy of developing an independent nuclear deterrent. Anglo–French col-laboration thus threatened to accelerate the gathering danger of a split within NATO between rival London–Paris and Washington–Bonn axes in the field of international arms co-development.

In the "Defence Review Memorandum" of 5th November 1965, Healey and Jenkins expressed their opposition to the Spey–Mirage due to its cost and intro-duction schedule. When *Time Magazine* carried an article on this model, Foreign Minister Michael Stewart urged Minister of Defence Denis Healey to inform the French in no uncertain terms that Britain had no intention of purchasing it. Stewart pointed to the diplomatic risks of adopting the Mirage. With continuing French objections to NATO, he argued, a British adoption of a French rather than an American aircraft as its next-generation nuclear delivery vehicle would give rise to severe political repercussions.[128]

The OPD meeting of 9th February 1966 focused on the manifold ramifications of this purchasing decision. Healey pointed out that, as part of the agreement, the US government would, indeed, remove the unique price differential of 50 per cent against foreign bids in the defence field for Britain. This would not only allow British arms to become much more competitive on the US market, but it would also give Britain a unique position within this market. British companies would be the only international companies able to compete on equal terms with American firms for defence contracts.[129]

Healey further reported on the status of Anglo–American negotiations, and also stressed that he was negotiating to offset the cost of the F-111 with sales of British-made aircraft to third countries, including Saudi Arabia. There was no doubt, he stated, that the US government had only agreed to co-operate with Britain in anticipation of the F-111 purchase.[130] He also observed that there were very good prospects for co-operative Anglo–American sales to Jordan and Libya. This essentially meant that proposed arms sales in the Middle Eastern market could be used to offset the cost of the F-111. This arrangement would, in turn, enable the British aircraft industry to enter the US, Middle Eastern and

106 *The British dilemma in military field, 1964–69*

German markets.[131] On 12th February 1966, British and American officials agreed on the purchase of a further 40 F-111s in addition to the originally contracted ten F-111s. The number of F-111s had thus been reduced from the 110 F-111s (an initial ten F-111s for training purposes and an optional 70–100 F-111s) agreed on 1st April 1965.[132]

At an OPD meeting on 13th February 1966, British ministers discussed the question of replacing the Canberra Bomber. Since the early 1950s, the Canberra had played a critical role in NATO's defence policy with respect to deterrent, early warning, reconnaissance and strike. By 1970, however, the aircraft would be unacceptably outdated, and it was envisioned that, by the mid-1970s, the AFVG would begin to take over the Canberra's functions. With this decision, the AFVG would become the operational and industrial core of Britain's long-term aircraft programme. Britain and France were both planning to purchase 150 such models, so in total, both countries were committed to purchasing 300 AFVGs.[133]

The Spey–Mirage had seemed to present an alternative in this area. However, in addition to problems with its capabilities, delivery date and cost, it also suffered from the familiar foreign exchange problem. Unlike the US government, the French had no intention of compensating Britain for its foreign currency outlays to purchase the Mirage. In order to bridge the temporal gap between the obsolescence of the Canberra and the completion of the AFVG, the British government decided to purchase 50 American F-111s. The British plan was that the F-111 would cover some of the tasks of the Canberra, especially early detection of an enemy's intentions from a distance.[134]

Delivery of the F-111s was expected in the mid-1970s, with the estimated cost pegged at $725 million. The US and British governments agreed that the United States would fully offset the cost by making direct purchases of military hardware valued at $325 million, and by participating in co-operative sales to third countries valued at $425 million. The most significant item on the list of co-operative sales was the Lightning fighter with Hawk missiles for Saudi Arabia.[135]

Britain, however, still had one foot on either side of the Atlantic, and still had to perform an increasingly precarious balancing act. Healey, for one, recognised that these deepening Anglo–American entanglements could prove alarming for the French. He stressed the importance of reassuring the French government that Britain's decision to purchase the F-111s would not have any adverse effect on Anglo–French joint aircraft projects.[136] On 16th February, Wilson personally wrote to de Gaulle to explain the British Cabinet's decision to purchase the American F-111 as a stopgap until the AFVG was flight-ready in the mid-1970s. "I wish to assure you", the Prime Minister stressed, "that I continue to see a great mutual advantage in our programme of aircraft cooperation".[137]

However, in a discussion between Mulley and the French General Fourquet, the latter expressed French anxiety that Britain's purchase of the F-111 would indeed damage the AFVG.[138] On 3rd March 1966, de Gaulle sent a private wire to Wilson which concluded with the following sentiment; "Let me say once again how much I appreciate your readiness to keep in close touch on the many

The politics behind the Plowden doctrine 107

problems which confront us".[139] Whether or not this was de Gaulle's diplomatic means of expressing his anger about the British decision is, unfortunately, impossible to discern from the currently available sources. Perhaps the French President appreciated the complexity of his British counterpart's predicament. And yet de Gaulle must have recognised that Britain's purchase of the F-111 meant nothing good for the vision of a European Defence Community.

That said, Wilson went to great pains to assure de Gaulle that Britain "continues to see great mutual advantage"[140] in the AFVG. Moreover, there were concrete signs in Britain's conduct that it, indeed, intended to honour its commitment to the French. Britain had limited the number of purchased F-111s to 50, and clearly intended this as a stop-gap until the AFVG became available in the 1970s. The Wilson government obviously hoped to secure Britain's fighter design capability through Anglo–French collaboration.[141]

On 9th March, six days after the exchange of messages between de Gaulle and Wilson, the French President sent yet another communique to his British counterpart. This time, however, he informed Wilson of France's intention to modify its participation in NATO – that is, to withdraw France from NATO's integrated military command.[142] The resulting crisis shook the framework of European fighter collaboration. The playing field on which Wilson's government had been operating now changed beyond recognition.

Conclusion

The aftermath of the cancellation of the TSR-2 was marked by a series of fateful British decisions in the realm of aerospace technology. These included the purchase of 50 F-111s, the offsetting of foreign exchange costs for these aircraft through the Saudi arms package, and the concluding of the US–UK V/STOL engine agreement. Collectively, these decisions transformed the very basis of British international co-operation in the field of military aviation. Anglo–American entanglement was significantly deepened. Jones in particular saw this as a strategy for extending Britain's bargaining power, and for maximising British arms sales as a feature of Anglo–American collaboration.

The implications of these measures were surely not lost on the French. That said, an examination of the historical record, and particularly of the activities of the Plowden Committee, reveals that British officials were still conflicted about their choice of long-term partner for aerospace collaboration. The minutes of the committee meetings show that, at this time, France was initially preferred. The final report also recommended that the Wilson government establish a European aircraft industry based on Anglo–French collaboration. And yet despite this, the British aircraft industry thereafter focused increasingly on Anglo–American collaboration in the civil sector and Anglo–German collaboration in the military sector.

Why were the recommendations of the Plowden Report not more vigorously taken up? It must have become increasingly clear even to members of the Committee that a "whole hearted", "roots and branch" collaboration between Britain

108 *The British dilemma in military field, 1964–69*

and France would be unacceptable to the United States. This realisation also had a significant symbolic manifestation – Jones' insistence that the draft of the Plowden Report be divested of the phrase which singled out co-operation with France as the "cornerstone" of Britain's future aeronautical sector.

The twists and turns in Britain's aeronautical defence policy during the 1960s had a greater historical significance than a mere rejection of co-operation with the recalcitrant French, however. Ultimately, this chapter has shown how Britain forged a new role for itself as an aero-engine supplier and developer of unique V/STOL technology. It is precisely here where we can more clearly make out the emerging contours of an active British military–industrial participation in a US-dominated process of globalisation.

Notes

1 Minister of Aviation, *Report of the Committee of Inquiry into the Aircraft Industry*, Cmnd. 2853 (London, HMSO, 1965), paras. 1–2; Jenkins (1991, pp. 166–67).
2 Sampson (1977, p. 155).
3 Dockrill (2002, p. 145).
4 Owen (1999, p. 313).
5 Owen (1999, p. 313).
6 Johnman and Lynch (2006, p. 125).
7 Edgerton ([2006] 2008, p. 242).
8 VG fighters are suitable at both low and high speed and V/STOL fighters are able to take-off from short runway or aircraft carrier, but both mechanisms are complex.
9 Reed (1973, p. 72).
10 TNA PREM13/714, Record of a Conversation between the Prime Minister and the President of France at the Élysée Palace at 11 a.m. on Friday, 2nd April 1965; TNA PREM13/714, Record of a Conversation between the Prime Minister and President de Gaulle at the Élysée Palace at 10 a.m. on Saturday, 3rd April 1965.
11 TNA AVIA97/18, Committee of Inquiry into the Aircraft Industry, Sub-Committee on International Co-operation, Minutes of a Meeting held at the Ministry of Aviation, Shell Mex House, on Tuesday, 6th April 1965.
12 TNA AVIA97/18, Sub-Committee on International Cooperation, Report of Visit to Paris, 5th May 1965.
13 PLDN5/7/1, Committee of Enquiry into the Aircraft Industry Sub-Committee on International Co-operation, 13th April 1965.
14 PLDN5/7/1, Committee of Enquiry into the Aircraft Industry Sub-Committee on International Co-operation, 13th April 1965.
15 TNA CAB148/21, OPD (65)80th, 30th April 1965.
16 On 26th May, BAC was named to develop the AFVG airframe, and the French Snecma and BSE were named to develop the AFVG engine (*AWST*, 24th May 1965, p. 18; Hayward (1989, pp. 108–10)).
17 TNA CAB148/21, OPD (65)80th, 30th April 1965.
18 TNA PRE13/714, Anglo–French collaboration: Strike/Trainer and Variable Geometry Aircraft (OPD (65)80), by Burke Trend, 3rd May 1965.
19 TNA CAB148/18, OPD (65)23rd, 4th May 1965.
20 Rohde (2004, p. 167).
21 TNA PREM13/118, Proposed U.S./U.K. Development for Advanced Lift Engine, S. Zuckerman to Prime Minister, 7th September 1965
22 NARA RG59/E5172/Box 21, UK Purchase of US Military Aircraft, 8th February 1965; NARA RG59/E5172/Box 17, U.K. Interest in US/FRG Advanced V/STOL

Development Studies, 26th February 1965; NARA RG59/E5172/Box 17, ADO12-US/German Agreement, From Healey to McNamara, 9th March, 1965; NARA RG59/E5178/Box 1, From Jeffrey C. Kitchen to The Secretary, 25th May 1965.

23 NARA RG59, E5172, Box17, US/FRG/UK Cooperative R&D on Advanced V/STOL Aircraft, 3rd March 1965.

24 NARA RG59, E5172, Box 17, Discussion with the Lord Plowden Committee on the Future of the British Aircraft Industry, 15th May 1965.

25 NARA RG59, E5172, Box 17, Discussion with the Lord Plowden Committee on the Future of the British Aircraft Industry, 15th May 1965.

26 TNA AVIA97/18, Sub-Committee on International Co-operation, Report of Visit to Washington.

27 NARA RG59, E5172, Box 17, Discussion with the Lord Plowden Committee on the Future of the British Aircraft Industry, 15th May 1965.

28 NARA RG59, E5172, Box 17, Discussion with the Lord Plowden Committee on the Future of the British Aircraft Industry, 15th May 1965.

29 NARA RG59, E5172, Box 17, Discussion with the Lord Plowden Committee on the Future of the British Aircraft Industry, 15th May 1965.

30 NARA RG59, E5172, Box 17, Discussion with the Lord Plowden Committee on the Future of the British Aircraft Industry, 15th May 1965.

31 NARA RG59, E5172, Box 17, Discussion with the Lord Plowden Committee on the Future of the British Aircraft Industry, 15th May 1965.

32 NARA RG59, E5172, Box 17, Discussion with the Lord Plowden Committee on the Future of the British Aircraft Industry, 15th May 1965.

33 NARA RG59, E5172, Box 17, Discussion with the Lord Plowden Committee on the Future of the British Aircraft Industry, 15th May 1965.

34 Ellison (2007, p. 23).

35 TNA AVIA97/18, Sub-Committee on International Cooperation, Report of Visit to Washington.

36 TNA AVIA97/18, Sub-Committee on International Cooperation, Report of Visit to Washington.

37 TNA AVIA97/18, Sub-Committee on International Cooperation, Report of Visit to Washington.

38 TNA AVIA97/18, Sub-Committee on International Cooperation, Report of Visit to Washington.

39 TNA AVIA97/18, Sub-Committee on International Cooperation, Report of Visit to Washington.

40 TNA PREM13/714, Foreign Office to certain of Her Majesty's Representatives, 18th May 1965.

41 PLDN5/7/3, Aubrey Jones to Lord Plowden, 24th May 1965.

42 PLDN5/7/3, Aubrey Jones to Lord Plowden, 24th May 1965.

43 PLDN5/7/3, Aubrey Jones to Lord Plowden, 24th May 1965.

44 PLDN5/7/3, Aubrey Jones to Lord Plowden, 24th May 1965.

45 PLDN5/7/3, Aubrey Jones to Lord Plowden, 24th May 1965.

46 PLDN5/7/3, Aubrey Jones to Lord Plowden, 24th May 1965.

47 TNA AVIA97/3, Minutes of a Meeting at the Ministry of Aviation, Shell-Mex House on Monday, 31st May 1965.

48 TNA AVIA97/3, Minutes of a Meeting at the Ministry of Aviation, Shell-Mex House on Monday, 31st May 1965.

49 TNA AVIA97/3, Minutes of a Meeting at the Ministry of Aviation, Shell-Mex House on Monday, 31st May 1965. De Gaulle suspected that British participation in European technological projects were "just strategies to get it into the EC by the backdoor" (Zimmermann (2000, p. 105)).

50 NARA RG59, E5172, Box 21, Draft Paper on V/STOL for Secretary McNamara, 19th May 1965.

110 *The British dilemma in military field, 1964–69*

51 TNA CAB148/22, OPD (65)111th, 16th July 1965.
52 NARA RG59, E5178, Box 1, Jeffrey C. Kitchen to the Secretary, 25th May 1965.
53 NARA RG59, E5178, Box 1, Jeffrey C. Kitchen to the Secretary, 25th May 1965.
54 NARA RG59, E5178, Box 1, Jeffrey C. Kitchen to the Secretary, 25th May 1965.
55 NARA RG59, E5172, Box 17, McNamara–Healey Visit, 29th May 1965.
56 NARA RG59, E5172, Box 17, McNamara–Healey Visit, 29th May 1965.
57 NARA RG59, E5172, Box 17, McNamara–Healey Visit, 29th May 1965.
58 NARA RG59, E5172, Box 17, McNamara–Healey Visit, 29th May 1965.
59 Zuckerman (1988, p. 200).
60 TNA AVIA97/8, Rolls-Royce Limited, Report to the Plowden Committee, June 1965.
61 Gardner (1981, pp. 122–25).
62 TNA CAB148/22, OPD (65)111th, 16th July 1965. When the Labour government cancelled the P.1154 V/STOL fighter on 1st February 1965, it decided to continue with the P.1127 V/STOL fighter (a subsonic version of the P.1154). However, the future of the P.1127 was uncertain at this time (TNA CAB148/22, OPD (65)111th, Annex A, 16th July 1965).
63 TNA CAB148/22, OPD (65)111th, 16th July 1965.
64 TNA AVIA97/7, Minutes of a Meeting at the Ministry of Aviation, Shell Mex House on Monday, 26th July 1965.
65 TNA AVIA97/7, Minutes of a Meeting at the Ministry of Aviation, Shell Mex House on Monday, 26th July 1965.
66 TNA AVIA97/7, Minutes of a Meeting at the Ministry of Aviation, Shell Mex House on Monday, 26th July 1965.
67 TNA AVIA97/7, Minutes of a Meeting at the Ministry of Aviation, Shell Mex House on Monday, 26th July 1965.
68 TNA AVIA97/7, Minutes of a Meeting at the Ministry of Aviation, Shell Mex House on Monday, 26th July 1965.
69 Zimmermann (2002, p. 252).
70 Zimmermann (2002, p. 252).
71 NARA RG59, E5178, Box 1, Military Export Sales Program, Germany (Draft), 23rd November 1965.
72 Zimmermann (2002, pp. 131–32).
73 NARA RG59, E5172, Box 21, Abortive Proposal for Munitions Control Policy Council, 26th May 1965; Minister of Aviation, *Report of the Committee of Inquiry into the Aircraft Industry*, Cmnd. 2853 (London, HMSO, 1965), para. 249; *AWST*, 24th May 1965, p. 19, 18th October 1965, p. 11.
74 TNA AVIA97/18, Sub-Committee on International Cooperation, Visit to Bonn, 1965.
75 TNA AVIA97/18, Sub-Committee on International Cooperation, Visit to Bonn, 1965.
76 TNA AVIA97/18, Sub-Committee on International Cooperation, Visit to Bonn, 1965.
77 TNA AVIA97/18, Sub-Committee on International Cooperation, Visit to Bonn, 1965.
78 TNA AVIA97/18, Sub-Committee on International Cooperation, Visit to Bonn, 1965.
79 TNA AVIA97/18, Sub-Committee on International Cooperation, Visit to Bonn, 1965.
80 TNA AVIA97/18, Sub-Committee on International Cooperation, Visit to Bonn, 1965.
81 TNA AVIA97/18, Sub-Committee on International Cooperation, Visit to Bonn, 1965.
82 TNA PREM13/716, Foreign Office and Commonwealth Office to Certain Missions, 11th August 1965.
83 *Flight International*, 12th August 1965, p. 244.
84 Gardner (1981, p. 135).
85 Gardner (1981, p. 135).
86 Gardner (1981, pp. 134–35); Gold (1995, pp. 72–73).
87 TNA PREM13/716, Foreign Office and Commonwealth Office to Certain Missions, 11th August 1965.
88 NARA RG59, E5178, Box 1, Jeffrey C. Kitchen to the Secretary, 25th May 1965.
89 NARA RG59, E5178, Box 1, Jeffrey C. Kitchen to the Secretary, 25th May 1965.

90 NARA RG59, E5172, Box 17, UK Proposal for Advanced Lift Engine, 28th July 1965.

91 NARA RG59, E5172, Box 17, McNamara to Jenkins, 12th August 1965.

92 NARA RG59, E5172, Box 21, DOD Procurement in the U.K., 23rd August 1965; NARA RG59, E5172, Box 17, R&D Cooperation with the United Kingdom, 11th October 1965.

93 TNA CAB148/22, OPD (65)111th, 16th July 1965; TNA PREM13/118, Proposed U.S./U.K. Development for Advanced Lift Engine, Note by the Minister of Aviation, 3rd September 1965.

94 TNA CAB148/22, OPD (65)111th, 16th July 1965; TNA PREM13/118, Proposed U.S./U.K. Development for Advanced Lift Engine, Note by the Minister of Aviation, 3rd September 1965.

95 TNA PREM13/118, Proposed U.S./U.K. Development for Advanced Lift Engine, Zuckerman to Prime Minister, 7th September 1965.

96 NARA RG59, E5172, Box 17, Jenkins to McNamara, 8th September 1965.

97 NARA RG59, E5172, Box 17, McNamara–Healey Visit 29th May 1965.

98 NARA RG59, E5172, Box 17, R&D Cooperation with the United Kingdom, 11th October 1965.

99 TNA PREM13/118, Proposed U.S./U.K. Development for Advanced Lift Engine, Zuckerman to Prime Minister, 7th September 1965; TNA PREM13/118, Foreign Office to Bonn, 8th October 1965.

100 NARA RG59, E5172, Box 21, Sale of British Aircraft to Saudi Arabia and Jordan, 8th October 1965.

101 NARA RG59, E5172, Box 21, DOD Procurement in the U.K., George S. Newman to Henry J. Kuss, 23rd August 1965.

102 NARA RG59, E5172, Box 21, DOD Procurement in the U.K., George S. Newman to Henry J. Kuss, 23rd August 1965.

103 NARA RG59, E5172, Box 21, DOD Procurement in the U.K., George S. Newman to Henry J. Kuss, 23rd August 1965.

104 NARA RG59, E5172, Box21, DOD Procurement in the U.K., George S. Newman to Henry J. Kuss, 23rd August 1965.

105 Sampson (1977, pp. 157–63); Stonehouse (1975, p. 50); Thayer (1969, p. 260).

106 NARA RG59/E5172/Box 21, British Arms Sales to Saudi Arabia and Jordan, 13th October 1965.

107 NARA RG59/E5172/Box 21, British Arms Sales to Saudi Arabia and Jordan, 13th October 1965.

108 Phythian (2000, pp. 205–7).

109 NARA RG59/E5172/Box 21, British Arms Sales to Saudi Arabia and Jordan, 13th October 1965.

110 TNA PREM13/1312, Saudi Arabian Deal and the F.111 Purchase, 26th April 1966.

111 NARA RG59, E5172, Box 21, British and U.S. Arms Sales to Saudi Arabia and Jordan, 12th October 1965.

112 NARA RG59, E5172, Box 21, British and U.S. Arms Sales to Saudi Arabia and Jordan, 12th October 1965.

113 Phythian (2000, p. 207); *AWST*, 8th November 1965, p. 32; *AWST*, 20th December 1965, p. 21; TNA PREM13/1312, Saudi Arabian Deal and the F111 Purchase, 26th April 1966.

114 Stonehouse (1975, p. 53).

115 TNA PREM13/1312, Saudi Arabian Deal and the F111 Purchase, 26th April 1966; 722 HC Deb., 21st December 1965, col. 1875.

116 TNA AVIA97/11, Minutes of a Meeting at the Ministry of Aviation, Shell Mex House on Monday, 23rd October 1965.

117 TNA AVIA97/11, Minutes of a Meeting at the Ministry of Aviation, Shell Mex House on Monday, 23rd October 1965.

112 *The British dilemma in military field, 1964–69*

118 TNA AVIA97/11, Minutes of a Meeting at the Ministry of Aviation, Shell Mex House on Monday, 23rd October 1965.

119 TNA AVIA97/11, Minutes of a Meeting at the Ministry of Aviation, Shell Mex House on Monday, 23rd October 1965.

120 TNA AVIA97/11, Minutes of a Meeting at the Ministry of Aviation, Shell Mex House on Monday, 23rd October 1965.

121 TNA AVIA97/11, Minutes of a Meeting at the Ministry of Aviation, Shell Mex House on Monday, 23rd October 1965.

122 TNA AVIA97/11, Minutes of a Meeting at the Ministry of Aviation, Shell Mex House on Monday, 23rd October 1965.

123 TNA AVIA97/11, Minutes of a Meeting at the Ministry of Aviation, Shell Mex House on Monday, 23rd October 1965.

124 TNA AVIA97/9, Minutes of a Meeting at the Ministry of Aviation, Shell Mex House on Monday, 25th October 1965.

125 Minister of Aviation, *Report of the Committee of Inquiry into the Aircraft Industry*, Cmnd. 2853 (London, HMSO, 1965), para. 248.

126 TNA AVIA97/9, Minutes of a Meeting at the Ministry of Aviation, Shell Mex House on Monday, 25th October 1965.

127 Jones (1985, p. 81).

128 TNA PREM13/716, Spey–Mirage IV, 13th December 1965.

129 TNA CAB148/25, OPD (66)11th, 9th February 1966.

130 TNA CAB148/25, OPD (66)11th, 9th February 1966.

131 NARA RG59, E5178, Box 1, Secretary of State to American Embassy in London, 23rd February 1966.

132 TNA CAB148/25, OPD (66)13th, 13th February 1966.

133 TNA CAB148/25, OPD (66)13th, 13th February 1966; Priest (2006, pp. 127–28).

134 TNA PREM13/714, Foreign Office to Washington, 15th February 1966.

135 TNA CAB128/41, CC (66)9th, 14th February 1966; TNA PREM13/714, Prime Minister's Personal Telegram, 3rd March 1966.

136 Britain restricts the number of F-111s to 50 in order to make room to procure the AFVG, TNA PREM13/714, Foreign Office to Washington, 15th February 1966.

137 TNA PREM13/714, Foreign Office to Paris, 16th February 1966.

138 TNA PREM13/714, Mulley to Healey, 21st February 1966.

139 TNA PREM13/714, Foreign Office to Washington, 3rd March 1966.

140 TNA PREM13/714, Foreign Office to Paris, 16th February 1965.

141 TNA PREM13/714, Foreign Office to Paris, 16th February 1965.

142 Bozo (2002, p. 165).

6 The "European Technological Community" and the Anglo–German MRCA project, 1966–1969

Introduction

Towards the end of the 1960s, several political and diplomatic developments caused London's search for a European collaborative partner in the realm of aircraft manufacturing to shift east, from Paris towards Bonn. For reasons that are explored in this chapter, this was a torturous process. The end result, however, was a success story. The most expensive European co-operative project in the military aircraft sphere during the 1970s was the Anglo–German–Italian Multi Role Combat Aircraft (MRCA) (Tornado) fighter. Why did such a huge European project exclude France, arguably the most important player in European aerospace? Why did the Wilson government choose Germany rather than France as Britain's principal partner in international collaboration? And why did this process of growing entanglement between London and Bonn prove so painful on both sides of the English Channel?

This chapter aims to answer these questions. It does so through an examination of the negotiations among the United States, the UK, France and West Germany with respect to two revolutionary technologies – VG and V/STOL. The chapter's focus is the process by which the UK switched its VG collaboration from France (AFVG) to West Germany (MRCA Tornado). VG aircrafts have "swing wings" that can be swept back and returned to their original position during flight, thereby enabling optimum speed either slow or fast. Therefore, these aircraft were sought because they were fit for both Air Force and Navy, which need aircraft carrier take-offs. The VG mechanism, however, is highly complex, and is one of its drawbacks. The V/STOL jump-jet ability is also good for aircraft carrier take-offs, and was especially urgent for the Luftwaffe in the event that runways were destroyed by first strike from the Eastern bloc, necessitating the use of Autobahns for take-offs.

Crucially, much of this occurred against the background of a profound crisis in the Atlantic alliance, largely initiated by France's withdrawal from NATO's integrated command structure.[1] Frédéric Bozo has pointed out that this crisis was really a conflict between de Gaulle's conception of a *force de frappe* and a US-advocated strategy of flexible response. The US strategy was also highly reliant on the BAOR, the core non-nuclear force at the centre of flexible response. At the

DOI: 10.4324/9781003127901-8

114 *The British dilemma in military field, 1964–69*

end of the 1960s, however, the continued existence of this force also seemed to be in doubt.[2] Moreover, and as Hubert Zimmermann has argued, during the 1960s and 1970s, it became increasingly apparent that the vision of a "Transatlantic Technological Community"[3] had failed. In its place, the idea of "European collaboration"[4] was gaining traction in key advanced technology sectors, such as fighters, space and nuclear power.

From the perspective of those British politicians concerned with aircraft policy, this was a minefield. Their response was familiar – a pragmatic attempt to keep one foot on either side of the Atlantic. Zimmermann has characterised the British position in the late 1960s as "ambiguous".[5] This chapter aims to add some empirical substance to this sense of British ambiguity through an examination of London's strategy concerning fighter research and development and European techno-co-operation.

"Perfidious Albion" and the Atlantic alliance in the 1960s

Part II of this book basically indicates that, during the 1960s, British governments made a succession of decisions which, from the perspective of some of its continental partners, certainly appeared "perfidious". The British decided to purchase American-made F-111s rather than the French Mirage, while a joint British–French VG project – the AVFG – quite literally failed to get off the ground. The UK's withdrawal from the European Airbus project in 1969 was apparently the last act in this decade of British betrayal. I argue here that Britain's apparent "perfidy" was rooted in an overall reorganisation of its fighter development programmes and aeronautical industry. It was also an – at times somewhat bewildered and desperate – attempt to navigate the twists and turns of the fraught politics of the Atlantic alliance.

This became particularly acute in the 1960s. It was caused not only by France's withdrawal from several key NATO structures in 1966, but also by de Gaulle's two vetoes to British membership of the European Economic Community (EEC) (14th January 1963 and 16th May 1966). In his rhetoric, de Gaulle denounced an Anglo–Saxon alliance. At the time of the French vetoes, he variously accused Britain "of being a bad European",[6] "America's Trojan horse",[7] and "not continental".[8] His words were not entirely without foundation because Britain did, indeed, support the US position during the confrontations of the 1960s.

In essence, these flashpoints formed part of the background to ongoing, highly complex diplomatic negotiations over the future of the transatlantic alliance. As Milward argues, these "negotiations did not spring from [Britain's] tactics but from direct conflict within its own worldwide strategy".[9] Bozo argues that these fissures in the Atlantic alliance owed to a basic conflict between two competing visions; one of an independent Europe, the other of a more thoroughgoing "Atlanticism" under[10] American leadership.

In her analysis of British decision making at the highest levels during the retreat from East of Suez, Saki Dockrill concluded that Britain's first priority between 1964 and 1968 was Europe rather than "the world".[11] But how can we

The Anglo–German fighter development, 1966–69   115

best understand this delicate British balancing act between "the world"[12] (that is, East of Suez), Europe and the United States during this period? Was *Perfidious Albion* as unfaithful as ever towards its continental neighbours?

As Ellison argues, any analysis of mid-1960s transatlantic relations must attach a key importance to the role of Germany. The containment of de Gaulle's challenge entailed the construction of "an Anglo–American–German relationship to solidify the Western alliance".[13] In essence, we are dealing her with a relational square, the four points of which were occupied by the United States, the UK, France and Germany. The manoeuvrings between these "four powers" shaped transatlantic relations during the mid-1960s.

Against this background, the following section examines the rise and fall of British–European aircraft industrial co-operation during the 1960s, with a particular focus on the procurement of fighter-bombers (British TSR-2, American F-111, UK–French AFVG and UK–German MRCA). In the 1960s, the "Four Powers" (the United States, the UK, France and West Germany) conducted hard negotiations in an attempt to achieve some kind of international collaboration over the development and production of fighter-bombers, precisely because such Mach 2.0 class vessels were still the most robust means of delivering a nuclear bomb. However, the Wilson government abandoned these major aerospace projects (although, in an interesting historical footnote, the Harrier V/STOL fighter commissioned by his government became one of the key factors in ensuring British victory during the Falklands War of 1982).

The West German military market was a coveted target for the British, French and Americans. The Germans were obviously seeking a successor to the F-104G.[14] Under the Potsdam conference in 1945, German aircraft-manufacturing capability was destroyed. However, with the start of the Cold War, the West German aircraft industry started to be resurrected. In 1958, Franz Josef Strauss, as German Minister of Defence, initiated the German selected Lockheed F-104G over the sales promotion by the French of their Dassault Mirage III as the Luftwaffe's fighter procurement.[15] As part of the F-104G Consortium of West Germany, the Netherlands, Belgium and Italy, West Germany produced 604 of a total of 849 aircraft and procured 210 of a total of 949 aircraft.[16] By licensed production granted by the F-104G Consortium, the West German aircraft industry had access to the "high-tech know-how"[17]of US fighter technology and was thereby able to be reactivated.[18] The United States and Germany co-operated over the developments of the ADO12 V/STOL fighter. Britain was far from enthusiastic about this prospective development of separate "London/Paris and Washington/Bonn" axes[19] in military technology. This chapter explains why and how the British shifted their VG co-developing partner from France (AFVG) to Germany (MRCA).

"White Heat" vs financial and diplomatic realities

Many scholars have been drawn to an analysis of the Wilson government's technology policy, which was perhaps most definitively symbolised in the Prime

116   *The British dilemma in military field, 1964–69*

Minister's "White Heat" speech at the 1963 Labour Party Conference. Of critical importance here was the Wilson government's military/civil high technology aerospace R&D, as well as both nuclear and computer technology.[20]

From November 1966, the Wilson government was a keen advocate of the "European Technological Community". By April 1968, however, the concept had manifestly failed.[21] Young has argued that "the basis for a European technology"[22] Community was, in fact, part of a Wilsonian charm offensive to achieve British accession to the EEC, and he quotes de Gaulle to the effect that: "If Britain, with its pro-American policies in Vietnam and NATO, joins the EEC, [de Gaule continued,] then it would work with Germany and Holland to subsume the Community into an Atlantic group".[23] Conversely, other studies have analysed the causes and failures of European technological co-operation during the 1960s, with Zimmermann concluding that a "transatlantic outlook was replaced by a European-centred view in most European countries".[24]

The question in the mid-1960s, however, was this: Where would the money for this grand European project come from? For its part, Wilson's Labour government was faced with severe budgetary and foreign exchange problems immediately upon assuming power in October 1964. Three substantial items presented themselves on the British balance sheet – military R&D (especially VG and V/STOL fighter), the maintenance of a British military presence East of Suez, and the BAOR. Moreover, budgetary allocation among the three items was profoundly shaken by the French announcement of withdrawal from the NATO Integrated Military Command Structures. This entailed both a wholesale US military departure from French territory and French withdrawal from German territory.

France's decision created no shortage of problems for the United States and NATO in Central Europe. The cohesion of the Atlantic alliance was threatened; American bases in strategic locations were lost; key areas of Central Europe would be left without a significant NATO presence.[25] From the British point of view, it was now clear that the BAOR's presence in Central Europe was absolutely essential and likely to get more expensive.[26]

To make matters worse, British fighter R&D was at this time beset by budgetary issues. Many of these problems were linked with Anglo–German offsetting negotiations on paying for the British military presence on the Rhine. Before the NATO Crisis of 1966, West Germany signed bilateral offset agreements with both the UK and the United States. These treaties obliged West Germany to purchase British and American arms in order to offset troop costs on German territory. But the agreements were fragile because they depended on West Germany's military budget and on the outcome of discussions in the Bundestag. As we shall see, these commitments increasingly constituted an onerous financial burden to Bonn.

In the 1960s, European co-operation for a next-generation fighter became an important issue. This owed partly to high European defence spending and the predicaments of European arms industries. De Gaulle's France, for example, had embarked on a programme to develop an independent nuclear deterrent (*force de frappe*). However, it soon became apparent that this would constitute an egregious budgetary burden for the French national economy.

Consequently, by the mid-1960s, Britain, France and West Germany were all suffering from severe defence spending problems. The defence budgets of all three countries were small compared to the United States, while the cost of the BAOR and the developmental costs of the next-generation fighter were escalating.

The NATO crisis of 1966

On 7th March 1966, a letter from de Gaulle to President Lyndon B. Johnson announced France's intention to withdraw from the NATO integrated Military Command Structure. According to Helga Haftendorn, the resulting crisis within the Western alliance was underpinned by three distinct features. First, it constituted a challenge from within the alliance to the idea of an exclusive US nuclear deterrent; second, it arose out of a basic conflict between US "Atlanticism" and the roles of both France and West Germany; and, third, it came against the background of US–Soviet détente and the continued irresolvability of the German Question.[27]

The French announcement on withdrawal from the NATO military organisation induced British Foreign Secretary Michael Stewart to propose a revision of the Anglo–French co-operation programme. The OPD committee of 5th April 1966 suggested that Britain should not start any new bilateral military projects with France. Stewart reiterated this stance during a discussion on the joint development of a new light helicopter at a second meeting on 4th May, when he stated that "France could no longer be regarded as a reliable ally and interdependence with France in the military field carries increased risks".[28] Prime Minister Harold Wilson, summing up the discussion at the OPD committee, further stated that, "[I]n view of current French policy toward NATO, we should not seek to extend collaboration with France and should only accept specific projects if they are markedly in our favour".[29] British–French relations would now be characterised by this basic sense of mistrust.

Unfortunately, at this point in time, Britain's relations with France's eastern neighbour were little better. Indeed, the profound problems around the Anglo–German offsetting relationship were exposed by the pound sterling crisis of July 1966. This crisis constituted the Wilson government's "severest economic challenge".[30] It seemed to place the continued existence of the BAOR in question. On 20th July, the Cabinet discussed a possible £100 million cut in British overseas expenditure, with targets including the Far East and the BAOR. In the House of Commons, Prime Minister Harold Wilson pledged to reduce his government's overseas spending. He further pointedly announced that, if the West German government would not agree to cover more of the costs of stationing the BAOR, then British forces would be withdrawn.[31]

On 28–29th July, at meetings held between Wilson and Johnson in Washington, Wilson once again raised the question of Britain's balance of payments,

118 *The British dilemma in military field, 1964–69*

emphasised Britain's reluctance either to devalue the pound or retreat from East of Suez, and openly mooted the withdrawal of the BAOR as an alternative solution. Johnson responded by promising to purchase around $100 million worth of British aero-engines for USAF fighters.[32] This represented the first concrete implementation of the US–UK F-111 offsetting agreement, whereby the United States had promised to purchase British arms valued at $325 million.[33]

With this commitment, the Johnson administration had rather unfortunately embroiled itself in the Anglo–German offsetting problem. This only added to the United States' own offsetting problems with the Bonn government. In the Senate, a group of Democrats led by Michael Mansfield showed themselves greatly disturbed by the mounting costs of these entanglements. They moved to reduce the size of US forces in Europe.[34] Johnson's only response was to point to West German progress in meeting the initially agreed upon offsetting targets. Behind the scenes, however, his anxiety was obvious. In a letter of 25th August to Erhardt, the US President urged his German counterpart to direct his efforts immediately towards the myriad offsetting problems between Germany, the United States and the UK.[35]

At this point, however, the redoubtably pro-American Erhardt government had just two more months left in office. A key reason for the fall of this government was an on-going crisis in the question of German offsetting of US troop costs. A mooted increase in taxes related to the procurement of US military goods, several public relations calamities resulting from successive crashes of the US-built F-104G fighters, and an enduring impasse in the US–German offsetting negotiations provided the necessary background to a government crisis in the autumn of 1966.

The trigger came in October 1966. Erhardt announced that his government would increase taxation by 2 billion Deutschmarks ($500 million) in order to meet the $892 million offset target for the period ending 30th June 1967.[36] The Chancellor had promised this to Johnson at a meeting on 26th September.[37] A scandal ensued, resulting in the resignation of several key government figures, including the Vice Chancellor. In the resulting confusion, a coalition government was cobbled together by Kurt Georg Kiesinger in December. Willy Brandt participated in this government as Vice-Chancellor and Foreign Minister, while Franz Josef Strauss assumed the role of Finance Minister. The Kiesinger government sought greater independence from its American ally. West Germany began to seriously reconsider its existing policy of purchasing mainly US military goods.

On 4th November 1966, at the same time as West Germany was descending into political crisis, Johnson sent a letter to Wilson. The President reiterated his request for a forestalling of the withdrawal of the BAOR in return for a US purchase of British arms to the value of $35 million – a sum that would be treated separately from the $325 million already agreed as part of the F-111 deal. Johnson's letter had the desired effect. At the end of November, the Wilson government decided to place a moratorium on withdrawal of the BAOR until June 1967.[38]

To add to this fraught atmosphere, the NATO crisis of 1966 meant that greater Anglo–German collaboration now appeared as essential to the survival of

The Anglo–German fighter development, 1966–69 119

the Western alliance. And yet Johnson's intervention with Wilson had not entirely resolved the fact that both Britain and West Germany continued to be bedevilled by serious offset problems relating to the BAOR. If London and Bonn failed to resolve this issue, then severe budgetary pressure would oblige the latter to cut or perhaps entirely withdraw its forces on the Rhine. The critical issue remained the German purchase of (or failure to purchase!) British military equipment. The key item here was the development of a next-generation VG fighter – which, in fact, was a joint British–French project.

Anglo–French discussions on the crisis of the AFVG project

The French announcement of withdrawal from NATO integration severely affected the AFVG project. Even before this announcement, Britain and France had been extremely worried about the AFVG's escalating development and per unit costs. Furthermore, as observed earlier in this chapter, the French announcement gave rise to an attitude of profound mistrust on the British side with respect to co-operation with France in the area of military high technology.

A joint paper on this issue was issued on 13th October 1966 by Healey, Minister of Defence, and Mulley, Minister of Aviation. This paper expressed considerable anxiety over the apparently diverging expectations that predominated between the UK and France with respect to the AFVG, as well as over its estimated costs. The British conceived of this primarily as a strike aircraft – they already had an interceptor in the form of the F-4. France, however, wanted the AFVG to have an interceptor capability – that is, a smaller, less powerful, single-engine airframe.[39]

There was further disagreement over the costs. Britain proposed a Rolls-Royce engine instead of the Snecma–BSE engine in order to reduce these, but France refused. Healey and Mulley had insisted on a revised estimated cost of between £1.5 million and £1.6 million.[40] Anxiety in London was growing. On 7th November, Healey met with Messmer, and it soon became clear that French budgetary problems might well cause an imminent breakdown in negotiations. As Healey and Mulley put it in their joint paper; "If the negotiations then break down, [Britain] will be under great pressure both politically and industrially to announce alternative plans quickly".[41]

In November 1966, Zuckerman visited Paris and met with Messmer, who insisted that the AFVG would cost more than Concorde. By this point, the French aircraft industry was already fully committed to the Concorde project, as well as to the Jaguar. According to Messmer, the French aero-engine maker Snecma was experiencing severe difficulties with AFVG's engine development. Snecma was inclined to approach the US company P&W, rather than Rolls-Royce, for assistance in this area.[42]

At this meeting, the redoubtably pro-American Zuckerman showed himself unexpectedly amenable to the idea of European integration. He believed that an arrangement between Rolls and Snecma would provide the key to success for the AFVG. He further noted that "a solution to the V.G. problem"[43] would certainly

120   *The British dilemma in military field, 1964–69*

aid in the realisation of Wilson's European "technological community". He argued for a deeper integration of the British and French aircraft industries, and an eventual procurement of the AFVG by countries such as West Germany, Holland, Belgium, Denmark and Italy.[44]

Unhappily from the British and French point of view, there were growing signs that the Dutch might switch from a purchase of the Anglo–French Jaguar to the American F-5. There was also a significant danger that the Belgians might follow them. This interesting variant on the Domino Theory that had led to US embroilment in Vietnam indicated that continental Europe's aircraft industry was in serious danger of being completely absorbed by the United States. The Americans offered licenced production of US fighters in European countries, just as they had for the F-104G.[45]

Messmer assured Zuckerman that the AFVG was the only VG project France had in the pipeline – although Dassault had actually developed a smaller single-engine VG aircraft (the Mirage F1) as a private venture. Pearson, Chairman of Rolls-Royce, and Blancard, President of Snecma, tried their best to reach a compromise whereby Snecma would take care of the manufacturing under the technical guidance of Rolls.[46]

On 21st November, Zuckerman sent a message to Wilson on this very topic. He stated that, though discussions with Messmer were still proceeding, the AFVG project was basically dysfunctional due to France's persistent budgetary difficulties. Zuckerman nonetheless stressed that monetary issues did not lie at the core of the AFVG's problems. He insisted that a solution still lay in British hands. He added that the French aircraft industry, a strong pressure group in French domestic politics, had fully committed to Concorde and the Jaguar. However, he also noted certain French misgivings with respect to the AFVG due to BAC's leading developmental role on the project.[47]

By this point, however, the UK was clearly beginning to tighten defence expenditures. This was indicated by the July pledge of £100 million, as well as a new spending ceiling of £1,850 million by 1970/71 (down from £2,100 million by 1969/70).[48] In a paper addressed to the OPD committee on 30th November, Minister of Aviation Fred Mulley proposed that the order of 60 P1127 V/STOL fighters at a cost of £60–65 million should be confirmed. Healey refused to back this proposal.[49]

In a second OPD paper issued on 2nd December 1966, Healey and Mulley reported that the AFVG project had run into significant difficulties arising from French budgetary problems. They suggested that Britain should make preparations to proceed with either a nationally independent VG programme or instead to make further purchases of the American F-111. In an annex to this OPD paper, it was pointed out that West Germany might enter the equation as a possible partner in such a project. This position was underpinned by the fact that, at this time, the Luftwaffe was undergoing a major review on procurement. German Air Staff were seriously considering the AFVG as a possible replacement for the F-104G.[50]

In his OPD paper on 2nd December 1966, Healey insisted that, should the French withdraw from the AFVG, then Britain should continue work on a

The Anglo–German fighter development, 1966–69   121

nationally independent VG. He conceded that the British defence budget could not afford to accommodate such a project in addition to the P.1127 V/STOL fighter, the subsonic version of the supersonic P.1154 V/STOL fighter which was cancelled in February 1965. However, given that the P.1127 was costly and had low priority, Healey recommended that it should be cancelled to make way for an exclusive British focus on the variable geometry project.[51] This would save an expected £300 million.[52] At the OPD committee on 9th December, Wilson concluded that Britain should continue to endeavour to secure French co-operation and, in case of a French withdrawal, should seek a more extensive collaboration with the Germans.[53]

At a meeting on 22nd December, the British Cabinet was faced with the choice of whether or not to cancel the P.1127 or to continue in line with the Cabinet paper of 20th December. The attendant ministers were divided into two camps. One faction insisted that the P.1127 was too expensive. Their opponents argued that, if Britain were, indeed, to cancel the P.1127, then it would lose its technological lead in V/STOL technology with respect to the Germans and Americans. On balance, the discussion produced a general determination to continue with the P.1127. The Cabinet placed an order for 60 models. This decision effectively indicated Britain's intention to go it alone in the development of V/STOL technology – a most expensive prospect.[54]

A possible German purchase of the Jaguar and the AFVG

In order to save the AFVG project, the UK and France demanded a commitment to purchase the aircraft on the part of West Germany and possibly certain F-104G countries. Such a purchase would entail expanding production numbers, as well as a decrease in developmental costs. In Bonn, a new, less pro-American government under Kieginger, Brandt and Strauss suddenly had the option to purchase European rather than American equipment.

On 10th January 1967, Strauss met Sir Frank Roberts, the British ambassador to West Germany, and conveyed the new intentions of his government with respect to Anglo–German co-operation. Strauss stressed that, at this point, the United States was in a position to absorb three-quarters of West Germany's military procurement budget due to the US–German offset agreement. Strauss freely admitted that this was closely connected to an American desire to exert control over Europe.[55]

Roberts urged Strauss to consider the importance of Anglo–German – or better yet, Anglo–German–French – co-operation in the form of projects such as the Jaguar and the AFVG. Moreover, Roberts recommended a German adoption of the British F-4 Phantom, which was equipped with a Rolls-Royce Spey engine. Robert essentially aimed to solve the Anglo–German offsetting problem by encouraging a German purchase of British or Anglo–French machines. Strauss "readily agreed".[56]

The AFVG was once again a topic of discussion at a meeting on 16th January 1967 between Healey, Mulley, and Messmer. The French delegation did not

122   *The British dilemma in military field, 1964–69*

raise any budgetary concerns. In fact, both sides agreed on the importance of partnerships with third parties, such as the Germans and the Dutch.[57] And despite the problematic situation, both parties expressed their determination to continue with the development of the AFVG.

These sentiments were reiterated at another Healey–Messmer meeting on 16th January 1967, at which Britain and France reconfirmed their commitment to the co-development of the AFVG. The British company BAC and the French manufacturer Dassault were pencilled in to co-operate on the airframe, while Snecma, Rolls-Royce and Bristol Siddeley would work together on the engine. The British and French delegates accepted the importance of attracting interested third parties to the project and stated their intention to hold high-level talks with the Germans and the Dutch. Again, the French made no mention of "budgetary problems".[58]

Cancellation of the AFVG

The AFVG negotiations quickly focused on the core questions of costs and German participation. On 10th May 1967, Healey composed a memorandum, which he presented to the OPD two days later. This document stated that, in October 1966, the estimation of the R&D costs for the AFVG stood at £200–215 million, with the estimated production costs at £1.5–1.6 million per aircraft.[59]

These cost estimations were to change, however. At the Healey–Messmer meeting in early May, the latter was at pains to point out that it was more difficult for France than for Britain to accept the degradation in the aircraft's performance. Britain could rely on the F-111 for the longest-range reconnaissance and strike missions. Moreover, in the F-4 Phantom, Britain already had a first-class interceptor. The French had no comparable aircraft, which meant that it was imperative for the AFVG to possess both the interceptor and strike roles.[60]

As a result of these demands, Healey indicated in the last section of his memorandum that the OPD "should note that the estimated unit production cost of a VG aircraft acceptable to both Britain and France has risen from £1.61 million to £1.75 million".[61] On 12th May, the OPD meeting decided that Britain should proceed with the project definition stage of the AFVG at the development cost of £120 million and a unit production cost of £1.75 million.[62] To solve the cost problem, the two sides agreed that "the Germans were the key to wider European collaboration. Not only would their requirement be large; but, if they accepted the AFVG aircraft, other European countries would probably follow their lead".[63]

And yet, little over a month after these positive discussions, the French government dropped a bombshell on 17th June 1967 by announcing in a letter that it "would be obliged to withdraw from the variable geometry programme".[64] France was pulling out of the AFVG project. A diplomatic telegram to the Foreign Office from Sir Patrick Reilly, the UK ambassador to France, revealed that the French government had decided to withdraw on "genuine financial grounds".[65] He reiterated this opinion in person to Healey on 29th June, explaining that "the French Government had been forced to make drastic economies in their planned expenditure for the years 1968–1970".[66] Nonetheless, this was a devastating development from the point of view of the AFVG's supporters.

The historians D. James and P. Judkins have exhaustively analysed the causes of the French retreat from the AFVG. First, there were fundamental differences between British and French requirements. The British needed heavy and expensive fighters which could be used East of Suez, whereas the French needed a cheaper model that could perform an interceptor role. Second, the French aerospace maker Dassault had been moving to build an original single-engined VG (the Mirage F1) with an Atar engine. This was the only model which France could sell abroad without any restrictions being applied by P&W.[67] Dassault, it seemed, had successfully lobbied the French government to sell its original Mirage IIIG VG instead of the AFVG. Third, Messmer, a key supporter of the AFVG, lost his seat in the 1967 General Election.[68]

In retrospect, it seems clear that, from the very beginning, Anglo–French collaboration was burdened by several serious conflicts. First, the joint programme was loaded with contradictory specifications with respect to military requirements, design leadership and cost escalation. Second, the French *force de frappe* constituted a heavy financial burden. From a budgetary point of view, the Anglo–French AFVG and Concorde had considerable difficulty competing with de Gaulle's planned independent French nuclear force. Third, and as we saw in Chapter 5, the French considered the British purchase of the American F-111 instead of the French Mirage to be a betrayal of the spirit of Anglo–French collaboration. Fourth, Dassault was successful in its advocacy of the Mirage IIIG (VG)/F1 instead of the AFVG.[69]

For Healey, however, the AFVG was "the core of [Britain's] long-term aircraft programme".[70] He was thus forced to seek a new partner for the VG fighter – or to proceed alone and bear the prohibitive costs.[71]

Anglo–German offsetting and the MRCA

The cancellation of the TSR-2 did not resolve the Wilson government's balance of payments problems. In terms of the defence budget, the choice was still being mulled between cuts to the BAOR, devaluation of the pound sterling, or a withdrawal from East of Suez. From the British perspective, the first of these presented the most apparently attractive option. The BAOR was a low priority for British defence. It also represented a heavy budgetary burden, especially given Germany's inability to meet its offsetting commitments.

At the end of 1966, Britain demanded a compulsory military purchase to the value of $215 million in order to meet the costs of the BAOR. The German offer, however, was a mere $90 million, meaning that the two Western European nations were some $125 million apart in their valuations. The political confusion in Germany led to a further stagnation in the Anglo–American offsetting

124 *The British dilemma in military field, 1964–69*

negotiations. This only made a complete withdrawal of the BAOR more appealing to an increasingly exasperated Wilson.[72]

However, the problem of Anglo–German offsetting was no mere bilateral issue between the two countries. It also represented a significant problem for the United States, because a continued British military presence in West Germany was a necessary precondition to settling the NATO crisis of 1966. These concerns were reflected in the McCloy Report, submitted to President Johnson on 21st November by John McCloy, the principal US negotiator at the offsetting talks. The McCloy Report assessed the level of forces in Europe and concluded that the NATO presence was sufficient to sustain the flexible response strategy. However, the Report also warned that any reduction of US forces on the continent would likely trigger a chain-reaction of troop reductions among America's allies. This might ultimately embolden the Soviets. Consequently, the McCloy Report recommended a new approach to the offsetting of the maintenance costs of US forces in Central Europe that would neutralise the deleterious effects of foreign currency expenditure on the balance of payments. McCloy was pushing for a change of approach.[73]

On 11th March, Johnson sent a letter to Chancellor Kiesinger which explained America's new principles and approaches with respect to troop offsetting. The three principles articulated in this letter were that, first, NATO was required to decide on the level of forces stationed in Europe from a purely military standpoint. Second, the foreign currency expenditure necessary to the US military presence in Germany had to be covered. As Johnson put it, "we recognize that the simple offset concept – an advance agreement for military purchases of prescribed amounts to offset the foreign exchange costs of U.S. troops in Germany – can be superseded by arrangements appropriate to full range financial relations which form the solid core of the Atlantic Community".[74] As recommended by the McCloy Report, this financial arrangement would proceed primarily through the *Bundesbank*.[75] Third, the West German government would henceforth be permitted to decide on its own policy of military procurement.[76]

In accordance with these three principles, the United States recommended restructuring the offsetting programme from military sales to a new financial arrangement. The third principle – German freedom with respect to military procurement – was intended to compensate for the second principle – a guarantee that US troop costs in Germany would be covered.

The Roberts Report of July 1967

The new US policy for offsetting its foreign currency spending with respect to stationing American troops thus consisted in the purchase of US treasury bills by the *Bundesbank*. The previous method for offsetting the total foreign currency spending of the United States for its stationed troops – that is, a compulsory West German purchase of US arms – had effectively been abandoned. This created a fundamentally new situation for the UK.

Precisely this point was made by Burke Trend, adviser to the UK Cabinet, to Prime Minister Harold Wilson after the conclusion of the trilateral offset negotiations. Trend suggested that, in the long term, this could prove to be an opportunity for the UK. In the following five years, the West German Army was scheduled to update its equipment, including its F-104G fighters. Trend considered it entirely possible that, in this update, the UK could take the place of the United States and become the West German Army's leading equipment supplier.

However, the problem the UK faced in selling arms to West Germany was whether its products met the needs of the West German Army. In this way, Britain's thinking about its preferred partner for European collaboration gradually shifted from France to Germany. The French withdrawal from the NATO military organisation, coupled with its persistent budgetary problems, as well as the obvious attractiveness of the German military market, all underpinned this shift in thinking.

On 13th July, Sir Frank Roberts, Britain's Ambassador to West Germany, submitted a report to the Cabinet on the Anglo–German offsetting arrangement. The essence of the new approach was to build up Anglo–German collaboration in advanced technology sectors. The hoped-for outcome was to bring about a situation in which German payments to the UK would occur naturally.[77]

In his Report, Roberts accepted the impossibility of a 100 per cent offset of the BAOR stationing costs through German arms purchases. He also contended that attempts to work towards this target were proving deleterious for Anglo–German relations. By contrast, France enjoyed natural German payments through co-operative aircraft and guided missile projects. This was the kind of scenario Britain needed to enact in its relations with the Bonn government.[78]

Roberts added here that Germany's changed political situation had brought two new factors into play. First, "a growing German disenchantment with the pro-Atlantic and pro-Anglo–Saxon policies of the Erhardt–Schröder–Von Hassel Government and its supersession by the Kiesinger–Brandt–Strauss team committed to improving relations with France"; second, West German freedom from compulsory purchases of American arms through the new US–German offset arrangement.[79]

In this new situation, Roberts proposed a new direction for the Anglo–German offset arrangements. Offset targets would be reached by building up Anglo–German – or, indeed, a broader Western European – collaboration in advanced technology at both the governmental and industrial levels. The report assumed that, in such a context of collaboration, German payments to Britain would arise naturally. In the long term, it might even be possible to dispense with formal offsetting agreements.

The Roberts report described this as "a new approach to offsetting".[80] It laid out three objectives for achieving this broader goal. The first was to seek offsetting payments through a thorough analysis of Germany's normal pattern of military requirements. The second was to establish "a partnership between British and German industry"[81] based on this analysis. The third was to aim for the creation of "a Western European base in advanced technology" in Britain.[82]

126 *The British dilemma in military field, 1964–69*

Overall, the Roberts Report concluded that "the solution to the offset problem should lie in joint, or Western European projects, if possible, in advanced technological fields. Joint projects, in meeting common requirements, would provide the natural element hitherto lacking; they would result in German firms being partners rather than rivals".[83]

The immediate goal was to establish some prospective Anglo–German co-operation projects for the 1970s. A promising area was the pending replacement of the F-104G fighter.[84] In the late 1960s, the American F-104G and Italian G.91 were the main fighters of NATO countries. But their impending replacement in the 1970s held out the prospect for huge procurements.

If West Germany procured the Anglo–French Jaguar as a replacement for the G.91, a minimum order of 100 Jaguars could be estimated. The Germans had 600 F-104Gs, so a replacement order for this model would be huge. Moreover, if West Germany decided to choose a British fighter as the replacement for the F-104G, then the F-104G Consortium countries such as Holland, Italy and Belgium might follow suit.

Discussions with the F-104G Consortium countries (Germany, Holland, Italy, Belgium and Canada) also got underway at the end of 1967. Britain had two principal aims in these discussions; the reconciliation of its requirements with those of its prospective partner countries, and the exploration of these prospective partners' industrial and management organisations with a view to the implementation of a collaborative project.[85] Another fortuitous development from the British point of view came in January 1968, when the United States and West Germany cancelled the US–German ADO12 V/STOL fighter project. They did so on the grounds that the ADO12 had proven too complicated to develop.[86] The Germans were thus forced to reconsider their fighter programme.

The MRCA was a key topic at a meeting between Healey and German Minister of Defence Gerhard Schröder on 9th and 11th October 1968. Healey outlined the UK's position on the multi-role combat aircraft. This was the biggest single defence procurement project over the next ten years: if Britain and Germany made a success of it, then they could realistically hope to jumpstart the concept of European defence procurement. Failure, however, would largely negate any chance of making this concept a reality.[87]

Britain had been prepared to compromise on the operational requirements to reach an agreement with the members of the F-104G Consortium.[88] In this spirit, negotiations for the MRCA continued between Britain, Germany, Italy and the Netherlands. NATO countries operating the F-104G had, indeed, been considering how to replace it for some time, with the Belgians and Canadians dropping out of the Consortium.[89] The MRCA could thus meet a common major European requirement and guarantee an order of perhaps 1,000 aircraft.[90]

In February 1969, as part of the Anglo–German offset negotiations, the UK pressed the Germans to accept the principle of technological collaboration for the longer term and to set as high a target figure as possible for defence procurement from the UK.[91] The German Chancellor and Foreign Minister both welcomed the notion of a long-term solution to the offsetting problem through

The Anglo–German fighter development, 1966–69   127

technological collaboration. However, when negotiations began in February 1968, it soon became clear that the UK had no hope of gaining any benefit from the principle of collaboration. The main reasons were as follows: first, the necessity of deferring decisions on major military procurement due to West Germany's budgetary problems; and, second, German industry's evident opposition to any attempt to tie the offsetting principle into any broader technological agreement. This was especially apparent with respect to the MRCA, with the German aircraft industry pressing for the biggest share of MRCA production.[92]

At an OPD committee meeting on 8th May 1969, Healey reported that the feasibility study of the MRCA project had been completed. He sought the Committee's approval to sign a General MoU covering the project as a whole "without any formal reservation"[93] on the choice of the engine between Rolls-Royce or the American P&W. But Benn, Minister of Technology, pointed out that the German aircraft industry was supporting the development of an American engine and the OPD Committee "should make it clear to the Germans that unless a Rolls-Royce engine was eventually adopted, we would not be able to continue with the project".[94]

Fortunately for the British, the problem of the choice of engine for the MRCA was finally settled in August 1969, when a Rolls-Royce RB199, rather than the P&W JTF16, was indeed selected. This would be co-produced by Rolls-Royce (32 per cent), Germany's MTU (52 per cent) and Italy's Fiat (16 per cent).[95] Less fortuitously, the Dutch soon expressed their preference for an American fighter, while the Belgians opted for a French model. Both countries dropped out of the project, leaving only the UK, West Germany and Italy.

The Anglo–German–Italian MRCA fighter provided a test case for the new approach to the offsetting problem as described in the Roberts Report. Its origins lay in an Anglo–French collaboration project that had been outlined in the Plowden Report. However, the MRCA would become the epoch-making European co-development fighter, as well as the most extensive European co-operation project of the 1970s. It ultimately took the form of an Anglo–German–Italian project that was very different from the Anglo–French model envisioned in the Plowden Report.

As mentioned above, the AFVG was ultimately cancelled, and French Dassault proceeded with the development of the Mirage F1 fighter. However, Dassault had almost no success in selling this model in continental Europe. In effect, the development of an independent European fighter based on Anglo–French collaboration had failed to materialise, while at the same time, recalcitrant France had been isolated within the Western alliance. The transfer of European aircraft co-operation ambitions from the AFVG to the MRCA comprised "[t]he politics of alliance solidarity and the isolation of France".[96] It also represented a significant political and commercial triumph for the United States.

Wilson's concept of a "European Technological Community" facilitated the British establishment of a bridgehead in Europe through the MRCA project. Ellison has further argued that the Gaullist challenge to a US-dominated Western alliance had the unintended effect of building "an Anglo–American–German

128 *The British dilemma in military field, 1964–69*

relationship to solidify the Western Alliance".[97] The tripartite offsetting agreement and the MRCA supplied the concrete evidence for the solidity of this American–British–German axis. Throughout the negotiations over the development of an international fighter which occurred between 1965 and 1969, the Wilson government consistently maintained the design capability of VG and V/STOL, and ultimately guaranteed Britain's position as the engine supplier to the MRCA.

Wilson's "European Technological Community"

Wilson's ambitious goal was to broaden the kind of Anglo–German co-operation envisioned in the Roberts Report in order to provide the basis for a European technological community. He expressed precisely these sentiments in a speech on 14th November 1966. The British Prime Minister proposed deeper co-operation between Britain and continental Europe in high-technology industries. His objective was to maintain European competitiveness in the face of an apparent US pre-eminence.[98]

Wilson also linked the development of such a community with a possible British entry into the EEC. Foreign Minister George Brown, for one, thought that Wilson's vision of a "European Technological Community" was devised almost solely with an eventual British application to the EEC in mind.[99] And the timing is clear; the Wilson government promoted the idea of a "European Technological Community" with particular gusto from September to December 1966, when Britain was also weighing up an application to join the EEC. This came in May 1967.

On 13th November 1967, Wilson made a speech on European techno-co-operation at the Lord Mayer's Banquet, Guildhall. He acknowledged the "technological gap" that existed between Europe and the United States and pointed to three highly instructive facts. First, one large American company spent more on R&D in a single year than the most significant European company in the same field. Second, the technological threshold became higher every year, so that no single European company could undertake comparable R&D and the attendant financial risks on a continental scale. Third, if Britain did not co-operate with European countries, British companies would face the danger of being absorbed by US competitors.[100]

Wilson further stressed that, though negotiations for British entry into the Common Market would take time, "the widening of the technological gap will not wait for a negotiating timetable".[101] Therefore, Wilson recommended that Britain should go ahead with bilateral and multilateral projects with any European partner to facilitate technological co-operation. Wilson made a renewed pitch for a "European Technological Community".

Unfortunately for Wilson and his vision of Britain at the heart of a "European Technology Community", in November of 1967 de Gaulle vetoed Britain's application to the EU – for the second time. De Gaulle insisted that "Anglo–European technological cooperation was possible without an ETC, and Britain was too

The Anglo–German fighter development, 1966–69   129

close to the Americans in areas like nuclear weapons and aerospace for its European commitment to be certain".[102] Moreover, de Gaulle suspected that British participation in European technological projects were "just strategies to get it into the EC by the backdoor".[103] He was not entirely wrong.

Retreat from East of Suez and cancellation of F-111

On 16th January 1968, after the two Cabinet meetings of 12th and 15th January, Wilson made a sensational statement in the House of Commons. He announced the cancellation of the British purchase of the US-built F-111, as well as his government's intention to accelerate the British withdrawal from Singapore, Malaysia and the Persian Gulf.[104] The escalating costs of the F-111, as well as the new promise of a European technological base oriented around the UK and West Germany, had apparently signalled a change in Britain's post-TSR-2 aircraft policy.

In the wake of this announcement, Anglo–American negotiations over the cost of cancellation began. Britain (somewhat optimistically) hoped to minimise these costs while ensuring the continued US purchase of British military equipment under the F-111 offset arrangements. Wilson was particularly concerned about the $35 million, plus the subsequent $19.6 million, promised by Johnson as part of the Tripartite offsetting negotiations.[105]

The British government and aircraft industry believed they had found a way to overcome the crisis of the escalation of military aircraft development costs while at the same time maintaining the UK's defence industrial base. The solution apparently lay in European collaboration – which would, by necessity, exclude the French. Furthermore, the British aircraft industry could apparently look forward to breaking into the vast American market with comparative advantage products, such as the V/STOL fighter. Moreover, this period saw two technological innovations which were to have long-term consequences. These were V/STOL and VG, both of which survived into the 1970s.

Overall, as the 1960s drew to a close, these developments formed the framework by which Anglo–German co-development of fighters proceeded apace, while the French were gradually squeezed out. The first of Churchill's "three circles" – the Empire – was gone forever. But the "special relationship", as well as a leading British role in Western Europe, were still on the table.

Conclusion

In the mid-1960s, against the backdrop of an increasingly fragile Western alliance, the British government was busily exploring the prospects for collaboration in the realm of military aviation technology. From the British perspective, persistent French budgetary problems, coupled with a basic French antipathy to "Anglo–Saxon" influence within the Western alliance, gradually tipped the scales away from France and towards its eastern neighbour. Amidst this transition, Anglo–German co-operation on the MRCA (Tornado) became the "next big

130 *The British dilemma in military field, 1964–69*

thing" for the British aircraft industry. In effect, the Gaullist challenge to US hegemony had the unintended consequence of positioning the UK and West Germany as the axis of a new European defence base. Realistically, however, no concerted European challenge to the United States in the realm of military aircraft could be successful without French participation. To some extent, then, Britain's trajectory throughout the 1960s tipped the balance of power away from Europe, specifically France, and ensured that the United States would maintain its hegemonic position within the Western alliance.

And yet the British position remained profoundly ambiguous, as *"Perfidious Albion"* sought to reap the maximum benefit from its US and European relations while committing wholeheartedly to neither. As the 1960s transitioned into the 1970s, the focus of European co-operation increasingly shifted from military to civil aerospace projects. The stakes – and the sums of money – were getting higher. British policymakers and officials would need all of their diplomatic skill and savvy in order to maintain their delicate balancing act between Western Europe and Washington.

Notes

1   Haftendorn (1996, pp. 224–26); Ellison (2007, pp. 34–39); Parr (2006, p. 72).
2   Bozo (2002, pp. 201–3).
3   Zimmermann (2000, p. 93).
4   Zimmermann (2000, p. 99).
5   Zimmermann (2000, p. 107).
6   Milward (2002, p. 483).
7   Milward (2002, p. 482).
8   Ellison (2007, p. 153).
9   Milward (2002, p. 483).
10   Bozo (2002, p. 246).
11   Dockrill (2002, p. 219).
12   Dockrill (2002, p. 219).
13   Ellison (2007, p. 190).
14   Zimmermann (2000, pp. 96–97).
15   Lockheed's dubious bribery to Strauss would be the key to the mystery of the *Spiegel* affair in 1962. The *Spiegel* affair was a German political conflict in the form of a test of press freedom, which resulted in the resignation of Strauss as Minister of Defence in October 1962. The F-104Gs caused several crashes and were called the "flying coffin" or "widow-maker", which played an important role in the fall of Chancellor Ludwig Erhardt in 1966; Sampson (1977, pp. 124–32).
16   NARA RG59, E5179, Box 4, Subject: Strike Aircraft, 19th June 1962.
17   Zimmermann (2002, p. 61).
18   Rohde (2004, p. 166).
19   TNA CAB148/22, OPD (65)111th, 16th July 1965.
20   Edgerton ([2006] 2008, pp. 239–40).
21   Shibazaki (2009, pp. 161–66).
22   TNA CAB164/159, Speech by the Prime Minister, the Rt. Hon. Harold Wilson, O. B.E., M.P., at the Lord Banquet, Guildhall, on Monday, 13th November 1967.
23   Young (2003, p. 107).
24   Zimmermann (2000, p. 109).
25   Haftendorn (1996, p. 226).

The Anglo–German fighter development, 1966–69 131

26 USNA RG59, E5178, Box 1, Effect on UK Balance of Payments of New UK–German Military Offset Agreement, 26th July 1965.
27 Haftendorn (1996, p. 4); Bluth (1995, pp. 101–4); Trachtenberg (1999, p. 382).
28 TNA CAB148/25, OPD (66)23rd, 4th May 1966.
29 TNA CAB148/25, OPD (66)23rd, 4th May 1966.
30 Ellison (2007, p. 74).
31 Dockrill (2002, pp, 164–65); Zimmermann (2002, pp. 188–89).
32 Johnson's promise was materialised as Rolls-Royce Spey engine for the USAF LTV A-7 Corsair II fighter (*Air View*, October 1966, p. 28). This contract amounted to $120 million and was the most significant overseas order in history for a British aero-engine (TNA PREM13/2003, The Arrangements for Offsetting the Dollar Cost of the F.111 Aircraft, the Secretary of the State for Defence).
33 TNA PREM13/2003, The Arrangements for Offsetting the Dollar Cost of the F.111 Aircraft, the Secretary of the State for Defence; NARA RG59/ E(A1)5603, Box 1, DEF12-5, Military Sales, The USAF Rolls-Royce Contract, 2nd August 1966; Zimmermann, (2002, pp. 188–89); TNA PREM13/2003, Offset Arrangements with the United States, 5th December 1967; Dockrill (2002, pp. 162–68, 88–89); Ellison (2007, pp. 78–81); Gavin (2004, pp. 144, 162).
34 Oberdorfer (2003, pp. 311–13).
35 *FRUS, 1964–1968, Volume XIII*, Document 202; Gavin (2004, pp. 144–45); Zimmermann (2002, pp. 194–99).
36 McGhee (1989, p. 194).
37 NARA RG59 CF1964–66, Box 2228, POL GerW 1/1/66, Memorandum of Conversation, 26th September 1966.
38 NARA RG59, E(A1)5603, Box 2, DEF12-5, US–UK Financial arrangement, 14th September 1967; NARA RG59, CF1967–69, Box 1539, DEF1 EUR, Katzenbach to Department of State, 18th February 1967; McGhee (1989, p. 199); Zimmermann (2002, p. 213); Dockrill (2002, p. 180).
39 TNA CAB148/28, OPD (66)99th, 13th October 1966.
40 TNA CAB148/28, OPD (66)99th, 13th October 1966.
41 TNA CAB148/29, OPD (66)129th, 2nd December 1966.
42 TNA PREM13/1937, Zuckerman to Wilson, 21st November 1966.
43 TNA PREM13/1937, Zuckerman to Wilson, 21st November 1966.
44 TNA PREM13/1937, Zuckerman to Wilson, 21st November 1966.
45 TNA PREM13/1937, Zuckerman to Wilson, 21st November 1966.
46 TNA PREM13/1937, Anglo–French Co-operation in the Aircraft Field, 25th September 1967.
47 TNA PREM13/1937, Zuckerman to Wilson, 21st November 1966; Zuckerman (1988, pp. 437–39).
48 Dockrill (2002, pp. 172–73).
49 TNA CAB148/29, OPD (66)127th, 30th November 1966.
50 TNA CAB148/29, OPD (66)129th, 2nd December 1966.
51 TNA CAB148/29, OPD (66)130th, 2nd December 1966.
52 Dockrill (2002, p. 174).
53 TNA CAB148/25, OPD (66)48th, 9th December 1966.
54 TNA CAB129/127, C (66)185th, 20th December 1966; TNA CAB128/41, CC (66)68th, 22nd December 1966.
55 TNA PREM13/1525, Sir F. Roberts to Foreign Office, 10th January 1967.
56 TNA PREM13/1525, Sir F. Roberts to Foreign Office, 10th January 1967.
57 TNA CAB148/31, OPD (67)7th, 3rd February 1967.
58 TNA CAB148/31, OPD (67)7th, 3rd February 1967.
59 TNA CAB148/32, OPD (67)35th, 10th May 1967.
60 TNA CAB148/32, OPD (67)35th, 10th May 1967.
61 TNA CAB148/32, OPD (67)35th, 10th May 1967.

132 *The British dilemma in military field, 1964–69*

62 TNA CAB148/30, OPD (67)19th, 12th May 1967.

63 TNA CAB148/32, OPD (67)35th, 10th May 1967.

64 TNA CAB148/33, OPD (67)51st, 3rd July 1967.

65 TNA PREM13/1937, Paris to Foreign Office, 17th June 1967. Healey maintained the reason why the French withdrew from the AFVG for financial reasons in House of Commons debates, but some MPs pointed out Dassault's move (750 HC Deb., 13th July 1967, col. 1029; Reed (1973, pp. 114–15)).

66 TNA CAB148/33, OPD (67)51st, 3rd July 1967.

67 TNA PREM13/1937, Anglo–French Co-operation in the Aircraft Field, 25th September 1967.

68 James and Judkins (2010).

69 Gardner (1981, pp. 136–39); James and Judkins (2010).

70 TNA CAB148/28, OPD (66)99th, 13th October 1966.

71 TNA CAB148/29, OPD (66)129th, 2nd December 1966.

72 Zimmermann (2002, p. 213); NARA RG59, CF1967–69, Box 1539, DEF1 EUR, Katzenbach to Department of State, 18th February 1967.

73 *FRUS, 1964–1968, Volume XIII*, Document 218; NARA RG59, CF1967–69, Box 1570, DEF4 NATO, John J. McCloy to the President, 21st November 1966; TNA PREM13/1525, Mr. McCloy.

74 NARA RG59, CF1967–69, Box 1539, DEF1 EUR, LBJ to Kiesinger, 11th March 1967.

75 NARA RG59, CF1967–69, Box 1539, DEF 1 EUR W, Trilateral Meeting, March 21, 21th March 1967.

76 TNA PREM13/1525, Mr. McCloy.

77 TNA PREM13/1526, Anglo–German offset arrangement, Sir Frank Roberts, 13th July 1967.

78 TNA PREM13/1526, Anglo–German offset arrangement, Sir Frank Roberts, 13th July 1967.

79 TNA PREM13/1526, Anglo–German offset arrangement, Sir Frank Roberts, 13th July 1967.

80 TNA PREM13/1526, Anglo–German offset arrangement, Sir Frank Roberts, 13th July 1967.

81 TNA PREM13/1526, Anglo–German offset arrangement, Sir Frank Roberts, 13th July 1967.

82 TNA PREM13/1526, Anglo–German offset arrangement, Sir Frank Roberts, 13th July 1967.

83 TNA PREM13/1526, Anglo–German offset arrangement, Sir Frank Roberts, 13th July 1967.

84 TNA PREM13/1526, Anglo–German offset arrangement, Sir Frank Roberts, 13th July 1967.

85 TNA CAB148/38, OPD (68)68th, 5th November 1968.

86 *Air View*, April 1968, p. 29.

87 TNA T225/3187, Note of Discussion between the Secretary of State for Defence and Dr G. Schröder, Federal German Minister of Defence, at 5 p.m. on 9th October and 9 a.m. on 11th October 1968.

88 TNA T225/3187, Note of Discussion between the Secretary of State for Defence and Dr G. Schröder, Federal German Minister of Defence, at 5 p.m. on 9th October and 9 a.m. on 11th October 1968.

89 Belgium procured the French Mirage 5 as next generation fighters on August 1968 (*Air View*, August 1969, p. 30) and later introduced the GD F-16s. The reasons why Canada did not participate in the MRCA were, first, budgetary strain, and, second, Canadian requirements were air-superiority fighters, different from the MRCA (essentially strike aircraft), so, American fighters would be cheaper. (*Air View*, February 1969, p. 30). Later, on September 1969, the Dutch withdrew from

the MRCA project because the Dutch requirements were fighters far different from the MRCA (*Air View*, September 1969, p. 26).

90 TNA CAB133/387, PMVB (69)5th, Prime Minister's Visit to Bonn, February 1969, Collaboration in Defence, 22nd January 1969.

91 TNA CAB133/387, PMVB (69)5th, Prime Minister's Visit to Bonn, February 1969, Collaboration in Defence, 22nd January 1969.

92 TNA CAB148/94, OPDO (69)2nd, 24th January 1969. Edgar concluded that the choice of the RB199 engine settled the Anglo–German offset problem for the next ten years, based on an *AWST* article (Edgar (1989, p. 56)).

93 TNA CAB148/92, OPD (69)20th, 2nd May 1969.

94 TNA CAB148/91, Defence and Overseas Policy Committee, Confidential Annex, OPD (69)7th, Minutes, Thursday, 8th May 1969; TNA CAB148/91, OPD (69)7th, 8th May 1969.

95 *AWST*, 8th September 1969, p. 19.

96 Wenger (2007, p. 227).

97 Ellison (2007, p. 190).

98 Shibazaki (2009, p. 161).

99 Shibazaki (2009, p. 161).

100 TNA CAB164/159, Speech by the Prime Minister, the Hon. Harold Wilson, O.B. E., M.P., at the Lord Mayer's Banquet, Guildhall, on Monday, 13th November 1967.

101 TNA CAB164/159, Speech by the Prime Minister, the Hon. Harold Wilson, O.B. E., M.P., at the Lord Mayer's Banquet, Guildhall, on Monday, 13th November 1967.

102 Young (2003, p. 109).

103 Zimmermann (2000, p. 105).

104 For more on the Cabinet discussions around the cancellation of the F-111, see Chapter 8. Initially, in the early 1960s, both the TSR-2 and the F-111 were designed to penetrate into Soviet territory at low-attitude over Mach 2.0 class speed, thereby avoiding the Soviet missile defence network. However, the Soviets were able to shoot down manned bombers such as the F-111 by the rapid development of missiles in the late 1960s. The Soviet Prime Minister Alexei Kosygin told Wilson that "the day of the bomber was over, the Soviet Union could shoot down any bomber in the sky" (TNA T225/3313, Record of a Conversation between the Prime Minister and the Soviet Prime Minister at the Opera in Moscow on the Evening of Tuesday, 23rd January 1968); Dockrill (2002, pp. 203–8).

105 Paul Nitze, US Secretary of the Navy, took a hard line here. Nitze sent a letter to Healey to the effect that the F-111's cancellation, combined with current US defence expenditures in the UK, would produce an unfavourable imbalance of $700 million during the intended period of the F-111 arrangement. After the negotiations, however, the cancellation charge comprised £11 million. Most existing offset items, which included $82 million to Rolls-Royce Spey for the USAF LTV A-7 Corsair II fighter, survived. (TNA T225/3313, Briefs for the Prime Minister, 25th January 1968; 784 HC Deb., 10th June 1969, col. 246; *AWST*, 22nd January 1968, pp. 17–19; Priest (2006, pp. 142–43).

Part III

European co-operative airliner projects and Anglo–American industrial collaboration, 1968–1982

As Parts I and II have shown, the post-war period was one of acute crisis and ambivalence for the British aircraft industry. And yet, by the 1980s, the rehabilitation of this industry was largely complete. How do we explain the transition from the apparent uncertainty of the late 1960s to the resurgence of the 1980s? Part III aims to answer this question by examining the British government's aviation-industrial strategy (airframe, aero-engine and airlines) in relation to continental Europe and the United States during the crucial decade of the 1970s. It shows how the British uncomfortably – but, ultimately, with some success – attempted to ride the "two horses" of deepened European collaboration and enhanced industrial entanglement with the Americans. By the mid-1980s, Rolls-Royce had emerged as an unlikely member of the "Big Three" aero-engine producers along with P&W and GE – a spectacular success for a non-American manufacturer.

DOI: 10.4324/9781003127901-9

7 The second jet age and the bankruptcy of Rolls-Royce, 1967–1971

Introduction

This chapter focuses on Britain's attempt to navigate difficult questions around wide-body airliner development during the mid-1960s and early 1970s. A characteristic ambivalence defined the UK's conduct in this field. On the one hand, Britain was deeply embedded in the European Airbus Consortium with France and West Germany. This was one component of a broader campaign to achieve integration into Europe, mirrored in Britain's application to the EEC in May 1967. Indeed, the Airbus represented an attempt to break the US monopoly on wide-body airliners. And yet, at the very same time, Britain was endeavouring to fit the US-manufactured Lockheed TriStar – a direct rival to the European Airbus – with a Rolls-Royce RB211 engine.

It could be argued that the British were in fact pursuing a consistent and vital interest: to maintain the position of Rolls-Royce as a leading aero-engine manufacturer that could compete equally with P&W and GE. It might also be argued that British companies were simply operating according to the logic of the free market, and that there was no reason why they should not simultaneously pursue the European and American options. And yet, as this book has tried to show, aircraft-industrial policy is more than merely a commercial enterprise; it has crucial geopolitical implications. And as Newhouse observes, "The largest single difficulty [of the European Airbus project] lay in Britain, more precisely with Rolls-Royce. This illustrious company mirrored Britain's deep and continuing uncertainty as to whether its larger political and commercial interests lay in Europe or the United States".[1]

Rolls-Royce's vacillation between European co-operation and the American TriStar thus amply symbolised British foreign policy, and Britain's place in the world more broadly. This ambivalence was to have severe consequences. Rolls-Royce's lack of success in staying on schedule in the development of a radical new jet engine for the Lockheed TriStar pushed the British manufacturer into bankruptcy, which was formally announced on 4th February 1971. This abject failure on the part of the primary symbol of post-war British high-technology constituted a severe blow to British national prestige – and, in the words of one government official, "was like hearing that Westminster Abbey had become a brothel".[2]

DOI: 10.4324/9781003127901-10

138 *US–European airliner projects, 1968–82*

There are many scholarly works on the battle over wide-body airliner manufacturing between the Americans and the Europeans. Owen has stressed that, despite the British withdrawal from Airbus, the confrontation between Atlanticists and Europeanists at the Department of Technology and Industry continued to splinter British political life.[3] Hayward has pointed out that the British government's absolute prioritising of the Lockheed project actually proved detrimental to the interests of British airframe manufacturers.[4] Lewis Johnman and Frances Lynch focus on the British factor, especially with regard to Rolls-Royce, in examining the establishment of Airbus. They conclude that the British government withdrew from the project in April 1969 due to the lack of a guarantee that the Airbus would be powered by a Rolls-Royce rather than an American engine.[5] Thornton has similarly explained British wide body airliner strategy as contorted over a basic ambivalence between "Europeanists" and "Atlanticists".[6]

This chapter offers an empirical contribution to this discussion. It first sets out to examine the broader competition over wide-body airliners that was raging toward the end of the 1960s, and aims to place Anglo–French negotiations about the engine for the European Airbus A300 within the context of this transatlantic competition. The second part of the chapter enquires into how Rolls-Royce was able to obtain the Lockheed TriStar contract amidst ongoing negotiations over a British withdrawal from the European Airbus project. The third part of the chapter explores the background to the first Rolls-Royce liquidity crisis in autumn 1970. The fourth and final part of the chapter examines Rolls-Royce's bankruptcy and the subsequent rescue of Lockheed–Rolls-Royce by the US government. At all times, the aim is to show how, at the beginning of the 1970s, Britain's on-going attempt to ride two horses – one European, one American – almost resulted in the complete dissolution of one of its most valuable assets in the field of aviation.

Wide-body airliners

In the early 1960s, the international long-range airliner market was dominated by Boeing and Douglas, two US airframe manufacturers, with their 707 and DC-8, respectively. The same two companies dominated the short- to medium-range airliner market with the 727/737 and the DC-9, respectively. The British and French governments grew increasingly concerned about this dominance. Indeed, this concern formed the basis of plans for the common European development of a next-generation airliner.

In the mid-1960s, expanding demand for air travel induced airframe manufacturers to introduce wide-body (two aisles) airliners into the short- to medium-range airliner market. These airliners had the advantage of low operating costs and massive passenger capacities. Before long, the market for wide-body airliners was the scene of an aggressive competition between four key units: the US McDonnell Douglas DC-10, the US Lockheed TriStar, the European A300/A300B, and the British BAC2-11/3-11. In 1964, the Europeans made some apparent advances. They first announced the co-development of a supersonic airliner, Concorde. Soon after, however, they announced the concept of the "Airbus" – a wide-body, short- to medium-range, subsonic aircraft with 250–300 seats.[7]

In April 1965, representatives of the British and French governments met to discuss the possibility of European collaboration. They also invited the Germans to participate. In July 1966, these three governments agreed to launch the European Airbus project. They selected Sud Aviation of France, HSA of Britain, and a Consortium of seven German companies as the main contractors. In October 1966, these companies announced the specifications for the first European Airbus, the A300, with two engines and 225–250 seats.[8]

The battle over wide-body airliners really got underway in April 1966. In this month, Pan Am ordered 25 Boeing 747s, and Frank Kolk, technical director of American Airlines, wrote to Boeing, McDD and Lockheed to ask if they were interested in a wide-body, twin-engine airliner which could carry 250 passengers.[9] The development of wide-body airliners triggered a competition not only among airframe manufacturers but also among air engine manufacturers. Work on the European Airbus was accompanied by intensive development of a next-generation big-fan engine. This competition was carried on mainly by the US firms P&W (JT9D) and GE (CF6) and British Rolls-Royce (RB207/RB211).

In 1965, the USAF stated its intention to procure a super-large transport aircraft, then known as the C-5A. Lockheed won the contract to develop the airframe in the face of competition from Boeing. Boeing subsequently decided on its own initiative to develop a long-range, wide-body commercial airliner (the 747). The contract for development of the C-5A's engine was the source of similarly intense competition, with two major US aero-engine manufacturers (P&W and GE) in contention. Ultimately, GE's bid was successful.[10] In March 1966, Boeing selected P&W's JT9D engine over Rolls-Royce's RB178 to power the 747.[11]

GE's developmental costs for the TF39 (a military version of the CF6) engine comprised $450 million, including $13 million prior to selection. These costs were fully funded by a contract from the US government. On top of this, GE was still receiving $25 million annually for the C-5A production contract. This money could be reinvested in the development of an engine for a civil wide-body airliner. Furthermore, P&W's JT9D engine for the Boing 747 was also generously funded by the US government to the tune of $11 million.[12]

What all of this amounted to was that both American companies, GE and P&W, had secured generous contracts to develop next-generation fan engines. Rolls-Royce, by contrast, had no such backing. In order to compete with P&W and GE, Rolls-Royce urgently needed to secure a similar contract for the development of a big-fan engine. The European Airbus became the source of the British company's ambitions.[13]

Anglo–French negotiations over the Airbus engine

Britain and France, however, vehemently disagreed over which engine should be incorporated into the A300. Britain insisted on the Rolls-Royce engine, while

140   *US–European airliner projects, 1968–82*

France demanded the inclusion of P&W's JT9D – which the French company Snecma was licensed to produce (P&W held a 10 per cent share in Snecma and had a seat on the company's board). BSE had already secured a guarantee that Concorde would be fitted with a BSE Olympus. Subsequently, BSE and Snecma put forward a joint proposal to construct the P&W JT9D for the European Airbus.[14]

It was against this background that, in February 1966, Denning Pearson, the Chief Executive of Rolls-Royce, sent a letter to Fred Mulley, the Minister of Aviation. Pearson stressed the importance of powering the A300 with a Rolls-Royce engine and warned of the incorporation of the rival JT9D. As he put it, "[w]e shall not only be losing our last chance to secure a foothold in the American large subsonic transport engine market of the future but will also be handing the Airbus engine market to Pratt & Whitney".[15]

In June 1966, Rolls-Royce even went so far as to propose a merger with BSE in order to strengthen the company's position. The apparent motivation for this was Rolls' "desire to prevent the American aero engine industry [from] obtaining a foothold in this country through possible collaboration between P&W and Bristol Siddeley".[16] Fortuitously for Rolls, BSE was by this point in severe financial difficulties. Indeed, the Bristol-based company needed a merger with Rolls in order to secure its own existence. This was completed in 1966, when Rolls bought the company for £2.8 million.[17] The American incursion into the British aircraft industry had apparently been headed off.

Momentum was gathering for the development of the European Airbus. In March 1967, the British Minister of Technology, Tony Benn, recommended to the Cabinet that the UK should participate in the Consortium. In deciding whether or not to take Benn's advice, the government considered several factors. First, would it be necessary for domestic manufacturers to join forces with overseas manufacturers in order for the British aircraft industry to survive? Second, did the proposed project constitute the best possible means of challenging American domination of the jet airliner market? Third, without the Airbus, would the British aircraft industry secure enough orders to maintain production lines? Fourth, was the Airbus project politically crucial with respect to broader European co-operation? And, lastly, did Britain have a vital interest in the selection of Rolls-Royce as the supplier of engines for the European Airbus/next-generation airliners?

In his recommendations to the Cabinet, Benn also suggested that some conditions be set before the British government agreed to join the Airbus Consortium. These comprised: (1) obtaining assurances from the three national airlines (Air France, BEA and Lufthansa) that they would purchase at least a total of 75 Airbuses; (2) obtaining assurances from the main contractors that the launching costs would not exceed the estimated £130 million; and (3) obtaining assurances from the French and German governments that the Rolls-Royce engine would be selected.[18]

On 9th May 1967, representatives of the three principal European parties to the Airbus project met to discuss their intentions. The main item on the agenda

Transatlantic rescue of Rolls-Royce, 1967–71   141

was the question of which engine should be used for the two-engine design of the European Airbus: the Rolls-Royce or the P&W. During these discussions, the British delegation proposed a three-engine design which would allow the Airbus to use the same model of Rolls-Royce engine as was being incorporated into Lockheed's three-engine TriStar.[19]

According to John Stonehouse, Minister of State for Technology, the French and Germans had an "extremely hostile reaction" to this proposal. They "realised immediately that we [Britain] were trying to *ride two horses* at the same time in order to put us in the most favourable position vis a vis Lockheed" (emphasis added).[20] Indeed, this was a totally transparent attempt by the British to avoid a duplication of R&D and to maximise profits by potentially fitting two different aircraft. Moreover, the adoption of a three-engine design by European Airbus would entail an outright competition with the Lockheed TriStar and McDD DC-10, and a subsequent loss of price competitiveness with respect to cheaper two-engine models.

At the same time as these negotiations were taking place, two American airframe manufacturers (Lockheed and McDD) were seriously considering the development of a new aircraft that would be broader and longer than the A300. In early 1967, Lockheed started to market its proposed wide-body airliner, the TriStar.[21] Table 7.1 sets out a comparison of wide-body (two-aisle) airliners and engines for airliners. The merger between the McDonnell and Douglas aircraft companies on 28th April 1967 was partially in response to fierce competition in

Table 7.1 Comparison of wide-body (two-aisle) airliners and engines for airliners

	Airframe	*Engine (thrust is shown in brackets)*
Long-range 400-seat class	Boeing 747[3]	P&W JT9D (50,000 lbs class)
Long-range 300-seat class	McDD DC-10[2] Lockheed TriStar[2]	GE CF6 (50,000 lbs class) (same as TF39) RB211 stretched version (50,000 lbs class)
Middle-range 300-seat class	McDD DC-10[2] Lockheed TriStar[2]	GE CF6 (50,000 lbs class) Rolls-Royce RB211-22 (40,000 lbs class)
Short- to middle-range 300-seat class	European A300[1]	Rolls-Royce RB207(50,000 lbs class)
Short- to middle-range 250-seat class	European A300B[1]	GE CF6 (50,000 lbs class) RB211 stretched version (50,000 lbs class)
	British BAC BAC3-11	RB211 stretched version (50,000 lbs class)

Source: Author.
Notes: (1) Two engines. (2) Three engines. (3) Four engines. The Lockheed TriStar, which has 300 seats and three engines, needed the 40,000-pound class RB211-22. The BAC BAC3-11 and the European A300B, which have 250 seats and two engines, needed the 50,000-pound class RB211-50 series.

142   *US–European airliner projects, 1968–82*

the airliner market. The merged company, McDD, had already lost the long-range, high-capacity market to Boeing's 747 and was at risk of losing the short- to medium-range airliner markets to Lockheed's TriStar.[22]

On 11th September 1967, Lockheed announced its readiness to take orders for the TriStar. McDD consequently decided that it was essential to proceed with a three-engine, wide-body airliner (the DC-10) in direct competition with Lockheed. What followed was a fierce commercial struggle. Both companies independently set criteria for initiating production: at least two of the four major American airlines (American Airlines, Trans World Airlines (TWA), Eastern Air Lines and United Airlines) would have to place a firm order for at least 20 aircraft. This constituted an essential precondition for launching a new airliner project and breaking even. Naturally, this also implied that any manufacturer which successfully secured three of the Big Four would force its competitors to withdraw from the bidding.[23] If Lockheed could secure three major airliners for the TriStar, McDD would have to cancel the DC-10 – and vice versa. This was a fateful moment for US aircraft manufacturing. If one party blinked, then the other would be able to establish a complete stranglehold over the 300-seat middle-range airliner market. The consequences for the loser would be calamitous and possibly terminal.

With respect to the development of a tri-engine wide-body airliner, the GE CF6 had taken the lead because it had been chosen for the US Air Force's C-5A transport. P&W, however, was less advanced in its development than both GE and Rolls-Royce. This was because P&W was concentrating on developing the powerful JT9D engine for the Boeing 747. But this was much more expensive than rival engines from GE (the CF6) and Rolls-Royce (the RB211). Lockheed leaned towards the RB211 because it would give them a doorway into the European market once Britain had, as expected, joined the EEC. At this stage, Rolls-Royce contented itself with a "dual programme" (the RB207 for the two-engine A300 and the RB211 for the tri-engine TriStar), and abandoned its cunning attempt to persuade European Airbus to adopt a single tri-engine model.[24]

McDD and Lockheed offered their customers a choice: the Rolls-Royce RB211, or the GE CF6. GE set a price for the CF6 at £280,000 per engine, whereas Rolls dropped the price of the RB211 to £200,000 per engine. 4[25] On 18th July 1967, Rolls officials discussed their plan for a dual programme which would incorporate the RB211 and RB207. Their forecast envisioned 3,289 engines; it was based on sales of 510 tri-engine TriStar and 500 twin-engine version TriStar, both assuming 30 per cent spare engines sales. Significantly, after Rolls' bankruptcy in 1971, a report published by the Department of Trade and Industry noted that "[t]he forecast plan was based on the hypothesis that there would be only one engine manufacture and one aircraft manufacturer supplying this market".[26] This was to prove a most quixotic assumption.

On 25th July 1967, representatives of the three principal European parties to the Airbus project met again and decided to initiate the project definition phase. At this meeting, the French and German representatives agreed to the adoption of the Rolls-Royce RB207 engine in exchange for the French being given leadership of the airframe design.[27] The European countries were, it seemed, unanimous in their determination to make a success of the Airbus. Indeed, two months later, on 26th September 1967, British, French and German ministers signed an MoU which signalled the beginning of the project definition phase. They set a deadline of July 1968 for deciding whether to continue to the next phase of the Airbus project.[28]

Despite this apparent harmony, however, there were growing problems behind the scenes. These were telegraphed by the fact that, throughout the negotiations, Britain and France had stubbornly focused on their respective vital interests, which were, respectively, adoption of the Rolls-Royce engine and designation of France as the leader in airframe design. Indeed, despite the signing of the MoU, Britain and France still had a rather glaring and unresolved issue. During the negotiations leading up to the MoU, the French Minister of Transport, Jean Chamant, demanded that the British government should not support the development of the BAC2-11, a 250-seat airliner fitted with two Rolls-Royce RB211 engines. The thrust provided by these two engines would be sufficient to power a 250-seater airliner. Despite the difference in seat capacity, the French evidently regarded the BAC2-11 as a competitor to the Airbus A300.[29]

On 14th December 1967, British ministers discussed this problem. The Cabinet faced the question of whether the British government should allow BEA to purchase the BAC2-11. Anthony Crosland, the President of the Board of Trade, insisted that BEA should be allowed to do so for two reasons: BEA had made the request, and the export prospects for the BAC2-11 were good. Opposing him was Benn, who also outlined two reasons for his position. First, the total development cost of the BAC2-11, with RB211 engines, was estimated to be £120 million over five years, so development would inevitably require substantial government subsidies. Second, the development of the BAC2-11 would damage the prospects of the Airbus.[30]

After much discussion, the Cabinet decided that the government should not assist with the development of the BAC2-11.[31] The British-national option was out, Churchill's "three circles" had narrowed to two, and the British government had effectively prioritised a European-collaborative project over an independent-national project. In the background, however, the American option was still alive and kicking.

The Lockheed/Rolls-Royce deal

At this time, the United States was suffering from a severe balance of payments problem which resulted in repeated dollar crises. By 1971, the integrity of the entire Bretton-Woods system was jeopardised. The US Senate leader Michael Mansfield suggested that significant budget cuts could be achieved through a withdrawal of US forces in Europe, especially if West European countries continued to refuse to contribute in this area.

In early 1968, GE tried to use the US balance of payments problem to achieve an advantage in the competition for dominance in the wide-body airliner market.

144 *US–European airliner projects, 1968–82*

Clearly, a purchase of Rolls-Royce engines by US airliners would entail a massive transfer of currency to Britain. From the perspective of American public opinion, this would be a difficult sell, to say the very least. GE lobbied senators and representatives in Congress to this effect.

In order to counter this argument, Lockheed was compelled to organise an "offset" order from Britain in order to justify powering the TriStar with a non-US engine.[32] In January 1968, Daniel J. Haughton, president of Lockheed, visited London with an offer for the British government. In return for Lockheed selecting Rolls-Royce's RB211 to power the TriStar, British airlines would commit to purchasing 50 of the aircraft once it was complete. This would balance the costs of importing the Rolls-Royce engine. Haughton presented his proposal directly to BEA and, simultaneously, to John Stonehouse, the Parliamentary Secretary to the Ministry of Aviation. However, Stonehouse rejected the proposal due to the British government's commitment to the European A300 project.[33]

On 25th January, Haughton and Sir Solly Zuckerman, the chief scientific adviser to the Cabinet Office, discussed Lockheed's proposal at the Cabinet Office with Pearson. Haughton explained that he expected to pay about $4 million per aircraft for the Rolls-Royce's engine and that he was confident Lockheed could sell at least 250 TriStar worldwide. Therefore, the total cost for the engines would be around $1 billion. British airlines' purchase of 50 TriStar at $16 million each would result in a total of $800 million in export earnings, thereby offsetting most of the engine purchase amount. Zuckerman pointed out that, if Britain accepted this proposal, it would effectively end up underwriting some of the cost of launching the TriStar.[34]

No decision was made on this proposal during Haughton's visit. In the United States, meanwhile, Congressman Robert Taft and Senator Frank Lausche, both of whom represented areas with GE plants, protested against US airlines' possible purchase of models fitted with British engines. They raised two objections: the negative impact on the US balance of payments, and the loss of American jobs. Both the US administration and board members of the US airliners were thus under considerable pressure to opt for a domestic engine supplier. Rolls-Royce was well-aware of this situation and realised that, without an offset purchase agreement, Lockheed would choose an American-based engine manufacturer.[35]

Of the four major airlines, American Airlines moved first. On 19th February, American ordered 25 DC-10s and took options on 25 more at a total cost of $400 million.[36] However, it did not specify an engine. At this critical moment, Rolls-Royce entered into negotiations with Lazard Brothers, British merchant bankers and financial consultant to Rolls-Royce, about an offset arrangement. It also drew on "the aerospace *old boy* network"[37] gathered around Air Holdings Ltd, a British aircraft purchaser.

The hour of the lords had struck! Lord Kindersley, Chairman of Rolls-Royce and a director of Lazard Brothers, approached Lord Cowdray, who was a major stockholder in Lazard and had interests in Air Holdings, with the mediation of Lord Poole, the Chairman of Lazard, for help in putting together the offset package for Lockheed.[38] Air Holdings agreed to order 50 TriStars. However, it

Transatlantic rescue of Rolls-Royce, 1967–71   145

stipulated that a deposit for each aircraft would only be paid under guarantee that it would be forfeited if the order was not taken up. Air Holdings thus had no intention of selling the TriStar, because Rolls-Royce agreed to indemnify any possible loss arising out of forfeiture of the deposit. This would expose Rolls-Royce to a risk of £12.5 million, inevitably forcing the British manufacturer back into the tender mercies of financial institutions.[39]

For its part, the British government was prepared to indemnify Rolls-Royce to a value of £5 million. This left Rolls with a potential loss of £7.5 million and would guarantee Air Holdings a fixed fee of $250,000.[40] As Newhouse put it in his *Sporty Game*, "[t]he Air Holdings deal cemented, as might a treaty, Lockheed's alliance with Great Britain".[41]

This deal ultimately encouraged the Johnson Administration to sign off on a US airlines purchase of the Rolls-Royce engine. Donald G. Agger, Assistant Secretary for International Affairs in the Department of Transport, took the lead on this and secured the support of the Departments of Defence and the Treasury. In his "engine memorandum", Agger outlined two key reasons for the US government's favourable view of the prospect of fitting the Lockheed TriStar with a Rolls-Royce engine. Obviously, such a move would open export markets for the model. Moreover, however, it would also strike a blow against the European Airbus.[42]

On 29th March 1968, Lockheed announced that it had already secured orders from Eastern Air Lines, TWA and Air Holdings for 168 TriStars. This deal amounted to $2 billion – the biggest in the history of American aviation.[43] These aircraft were to be powered by the RB211. McDD, by contrast, had secured only one order from American Airlines for 25 of its GE-powered DC-10s. Of the four major airlines, only one – United Airlines – was yet to place an order. If United Airlines opted for the TriStar, it would surely signal the end of the DC-10.[44]

Eastern Air Lines and TWA exerted heavy pressure on United Airlines to join them in buying the TriStar. They knew that this would effectively put McDD out of business. Industry heads were firmly convinced that "one financially healthy airbus builder would be better than two sick ones"[45] Significantly, however, one of the largest shareholders in United Airlines was Morgan Guaranty, a bank closely linked to GE. It thus came as little surprise when, on 25th April 1968, United Airlines announced that it had ordered 40 DC-10s.[46]

Many years after the commercial wars of the late 1960s, Houghton observed that Lockheed's failure to offer United Airlines the TriStar fitted with GE's engine was "the second of the two biggest mistakes of his life".[47] United Airlines' order effectively enabled McDD to launch the DC-10 project. Lockheed and McDD had each secured two of the big four airliners, splitting the US wide-body market in two. The result was that two aircraft (TriStar and DC-10) with almost identical specifications would enter a – by no means expansive – market.[48]

Rolls-Royce and GE had thus been selected to provide engines for, respectively, Lockheed's and McDD's new wide body aircraft. These two mighty alliances now entered into a fierce competition to secure a sufficient number of orders to reach at least the breakeven point and avoid significant losses. It was

146 *US–European airliner projects, 1968–82*

with this goal in mind that both sides turned to the European long-distance market.

Rolls-Royce, however, faced an additional problem; how was it possible to find enough resources to develop both the RB207 for the A300 and the RB211 for the TriStar? The French, who were developing the A300 airframe, were not entirely confident of Rolls' ability to handle both projects. This only deepened their existing suspicion around the British attitude to the European Airbus.

Indeed, the French scepticism was not entirely unwarranted. To be sure, immediately after securing the contract with Lockheed in March 1968, Rolls-Royce was in an extremely healthy position. The company had short-term banking facilities of £70 million (£50 million bank overdrafts and a £20 million acceptance facility), as well as abundant money entering the company from Lockheed.[49] However, the division of the 300-seat market between the TriStar and the DC-10 meant that number of projected aircraft sold, and the sale price of each individual aircraft, dropped below the initial estimate. The clouds were already beginning to gather over the TriStar – and over Rolls-Royce.

The project definition stage of the European Airbus

Rolls-Royce had pulled off an apparent coup in securing the engine contract for the TriStar. And yet this very success plunged the company's two-pronged development programme – of the RB207 for the European Airbus, and the RB211 for the TriStar – into uncertainty. Five days after the TriStar deal was announced, Benn stated in the House of Commons that "[t]he securing of the RB211 order by Rolls Royce does not lessen in any way our support for the European Airbus".[50] In fact, however, Rolls had bitten off more than it could chew by taking on both projects.

It was obvious to everyone that the Lockheed order for TriStar engines would dwarf any conceivable order from a gamut of less-than-enthusiastic European national airlines for the Airbus. Only 75 orders at the most were forecasted for this latter project. And the reality was that the combined development of the RB207 and RB211 lay beyond Rolls-Royce's financial capacities. There was little question that, faced with this choice, Rolls would concentrate overwhelmingly on the much more lucrative TriStar deal. As Hayward put it: "The Lockheed order had removed Rolls' worries about remaining an important manufacturer of large civil engines. The existence of a second project, the RB207, in fact was a growing embarrassment".[51]

The French, at least, were well aware of this, and they took action. In May 1968, Roger Béteille, Chief operating officer of Sud Aviation, visited Derby, the site of Rolls-Royce's factories, in an effort to uncover the company's real intentions. He quickly concluded that Rolls had decided to devote all its efforts to the Lockheed TriStar engine (the RB211) and that "the RB207 was dead".[52] Significantly, Rolls-Royce was demanding the same price for two RB207s as it was for three of the TriStar's RB211s. The damage thereby done to the European Airbus' price competitiveness was unmistakeable. Arnold Hall of HSA warned

Henri Ziegler, Head of Sud Aviation, that the Europeans were "in serious danger of building the world's biggest glider".[53] The TriStar deal also seemed to effect a personal change in Benn, with the "modernizing, pan-European technocrat of 1967" transitioning into "the Francophobe, little Englander of 1969".[54]

Uncertainty over the engine was not the only problem facing the A300 in the summer of 1968. According to the MoU, the European Airbus was not exactly being warmly embraced by the carriers who were ultimately expected to operate it (BEA, Lufthansa and Air France). BEA had misgivings over the aircraft's excessive capacity, while Lufthansa informed the German government that it could use only six models. Furthermore, estimated development costs had risen from £130 million to £255 million. In short, as the project definition stage neared an end, the A300 project was bedevilled by a multitude of problems; engine uncertainty, diminishing prospects for attracting customers, and escalation of development costs.[55]

On 2nd August 1968, a trilateral ministers' conference brought French, British and German officials to Paris. The three participating countries agreed to postpone the decision on whether they should go ahead with the Airbus project in order to give their governments more time to negotiate with the airlines. However, at this very conference, some basic divergencies between the different parties became uncomfortably apparent. British representatives maintained that the project had to be economically viable. The French and Germans, however, insisted that the project should proceed even if it was unlikely to break even.[56]

Fault lines were beginning to appear in the European Airbus project. For the French in particular, this project represented Europe's last chance to preserve its independent commercial aircraft development.[57] Heartened by the A300's gathering difficulties, and especially by the pessimism of the British government, BAC announced the development of the BAC3-11 in July 1968. The BAC3-11 was designed to carry 250 passengers and would be powered by twin RB211 engines. BAC believed that this aircraft would not compete with either the DC-10 or the TriStar because it was somewhat smaller than either model. Indeed, in addition to BEA's interest in the BAC3-11, BAC actually planned to collaborate with Lockheed to market the aircraft in the United States.[58]

Soon after returning to Paris, Béteille decided to organise a secret "pirate team" in Sud Aviation to redesign the Airbus. Ziegler was aware of this initiative; his goal was to develop an "off the shelf" engine for the A300. He believed that Rolls-Royce's proposal to introduce the RB207 – a totally new engine – for the European Airbus was too risky. He wanted to fit the European aircraft with a proven model, such as P&W's JT9D, GE's CF6, or Rolls-Royce's RB211.[59] Rolls and the Europeans were simultaneously turning their backs on each other.

The Airbus shrinks

On the 9th and 10th December 1968, a group of associated contractors called the Airbus Steering Committee met in London. The meeting began with a recommendation from the airframe companies that the A300 be scaled down to 250

148　*US–European airliner projects, 1968–82*

seats, and that it should be renamed the A300B. This model would be powered by a "stretched" version of Rolls-Royce's RB211 engine (47,000-lb thrust) and not by the RB207 (over 50,000 lb). Scaling down to 250 seats would make this engine switch possible.[60]

From a British perspective, this seemed a most welcome development, because the RB211 was also destined for the Lockheed TriStar. Nevertheless, Benn sensed that the committee members were weighing the idea of using a US engine for the European Airbus. Ziegler pointed out that versions of the P&W JT9D and GE CF6 could be fitted into the Airbus if national airliners insisted on it. Furthermore, the downscale to 250 seats clearly indicated that the A300B was intended as a direct competitor to the BAC3-11.[61]

On 12th December 1968, Benn stated in the House of Commons that "the withdrawal of the A300 design presents the three governments with a *new situation* which they will have to consider" (emphasis added).[62] On 8th January 1969, Benn proposed to the French and Germans that the BAC3-11 be reimagined as a European collaborative project, perhaps in place of the A300.[63] This proposal was roundly rejected at a meeting between Klaus von Dohnanyi, Secretary of State at the Federal German Ministry of Economic Affairs, and Chamant in Paris on 17th January. The French indicated that they would proceed with the A300B project even without British participation.[64]

On 5th February, the German government also decided to go ahead with the A300B project in partnership with the French, irrespective of the British position.[65] On 13th February, at a top-level conference in Bonn, Wilson informed his German hosts that "it would be a great mistake for the Federal Republic to agree to build an Airbus which could not be sold".[66] In response, German Minister of Finance Franz Josef Strauss insisted that Europe needed to maintain a degree of technological and financial independence from the United States. European collaboration was essential to achieving this. Strauss also expressed the view that France would never agree to build the BAC3-11 because the French saw this model as unalterably *British*.[67] And yet, though a French/German conference on 13th and 14th March once again reaffirmed the two countries' commitment to the Airbus, they continued to hope that the British would remain on-board.[68] They were to be disappointed.

British withdrawal from the European Airbus

The main topic of conversation at the British Cabinet meeting on 25 March was Benn's memorandum on the European Airbus. Ministers agreed that, for several reasons, it would be inappropriate to proceed with the project. First, it would not be possible to force national airlines to purchase the aircraft. Second, the BAC3-11 project was more promising. BEA had expressed a clear interest in this model, while BAC and Lockheed were in advanced discussions over its joint development. Third, France and Germany obviously intended to design the A300B flexibly enough for it to be fitted with an American engine. This implied that there was no guarantee that the A300B would be powered by Rolls-Royce. If indeed the European Airbus Consortium went with a Rolls engine, then they had already indicated their desire to use a "stretched" version of the RB211. This same engine had been earmarked for the long-range version of the TriStar – but Lockheed was yet to confirm its intention to launch such an aircraft.[69]

The case against continued British participation in the European Airbus project seemed compelling. In the end, the Cabinet instructed Benn to inform the French and German governments that Britain would withdraw.[70] On 10th April, at the Tripartite Ministerial Meeting in London, Benn reported that the British government was not satisfied with the A300B project due to a weak market and economic prospects, high development costs, and the lack of a firm commitment to a Rolls-Royce engine. The French and German governments made it clear to their hosts that they would continue with the A300B project on a bilateral basis. Significantly, they also signalled their intention to "leave the door open to us [Britain] for an unspecified period".[71]

After the withdrawal of the British, the A300B project faced a dilemma. HSA, a British company and chief contractor for the development of the aircraft's wings, was suddenly left without government support. The company nonetheless hoped to remain within the project on a private basis. It had good reason for its optimism, because it was not possible for France and Germany to proceed without it. The wings are the most complicated part of an airframe, and it was too late to find another company to produce them. Strauss arranged for the German government to cover £18 million of the £31 million needed to develop the wings. More than half of HSA's costs were thus accounted for. With this complication settled, on 29th May 1969, the French and German governments agreed to establish Airbus Industrie as the managing organisation for the A300B.[72]

Britain's position throughout this manoeuvring was, to some extent, remarkably consistent. The British government's vital interest was to maintain Rolls-Royce's position as a leading aero-engine manufacturer that could compete on an equal footing with P&W and GE. Before Rolls-Royce secured the TriStar order, the British government had believed that this could best be achieved by supporting the European Airbus. But the securing of the Lockheed contract in March 1968 effectively reduced the A300 to a non-priority – indeed, to an inconvenience.[73] The Airbus Steering Committee's decision to scale down the 300-seat A300 to the 250-seat A300B, and to indicate a possible selection of an American engine, was little more than the straw which broke the camel's back and sealed Rolls' withdrawal from the European Airbus project.[74]

At the time, this must have seemed like a victory for the British. Rolls-Royce had secured an apparently perfect airframe to adopt its next-generation engine, and under extremely lucrative conditions. It had accomplished this by *riding two horses*: the European Airbus and the Lockheed TriStar.[75] However, the failure to make the hoped-for link between the two projects and provide the engines for both would come back to haunt Rolls-Royce. This failure sowed the seeds of a close association between the continental European aircraft industry and the American firm GE.

150 *US–European airliner projects, 1968–82*

The TriStar's European failure

By the spring of 1969, the four major American airlines had decided which way to go. For Lockheed and McDD, the competition now shifted to the European long-range market. They planned to market the TriStar and DC-10 in both short-to-medium range and long-range versions. Certainly, the long-range wide-body market had been monopolised by Boeing 747. Nonetheless, Lockheed and McDD believed that their more cost-effective models would be able to compete with the 747. In this confrontation, however, Lockheed was at a certain disadvantage. The TriStar still awaited Rolls-Royce's development of a stretched engine, the RB211. Conversely, GE already had quite some experience of creating the powerful CF6 engine for the giant C-5A transport.[76] McDD was ahead of its rival from the start.

The Lockheed TriStar was fitted with 300 seats and needed three 40,000-lb thrust engines (the standard version of the RB211). The European A300B and BAC BAC3-11 each carried 250 seats, and both required two stretched RB211s (about 50,000 lb of thrust). In the long-range category (trans-Pacific and trans-continental flights), a monopoly was held by Boeing's 400+-seat 747. This gargantuan aircraft had four engines – the P&W JT9Ds. Lockheed and McDD were left to fight it out over the medium-range, 300-seat class aircraft market, with the DC-10 and the TriStar.

The medium-range, 250-seat class market was already monopolised by the European A300B. This was precisely the market that the BAC3-11 aimed to enter. Rolls-Royce's priority was the RB211 for the medium-range TriStar. However, a lack of funds was hampering the British engine maker from developing a stretched RB211 for the long-range TriStar. Rolls was apparently unable to power long-range, 300-seat class airliners as well as medium-range, two-engine 250-seat class airliners.

There was thus little chance of Rolls being able to compete with its principal rivals, P&W and GE, in the long-term. To make matters worse, Lockheed had no prospects for entering into the long-range, 300-seat class market because of the company's fund shortage and the absence of a stretched version of the RB211. This meant that, when it came to the variety of airliners on offer, the Lockheed TriStar was inferior to the McDD DC-10. That said, Rolls' RB211 had some technical superiority over the P&W JT9D and the GE CF6, especially in terms of thrust speed and quietness.

In mid-1969, the commercial competition between Lockheed/Rolls and McDD/GE came to centre on key airliners of the so-called "KUSS" countries – KLM (Holland), UTA (France), Swissair (Switzerland) and SAS (Scandinavia). This group had been formed in order to strengthen the respective airliners' bargaining position in negotiations with the aircraft manufacturers. Ultimately, McDD/GE secured the KUSS group's orders, primarily because GE offered the most generous credit terms. These comprised ten-year repayment plans at substantially below the New York prime rate to airlines.[77]

This represented yet another loss for Lockheed. The company now endeavoured to revise its strategy for marketing the long-range TriStar in Europe. The aim was to ensure that the A300B and the TriStar would use the same engine, in order to secure the orders of the ATLAS group (Air France, Lufthansa, Alitalia (Italy) and Sabena (Belgium)).[78]

On 9th July 1969, representatives of Lockheed and the British government met to discuss this new plan. Haughton stressed the importance of securing ATLAS group orders for the long-range version of the TriStar. At Lockheed, the opinion had apparently formed that, if Air France and Lufthansa placed orders, then Alitalia and Sabena would surely follow. This would be sufficient to launch the long-range version of the TriStar.[79]

Haughton's analysis showed that it was essential for Rolls-Royce to secure the Air France and Lufthansa engine orders for the A300Bs. He believed that the TriStar's success was closely tied to that of the A300B. If Air France and Lufthansa selected the RB211 for their medium-range A300Bs, then they would almost certainly order the long-range TriStar due to the commonality of engine types. This is an essential factor in an airline's decision when purchasing an aircraft, because spare parts costs are enormously influenced by commonality.[80]

For the exact same reason, however, GE was also diligently working to secure the Air France and Lufthansa engine orders for the A300Bs and the long-range DC-10s. In short, Air France and Lufthansa faced two choices for engine/aircraft combination: the medium-range A300B and the long-range TriStar with the powerful version of Rolls-Royce RB211, or the medium-range A300B and the long-range DC-10 with the GE CF6. Their decisions would more or less decide the destiny of the TriStar/RB211 project.[81]

Unsurprisingly, then, the competition between GE and Rolls-Royce for the Air France and Lufthansa orders was extremely fierce. When it came to the A300B, however, there was a significant difference between their proposals. The Rolls-Royce offer for the A300B was conditional on Air France and Lufthansa selecting the TriStar with the RB211 for their long-range aircraft. After estimating the total developmental costs for the powerful version of the RB211, Rolls-Royce concluded that it would have the resources for developing a stretched version of this engine only if it was possible to secure orders for the long-range version of TriStar and the twin-engine A300B. However, the development of a stretched version of the RB211 made no business sense if it was possible to secure the order for the A300B alone.[82]

By contrast, GE's offer was unconditional. GE had already secured the KUSS group orders. Both Air France and Lufthansa disliked the conditional nature of the Rolls-Royce proposal, and they urged for these conditions to be removed. For Rolls to make its offer unconditional, however, it needed Air France and Lufthansa to order the long-range version of the TriStar. Even more inauspiciously for Lockheed and Rolls, GE was making its offer yet more attractive by indicating that it might allow French and German companies to manufacture the CF6 engine for the A300B under a sub-contracting agreement with French Snecma and German MTU.[83]

The Anglo–German offset fund proposal

Lockheed's goal was clear; to secure Air France and Lufthansa's long-range aircraft orders. With this in mind, company representatives approached Béteille and

152   US–European airliner projects, 1968–82

Ziegler with respect to sales collaboration between Lockheed and Airbus. This represented a blatant attempt by Lockheed to switch partners from BAC to Airbus. Unfortunately for the Americans, the French proved distinctly unenthusiastic about Lockheed's scheme. They believed that the A300B could be sold on the US market on its own merits. They were also already eyeing up either a GE or a Rolls-Royce engine for the Airbus.

On the other hand, the German response proved more encouraging for Lockheed. They were interested in the plan to fit both the Airbus and the long-range TriStar with the RB211 engine, and for Air France and Lufthansa to make use of both models.[84] Less publicly, the Germans were also holding out for an eventual British return to the Airbus project in order to counterbalance the overweening French.

In this spirit, British and German officials began to closely examine the prospects of selling the long-range TriStar with RB211 to the ATLAS group. This would have involved Germany diverting payments for the BAOR in order to subsidise TriStar/RB211 sales to the ATLAS group. Precisely this scheme was on the agenda at a meeting on 5th September 1969 between an unnamed British official and Klaus-Dieter Reichardt, Chairman of the Airbus Steering Committee and a key figure at the Federal Ministry of Economics.[85]

The British official raised the idea that, under Article 4 of the Anglo–German offsetting agreement, money could be used to subsidise the Rolls-Royce offer. Reichardt proposed that some proportion of the German offsetting payments to Britain for the BAOR could be used to help Air France and Lufthansa purchase the TriStar and the RB211.[86] On 26th September 1969, a further meeting of Anglo–German officials took place in Bonn. Their discussion centred on the possible use of Anglo–German offsetting funds to help Lufthansa purchase the TriStar fitted with the RB211.[87]

The mood changed in early October, however. Ziegler of Airbus Industrie stated that he would not recommend the adoption of the RB211 as the primary engine for the A300B. He favoured GE's CF6 engine, because it was "offered without strings attached".[88] Ziegler's statement meant that Lufthansa and Air France's selection of an engine for the European Airbus would depend on which long-range airliner they decided to purchase: the DC-10 or the TriStar.[89] At this stage, the crucial question was whether or not Anglo–German offset money could indeed be used to help Lufthansa purchase the long-range version of the TriStar. If it could, Rolls-Royce could render unconditional its offer to Lufthansa and Air France about using a stretched version of RB211 for the A300B – no strings attached.[90]

However, once the US government found out about Anglo–German plans for the offset money, strident objections were raised. On 11th September, the US embassies in London and Bonn delivered notes protesting the proposed use of offset funds to subsidise British aircraft exports. According to the note, this would be contrary to "internationally accepted trading practices as outlined in the GATT".[91] Apparently, such a course would violate the export subsidy clause in the terms of Article XVI:4. In this clause, the subsidy is clearly in the sales of covered products "for export at a price lower than comparable price charged for the like product to buy in the domestic market".[92] There is little doubt that, in making this move, the US administration was "under pressure from the American aircraft industry".[93] But this pressure worked. In November 1969, Reichardt was forced to inform the British that he "had to accept defeat".[94]

This meant that Rolls-Royce's offer to Airbus for the RB211 was still conditional. GE, meanwhile, had a different strategy for ensuring that its engines ended up in the Airbus. GE representatives tried to convince Ziegler to fit the Airbus with the nacelle (the pod which houses the engine) from the GE-powered DC-10. This would help Airbus financially and see the CF6 sub-contracted to Snecma.[95] Indeed, this was the basis for an alliance between GE and Snecma which aimed to see P&W and Rolls-Royce entirely excluded from the European Airbus project.[96]

In January 1971, GE reached an accord with French Snecma and German MTU to sub-contract 40 per cent of the CF6 production for the A300B.[97] From November 1971 to May 1973, Air France and Lufthansa ordered A300Bs fitted with the GE CF6. This set the tone for the following two decades, during which time GE cemented itself as the prime engine provider for the European Airbus. GE's civil aircraft engine business greatly expanded as the European Airbus grew.[98]

Conversely, Rolls-Royce had effectively lost the contest to ensure that its engines would dominate Europe's long-range airliner market. Indeed, if the original aim was to prevent American manufacturers from penetrating the European market, then Rolls had failed signally. GE entered the 1970s with a strong foothold in Europe. It would no longer be possible for Lockheed and Rolls-Royce to launch the development of the long-range TriStar and a stretched version of RB211. As Rolls-Royce's developmental costs escalated, company executives began to look nervously at their accounts.

Rolls-Royce's first liquidity crisis in October 1970

The defeat of Lockheed and Rolls-Royce on the European long-range market piled on the pressure. Projections for the RB211 programme were no longer above the breakeven point. Rolls-Royce was manifestly unable to absorb the escalation of the development costs of the RB211 project. This became uncomfortably apparent to a team from the Ministry of Technology which visited Rolls' Derby Engine Division from 24th to 27th August 1970. The situation around the RB211 was explained to this team in no uncertain terms.[99]

On 17th September 1970, Rolls-Royce reported to the Ministries of Aviation and Supply that the escalating costs of developing the engine for Lockheed were driving the company into a liquidity crisis. Rolls stated that the developmental expenses of a standard RB211 project had risen from £74.9 million to a staggering £137.5 million. Company executives concluded that, without £60 million in additional loans, bankruptcy was on the horizon.[100]

On 15th October 1970, the Cabinet met to discuss this and other issues around the British aircraft industry. If the British government decided to assist in

154   *US–European airliner projects, 1968–82*

the development of a standard version of the RB211, then this gave rise to a critical question: Was the government prepared to finance the BAC3-11 *and* a stretched version of the RB211? This alternative held out the best chance for the preservation of Britain's capacity to manufacture large civil subsonic aircraft and large civil aero-engines. But it would cost around £150 million.[101]

The Cabinet's focus at this meeting lay on a paper entitled "Airbuses and the RB211-61 Engine" (the RB211-61 was the stretched version of the standard RB211-22).[102] The author of this report was Burke Trend, Secretary of the Cabinet. Trend's report observed that the BAC3-11 would provide alternative work for the British aircraft industry in the event of a cancellation of Concorde. However, the unilateral cancellation of Concorde and the development of the BAC3-11 as a competitor to the Airbus would be enormously complicated in light of the British relationship with France. Another possibility was to finance the development of the A300B and support a stretched version of the RB211. This would cost the government £70–90 million. Either way, Trend urged an immediate Cabinet decision on this matter, because, without financial support, BAC would be unable to continue work on the BAC3-11 after the end of October.[103]

At this point, John Davies, Minister of Trade and Industry, proceeded to inform his colleagues of the scale of Rolls-Royce's problems. Rolls executives had informed Davies in mid-August that the company was facing huge losses on the contract with Lockheed for a standard RB211 for TriStar. The development costs of the RB211 had doubled to £140 million. To complete the contract with Lockheed, Rolls-Royce would need £60 million in additional funding.[104]

The Cabinet meeting of 19th October thus had to make two urgent decisions. First, should the government support the development of a standard version of the RB211-22 for TriStar? Second, should the government support the development of a stretched version of the RB211 for the BAC3-11 or the A300B? Taking the second option would inevitably give rise to another question – Should the British government support the BAC3-11, a clear rival to the Franco–German A300B?[105]

The sums involved were astronomical. Davies suggested an aggressive course of action: governmental support for both the BAC3-11 and a stretched version of the RB211, at a cost of £144 million. He accepted that the government was extremely unlikely to recoup this outlay. However, he insisted that this double project offered the best chance for the British aircraft industry to retain its capability in manufacturing large civil subsonic aircraft and large civil aero-engines. It might be possible for Britain to maintain its aircraft industry without the BAC3-11 and a stretched version of the RB211 but, in such a scenario, the French and Germans would almost certainly assume European leadership in these fields.[106]

The Chancellor of the Exchequer, Anthony Berber, took the opposite view to Davies. He insisted that, if Britain was unable to disengage from Concorde for the foreseeable future, and if these costs were coupled with government support for the BAC3-11 as well as a stretched version of the RB211, then there was almost no chance of Britain achieving the targets outlined in the "White Paper on Public Expenditure".[107] Even if the government were full-throated in its support for a stretched version of the RB211 then, Berber suggested, the outcome would still be bleak. Such support would only be sufficient to keep Rolls-Royce in the "big leagues" along with P&W and GE for a limited period before the next generation of engine development started. Support now would only mean a temporary stay of execution.[108]

Berber then proceeded to introduce the view of Leslie O'Brien, the Governor of the Bank of England. O'Brien stated that, if the government decided to back a stretched version of the RB211 for the BAC3-11 as well as a standard RB211, then support could be expected from the gamut of financial institutions known as the City of London. The Bank of England – "the official channel of communication between governments and City"[109] – would pay another £10 million, and then the government would pay £40 million for a standard RB211 and at least £150 million for the BAC3-11 and a stretched version of the RB211. However, if the government supported only a standard RB211, then the City would pay just £10 million. This would leave the British government with a remaining bill of £50 million to save Rolls-Royce. This was the course that Berber recommend to his colleagues.[110]

At this Cabinet meeting, there had thus emerged three alternative courses of action with respect to Rolls-Royce. These were: (1) let Rolls go into liquidation; (2) support a stretched version of the RB211 for the BAC3-11 (Davies' position); and (3) limit support to a standard version of the RB211 for TriStar and draw on substantial support from City institutions (Berber's position). During the ensuing discussion, it became increasingly apparent that several British Ministers were of the view that City institutions, which already provided long-term finance to Rolls-Royce and were also committed to the Air Holdings/Lockheed arrangements, should contribute to the completion of the RB211.[111]

At the end of this exhausting exchange, Heath summarised the discussion and concluded the following. First, the government should support a standard RB211 to avoid the immediate liquidation of Rolls-Royce. Second, the Cabinet would not agree to support the BAC3-11 with a stretched version of the RB211, due to the excessive costs of such a move. Consequently, the problem remained Davies' position – a stretched version of RB211 for BAC3-11 or the A300B.[112]

On 27th October, the Cabinet met again to discuss the French and German proposal that Britain re-enter the Airbus project. Davies considered the terms offered to be "unattractive". There was, he pointed out, no assurance that European airlines would change the engines of the A300B from GE's CF6 to Rolls-Royce's RB211. Accordingly, Davies reiterated his view that the government should support the BAC3-11 and a stretched version of the RB211.[113]

Indeed, the consensus at this Cabinet discussion was that the A300B option was "unacceptable". Even if 250 A300Bs were sold, and 100 of them were equipped with the RB211, then the net loss would still amount to £65 million. Heath concluded that the government should not support the RB211 without securing a firm commitment from the City of London. He insisted that British financial institutions had a responsibility to pay more to Rolls-Royce.[114] The Heath government was thus faced with the difficult task of negotiating with the

156 *US–European airliner projects, 1968–82*

City on behalf of Rolls-Royce. Matters were not made any easier by the Franco–German request for British re-entry into the European Airbus Consortium, which would have required Rolls-Royce to develop a stretched version of the RB211 for the A300B. The costs were piling up.

A £60 million relief package

On 28th October, a meeting took place at number 10 Downing Street between Heath, Berber and representatives of the City. Their focus was the Rolls-Royce liquidity crisis. Heath began by making the following points about Rolls' financial predicament: (1) company losses in the event of the development of a standard RB211 were likely to be around £61 million; (2) losses on the production of 500 standard RB211s were likely to be £45 million, with the company needing to sell all 500 models in order to break even; and (3) Rolls ultimately needed a cash injection of around £60 million in order to avoid bankruptcy.[115]

After this rather sobering introduction, Heath stated that the future of Rolls-Royce did not depend on the BAC3-11, or on a stretched version of the RB211. The City bankers claimed that if the government put up the additional £61 million of launching aid for a standard RB211, they would continue existing facilities of £70 million, including the £18 million that Rolls had not yet drawn. However, if the government refused to put up the cash, then the bankers would be considerably more reluctant to put up anything beyond the £52 million (i.e. £70 million minus £18 million) which had already been lent.[116]

Heath made it clear to the bankers that the government could not accept "an open-ended commitment". In response, the City representatives suggested that the original proposition – i.e. that they would put up £40 million against the government's £20 million – was effectively dead. After all, this depended on a government decision to support the BAC3-11 and a stretched version of the RB211.[117]

Heath attempted to persuade his guests that the government had no commercial interest in the workings of Rolls-Royce. He insisted that it was incumbent on the City to share the provision of the additional amount required. But the bankers would not budge. They maintained their position that Rolls-Royce's reserve and capital position did not justify them injecting any further money beyond what had already been committed.[118]

At another Cabinet meeting on 3rd November – and with the situation becoming ever more critical – ministers came to some basic conclusions on the way out of the crisis. First, it was essential to appoint a new chairman to rebuild the company. This task fell to Lord Cole, former Chairman of Unilever. Second, it was necessary to appoint an independent accounting firm in order to precisely determine the minimum additional sum required for completion of the standard RB211 contract. The Cabinet apparently believed that, if the government provided 70 per cent of the additional cost (i.e. £42 million), then the City was morally obliged to find the additional £18 million (assuming, of course, that the accountants confirmed that £60 million was, indeed, the required amount).[119]

On 4th November, O'Brien and Cole met Heath. They informed him of the terms that had to be met in order for Midland and Lloyds and the Bank of England to sanction special loan facilities of £18 million for Rolls-Royce.[120] On 9th November, the Heath Cabinet, the Bank of England, Midland Bank and Lloyds Bank agreed to provide a £60 million rescue package to Rolls-Royce. The first liquidity crisis of Rolls-Royce was thereby settled.[121] Unfortunately, it was not to be the last.

The bailing out of Rolls-Royce had not solved the Heath Cabinet's other aeronautical dilemma. The Airbus was still a problem. The French and German governments were still urging the British to return to the Consortium. The first option was to accept this proposal – and thus, to embroil the Heath government in support for the European Airbus *and* a stretched version of the RB211. The second choice was to support BAC in the development of the BAC3-11 (the rival machine to the A300B) and the development of a stretched version of the RB211 to equip the BAC3-11. Incidentally, this second option was the favoured position of the City, because they were already financially entangled with the British aircraft industry and they naturally liked the idea of a powerful guarantor, the British government, joining them in this entanglement. The third choice was to support neither the A300B nor the BAC3-11.

The Heath government took the view that Rolls-Royce was not capable of developing both a standard RB211 for the TriStar and a stretched version of the RB211 for the A300B or BAC3-11. Therefore, on 1st December, the Cabinet decided not to support a powerful version of the RB211 for the BAC3-11 *or* the A300B due to the vast government outlay that would be required. This left the beleaguered Rolls-Royce with little option but to focus exclusively on developing a standard RB211 for the TriStar.[122]

Rolls-Royce between Cooper Brothers investigation and second liquidity crisis

During the autumn of 1970, an ominous question began to enter the minds of British policymakers and bankers: Would the £60 million rescue package agreed by the British Government and the City of London be enough to cover the development of a standard RB211?[123] At this time, the accountancy practice Cooper Brothers was carefully examining Rolls-Royce's 1971–1975 forecast. Their report was due to be submitted for approval to the main board of Rolls-Royce on 26th January 1971.[124]

Long before the report was complete, however, it was becoming obvious to all concerned that Cooper Brothers were finding more and more reasons to revise upwards the expected cost of developing the RB211. For a start, a production cost estimate, produced on 4th December 1970, showed that the estimated cost of the RB211 had increased £17,200 per engine compared to a comparable estimation made fewer than four months previously, on 10th August.[125]

Then, on 9th December, Cooper Brothers obtained a copy of the RB211 profit plan. This was largely unchanged from the earlier version submitted on 10th

158   US–European airliner projects, 1968–82

September. It assumed sales of 976 RB211s (813 installed engines and 163 spare engines), whereas firm orders totally only 540 RB211s (450 installed engines and 90 spare engines). Unless these figures changed, it would represent a further loss of £44.4 million.[126] Cooper Brothers concluded the Rolls-Royce's forecasting was "over optimistic and that the forecasts reflect management targets rather than likely performance".[127] In fact, Rolls-Royce would probably need a further £62.6 million to stay afloat.[128]

On 19th January 1971, the executive committee of Rolls-Royce met to discuss the 1971 profit plan. On this day, the company's forecast for 1971–1975 became available. This showed that, in 1971, a peak requirement of £121.9 would arise. The proposed facilities of £88 million would be unable to match this, leaving a total deficit of at least £33.9 million.[129]

On 20th January, Cole explained the situation to Benson of Cooper Brothers. From the perspective of Rolls-Royce, only two ways forward now remained: to call a complete halt to the RB211 programme, or to negotiate for more time in which to complete it. In the first case, the basis for acquiring the additional launch aid of November 1970 would disappear. In either case, heavy compensation claims from Lockheed and other airlines could be expected. These would probably total £50 million for a delay, and £300 million for a complete cancellation.[130]

On 22nd January, Cole and Benson reported to Sir Ronald Melville, Ministry of Aviation Supply, that Rolls-Royce was rapidly falling into yet another severe liquidity crisis. From a technical standpoint, completion of the RB211 was possible. However, it required more time and money (estimated at over £150 million in addition to the £60 million rescue package in November 1970). The only remaining options were to either postpone or terminate the project. Even a postponement would require some kind of input from Lockheed and other airliners, because they were expecting to fit their aircraft with the Rolls engine.[131]

On 26th January, Rolls-Royce held yet another critical board meeting. The board took the same view as that agreed upon by the Executive Committee on 19th January. If the RB211 project proceeded, the board estimated that £100 million in funding was needed. Any penalties for breach of contract with Lockheed and the other airlines could be added to this sum.[132]

Three days later, an emergency meeting of the Cabinet was held. Frederick Corfield, Minister of Aviation Supply, argued that a continuation of the RB211 programme would cost an estimated £110 million. Corfield was making the rather dubious assumption that Lockheed would make no attempt to gain compensation for Rolls-Royce's breach of contract. The only alternative to this, Corfield stated, was to allow Rolls-Royce to go into receivership. The government would assume control of the military divisions of the company. Heath confirmed that this would, indeed, be the way forward.[133]

The fate of Rolls-Royce now effectively depended on whether or not Lockheed was prepared to accept a postponement and an increase in the price of the engine. At this time, however, Lockheed was also confronted by severe financial problems. In early 1970, Lockheed had run into problems at the US Department

Transatlantic rescue of Rolls-Royce, 1967–71   159

of Defense due to the escalating developmental costs of the C-5A. To save the manufacturer, David Packard, Deputy Secretary of Defense, turned to the financial sector. Lockheed arranged for a $400 million line of credit from a Consortium of 24 banks.[134] However, this credit was conditional on the Pentagon paying Lockheed for military contracts, including the C-5A.[135]

On 1st February, Haughton settled negotiations with the Pentagon on the C-5A and several other military projects. He agreed to reimburse the company for over $757 million. This agreement with the Pentagon was effectively what allowed Haughton to proceed with the TriStar programme, and the collaboration with Rolls-Royce. The day after he concluded his business at the Pentagon, Haughton flew from Los Angeles to London to let Rolls know the good news in person.[136] He was in understandably jubilant mood, given the imminent injection of a new $150 million loan from America's banks.[137] Unfortunately, while he was still airborne, Ted Heath made a phone call to National Security Advisor Henry Kissinger to inform him of Rolls-Royce's impending bankruptcy.[138]

On the morning of 2nd February, Cole phoned Haughton at the Hilton Hotel to ask if he would mind arriving at Grosvenor House 30 minutes early, alone, for a private chat. Any suspicions Haughton may have fostered as a result of this call were duly confirmed that morning, as Lord Cole informed him that Rolls-Royce's problems seemed insoluble. The company would formally declare bankruptcy in two days.[139] Haughton agreed to meet representatives of the British government the following morning, by which point most parties expected him to have accepted defeat.[140]

But they had underestimated Haughton. That evening, he called together a small team of Lockheed officials at the Hilton Hotel. He was in defiant mood, stating that "[w]e've a lot of possums running around out there: Rolls, the government, banks, airlines, everybody. What we're going to do is get all those possums up the tree at the same time. The L-1011 [TriStar] program is going to go on".[141] These were fighting words, but where would the money come from?

The Lockheed/Rolls-Royce showdown

At 9:30 a.m. on 3rd February, Haughton met with representatives from Rolls-Royce. They agreed that if the British government did not pay over £100 million, and if Lockheed did not make some serious concessions (advance pay of engine prices, acceptance of a 12-month delay, and renunciation of all breach of contract claims), then Rolls-Royce would go bankrupt. Lockheed, however, could not make such concessions without consulting its creditors. Moreover, the intentions of those other airlines such as Eastern Air Lines and TWA which had ordered the RB211-fitted TriStar remained uncertain. Lastly, such a move was unlikely to enjoy the support of the Nixon Administration. Even if Nixon was willing to support Lockheed, then congressional backing was still required (and equally uncertain).[142]

On the morning of 3rd February, the decisive Cabinet meeting took place. Its task was to decide between two alternative courses of action. The first course of

160 US–European airliner projects, 1968–82

action would see the United States and the UK take the following measures: the Nixon administration would give Lockheed financial support; Lockheed would agree to pay a higher price for each engine, accept a delay on delivery of up to 12 months, and (along with other airlines that had purchased the RB211) renounce all claims for breach of contract. Moreover, the British government would provide additional financial support of up to £100 million to Rolls-Royce, thereby saving the manufacturer. The government would not, however, provide any guarantee for the technical success of the engine.[143]

The second course of action basically consisted of putting Rolls-Royce into receivership. A trustee would be appointed on 4th February and promptly terminate the RB211 contract. The British government would proceed to buy the military engine division of Rolls-Royce. Lockheed would then negotiate any compensation with – to all intents and purposes – the Heath government.[144]

In the meantime, the predicament of Rolls-Royce had become public knowledge. The Cabinet had to make an immediate decision. Heath told his ministers that he intended to put Rolls into receivership.[145] At 12:15 p.m., he called Nixon. He stated that Rolls-Royce was insolvent, and that the appointment of trustees would proceed immediately, by the letter of the law.[146]

Heath stressed the possible impact of Rolls' bankruptcy on Lockheed. In his meeting with Haughton, Heath had indicated that it would be possible to conclude a new contract with a government-administered Rolls-Royce. Nixon asked for confirmation of this position – Heath duly provided it. Nixon expressed the hope that Rolls-Royce would enter into a new contract with Lockheed. The administration's goal, he said, was to ensure that Lockheed could continue to develop and produce aircraft, and Britain and the United States "should be as positive as possible" in trying to achieve this. Heath agreed.[147]

The Prime Minister went back to his Cabinet. He explained that, if Lockheed could offer satisfactory terms for ensuring a government-administered Rolls-Royce's completion of the RB211, then it might be possible to negotiate a new contract. Heath assured his ministers that President Nixon would personally involve himself in trying to meet British requirements, which might involve providing Lockheed with additional finance.[148]

At 1:30 p.m., Haughton and Heath met yet again. Haughton explained that he had come to England to take the measure of the difficult situation at Rolls-Royce. He stated that the TriStar could still go ahead without the RB211, but that this would delay the project for over a year. The bank Consortium would continue to lend money to Lockheed if Lockheed could guarantee the eventual delivery of the RB211. For this, however, Lockheed would have to inject more cash into Rolls-Royce. This required Haughton to explain the situation to the Board of Lockheed, the banks and the airliners.[149]

Heath said that British government had already provided substantial assistance to Rolls-Royce. The previous Labour government had injected £47 million into the company, while Heath's administration had provided a further £42 million. Heath then outlined a possible legal basis for withholding any further support to Rolls. The company's directors were personally liable if they continued to trade despite the company's state of virtual insolvency. If funds continued to be injected into the ailing engine manufacturer, then the British government would almost certainly end up footing the bill. Overall, however, Heath stressed that the crucial factor was Lockheed's readiness to make contractual concessions to Rolls. Without a guarantee from Lockheed that it would accept a delay, escalating costs, and waive any breach of contract claims, the British government was not able to justify any further financial support for Rolls-Royce.[150]

The reality was that the cancellation of the RB211 would also bring about the bankruptcy of Lockheed. The survival of TriStar thus depended upon Haughton's personal ability to organise a rescue operation on a scale perhaps unprecedented in the business histories of either the United States or Britain. He had to persuade two governments, 24 banks, ten customers and 25 significant suppliers to lend their assistance. Fortunately for Haughton, Lockheed's customer airlines and suppliers had invested a total of $550 million in the TriStar – the airlines through advance payments and the sub-contractors through building up inventories. They were as anxious as he was to save the project. Indeed, many of them also faced bankruptcy if the rescue operation failed. Moreover, in the event of a termination, Lockheed's bankers stood to lose most or even all of the $400 million they had already loaned the company.[151]

The elephant in the room after these fairly optimistic discussions, however, was the fact that the agreed course of action would not save Rolls-Royce from receivership. The next day, 4th February, a declaration to this effect was made by the company. Rolls-Royce was bankrupt.

The British government reinvestigates the RB211

On 5th February, the day after Rolls-Royce declared bankruptcy, Heath appointed Defence Secretary Peter Carrington to deal with the increasingly problematic company.[152] Five days later, Carrington held a telephone call with Packard to learn more about the position of the US airline industry. He was pleasantly surprised; US airliners were not yet seriously concerned about the delay to the TriStar. However, they did want reassurances from Rolls and the British government with respect to the RB211's delivery time, price and performance. Carrington launched an independent inquiry into the engine, chaired by Sir William Cook. He wanted to know the exact costs of continuing its development.[153]

The British government's decision to allow Rolls-Royce to go into receivership gave rise to considerable consternation within the American financial sector. After all, US banks had a significant stake not only in the domestic aircraft industry, but in this specific model. On 12th February, British merchant banker Sir Kenneth Keith (later Chairman of Rolls-Royce) made this extremely clear to the British government in a telephone conference with Robert Armstrong, Heath's private secretary. Keith warned that he was "actually in Augusta [right now] with a group of businessmen and bankers and everyone is watching".[154]

The day prior to this phone call, Keith had the opportunity to consult with William Moore, President of The Bankers Trust, the organisation that

162 US–European airliner projects, 1968–82

represented the banks involved in the TriStar financing deal. According to Moore, Lockheed's technical staff still had confidence that the RB211 would soon be operational. There was also a basic conviction that other airlines would be able to pay a bit more for the engines – and that the banks would come through with extra funding.[155]

That said, Moore saw a possible stumbling block in a lack of co-operation on the British side. This would surely result in the bankruptcy of Lockheed. "Nobody has suggested that by putting Rolls into liquidation we [Britain] have slightly evaded our responsibilities", he said. However, "if, through any lack of co-operation on the British part this thing falls down, and Lockheed goes under, repercussions here will be very serious and we will not be forgiven for very, very many years".[156] Armstrong promised to convey Keith's views directly to Carrington and Heath.[157]

The banks, at least, were in a generous mood. In mid-1969, the group of 24 arranged a $400 million credit line for the TriStar project. Roy A. Anderson, an accountant at (and later chairman of) Lockheed, estimated that an injection of $350 million in addition to the $400 million credit line would allow Lockheed to proceed with TriStar. He anticipated that, with government guarantees in place, the 24 would lend another $250 million, while the three TriStar customer airlines – TWA, Eastern Air Lines and Delta Airlines – would make a $100 million prepayment. If Lockheed did go bankrupt then these airlines would most probably (and, in the case of Eastern, almost certainly) go down with the manufacturer, given that they had already prepaid $200 million.[158]

The Bankers Trust and Chase Manhattan Bank, two major banks among the group of 24, agreed to lend the necessary cash to TWA and Eastern Air Lines, respectively. Delta Airlines' financial position was already relatively strong. And so it was that, when it came to the crunch, the banks and the airliners agreed to inject yet more cash into the TriStar project.[159]

On 12th February, US Treasury Secretary John Connally gave his views on the Rolls-Royce bankruptcy to Lord Cromer, British ambassador to Washington. According to Connally, when Rolls' impending insolvency first became apparent, Lockheed seriously considered switching to either a P&W or a GE engine. However, the company's engineers soon realised that this would require significant changes to the airframe's design. Proceeding with the RB211, even if delayed, was the only realistic option.[160]

Connally also outlined some intimidating figures. Lockheed had liability for $200 million to customer airlines (TWA/Eastern Air Lines), $750 million to sub-contractors, and $350 million to the banks. Indeed, Lockheed owed money to the same banking group that had lent to the airlines and sub-contractors. The cancellation of the TriStar would, Connally warned, cause the bankruptcy of Lockheed. This would lead to a train reaction of bankruptcies among the customer airlines, and perhaps do significant damage to the US economy.[161]

According to Connally, in general, the United States was unhappy with the way Rolls-Royce had handled the crisis. Haughton had been given only one day to re-negotiate the RB211 contract. As Connally rather darkly observed, a cynical observer might assume that the British government had known well in advance about Rolls' mounting problems. Cromer insisted that this was not the case, and he rejected any intimations that there had been a conspiracy of silence between Rolls and the British government. Connally declared himself "glad to hear this"[162] – but he nonetheless reemphasised the seriousness of the situation and the possibly catastrophic consequences of Rolls' failure to deliver the RB211.[163]

From this meeting, Cromer drew the conclusion that Connally was the leading figure within the US government with respect to the Rolls-Royce question. Packard, it seemed, was more responsible for its technical dimensions. When Heath learned of the content of this discussion, he instructed Connally to relay to Washington that, when it came to the Lockheed/Rolls problem, the British government was not pessimistic or defeatist, but *realistic*. Above all, according to Heath, the British government was as anxious as anyone in Washington to ensure the survival of the TriStar/RB211 project.[164]

On 19th February, Moore, along with R. G. Ross, the vice president of the Bank of America, visited O'Brien and explained the situation on the US side. The Bankers Trust and the Bank of America were joint heads of a group of financiers who were prepared to lend to Lockheed and the three TriStar customer airliners. Moore pointed out that around $1.5 billion in credit facilities had been extended, and that more than two-thirds of this sum had already been withdrawn.[165]

Above all, it was abundantly apparent that the banks were extremely fearful of the consequences of the RB211's failure. If the airlines decided against purchasing the TriStar – and if any single customer decided to "cut and run"[166] – then, given the financial commitments already made, heavy losses would ensue. Much like the banks, the US government had a strong interest in the survival of Lockheed for reasons of defence, domestic employment and balance of payments. Given all of this, Moore emphasised the need to bring the RB211 project to a timely completion.[167]

O'Brien promised to convey US banking and official opinion to the British government.[168] At the same time, Lockheed began negotiations with its customer airlines (TWA, Eastern Air Lines, Delta Airlines and Air Canada) about possible prices and operating dates. It also entered into negotiations with the banks, as well as the British and US governments, about further loans. These were needed to increase the engine price.

On 17th February 1971, the Rolls-Royce (Purchase) Act was passed and a new company, Rolls-Royce (1971) Ltd., was created to assume control of the business acquired by the British Government.[169] The negotiations with Lockheed that would now ensue were the focus of a Cabinet meeting on 25th February. Carrington – Defence Secretary and the chair of the Ministerial Committee on Rolls-Royce – first reported the findings of the Cook Investigative Commission. This commission had been asked to scrutinise three issues. First, was the RB211 engine a viable project? Second, if it was feasible, when could it be completed? Third, if serious losses were to be avoided, by how much did the engine price need to be increased from the original contract?[170]

164   *US–European airliner projects, 1968–82*

In response to these questions, Cook had reached the following conclusions. First, technical problems in engine development could definitely be overcome. Second, with respect to delivery time, engines with an output thrust of 37,000 lbs would be ready six months later than initially agreed, while those with an output thrust of 42,000 lbs would be ready in 1973. Third, it was estimated that a price increase of £150,000 per engine was necessary in order for the initial production costs to be recovered.[171]

On this basis, Carrington made the following policy recommendations with respect to the upcoming negotiations. First, the price per engine should be increased to cover the full cost of engine production. Second, the share of the remaining development costs should be split at 50:50 between Lockheed and the newly nationalised Rolls-Royce company. Third, Lockheed should renounce any claims for breach of the original contract. Fourth, delivery delays on the original contract of nine months – and up to 12 months – should be accepted without any penalties accruing. Fifth, the UK should seek adequate guarantees of Lockheed's financial condition and capacity to follow through with the contract.[172] These were stiff conditions.[173]

From 3rd to 4th March, initial negotiations between Haughton and representatives of the British government took place. On the afternoon of 3rd March, Carrington first presented the rather severe proposals outlined at the Cabinet meeting in February. First, he accepted that the UK government would finance additional development costs of up to £60 million. But he also indicated that Lockheed would have to pay even more in this area. Second, he stressed that Rolls-Royce (1971) Ltd., the name of the nationalised successor company to Rolls-Royce, would jointly operate the RB211 project with Lockheed. Profits and losses would be pooled between the two companies. Third, the price per engine had risen to £140,000, making a total of £91 million for 646 bases. Fourth, both sides would provide certain guarantees around their financial solidity and capacity to carry out the plan. Fifth, the penalty for delivery delays in the original contract would be null and void.[174]

Haughton rather diplomatically described these proposals as "very difficult".[175] They represented an additional, objectionable financial burden for Lockheed. The engine price of £140,000 was unrealistic, and would increase the price per aircraft to around $1 million. These costs were exacerbated by a depreciation of the pound sterling in 1967. This resulted in a stabilisation of the pound–dollar exchange rate at around £1 = $2.4. Consequently, three RB211 valued at £140,000 each totalled around $1 million. Lockheed was prepared to pay up to £42,000 per engine – a difference in valuation of almost £100,000. The prospect of a joint company operating the RB211 project was also unacceptable. The airlines would not trust such a company, while the banks would almost certainly cut their losses and extend no further credit to Lockheed. Lastly, Haughton pointed out the virtual impossibility of securing a guarantee from the US government or the banks to ensure the completion of the TriStar project.[176]

Carrington went back to the Cabinet on 18th March with a renewed plan. The initial meeting with Haughton, it seemed, had not softened the British position.

Transatlantic rescue of Rolls-Royce, 1967–71   165

Carrington accepted that the British government was responsible for all additional costs necessary in order to achieve a thrust of 42,000 lbs. But he continued to insist that Lockheed bear a price per engine of £150,000, and that any contractual financial penalties for lateness of delivery be waived. Moreover, Carrington still sought a debt guarantee for Lockheed from US banks or even the government. This last condition was decisive; without it, the risk of failure of the project and the bankruptcy of Lockheed would be transferred to the British government.[177]

These tense negotiations continued throughout February and March 1971. Furthermore, even as negotiations with the Heath government were on-going, Lockheed opened talks with the customer airlines (TWA, Eastern Air Lines, Delta Airlines, Air Canada) about the price and delivery date of the RB211-fitted TriStar, and with US banks over a new and sizeable loan. A compromise over the engine price was eventually reached. However, there was deadlock with respect to a debt guarantee from US banks or from the Nixon administration.

Guaranteed problems

Heath still wanted the Nixon administration to guarantee the loan given to Lockheed by US banks. This was the topic of another conversation between Connally and Cromer on 22nd March. Cromer pointed out that, should Lockheed fail, then the British state was liable for around £200 million, including a total of £100 million in R&D expenses. Connally conceded that US banks would not make any guarantees without the backing of the US government. The question, however, centred on which government agency was actually responsible for providing such guarantees. Connally suggested that no single agency had such authority, and that the President would have to give it the green light. Indeed, even with Presidential backing, congressional authorisation would still be necessary.[178]

On 25th March, Carrington lead a negotiating team to Washington to meet with Haughton and Connally. At the first meeting with Haughton, Carrington first suggested a lowering of the production price increase from £97 million (this had already risen again from £91 million on 4th March) to £80 million (which worked out at around £124,000 per engine). Haughton, however, said that raising the total price by £80 million would render the aircraft uncompetitive. He suggested that airlines should be quoted a price of around a ceiling of £81,000 per engine, at a total cost of £50–60 million, with a total production batch of around 555 engines.[179]

On the same day, Carrington met Connally, who revealed that he was making every effort to obtain legislative authority over a congressional guarantee for the TriStar plan. Peter Rawlinson, Attorney General, pointed out that the British government was willing to support Rolls-Royce (1971) Ltd.; if the US government was ready to offer similar backing to Lockheed, then US banks would prop up the TriStar plan.[180]

Carrington then proceeded to suggest that the two key issues – over the engine price, and over government guarantees – should be considered as a single

166 US–European airliner projects, 1968–82

problematique. He reiterated the Heath Cabinet's position that no engine price would be agreed without the appropriate guarantees from Washington. Connally accepted, in principle, that the TriStar project could not be brought to completion without the support of the US government. Washington would have to guarantee $250–300 million in loans in order to persuade the banks to extend Lockheed's lending from $350 million to $500 million.[181]

At this point, Connally repeated his assertion that both Presidential and Congressional approval would be needed for such a guarantee. The priority, he insisted, was that the UK government and Lockheed agree on an engine price. This would allow Lockheed to quote prices to airlines and provide plausible projections to the banks. After Lockheed had reached a satisfactory agreement with these parties, the US government would be able to work with Congress on putting together a guarantee.[182]

On 29th March, Carrington communicated the results of this meeting to the British Cabinet. He was now convinced that Lockheed's reverse proposal for engine prices – £50–60 million – was their last offer. The manufacturer, he contended, could not draw on any further reserves of cash; and anyway, a higher price than this would make the TriStar uncompetitive against the DC-10.[183]

Carrington then broached the increasingly painful question of a government guarantee for Lockheed's loans. He expressed some confidence that Connally would be able to successfully pressure the US banking group into increasing Lockheed lending from $350 million to $500 million. Carrington also hoped that Connally would secure presidential and congressional backing for an official guarantee of Lockheed's loans, giving banks the confidence to lend further. The upshot of all this was that any new agreement between Lockheed and the British government would be underwritten by the American government. This was about as secure as any financial transaction could get and, from a British point of view, would totally eliminate any element of risk.[184]

Carrington thus pressed Heath to accept Lockheed's final offer on the engine price subject to a guarantee from the US government. Heath concluded that a rejection of Lockheed's latest proposal would have serious consequences. There was, he believed, no better option than the one Carrington had carved out in Washington.[185] Later that day, in a telephone meeting with Cromer, Carrington conveyed British government acceptance of Lockheed's revised proposal to increase the engine price by £50 million – on the condition that a US government guarantee was forthcoming.[186] But there were still many hurdles to be jumped through.

Hurdles in Washington

On 6th April, Connally informed The Bankers Trust and the Bank of America about Lockheed's financing issues. The bank had already loaned $350 million to the manufacturer and was weighing an additional $150 million loan. Connally asked if a further $300–350 million loan would be possible. The bankers said that this would be subject to a guarantee from the US government. Before such a guarantee could be acquired, however, it was necessary for the customer airlines to order the TriStar in the face of rising engine prices. Once these conditions were met, Nixon's approval would surely be obtained.[187]

In mid-April, Connally constructed the following three-step plan for saving the TriStar project. First, an agreement would be reached on terms and conditions between Rolls-Royce (1971) Ltd. and Lockheed. Second, the banks would extend an additional $150 million loan *without* a guarantee from the US government and, once such a guarantee was obtained, would provide a further loan. Third, the airlines would commit to ordering the same number of machines they had already asked for, but at the new (higher) price.[188]

On 28th April, Carrington met with Haughton and asked about the progress of negotiations with banks and airlines. Haughton said that the banks had, indeed, agreed to a $50 million additional loan. Any more than this, however, required a government guarantee. Haughton expected this to be forthcoming, just as he expected TWA and Eastern Air Lines to agree to the new price-per unit. Delta Airlines would also sign if further loans were offered. Air Canada was a problem case because it had raised considerable concerns about the financial predicament of Rolls-Royce (1971) Ltd. But for now, this could be overlooked.[189]

On 5th May, further intensive negotiations took place in Washington between British and US officials. With these discussions concluded, Connally finally took the plunge and asked congressional approval for a debt guarantee of $250 million for Lockheed.[190] On 10th May, Carrington announced to the House of Commons that if the US Congress sanctioned a $250 million guarantee, and if the airlines agreed to the new terms, then the British government would make an analogous financial commitment to Rolls-Royce.[191] The wheels were now in motion. All eyes now turned to Congress.

And here there were problems. The deal was not to everybody's liking. In early May, GE began an offensive against the US government's debt guarantee. Nixon and Connally both received letters from the engine manufacturer which called for an "American solution"[192] to the crisis. If American engines were not being used, then why should the American Congress pick up the tab?[193]

On 4th June, the US bank group agreed to provide a new $250 million loan to Lockheed subject to a debt guaranteed by the US government. In effect, the government's guarantee would be the condition for $250 million in excess of the $400 million already loaned.[194] These were staggering sums, but the involvement of the US government (and its enormous reserves of cash) was decisive. The new loan effectively meant that Lockheed could now confidently raise the price of the RB211 engines and complete the contract with Rolls-Royce.

Strong criticism also came from Wright Patman, the Chairman of the House Committee on Banking and Currency, who asked why the US government should become embroiled in saving a specific (private) enterprise. William Proxmire, Senate Committee on Banking, Housing and Urban Affairs, opposed the bill for much the same reason.[195]

168   US–European airliner projects, 1968–82

It was against this background that the bill entered Congress. On 15th July, at a hearing of the House Committee on Banking and Currency, Moore insisted that "[n]o bank, no group of banks, no matter how large, could take such a risk"[196] – i.e. assume responsibility for the enormous aircraft industry. He urged that the bill be passed.[197] Decisively, in mid-July, Patman changed his position.[198] The consequences of Lockheed's bankruptcy would, he now felt, be catastrophic in terms of unemployment. He too urged that the bill be ratified. Ultimately, the debt guarantee bill made it through the House of Representatives on 30th July. It passed by a hair's breadth – 192 to 189 votes. Its passage through the Senate on 2nd August was even more nail biting – 49 to 48 votes.[199]

On 14th September, the new contract between Rolls-Royce (1971) Ltd. and Lockheed came into force.[200] Lockheed was now under the control of an Emergency Loan Guarantee Board composed of the Secretary of the Treasury, the Chairman of the Board of Governors of the Federal Reserve System and the Chairman of the Securities and Exchange Commission.[201] These were the three most significant economic entities in the US state. This position under the stewardship of the state was surely humbling for venerable institutions such as Lockheed and Rolls-Royce. But the crucial fact was that their bankruptcy had been averted.

Conclusion

As the 1960s became the 1970s, the British aerospace industry was still trying to ride two horses. British co-operation with the French and Germans on the European Airbus Consortium was a clear attempt to break the monopoly on widebody airliners operated by US manufacturers. And yet, at the same time, the British were endeavouring to power the American-produced Lockheed TriStar with a Rolls-Royce RB211 engine. Indeed, once Rolls secured the TriStar order in March 1968, this dilemma seemingly became a moot point. The British government promptly withdrew from the apparently much less lucrative European Airbus project.

Ironically, however, it was precisely this neglect of continental Europe which resulted in Lockheed–Rolls-Royce ceding the European long-range wide-body market to McDonnell–GE. The long-term result of this was a profound liquidity crisis within both Lockheed and Rolls. Only an extraordinary intervention by government and financial sectors on both sides of the Atlantic ensured that the catastrophic bankruptcy of both companies was averted.

In retrospect, the UK's withdrawal from the European Airbus in April 1969 signalled a watershed moment in Britain's flirtation with European collaboration. The Wilson government, armed with the Plowden Report and bewitched by the vision of a "European Technological Community", had been a keen proponent of such collaboration. At the beginning of the 1970s, however, this vision seemed increasingly fanciful. That said, Rolls-Royce's liquidity crisis showed that, even though the big money seemed to be in the United States, bad things happened when Britain tried to turn its back on the continent completely. The

Transatlantic rescue of Rolls-Royce, 1967–71   169

dawning of a new decade had not resolved the British dilemma, which remained as acute as ever.

During the 1970s, the Airbus was not the only challenge to US hegemony in aerospace touted by the Europeans – including their reluctant British partners. Chapter 8 examines another such challenge: the Anglo–French Concorde, a significant civil aircraft project which co-existed alongside the wide-body initiatives that have been the subject of this chapter.

Notes

1 Newhouse (1982, p. 126).
2 *Fortune*, June 1971, p. 68.
3 Owen (1999, p. 318).
4 Hayward (1983, p. 91).
5 Johnman and Lynch (2006, p. 40).
6 Thornton (1995, p. 42).
7 Lynn ([1995] 1998, p. 103).
8 Hayward (1983, pp. 78–79).
9 Newhouse (1982, pp. 120–22); Aris (2002, p. 3).
10 Department of Trade and Industry, *Rolls-Royce Limited, Investigation under Section 165(a)(i) of the Companies Act 1948, Report by R A MacCrindle P Godfrey FCA* (London, HMSO, 1973), para. 200.
11 Department of Trade and Industry, *Rolls-Royce Limited, Investigation under Section 165(a)(i) of the Companies Act 1948, Report by R A MacCrindle P Godfrey FCA* (London, HMSO, 1973), paras. 197–201.
12 Department of Trade and Industry, *Rolls-Royce Limited, Investigation under Section 165(a)(i) of the Companies Act 1948, Report by R A MacCrindle P Godfrey FCA* (London, HMSO, 1973), p. 19 of Appendix 11.
13 TNA AVIA65/2007, Rolls-Royce to Frederick Mulley, 17th February 1966; Hayward (1986, pp. 129).
14 Hayward (1986, pp. 128–29).
15 TNA AVIA65/2007, Denning Pearson to Frederick Mulley, Minister of Aviation, 17th February 1966.
16 TNA PREM13/1936, Aero Engines, Frederick Mulley to Prime Minister, 29th June 1966.
17 Pugh (2001, p. 102).
18 TNA CAB129/128, C (67)30th, The Airbus, Memorandum by Minister of Technology, 14th March 1967.
19 TNA PREM13/1939, Airbus Discussions in Paris on 9th May, 12th May 1967.
20 TNA PREM13/1939, Airbus Discussions in Paris on 9th May, 12th May 1967; Lynn ([1995] 1998, p. 105); *AWST*, 15th May 1967, p. 31.
21 Eddy et al. (1976, p. 68); Newhouse (1982, p. 141).
22 Eddy et al. (1976, pp. 66–67).
23 Newhouse (1982, p. 149).
24 Hayward (1983, p. 88). Department of Trade and Industry Investigation Report found "no evidence" that during this period the main board of Rolls-Royce sought to evaluate the possible financial risks inherent the proposed RB211/207 dual programme (Department of Trade and Industry, *Rolls-Royce Limited, Investigation under Section 165(a)(i) of the Companies Act 1948, Report by R A MacCrindle P Godfrey FCA* (London, HMSO, 1973), para. 230).
25 Reed (1973, p. 128).

170 *US–European airliner projects, 1968–82*

26 Department of Trade and Industry, *Rolls-Royce Limited, Investigation under Section 165(a)(i) of the Companies Act 1948, Report by R A MacCrindle P Godfrey FCA* (London, HMSO, 1973), para. 220.

27 TNA PREM13/1939, Airbus, to the Minister of Technology, 26th July 1967; Gardner (1981, pp. 168–69); Hayward (1983, p. 76).

28 TNA CAB134/2609, European Airbus, AI (68)2, Memorandum by the Minister of Technology, 24th May 1968.

29 TNA PREM13/1939, Airbus, 26th July 1967. In mid-1967, BAC, which was not named a European Airbus contractor by the British government, started marketing the BAC2-11, the successor to the successful BAC1-11. TNA T225/3163, Benn to M.J. Chamant, 14th September 1967; TNA T225/3163, Airbus, 20th September 1967; Hayward (1983, pp. 85–86); *AWST*, 2nd October 1967, p. 30.

30 TNA CAB128/42, CC (67)70th, 14th December 1967.

31 TNA CAB129/134, C (67)191st, British European Re-equipment, Memorandum by the Minister of Technology, 12th December 1967; TNA CAB128/42, CC (67) 70th, 14th December 1967; Gardner (1981, pp. 170–71).

32 Department of Trade and Industry, *Rolls-Royce Limited, Investigation under Section 165(a)(i) of the Companies Act 1948, Report by R A MacCrindle P Godfrey FCA* (London, HMSO, 1973), para. 243.

33 *AWST*, 8th April 1968, p. 34.

34 TNA PREM13/1936, Notes of meeting held at the Cabinet Office, S.W.1., at 10:30 a.m. on 25th January 1968.

35 TNA T225/3438, Washington to Foreign Office, 14th February 1968; TNA T225/ 3438, Washington to Foreign Office, 6th March 1968.

36 When American Airlines ordered the DC-10, it did not specify the engine, the GE CF6 or the Rolls-Royce RB211, for the DC-10. *AWST*, 26th February 1968, pp. 26–29; TNA T225/3438, Foreign Office to Washington, 19th February 1969; Department of Trade and Industry, *Rolls-Royce Limited, Investigation under Section 165(a)(i) of the Companies Act 1948, Report by R A MacCrindle P Godfrey FCA* (London, HMSO, 1973), para. 247.

37 West (2001, p. 70).

38 *AWST*, 8th April 1968, p. 34.

39 Department of Trade and Industry, *Rolls-Royce Limited, Investigation under Section 165(a)(i) of the Companies Act 1948, Report by R A MacCrindle P Godfrey FCA* (London, HMSO, 1973), para. 243.

40 Department of Trade and Industry, *Rolls-Royce Limited, Investigation under Section 165(a)(i) of the Companies Act 1948, Report by R A MacCrindle P Godfrey FCA* (London, HMSO, 1973), para. 243.

41 *AWST*, 26th February 1968, pp. 26–29; *AWST*, 29th April 1968, p. 30; Newhouse (1982, pp. 153–54); Stonehouse (1975, p. 75). Lazard and Rothschild organised the Air Holdings deal (TNA T225/3438, Foreign Office to Washington, 15th February 1968; TNA T225/3438, R.B.211, I.P. Bancroft, 15th February 1968).

42 *AWST*, 18th March 1968, p. 325.

43 Newhouse (1982, p. 155); Eddy et al. (1976, p. 78).

44 Eddy et al. (1976, pp. 78–79).

45 Eddy et al. (1976, p. 79).

46 Eddy et al. (1976, p. 80).

47 Newhouse (1982, p. 156).

48 *AWST*, 29th April 1968, p. 34; 6th May 1968, pp. 39–40.

49 Department of Trade and Industry, *Rolls-Royce Limited, Investigation under Section 165(a)(i) of the Companies Act 1948, Report by R A MacCrindle P Godfrey FCA* (London, HMSO, 1973), para. 334.

50 762 HC Deb., 1st April 1968, col. 45.

51 Hayward (1983, p. 92).

Transatlantic rescue of Rolls-Royce, 1967–71   171

52 Aris (2002, p. 33).
53 Aris (2002, p. 34).
54 Aris (2002, p. 37).
55 TNA CAB129/138, C(68)91st, 29th July 1968; *AWST*, 17th June 1968, p. 29.
56 *AWST*, 12th August 1968, p. 46.
57 *AWST*, 12th August 1968, p. 46.
58 *AWST*, 29th July 1968, p. 29; Hayward (1983, p. 92).
59 Aris (2002, pp. 37–38); Magaziner and Patinkin (1989, pp. 240–41).
60 This "stretched" version of the RB211 was later offered by Rolls-Royce to Lockheed for the long-range version of the TriStar. (TNA CAB129/141, C(69)28th, 17th March 1969.)
61 TNA T225/3258, European Airbus: Draft Statement for SEP Committee 9th December 1968 by Minister of Technology; TNA AVIA63/159, Airbus Directing Committee: Minutes of the Meeting with the Associated Contractors in London on 10th December 1968.
62 775 HC Deb., 12th December 1968, col. 203.
63 TNA T225/3166, Technological Collaboration with Germany in Civil aircraft, 16th January 1968.
64 *AWST*, 27th January 1969, p. 30; TNA FCO46/410, Bonn to Foreign and Commonwealth Office, 22nd January 1969.
65 TNA T225/3166, (b) Civil aircraft; TNA T225/3166, Bonn to Foreign and Commonwealth Office, 5th February 1969.
66 TNA T225/3166, Record of a Meeting between the Prime Minister and the Federal German Chancellor at the Federal Chancellery, Bonn, at 10 a.m. on Thursday, 13th February 1969.
67 TNA T225/3166, Record of a Meeting between the Prime Minister and the Federal German Chancellor at the Federal Chancellery, Bonn, at 10 a.m. on Thursday, 13th February 1969.
68 TNA PREM13/2484, Paris to Foreign and Commonwealth Office, 15th March 1969.
69 TNA CAB129/141, C (69)28th, 17th March 1969; TNA CAB128/44, CC (69) 14th, 25th March 1969.
70 TNA CAB128/44, CC (69)14th, 25th March 1969.
71 TNA T225/3259, Airbus Tripartite Meeting 10th April 1969; TNA FCO46/413, Minute of a Meeting Between the British, German and French Ministers Held in London on 10th April 1969.
72 Lynn ([1995] 1998, p. 108); TNA T225/3442, Bonn to Foreign and Commonwealth Office, 29th November 1969.
73 Hayward (1983, p. 92).
74 TNA CAB128/44, CC (69)14th, 25th March 1969.
75 TNA PREM13/1939, Airbus Discussions in Paris on 9th May, 12th May 1967.
76 TNA T225/3441, RB211-Applications in Developed Versions in Lockheed Trijet and A300B.
77 TNA FCO70/18, Washington to Bonn, 24th June 1969; TNA FCO70/18, Commercial – In Confidence, B.V. Bull, 23rd June 1969; Hayward (1986, p. 130).
78 TNA FCO70/18, Commercial – In Confidence, B.V. Bull, 23rd June 1969.
79 TNA FCO70/18, Lockheed, The Airbus and The RB211, 9th July 1969.
80 TNA FCO70/18, Lockheed, The Airbus and The RB211, 9th July 1969.
81 TNA T225/3442, RB.211, F. R. Barratt, 8th August 1969; TNA FCO70/18, Commercial – In Confidence, B.V. Bull, 23rd June 1969; TNA FCO70/18, Washington to Foreign and Commonwealth Office, 24th June 1969; TNA FCO70/18, Note of a Meeting in Millbank Tower on Wednesday, 9th July 1969.
82 TNA T225/3441, Stretched RB211, 5th August 1969.
83 TNA T225/3441, Stretched RB211, 5th August 1969.

172 *US–European airliner projects, 1968–82*

84 TNA T225/3442, The Stretched RB211 (RB211–50 Series). The motivation behind Germany's support for Rolls-Royce was mainly political in that British participation in the European Airbus project led to British commitment to Europe (Aris (2002, p. 46)).

85 TNA T225/3260, Bonn to Foreign and Commonwealth Office, 6th September 1969.

86 TNA T225/3260, Bonn to Foreign and Commonwealth Office, 6th September 1969; TNA T225/3443, Anglo–German Offset – Article 4, Ann Toulmin, 11th February 1970.

87 TNA T225/3260, Bonn to Foreign and Commonwealth Office, 6th September 1969.

88 TNA FCO46/413, L. Williams to F. R. Barratt, 10th October 1969.

89 TNA FCO46/413, L. Williams to F. R. Barratt, 10th October 1969.

90 P&W withdrew from the competition because of price. TNA T225/3260, Bonn to Foreign and Commonwealth Office, 6th September 1969; TNA FCO46/413, Bonn to Foreign and Commonwealth Office, 21st October 1969; TNA FCO46/413, Bonn to Foreign and Commonwealth Office, 26th November 1969.

91 TNA T225/3442, OPD (69)59th, J. F. Slater, 6th November 1969.

92 NARA RG59, CF 1967–69, Box 757, FN12 GER W, Rogers to American Embassy Bonn, 9th September 1969.

93 TNA T225/3443, Anglo–German Offset – Article 4, Ann Toulmin, 11th February 1970.

94 TNA FCO46/413, Bonn to Foreign and Commonwealth Office, 26th November 1969; NARA RG59, CF 1967–69, Box 757, FN12 GER W, Rogers to American Embassy Bonn, 9th September,1969. Boeing pushed the Department of State to oppose the use of the Anglo–American offset fund. This might be because, for Boeing, Lufthansa had been a major customer.

95 Aris (2002, p. 47).

96 Hayward (1986, p. 126).

97 Endress (1999, p. 124); Garvin (1998, pp. 56–57).

98 Endress (1999, pp. 66, 89).

99 Department of Trade and Industry, *Rolls-Royce Limited, Investigation under Section 165(a)(i) of the Companies Act 1948, Report by R A MacCrindle P Godfrey FCA* (London, HMSO, 1973), para. 415.

100 Department of Trade and Industry, *Rolls-Royce Limited, Investigation under Section 165(a)(i) of the Companies Act 1948, Report by R A MacCrindle P Godfrey FCA* (London, HMSO, 1973), para. 417, appendix 11; TNA CAB134/3447, Events Leading up to £60 million support for Rolls-Royce, 14th May 1971; TNA CAB128/47, CM (70)30th, 15th October 1970.

101 TNA CAB128/47, CM (70)30th, 15th October 1970.

102 TNA CAB129/152, CP (70)74th, Airbuses and the RB211-61 Engine, 8th October 1970.

103 TNA CAB129/152, CP (70)74th, Airbuses and the RB211-61 Engine, 8th October 1970.

104 TNA CAB128/47, CM (70)30th, 15th October 1970.

105 TNA CAB128/47, CM (70)31st, 19th October 1970.

106 TNA CAB128/47, CM (70)31st, 19th October 1970.

107 The Chancellor of Exchequer, *New Policies for Public Spending*, Cmnd. 4515 (London, HMSO, 1970).

108 TNA CAB128/47, CM (70)31st, 19th October 1970.

109 Cain and Hopkins (2002, p. 122).

110 TNA CAB128/47, CM (70)31st, 19th October 1970.

111 TNA CAB128/47, CM (70)31st, 19th October 1970.

112 TNA CAB128/47, CM (70)31st, 19th October 1970.

Transatlantic rescue of Rolls-Royce, 1967–71 173

113 TNA CAB128/47, CM (70)33rd, 27th October 1970.
114 TNA CAB128/47, CM (70)33rd, 27th October 1970.
115 TNA PREM15/3, Note of a Meeting at 10 Downing Street on Wednesday, 28th October 1970 at 4.30 p.m.
116 TNA PREM15/3, Note of a Meeting at 10 Downing Street on Wednesday, 28th October 1970 at 4.30 p.m.
117 TNA PREM15/3, Note of a Meeting at 10 Downing Street on Wednesday, 28th October 1970 at 4.30 p.m.
118 TNA PREM15/3, Note of a Meeting at 10 Downing Street on Wednesday, 28th October 1970 at 4.30 p.m.
119 TNA, CAB128/47, CM (70)35th, 3rd November 1970; Department of Trade and Industry, *Rolls-Royce Ltd and the RB211 Aero-Engine*, Cmnd. 4860 (London, HMSO, 1972), Annex C.
120 TNA, CAB134/3447, Events leading up to £60 million support for Rolls-Royce, 14th May 1971.
121 Department of Trade and Industry, *Rolls-Royce Ltd and the RB211 Aero-Engine*, Cmnd. 4860 (London, HMSO, 1972), para. 10.
122 TNA CAB129/152, CP (70)74th, Airbuses and the RB211–61 Engine, Note by Secretary of Cabinet, 8th October 1970; TNA CAB128/47, CM (70)42nd, 1st December 1970.
123 Department of Trade and Industry, *Rolls-Royce Limited, Investigation under Section 165(a)(i) of the Companies Act 1948, Report by R A MacCrindle P Godfrey FCA* (London, HMSO, 1973), para. 439.
124 Department of Trade and Industry, *Rolls-Royce Limited, Investigation under Section 165(a)(i) of the Companies Act 1948, Report by R A MacCrindle P Godfrey FCA* (London, HMSO, 1973), para. 442.
125 Department of Trade and Industry, *Rolls-Royce Limited, Investigation under Section 165(a)(i) of the Companies Act 1948, Report by R A MacCrindle P Godfrey FCA* (London, HMSO, 1973), para. 451.
126 Department of Trade and Industry, *Rolls-Royce Limited, Investigation under Section 165(a)(i) of the Companies Act 1948, Report by R A MacCrindle P Godfrey FCA* (London, HMSO, 1973), paras. 452–53.
127 Department of Trade and Industry, *Rolls-Royce Limited, Investigation under Section 165(a)(i) of the Companies Act 1948, Report by R A MacCrindle P Godfrey FCA* (London, HMSO, 1973), para. 464.
128 Department of Trade and Industry, *Rolls-Royce Limited, Investigation under Section 165(a)(i) of the Companies Act 1948, Report by R A MacCrindle P Godfrey FCA* (London, HMSO, 1973), para. 467.
129 Department of Trade and Industry, *Rolls-Royce Limited, Investigation under Section 165(a)(i) of the Companies Act 1948, Report by R A MacCrindle P Godfrey FCA* (London, HMSO, 1973), para. 474.
130 Department of Trade and Industry, *Rolls-Royce Limited, Investigation under Section 165(a)(i) of the Companies Act 1948, Report by R A MacCrindle P Godfrey FCA* (London, HMSO, 1973), para. 475.
131 TNA T225/3675, Rolls-Royce; TNA CAB130/504, GEN16(71)1st, Rolls Royce, Memorandum of the Minister of Aviation Supply, 28th January 1971.
132 TNA PREM15/228, Rolls-Royce Limited Minutes of a Meeting of Directors in London on 26th January 1971.
133 TNA CAB130/504 GEN16(71)1st, Memorandum by Minister of Aviation, 28th January 1971; TNA CAB130/504, GEN17(71)1st, 29th January 1971.
134 *Business Week*, 26th June 1971, pp. 70–72; Rice (1971, p. 185).
135 Rice (1971, pp. 193–94).
136 Hartung (2011, p. 97); West (2001, p. 110).
137 Rice (1971, p. 194).

174 *US–European airliner projects, 1968–82*

138 TNA PREM15/229, Telephone Conversation between the Prime Minister and Mr. Kissinger at 2.30 p.m. on Monday, 1st February 1971.
139 Eddy et al. (1976, p. 101).
140 TNA PREM15/229, Rolls-Royce and Lockheed: Summary Note of a Meeting at 4.30 p.m. on 2nd February 1971.
141 West (2001, p. 116).
142 TNA CAB128/49, CM (71)7th, Annex I Report by Sir Henry Benson. Read to, and accepted by, both the Rolls-Royce Board and Lockheed Representatives, 3rd February 1971.
143 TNA CAB128/49, CM (71)7th, 3rd February 1971.
144 TNA CAB128/49, CM (71)7th, 3rd February 1971.
145 TNA CAM128/49, CM (71)7th, 3rd February 1971.
146 TNA PREM15/229, Record of Telephone Conversation between the Prime Minister and President Nixon on Wednesday, 3rd February 1971 at 12.15 p.m.
147 TNA PREM15/229, Record of Telephone Conversation between the Prime Minister and President Nixon on Wednesday, 3rd February 1971 at 12.15 p.m.
148 TNA CAB128/49, CM (71)7th, 3rd February 1971.
149 TNA PREM15/229, Note for the Record, 5th February 1971.
150 TNA PREM15/229, Note for the Record, 5th February 1971.
151 Eddy et al. (1976, pp. 102–3).
152 TNA CAB129/155, CP (71)18th, 5th February 1971.
153 TNA PREM15/229, Note for the Record, 11th February 1971.
154 TNA PREM15/230, Record of Conversation between Mr. Robert Armstrong and Sir Kenneth Keith at 2.45 p.m. on Friday, 12th February.
155 TNA PREM15/230, Record of Conversation between Mr. Robert Armstrong and Sir Kenneth Keith at 2.45 p.m. on Friday, 12th February.
156 TNA PREM15/230, Record of Conversation between Mr. Robert Armstrong and Sir Kenneth Keith at 2.45 p.m. on Friday, 12th February.
157 TNA PREM15/230, Record of Conversation between Mr. Robert Armstrong and Sir Kenneth Keith at 2.45 p.m. on Friday, 12th February.
158 West (2001, pp. 121, 123–25).
159 West (2001, pp. 129–32).
160 NARA RG59, E(A1)5603, Box 1, AV Rolls Royce 1971–1972, Subject: Rolls Royce Problem, 16th February 1971.
161 NARA RG59, E(A1)5603, Box 1, AV Rolls Royce 1971–1972, Subject: Rolls Royce Problem, 16th February 1971.
162 NARA RG59, E(A1)5603, Box 1, AV Rolls Royce 1971–1972, Subject: Rolls Royce Problem, 16th February 1971.
163 NARA RG59, E(A1)5603, Box 1, AV Rolls Royce 1971–1972, Subject: Rolls Royce Problem, 16th February 1971.
164 TNA PREM15/230, Personal from the Prime Minister.
165 TNA T225/3677, Note for Record, 19th February 1971.
166 TNA T225/3677, Note for Record, 19th February 1971.
167 TNA T225/3677, Note for Record, 19th February 1971.
168 TNA T225/3677, Note for Record, 19th February 1971.
169 Department of Trade and Industry, *Rolls-Royce Ltd and the RB211 Aero-Engine*, Cmnd. 4860 (London, HMSO, 1972), para. 39 (https://www.legislation.gov.uk/ukpga/1971/9/introduction/enacted [accessed 13.8.2020]).
170 TNA CAB128/49, CM (71)11th, 25th February 1971.
171 TNA CAB128/49, CM (71)11th, 25th February 1971.
172 TNA CAB129/155, CP (71)24th, Aircraft Industry: The RB-211, Note by the Secretary of State for Defence, 24th February 1971; TNA CAB128/49, CM (71) 11th, 25th February 1971.
173 TNA CAB128/49, CM (71)11th, 25th February 1971.

Transatlantic rescue of Rolls-Royce, 1967–71 175

174 TNA CAB134/3446, Record of a Meeting with Representatives of the Lockheed Corporation at 1530 hours 3rd March 1971.

175 TNA CAB134/3446, Record of a Meeting with Representatives of the Lockheed Corporation at 1530 hours 3rd March 1971.

176 TNA CAB134/3446, Record of a meeting with representatives of the Lockheed Corporation at 1530 hours 3rd March 1971; TNA PREM15/230, RB211 Engine: British Proposal, 4th March 1971; TNA PREM15/230, Note of a Meeting at 10 Downing Street, S.W.1 on Thursday, 4th March 1971, at 2.15 p.m.; TNA CAB128/49, CM (71)12th, 4th March 1971.

177 TNA CAB128/49, CM (71)15th, 18th March 1971.

178 TNA PREM15/231, From Cromer, 22nd March 1971.

179 TNA PREM15/231, Meeting of the Defence Secretary and the Attorney General with the Lockheed Corporation in Washington, 25th March 1971.

180 TNA PREM15/231, Meeting of the Defence Secretary and the Attorney General with the US Secretary of the Treasury in Washington, 25th March 1971.

181 TNA PREM15/231, Meeting of the Defence Secretary and the Attorney General with the US Secretary of the Treasury in Washington, 25th March 1971.

182 TNA PREM15/231, Meeting of the Defence Secretary and the Attorney General with the US Secretary of the Treasury in Washington, 25th March 1971.

183 TNA PREM15/232, Record of Telephone Conversation between the Defence Secretary & Lord Cromer, 29th March 1971.

184 TNA PREM15/232, Record of Telephone Conversation between the Defence Secretary & Lord Cromer, 29th March 1971.

185 TNA CAB128/49, CM (71)18th, 29th March 1971.

186 TNA PREM15/232, Record of Telephone Conversation between the Defence Secretary & Lord Cromer, 29th March 1971.

187 NARA RG59, E(A1)5603, Box 1 AV Rolls-Royce 1971–1972, Memorandum for the Files – #9, Subject: Rolls-Royce Problem, 8th April 1971.

188 TNA PREM15/232, Sir Alec Douglas-Home to Washington, 15th April 1971; TNA PREM15/232, Cromer to FCO, 19th April 1971.

189 TNA T225/3559, Note of Meeting of the Defence Secretary and the Minister for Aerospace with the Chairman of the Lockheed Aircraft Corporation, 28th April 1971.

190 TNA T225/3687, Washington to FCO, 5th May 1971.

191 318 HC Deb., 10th May 1971, cols. 622–23.

192 TNA T225/3687, Franklin to FCO, 5th May 1971.

193 *Congressional Quarterly Almanac*, 92nd Congress, 1st Session, 1971, v. 27 (Washington, Congressional Quarterly Inc., 1972), p. 154.

194 TNA T225/3691, Summary of Terms of Proposed Bank Loan to Lockheed Corporation.

195 *Congressional Quarterly Almanac*, 92nd Congress, 1st Session, 1971, v. 27 (Washington, Congressional Quarterly Inc., 1972), p. 152).

196 *Congressional Quarterly Almanac*, 92nd Congress, 1st Session, 1971, v. 27 (Washington, Congressional Quarterly Inc., 1972), p. 154).

197 *Congressional Quarterly Almanac*, 92nd Congress, 1st Session, 1971, v. 27 (Washington, Congressional Quarterly Inc., 1972), p. 154).

198 TNA T225/3691, Cromer to FCO, 16th July 1971. Young (2000, p. 262).

199 *Congressional Quarterly Almanac*, 92nd Congress, 1st Session, 1971, v. 27 (Washington, Congressional Quarterly Inc., 1972), pp. 152, 161).

200 Ingells (1973, p. 213).

201 PL 92–70, §2, 9th August 1971, 85 Stat. 178 (https://www.law.cornell.edu/uscode/text/15/1841 [accessed 21.5.2021]).

8   Trapped in a loveless marriage
The Anglo–French Concorde crisis of 1974

Introduction

The term "Concorde fallacy" was coined by the famous British biologist Richard Dawkins to describe a curious subset of animal behaviour. This behaviour comprises continued heavy investment in particular projects or courses of action not because of expected future returns, but purely on the basis of previous heavy investment. The animal continues to expend considerable effort in a given undertaking even though there is no realistic chance of gaining anything from it. Instead, it seems, the prospect of quitting without gains appears as too distressing, given the amount of already-expended effort. And so the animal ploughs on in a senseless endeavour, unable to face the truth of the futility and waste it has engaged in.

Dawkins derived this term from a development in the British aviation industry during the 1960s and 1970s – the UK's continued involvement in the catastrophic Anglo–French Concorde project.[1] At one point, Concorde had 74 options from an illustrious list of 16 major airlines which included BOAC and Air France as well as Pan Am. At the time of its cancellation, it was little more than a source of protracted conflict between Britain and France, and was widely considered a complete commercial failure.

This chapter focuses on the doomed Concorde project, and on its diplomatic and economic implications. Why did this revolutionary aircraft technology not herald the age of SST in aviation? Why did successive British governments persist in this burgeoning commercial disaster? And how did these governments ultimately steel themselves and put the brakes on the whole project – a move which signalled the end of over a decade of Anglo–French aerospace co-operation?

Part of the answer is that Concorde was ahead of its time. It surely looked very impressive on the drawing board in the late 1950s and early 1960s. However, the aircraft that rolled off the assembly line in the 1970s was too noisy, too expensive and required too much fuel, in an era of extreme sensitivity around energy expenditure. As a result, the American Federal Aviation Administration (FAA) took a dim view of the aircraft's landing rights, which effectively prevented the model from selling on a global scale.

DOI: 10.4324/9781003127901-11

Trapped in a loveless marriage 177

The fact that these issues proved so important was, first, testament to the rise of an increasingly influential environmental movement across the West and in the United States itself. But Concorde's failure to acquire landing rights in the United States also reflected "a web of technical, legal, social, economic, and political issues" as Donald G. Agger,[2] the US Assistant Secretary of Transportation for International Affairs and Special Programs, has noted.[3] This chapter thus focuses on what might be termed the *supersonic politics* of the United States, Britain and France from the 1960s to the 1970s. It also examines how these politics impacted global co-operation in aircraft development over the long term, though the focus naturally lies chiefly on the British perspective.

Johnman and Lynch have extensively analysed the Anglo–French Treaty of 1962 (1962 Treaty), which set out a collaborative plan to develop a supersonic airliner. They have offered their own explanation for the long and apparently self-injurious British adherence to the project. First, they suggest that leading British politicians were initially convinced that cancellation would prove more expensive than continuing with the project. When it became obvious that this was not true, technological and political motives increasingly supplanted economic concerns.[4] By contrast, Annabelle May has suggested that Britain's support for the Concorde project was, from the very start, linked to largely non-economic criteria, such as short-term foreign policy goals and deeper-rooted British "delusions"[5] around its role and influence in the post-Suez world.[6]

Another key factor in the history of Concorde from the British side is that, from its inception in the early 1960s until its termination some ten years later, the project was at the mercy of repeated changes in government. This period was presided over by four different administrations: a Conservative government under Harold Macmillan, a Labour government under Harold Wilson, a second Conservative government led by Ted Heath, and finally the return of Wilson to Downing Street in 1974. Generally speaking, the Conservatives were sympathetic to the Concorde project, whereas Labour was much cooler (with the apparent exception of Tony Benn, Wilson's Minister of Technology). On the whole, Wilson's second government in particular had little enthusiasm for Concorde. This was to be expected because, by 1974, the project was saddled with a veritable litany of problems.

France, however, did not waiver from its dream. Until the bitter end, the French continued to push for the completion of the project as initially agreed upon. Indeed, they even tried to expand it. And so, like the monarchs of Medieval Europe, Britain and France found themselves trapped in a "loveless marriage of convenience". A key role in this loveless union was played by what might be considered the original marriage certificate. This took the form of a single treaty, first essayed in 1962.

The 1962 Treaty

The British took great pride in introducing the Comet, the world's first commercial jet aircraft, to the market in the early 1950s. This achievement seemingly

178 *US–European airliner projects, 1968–82*

cemented the British position as the undisputed leader in the field of civil aviation. Unfortunately, pride quickly turned to horror when approximately one-third of the Comet fleet was involved in a series of fatal accidents. Britain launched one of the first and most extensive accident investigations, which swiftly determined that metal fatigue was a significant factor in the accidents.

The demise of the Comet constituted a significant dent to British pride. It also represented a massive setback to the UK's aspirations to leadership in the global field of civil aviation. Despite this setback, in November 1956 the British turned their attention to an even more challenging and forward-thinking project – SST.[7] At this time, the US companies Boeing and Douglas had moved to the top of the civil aviation market with the 707 and DC-8. Macmillan's Conservative government was determined to counter this development. It funded a few select British companies with the objective of re-entering the civil aviation market.[8]

In the late 1950s, it was expected that SST technology would revolutionise air travel. British policymakers believed that this technology could provide the key to overtaking the United States. In September 1959, Duncan Sandys, Minister of Aviation, ordered SST prototypes from Bristol and Hawker Siddeley. Bristol's design was chosen and passed on to the BAC. This became the forerunner of Concorde.[9]

As they jockeyed for the sole lead in civil aviation, however, British decision-makers realised that they could not embark on an SST project alone: they needed a partner. Britain had initially hoped to work with the United States, so it approached the US government in 1959 with a plan to collaborate on SST development.[10] At a Cabinet meeting in July 1960, Prime Minister Harold Macmillan went so far as to authorise design studies for a Mach 2.2 supersonic airliner.[11]

From the perspective of the United States, however, SST was a coveted trophy of technological achievement which it intended to win alone. The United States was competing with the Soviets in this area, as the USSR started its own supersonic project – the Tu-144 – at around this time. Indeed, the United States had already set its sights on producing a much more ambitious Mach 3 SST. The Americans were thus inclined to go it alone with an all-American project. The British courtship of the Americans was in vain.[12]

France represented a second, and final, hope for international partnership. At the Paris Air Show of June 1961, Sud Aviation displayed a model of a Super-Caravelle, which was able to fly at supersonic speeds. After this air show, British and French designers and engineers embarked on intensive projects of technical communication, both in airframe and engines. However, these projects were bedevilled by technical problems, especially with respect to the airframe.[13]

At this point, political considerations came into play. The British government was mulling an application to the EEC. A joint British–French undertaking in SST might prove facilitative to this goal. From de Gaulle's perspective, a Franco–British partnership in SST would constitute an assertion of European technological superiority over the United States.[14] Indeed, the United States showed some degree of anxiety over this development. Eugene R. Black, the former US President of the World Bank and unofficial chairman of the American SST commission, attempted to persuade Julian Amery, British Minister of Aviation, not to embark on the Concorde project. Amery, however, also saw the connection between Concorde and a possible British accession to the EEC. This, he opined, was "really part and parcel of the same thing".[15]

It was against this background that Britain and France decided to move ahead with an SST project.[16] However, they took the telling step of protecting themselves and their interests by formalising the commercial agreement via an international contract. The Anglo–French MoU of 29th November 1962 was registered as a treaty at the United of Nations, enforceable by the International Court of Justice.[17] It was signed in 1962, creating a legal basis for Anglo–French SST development. It also added a further layer of protection from American pressure through the FAA's certification on Concorde, via its registration with the United Nations.[18] The 1962 Treaty marked the official beginning of the Anglo–French Concorde project. A glaring omission was the absence of a provision expressly permitting either party to withdraw.

Ultimately, Concorde was intended as a symbol of Anglo–French co-operation (and thus European prowess) in the field of advanced technology. This aircraft promised to hold its own, even against US aircraft. However, if the British hoped that participation in this project would bring immediate diplomatic rewards, they were to be sharply and swiftly disabused. In January 1963, just six weeks after the 1962 Treaty was signed, de Gaulle announced his veto of British entry into the EEC. He justified this with reference Britain's unpalatably close ties with the United States. This did not auger well for the Concorde project.

The international politics of SST

Juan Trippe, the chairman of Pan Am, had gained a reputation for making some courageous commercial decisions. He had effectively introduced jet air travel to commercial flights through his purchase of the 707/DC-8, as well as wide-body travel by buying the 747. He was now determined to take a similar step forward with SST. His strategy for encouraging American manufacturers to embark on the construction of an SST was to order Concorde. He had played a similar trick many years before, by ordering the Comet in an attempt to strong-arm Boeing into developing the 707. Trippe also knew that such a move would have an impact on President Kennedy, who was reputed to be ambivalent about the prospects of American SST.[19]

Trippe announced a Pan Am order of six Concordes on 5th June 1963 – the day Kennedy was due to give a statement on American SST. The President was understandably furious at this development. Nonetheless, Kennedy stated that the United States would embark on the construction of an SST: "This commitment, I believe, is essential to a strong and forward-looking Nation, and indicates the future of manned aircraft as we move into a missile age as well".[20]

Shortly after Kennedy's announcement, Trippe signed Pan Am up for 15 American SSTs at 1,800 miles per hour (Mach 2.4) with 200 passengers. Trippe

180   *US–European airliner projects, 1968–82*

had successfully hedged his bets between the United States and Europe, but he likely hoped that an American-built SST would be faster and larger than the European model. He envisioned that such technology would be readily available by the early 1970s.[21]

In August 1963, Kennedy formally appointed Eugene R. Black and Stanley de J. Osborne as special advisers on the financial aspects of the commercial SST programme. On 29th February 1964, Black and Osborne's report was made public by President Johnson. It stated:

> We recommend that the United States proceed with the Supersonic Transport program. It is in the national interest so to do, it is of great economic importance to the nation, and failure to do so might well leave our important airline and aircraft industries in potentially dangerous competitive situations.[22]

Black and Osborne did not believe that it was necessary for the United States to join the Anglo–French Concorde Consortium. They were convinced that the United States would be able to build a superior aircraft, which would be available within two to three years of the first Concorde deliveries. In the long-run, they were confident that the US SST could dominate the world market.[23] President Johnson apparently shared their confidence; he formed an Advisory Committee on Supersonic Transport, chaired by US Secretary of Defense Robert McNamara.[24]

It was in Spring 1964 when Concorde's cost escalation problems first began to emerge. Amery revealed a new cost estimation of £250 million, compared to £85 million in November 1962.[25] In the 1962 Treaty, the British share of the developmental costs was envisioned to be £80 million, on the principle of a 50–50 split with France. By 1964, this figure had risen to £140 million.[26] And yet the British and French were not the only ones who quickly ran into difficulties with the costs and technicalities of SST. The Americans were also soon confronted with the problem of the technology's extreme volume – the "sonic boom".

Against this background, the United States, Britain and France held a series of informal meetings on SST during 1964. The third of these took place in Paris in June of that year. One of the US representatives, Assistant Secretary Alexis Johnson, was given explicit direction by Dean Rusk, US Secretary of State, on how he should approach the talks. Rusk believed that the SST situation was "still fluid".[27] He advised Johnson to be "noncommittal on any possible U.S. collaboration with the Concorde program, hearing out the British and French without taking any particular position".[28] At the same time, however, Rusk advised Johnson "to avoid giving the impression that the door is already closed to U.S. collaboration".[29] Overall, Rusk believed that America's interests were best served by "[leaving] the issue open, pending further study here and further developments in the UK and France".[30] Evidently, there was still considerable doubt around SST technology even as late as the mid-1960s.

Trapped in a loveless marriage 181

In 1964, a General Election was held in Britain and was won by Labour. During the campaign, Labour had launched into a frontal assault against expensive "prestige projects" such as Concorde and the TSR-2.[31] On 24th October 1964, soon after moving into 10 Downing Street, Wilson sent a telegram to President Johnson. Wilson informed his opposite number that the British government was "communicating to the French Government their wish to urgently re-examine prestige project",[32] among which could be numbered Concorde. Wilson's goal was to immediately improve the British balance of payments and cut expenditure on items of low economic priority.

Trouble was brewing with the French, however. On 13th November, Charles Bohlen, US Ambassador to France, reported to the State Department that the British Ambassador had shared with him a message from French Prime Minister Georges Pompidou to Wilson: "Message stated in effect that since appears UK may not wish to go through with project French would appreciate yes or no answer on British intentions".[33] France, it seemed, might go ahead even without British involvement.

On 5th December, Hervé Alphand, French Ambassador to the United States, made several statements to US General Elwood Richard Quesada with respect to the SST project. He first conceded that the French were highly disturbed about Britain's apparent ambivalence over Concorde. Should the British pull out completely, he doubted that the French would continue alone. He also asked that the United States communicate directly with France about the SST, rather than using the British as an interminable interlocutor. He even hinted at possible American–French co-operation over SST.[34]

On 11th January 1965, a new Minister of Aviation, Roy Jenkins, secretly visited France for a discussion with Marc Jacquet, Minister of Public Works and Transport.[35] Jenkins later noted that this meeting was "not nearly as bad as I had feared".[36] Jacquet, he observed, was "even friendly throughout".[37] But this only served to raise Jenkins' suspicions. He knew that Najeeb Halaby, the US FAA administrator, planned to visit Paris on 11th–12th February. The possible subject of Halaby's visit might be American–French SST co-operation – with the penny-pinching British left out in the cold.[38]

On 19th January 1965, Jenkins informed David Bruce, US Ambassador to the UK, that the new Labour government's initial determination to cancel Concorde had been reversed after significant French political pressure.[39] Ten days later, Jenkins formally and publicly announced this intention.[40] At the same time, however, the US Embassy in London reported to the State Department that Jenkins had been "careful not to commit govt. on whether original program would or would not be maintained".[41] According to this report, the purpose of the British government was to "maintain flexibility to adjust course of action in light further discussions with French and possibly US".[42]

On 21st January, Jenkins appealed to Bruce that the NATO allies should try to minimise the economic pressures of a competitive struggle for dominance over SST. The US and European programmes should be staggered to avoid reciprocal

182 US–European airliner projects, 1968–82

pressure, with Britain planning to "reduce at least near term commitments".[43] Jenkins also called for additional research into SST's technical problems, especially the sonic boom.[44] The following day, Bruce relayed Jenkins' position to the State Department. SST, he contended, was not a mere aviation topic, but rather a question of national prestige. Jenkins questioned the wisdom of allowing the United States to slip too far behind its European partners (and rivals) in this area.[45]

From 2nd to 3rd April, Wilson and de Gaulle met to discuss Anglo–French aerospace co-operation. Wilson explained to the French President that the primary purpose of cancelling the TSR-2 was to release resources for Anglo–French projects. He insisted that these projects would in no way be negatively impacted by the British decision on the TSR-2.[46] Wilson's position was apparently not very gratifying to the US Department of Defense. This became clear from comments made by Henry J. Kuss Jr., Deputy Assistant Secretary of Defense for international security affairs and head of the ILN, at a meeting of the Plowden Committee on 15th May. Kuss stated in no uncertain terms that Britain should compete on the US market and warned that, "if [the UK collaborates] with the French, recognise the threat of U.S. competition, like on the Concorde. We might still undersell you because the U.S. defense budget is five times that of the U.K. plus France".[47]

The Plowden Report was due to be published in November 1965. On 22nd October, Bruce sent a telegram to the State Department which dealt explicitly with the impending report. His telegram made for uncomfortable reading in Washington. The main recommendation of the report, Bruce warned, was that co-operation between the UK and Europe should be deepened. It advised against extensive collaboration with the apparently more difficult Americans. And yet Bruce also observed that a "minority of the Plowden Committee does not support the conclusions of the majority".[48] He even predicted the possible release of a minority report calling for co-operation with the United States as well as the continent.[49]

The "minority" that Bruce had in mind was led by Aubrey Jones, the most ardent proponent of Anglo–American collaboration on the Plowden Committee. Bruce believed that the US Department of Defense economic study of SST (titled *The Limited Market for Concorde*) would dramatically expose the deficiencies in the Plowden Report's recommendations. This, he hoped, would strengthen the position of the pro-American minority.

On 11th November, Willis Armstrong, Minister for Economic Affairs at the Embassy in London, gave two copies of the US Department of Defense study report to Jenkins. Armstrong later observed that, in giving the report to Jenkins:

> ... we were not attempting to "shoot down the Concorde." I told him simply that the embassy had been acquainted with a study of SST problems being made by the Defence Department, and that we had asked for permission to give [it] to the British Government, whatever our authorities in Washington thought suitable, and this was the result.[50]

Trapped in a loveless marriage 183

Armstrong thought that Jenkins would pass the US Department of Defense report to the Plowden Committee.[51] Sure enough, when the report was finally published, it did not rule out the possibility of Anglo–American co-operation, even though it continued to prioritise collaboration with the French. None of this helped to remedy the increasing cloudiness and ambivalence that had descended upon Anglo–European aerospace co-operation in general and Concorde in particular.

The Benn/Chamant correspondence of 27th September 1968

The backdrop to these diplomatic machinations was the fact that Concorde was not getting any cheaper. Indeed, by mid-1966, the estimated cost of the project had risen to £250 million. Moreover, the prospect of a return after sales was very poor. This remained so even if the selling price of the aircraft were set at £6.5 million, with a sales forecast of 150 aircraft – optimistic figures, indeed.[52]

Before the scheduled London meeting in July 1966 between Wilson and Pompidou, the British Cabinet had to come to a consensus on the future of the project. This important meeting occurred on 30th June. Fred Mulley, Minister of Aviation, took the view that the 1962 Treaty effectively locked Britain into the project. He advocated for a £145 million, five-year development programme.[53] Similarly, in a paper given to the Cabinet on 27th June, Michael Stewart, Secretary of State for Foreign Affairs, emphasised the significant damage that a unilateral British withdrawal from the project might cause to European diplomatic relations.[54] Elwyn Jones, Attorney-General, echoed Mulley in offering a legalistic appraisal of the project. There was, he contended, no legally defensible way for Britain to withdraw. If it did so, the UK might face sanction from the International Court of Justice and be required to pay compensation to the French of around £140–200 million. This might enable France to complete the project without British involvement, but with British funds – an unconscionable prospect.[55]

After this discussion, Prime Minister Harold Wilson made a commitment to raising the Concorde question in his forthcoming discussion with Pompidou. Wilson wanted to know the French Prime Minister's view on the matter. He also planned to wait for the impending publication of a report by the Minister of Aviation on the commercial aspect of Concorde and the effect of the sonic boom. With this information, the Cabinet would be better placed to evaluate the issue further.[56]

The discussion with Pompidou in London left no room for ambiguity about the French position. From their point of view, there was zero possibility of cancellation. However, the French did agree to establish a joint committee on the commercial aspects of the project. Furthermore, by 21st July 1966, the Cabinet was able to draw on the Minister of Aviation's report. This confirmed that the sonic boom did not constitute a technical drawback to completing the aircraft, though the success of the project did depend on public acceptance of its sheer volume. Overall, the prospects for a British withdrawal from Concorde seemed remote.[57]

184 US–European airliner projects, 1968–82

Meanwhile, contenders for the American SST contract consisted of the Boeing 2707 and the Lockheed L-2000, with the former eventually being selected in December 1966.[58] In December 1967, the Concorde prototype finally rolled off the assembly line. BOAC and Air France immediately picked up options for purchasing. They were soon followed by leading American and world airlines such as Pan Am, Continental Airlines, American Airlines, Air India, Japan Airlines, Sabena and Lufthansa. These preliminary orders reached a total of 74. A further 122 order options had been placed by Boeing.[59]

By the beginning of 1968, however, Concorde was faced with the prospect of total cancellation. This was largely because the British Cabinet had begun to mull massive expenditure cuts. The possible victims of these cuts included one or both of the Concorde and F-111 projects. On 3rd January, this decision was embodied in a confrontation between Denis Healey, Minister of Defence, and a key supporter of the F-111, and Tony Benn, Minister of Technology, a strong proponent of Concorde. Benn warned Healey that, if Concorde were cancelled, it would lead to the complete termination of the entire Anglo–French defence package (Jaguar). The Minister of Defence responded with some "very crude politicking":[60] if Benn supported the F-111, then Healey would endeavour to preserve Concorde.[61]

On 4th January, the Cabinet met to discuss the cancellation of the F-111. Ten ministers were in favour of keeping the F-111, while nine were against. According to his diary, Benn held the decisive vote. His view was that, if the F-111 were to continue, Britain would be forced to cut either the Polaris submarine or the Harrier. The latter had significant export potential, which gave Benn cause to vote against keeping the F-111. The Cabinet was split straight down the middle, with Wilson casting his deciding vote for cancelation.[62] In effect, Benn had helped to eliminate a key competitor to Concorde from the British budget.

But the fate of the project still hung in the balance. Benn knew that George Brown, Secretary of State for Foreign Affairs, had sent telegrams to British ambassadors in all six EEC countries about a possible unilateral cancellation of the project. The responses were unanimously unfavourable. Frank Roberts, the British Ambassador to West Germany, said that such a withdrawal "would confirm all the French suspicious about us being bad Europeans and would destroy our credibility as a technological partner".[63]

The Cabinet met again on 5th January 1968 to reach a consensus on whether Britain should continue the Concorde project beyond the spring or early summer of 1969. Brown was alarmed at the prospect of four EEC governments interpreting British unilateral withdrawal as "motivated mainly by pique at the French veto"[64] of the British application to join the EEC. He also feared that the Europeans would conclude that the British were no longer seriously interested in meaningful technological collaboration.[65]

To no one's surprise, Benn also expressed opposition to immediate cancellation. He stressed the diplomatic and financial implications of such a move. He also pointed to the vital interests of the airframe and aero-engine industries. He did recognise, however, that Britain needed to lay down some conditions to the

French for continuation of the project beyond the spring or early summer of 1969. By this point, the results of the first Concorde flights on 2nd March would be available. Benn drew his comments to a close by adding that, if Britain withdrew from Concorde, then a departure from the Airbus project would surely follow. This would spell the end of British involvement in civil aerospace projects.[66]

The Cabinet agreed that Britain should not withdraw from Concorde at that juncture. Benn was asked to outline the conditions which, in his view, should be put to the French.[67] After some consultation with the other ministers, Benn formulated two criteria: (1) An upper limit of £600 million (1966 prices) on developmental costs; and (2) the receipt by 31st December 1969 of firm orders from four major airlines, one of which should be based in the United States.[68]

On 24th September 1968, Benn and Jean Chamant, French Minister of Transport, had met in London for a (apparently rather cordial) eight-hour discussion. According to Chamant, the French government had never regarded Concorde as a prestige project, though it was undoubtedly a "source of pride".[69] In the discussion, Chamant acknowledged that, if there were insufficient orders by the end of 1969, then Concorde would have to be cancelled. Benn raised the prospect of a possible British withdrawal from the project. Chamant gave the impressively political response that, although there was a readiness among French officials to "*recommend* to their Government that the other side be discharged from the obligation to continue" (original emphasis), there was equally "no *commitment* that this action would be accepted by the French Government" (original emphasis).[70]

Benn came away from this meeting with the clear impression that Chamant and his favoured project had some enemies in France. The French Prime Minister Maurice Couve de Murville, for example, was extremely hostile to Concorde. Nonetheless, Benn noted in his diary that the negotiations had been "really quite [...] successful and rather [...] enjoyable".[71] Indeed, Chamant and Benn continued to exchange correspondence and tried to shape the criteria according to which the commercial prospects of the aircraft would be measured. In a letter dated 27th September 1968, Chamant agreed that, for the project to continue, it needed to secure orders from four major airlines, including at least one US airline. If such orders failed to materialise, the project would be cancelled. Similarly, if the estimated costs exceeded more than £600 million, then Benn and Chamant would suggest to their respective governments that the 1962 Treaty be amended. Such an amendment would allow either party to withdraw without incurring any legal consequences. Again, however, Benn and Chamant reserved only an advisory function for themselves – they made no promises to each other.[72]

Concorde, A300B/BAC3-11 and the MRCA

The spring of 1969 was now the unofficial deadline for a Cabinet decision on continued British involvement with Concorde. In early 1969, however, certain connections began to form between the BAC3-11, BAC's planned 250-seater

186 *US–European airliner projects, 1968–82*

airliner, and three major collaborative European aerospace ventures (Anglo–French Concorde, Anglo–French–German A300B and Anglo–German MRCA). This was to have a profound influence on the Cabinet's decision-making process.

In a first development, the Concorde Directing Committee reported that the cost estimate of the Concorde development programme had risen to £596 million. This was perilously close to the £600 million ceiling negotiated by Benn and Chamant. It now seemed certain that cancelling Concorde would strengthen the case for proceeding with either the A300B, the MRCA or, given the astronomical figures of the Concorde project, perhaps even both.[73]

Then, in December 1968, the Airbus Consortium (Sud Aviation of French, the Deutsche Airbus Group and British Hawker Siddley) announced a downscale of the 300-seat A300 to a 250-seat A300B, which would likely be powered by a US-produced engine (from P&W or GE). This represented direct competition to the BAC3-11.[74] The Anglo–German MRCA was not an urgent problem because its production was scheduled for much later. Nonetheless, it still represented a source of considerable expenditure to the British government.[75]

Britain was thus confronted by a range of civil and military aerospace projects which had to be paid for out of diminishing funds. Cabinet discussions on 20th and 25th March 1969 focused on this problem. At these meetings, Benn once again positioned himself as a staunch defender of Concorde, despite its mounting costs. However, Chief Treasury Secretary John Diamond opposed Benn on the grounds that Concorde would almost certainly require an additional £100 million by mid-1970. Elwyn Jones, Attorney-General, anticipated that, if Britain withdrew at this stage of the project, it stood a 50–50 chance of being indicted at the international court for breaching the 1962 Treaty with France.[76]

The Anglo–German MRCA presented fewer problems. This project had not yet shifted from the definition to the developmental stage. The Germans seemed to favour an American instead of a Rolls-Royce engine, which was a potential source of conflict, but nothing serious at this stage. A more difficult question was the development of a European 250-seater aircraft. The French and Germans had invited Britain to co-operate in the development of the A300B, and even to guarantee the inclusion of a Rolls-Royce engine. This, however, would imply an abandonment of the BAC3-11. This was a sticking point because British ministers evidently regarded the BAC3-11 as a hugely promising project. BEA and US Eastern Airlines both liked it, while collaboration on the model between BAC and Lockheed was continuing apace. Eastern Airlines had already indicated that it wanted 50 models, while the co-operation with Lockheed virtually guaranteed high sales on the US market. And yet prioritising the BAC3-11 would imply a rejection of European co-operation over a 250-seater aircraft.[77] Not for the first or last time, riding two horses was proving difficult.

Overall, it seemed clear that, if Britain withdrew from both the Concorde and A300B projects, the political and diplomatic consequence would be serious. On 25th March 1969, the Cabinet thus decided to postpone a decision on Concorde until the end of the year. As we saw in Chapter 7, however, a firm commitment was made to withdraw from the A300B, though this decision would not be made public until the collaboration between Lockheed and BAC had yielded more concrete results. This meant that Benn would have to – somewhat disingenuously – buy time with the French and German governments in terms of a British commitment to the European Airbus. Healey, meanwhile, was authorised to advance British participation on the less controversial MRCA.[78]

Concorde was still alive. And yet, toward the end of 1969, differences between the French and British governments began to intensify. Chamant relayed to Benn that, if he indeed tried to persuade the French government to amend the 1962 Treaty in keeping with a £600 million ceiling for the project, then he would almost certainly be rebuffed. The French, it seemed, were less concerned with the economic sustainability of Concorde than their British partners. These differences remained unresolved at this point, with Wilson scheduling a reassessment of the project for June 1970.[79]

There is an unmistakeable irony here. The British had been the prime movers behind the Concorde project. In 1962, they had aggressively courted the French. Ten years later, however, and with Concorde on the verge of being launched, the British were grappling with the stark reality that the whole project was doomed to failure. But their partners refused to call it to a halt. The French considered Concorde a symbol of national prestige and an engine of employment. Above all, the 1962 Treaty still hung over the British like a sword of Damocles, rendering their withdrawal potentially more expensive than further participation.

Meanwhile, the United States was keeping a watchful eye on these proceedings.[80] Washington remained deeply concerned that it should maintain its position as the global innovator in space and aviation technology. There was little question of applauding the advances achieved within the context of the Concorde project. On the contrary, it was likelier that the United States would erect roadblocks to its successful launch.

Continuing Concorde

During the 1970s, governmental power in Britain frequently changed hands between Labour and the Conservatives. This, of course, had a significant impact on British policy with respect to Concorde. Most of the negotiations of the early 1970s were carried out by Ted Heath's Conservative government. Despite obvious problems with the project, as well as a burgeoning political and public desire to cancel the whole thing, Heath's government preferred to punt the ultimate decision on withdrawal down the road. It is safe to say that ongoing negotiations vis-à-vis British entry into the EEC played an important role here.

A key question was posed by Attorney General Peter Rawlinson in his paper to the Cabinet on 17th July 1970. If Britain withdrew unilaterally at this stage of the project, would the International Court of Justice hold it liable for damages to France? Rawlinson's assessment was optimistic. In his view, there had been such a fundamental change in situation since 1962 that the Treaty signed in that year was surely no longer binding. Moreover, the commercial and developmental cost ceiling of £600 million agreed in the Benn/Chamant correspondences would

188 US–European airliner projects, 1968–82

obviously be exceeded. Given these factors, Rawlinson felt that the odds were six to four in favour of no action being taken should Britain withdraw. Likely cancelation charges would be around £20–30 million.[81]

Given the enormous sums already invested in the project, however, it was very clear to British politicians that both withdrawal and continuation were equally unpalatable options. This was the subject of a Cabinet meeting held on 28th July 1970. The drawbacks to unilateral withdrawal included irreparable damage to the Anglo–French relationship, a heavy blow to the international position of the British aerospace industry, and a stain on Britain's broader national prestige. Rawlinson once again brought up the possibility of Britain being hauled before the International Court of Justice and facing a damages payment of anything between £40–230 million. Heath intervened to point out the likely effects of British withdrawal on the continuing, and delicate, EEC negotiations.[82]

The main topic of the Cabinet meeting on 30th July was a US congressional debate over whether or not to continue providing government subsidies to the US SST (Boeing 2707). These debates had created some strange bedfellows. Opposed to continued subsidies were Democratic Senator William Proxmire, the environmental lobby lead by Professor William A. Shurcliff, the Citizens' League Against the Sonic Boom (CLASB), and free-market Republicans who opposed government intervention on principle.[83]

The makeup of this exotic coalition was not the primary concern of the British Cabinet, however. It seemed certain that, if Congress decided against continued subsidisation of the SST, then order options for the US Boeing 2707 would collapse. The consequences of such a development were uncertain. On the one hand, the termination of an American SST would be grist to the mill of the environmental lobby. They would push hard against any and every project which threatened to bring the dreaded "sonic boom" to American shores. Concorde would be a non-starter on the world's biggest aviation market. On the other hand, the lack of a domestic SST programme might force some US airlines to turn to Concorde as an alternative.[84]

The Cabinet could not predict the future. Indeed, the only concrete result of this meeting was the entirely predictable postponement of any decision on Concorde until the end of the summer. September 1970 was set as the target date.[85] As the summer drew to a close, however, the full implications of either unilateral withdrawal or continued participation were becoming uncomfortably apparent. Burke Trend, the Cabinet Secretary, clarified these implications in a memorandum dated 10th September 1970. His assessment of the future of the project was bleak indeed. Existing losses were already massive, and would be added to by any future expenditure. Trend outlined two options – immediate withdrawal, or yet another postponement of the decision until 31st March 1971.[86]

The Cabinet meeting of 17th September would at least be able to base its decision on the results of upcoming flight tests, and also on the reaction of various airlines to these results. By the time of this meeting, however, the full scale of Concorde's failure as a profitable venture was unmistakeably apparent. The

Trapped in a loveless marriage   189

discussion basically revolved around the wisdom of continuing to support a project that was no longer economically feasible.[87]

At this meeting, an apparent consensus emerged that the key problem was the binding nature of the 1962 Treaty. Ministers were also groping toward the conclusion that an exit strategy was becoming increasingly necessary. That said, John Davies, Minister of Technology, firmly backed Trend's second option for a postponement until March 1971. His colleagues also drew back from the monumental step of cancelling the project at that juncture. Instead, they called on the Central Policy Review Staff (CPRS), a think tank under the direct control of the Prime Minister,[88] to prepare an assessment of Concorde.[89]

At the 17th September Cabinet meeting, Heath stated that the project would continue at least until test results were received in March 1971. By the time the winter of 1970/71 had come and gone, however, little had changed. As Frederick Corfield, Minister of Aviation Supply, noted in a Cabinet meeting on 18th March 1971, the options remained basically the same as they had been the previous September.[90]

This March Cabinet meeting was intended to thrash out a British position for upcoming talks with Jean Chamant in London on 29th March. Option one was to inform Chamant that Britain wished to withdraw from the agreement, and thereby risk being brought before the International Court of Justice. Option two was to tell Chamant that a firm decision would be postponed until all the facts were available on technical matters, such as payload and noise level. Such information would presumably deliver a clearer picture of Concorde's commercial prospects.[91]

Heath flatly rejected the idea of outright cancellation because he did not want to risk Britain being hauled before the International Court of Justice. Only the second option was acceptable.[92] And yet it was clear to the British government that the passing of time would not make Concorde more economically viable. The can was thus kicked down the road again, to 7th December 1971, when Corfield was due to meet Chamant.[93]

At the end of November 1971, Lord Rothschild (Nathaniel Mayer Victor Rothschild), Head of the CPRS, finally submitted the report that had been commissioned over a year before. He strongly recommended an immediate unilateral cancellation of Concorde. He did not mince his words; the project was "a commercial disaster"[94] that "should never have been started".[95] Taxpayers' money to the value of £350–475 million had disappeared into a black hole. No diplomatic, legal or prestige-related concerns could justify such grave damage to public finances. He stated that, "at the moment, the British government is getting the worst of both worlds – having to pay up and getting no credit for doing so".[96] Unfortunately, "much of the milk is already split"[97] – the government could now only save what remained to be saved. Any other project – the Channel Tunnel, the maintenance of the BAOR for two years, or even the purchase of 200 MRCAs – could be undertaken with the money that was due to be poured into Concorde.[98]

And yet there were still strong indications that Rothschild's economic logic was not shared by important members of the Cabinet. For example, John Davies,

190   *US–European airliner projects, 1968–82*

Secretary of State for Trade and Industry, remained staunchly committed to Concorde. On 30th November, he stated in a memorandum that any unilateral pull-out would irredeemably harm the UK's relationship with France. Davies somewhat cynically observed that such a risk could be taken only *after* British membership of the EEC was ratified.[99]

On 2nd December 1971, the Heath Cabinet finally brought an end to the interminable round of reviews that constituted official discussion of Concorde. In a dramatic and somewhat surprising move, the Cabinet decided to express its wholehearted support for the project. The key factor here was undoubtedly Britain's attempt to join the EEC. The Cabinet did draw the line at committing to further technological development of Concorde beyond the original agreement. Indeed, at this time, France was pushing for the development of a "stretched" version of Concorde.[100]

Nonetheless, 1971 drew to a close with the British government apparently accepting that the Concorde project simply could not be cancelled. The short-term future of the aircraft was assured and the French were placated. Most importantly from Heath's perspective, Concorde would not serve as a possible obstruction to British entry into the EEC.

The build up to the 1974 crisis

The circumstances surrounding SST changed considerably in the early 1970s. First, there was no easing of the existing litany of environmental concerns. On the contrary, it became increasingly apparent that Concorde had no hope of meeting existing US environmental protection standards for residential areas. The US government at both the state and national levels showed no inclination to weaken these standards and make an exception for a European-built SST.[101] To make matters worse, the introduction of a new form of technology – wide-body jets – would prove an almost insurmountable obstacle to the success of Concorde.

As we saw in the previous section, at the beginning of the 1970s, the United States was becoming unequivocally negative in its attitude toward SST, due in large part to pressing environmental concerns. This was the background to the congressional vote of 24th March 1971 against US government funding of SST, which signalled an end to Boeing's forays in this area.[102] After this vote, William Shurcliff of CLASB set his sights on "shooting down the Concorde".[103]

By early 1971, the Nixon administration was sandwiched between, on the one hand, Anglo–French pressure for approval to fly Concorde on US domestic and international routes and, on the other, US congressional and public pressure to ban Concorde for environmental reasons. Nixon had already indicated to Prime Minister Edward Heath that Concorde would be permitted to "compete for sales in this country on its merits".[104] In fact, however, a proposed ruling from the FAA would bar US airlines from flying Concorde on US domestic routes such as California to Hawaii. In the end, Concorde's virgin flights would be to New York – despite the fact that US environmental standards made the aircraft more or less impossible to sell on the US market.[105]

Trapped in a loveless marriage 191

A further headache from the point of view of Concorde's manufacturers was the removal of Juan Trippe as Chairman of Pan Am. Trippe was an evangelist for supersonic. Unfortunately, his purchase of the Boeing 747 had proven disastrous. The airline had incurred losses of $45.5 million for 1971 and an accumulated deficit of $120 million over the previous three-year period.[106] Concorde had lost perhaps its biggest supporter on the Western side of the Atlantic.

1972 was uneventful, with little movement on either side of the Concorde issue – if we overlook the vast sums of money that continued to be poured into it. A considerable crisis, however, was triggered on 30th January 1973, when Pan Am announced that it would not exercise its options on Concorde. Pan Am's tendencies toward gleeful risk-taking in the introduction of new aircraft had apparently been expelled from the company along with Trippe.[107] But the airline remained influential. Soon after its announcement, other airlines quickly followed suit by choosing not to exercise their options. Before long, only the national airlines of Britain and France – BOAC and Air France – retained firm commitments to purchase the aircraft.

Concorde was already economically problematic. This flurry of cancellations rendered it a virtual lame duck from a commercial point of view. The British were quick to recognise the hopelessness of the situation, but the French response was strikingly different. The British Foreign Office determined that French President Pompidou was unwavering in his support of the project. Pompidou apparently felt that cancellation would be damaging to the prestige of both France as a nation and himself as an individual. Nor did the French government believe that the on-going energy crisis necessitated any review of the project's status.[108]

It also appeared that the immediate concerns of the French were closely related to employment in the Toulouse area, where the national aerospace industry was located. There was also some anxiety within the political class around the maintenance of France's perceived position as an international leader in advanced technology, independent of the United States. Cancellation would be viewed by the French as a capitulation to American pressure, and any such submission was entirely unacceptable.[109]

In early 1974, Harold Wilson returned to Downing Street as Prime Minister under a Labour government. The new administration wanted to cancel the entire Concorde project, even though the aircraft was scheduled to go into service in 1976. As we saw elsewhere in this chapter, Wilson had never been a fan of Concorde. In January 1965, only fear of possible American–French co-operation on the (at the time, innovative) SST technology had deterred him from terminating the project. In January 1969, with estimated developmental costs nearing £600 million, Wilson had again moved to cancel it. Only concerns about the diplomatic damage of a withdrawal had stayed his hand.

The year 1974 represented the last chance for Wilson to cancel the ruinous "prestige project" of his Conservative predecessors. To be sure, inside the Cabinet, Tony Benn was still a keen supporter of the project. Overall, however, the

192   *US–European airliner projects, 1968–82*

new Labour Cabinet was convinced that the cancellation of Concorde was a matter of time. There was a recognition, however, that a review of the project was necessary before a final decision could be made.

Benn pushed hard against cancellation and used every trick in the book to achieve a stay of execution. The two key cards in his deck were the trade union card and the French relations card. On 19th March 1974, Benn made a last ditch attempt to preserve Concorde by using his close links with the British aircraft industry, noting in his diary that:

> If the Cabinet do decide to cancel, then I might have to declare my intention to consult my people in Bristol [Bristol division of Rolls-Royce] and let them decide whether I should continue in the Government or not.[110]

At a Cabinet meeting on 21st March 1974, it soon became apparent that Wilson's government was faced with the exact same choices that had confronted his Conservative predecessor: unilateral withdrawal, or continuation with an economic no-hoper. Benn argued for yet another postponement of a final decision. He reminded his colleagues of the legal risks to which Britain would expose itself by unilaterally withdrawing from an international treaty. Elwyn Jones, Lord Chancellor, also emphasised the enormous political fallout that Britain would suffer as a result of unilateral withdrawal.[111]

Cold water was promptly poured over these tentative indications of support for Concorde by Chancellor of the Exchequer Healey, however. Healey pointed out that the economic case for cancellation was simply overwhelming. If the Concorde project moved forward, then huge losses would be incurred on the production, sale and operation of the aircraft. Cancellation would constitute a catastrophic write-off of the substantial sums already invested, but it would have only a modest impact on employment within the aviation industry. Overall, the Chancellor estimated that continuation of the project would prove more costly to Britain than actually paying the cancellation penalty to France.[112]

Wilson concluded that the broad consensus within the Cabinet was in favour of cancellation. However, he also acknowledged that the time was not right to make such a momentous and far-reaching decision. First, the social, industrial and regional implications all needed to be carefully studied, along with the impact on the British aircraft industry. A further review was needed. Trend was tasked with arranging an interdepartmental group of officials to examine the social, industrial and regional results of a cancellation.[113] Wilson's government had kicked the can yet further down the road.

The report commissioned by Trend was published on 24th April 1974. This report carefully examined the effects that a cancellation would have on the size and shape of the British aircraft industry. It concluded that the Concorde programme played a relatively minor role within this industry, which was already saddled by a very substantial amount of work from other sources. Cancelling Concorde would not, it seemed, have much of a domestic impact.[114]

The French say "*oui*"

The British had spent the first half of the 1970s wanting to withdraw unilaterally from the Concorde project. However, they had been forced to accept that, even though the project was economically unfeasible, unilateral withdrawal was politically unfeasible. From 1974, however, a possible solution to this impasse began to develop among British policymakers. This solution would allow the UK to staunch the haemorrhaging of funds, while simultaneously allowing the French to present the Concorde project as an ongoing symbol of national pride.

From the British perspective, the chief problem was that the French would probably not entertain the idea of outright cancellation, despite the project's gloomy financial prognosis. Indeed, the French actually wanted to extend the project by adding an additional three aircraft to the existing production plan of 16. Two of these would be reserved for in-house testing and would not go onto the market, while BOAC and Air France had ordered five and four models, respectively. The three additionally planned aircraft would raise the total number of Concordes to 19.[115]

The British attitude was further coloured by the recognition that losses on the project would continue to mount even after Concorde was in operation. BOAC estimated that it would incur operating losses of £110 million over ten years.[116] In a memorandum dated 21st May 1974, Elwyn Jones, the chairman of the Committee of Ministers on Concorde, observed that Britain was under no obligation to authorise more than 16 aircraft. According to the committee, the UK had two "realistic choice[s]"[117] in this scenario – complete 16 aircraft, or terminate the project entirely. In their view, the former option would represent "the right course".[118] Nonetheless, the committee acknowledged that the project was guaranteed to incur further serious losses, with any Concordes that were manufactured likely to become "white elephants".

At the Cabinet meeting on 23rd May 1974, ministers focused on trying to identify a reason for cancellation that the French would agree to while still "saving face". Benn continued to insist on proceeding with Concorde but, by now, the game was most definitely up. As if to emphasise this, Healey delivered a long speech on the inescapable economic logic of cancelling Concorde and the folly of continuing with it. Jenkins agreed with him, while Elwyn Jones underscored the case for withdrawal by raising the difficult question of landing rights in New York, Tokyo and Sydney. The British could make the argument that not only was the production of Concorde unprofitable, but also that those already in operation would have nowhere to land.[119]

As if to sign off on the inevitability of British withdrawal, Wilson made plain his desire to work with the current French government, rather than starting new negotiations with the next government. All agreed that it was important to secure French consent for withdrawal – but, crucially, that it was not absolutely necessary. The Cabinet did discuss the negative implications of unilateral withdrawal, and briefly considered the prospect of completing 16 aircraft. Overall, however, it was clear that an overwhelming majority inclined toward cancellation.[120]

194 *US–European airliner projects, 1968–82*

This position was apparently unaffected by the presence outside 10 Downing Street of a massive crowd of Concorde workers. Benn "went and had a chat with them, then slipped out through a side door to the main body of Ministers".[121] The Secretary of State for Industry, however, had still not given up on saving the aircraft – even if certain dirty tricks were required. On 10th June, Benn met George Edwards of BAC and made the following comment:

> The cabinet have told me to suggest we discontinue, but if the French insist on producing sixteen planes we shall go ahead. Therefore, without breathing a word that you have heard from me, your job is to persuade the French to make such a demand and we shall have to build them [...] George did his job.[122]

On 26th June 1974, Wilson met French Prime Minister Jacques Chirac in Brussels. Despite the British desire to cancel or freeze the project, Chirac made it clear that the French wanted to produce three additional Concordes. In his opinion, the environmental argument was nothing more than "an excuse".[123] He was convinced that airline orders would pick up once the immediate petroleum crisis was overcome.[124] Wilson reiterated that, in the view of his government, Concorde was economically unsustainable. He was not convinced that further advances in technology would materially change the project's economic prospects.[125] "What would you say if we suggested that we discontinue it? What would your answer be?", Wilson asked. "*Negatif, negatif*" (original emphasis), was the reply.[126]

Clearly, British withdrawal from this burgeoning commercial disaster would be anything but straightforward. Wilson reported his discussion with Chirac to the Cabinet on 27th June. The French Prime Minister, he said, had spoken of "producing two hundred Concordes".[127] He was extremely unlikely to let Britain (and its considerable sums of money) leave the project without a fight. To be sure, the final decision rested with French President Giscard d'Estaing. Overall, however, it seemed certain that any attempt on the part of Britain to cancel the project would be overwhelmingly rejected by their partners.[128]

There was thus a growing, grudging acceptance within the Cabinet that unilateral withdrawal was no longer a viable option. The government's energies would be better used in figuring out how to persuade the ambitious French to freeze production at sixteen aircraft. Moreover, measures were needed that would protect the financial interests of the British and cap their liabilities.[129]

On 12th July, Lord Chancellor Elwyn Jones released a memorandum which outlined the history of Concorde and weighed up the options available to the British government. He noted that French President Giscard d'Estaing would almost certainly not entertain any notion of cancellation. The objective of the British in the upcoming meeting scheduled between Wilson and Giscard d'Estaing was to accept the continued production of the agreed-upon 16 aircraft, but to rule out any increase of this number. Indeed, British accession to the production of sixteen Concordes would be "conditional on an Exchange of Letters which made it clear that there was no legal obligation on either side to agree to any development or production work beyond this programme".[130]

Elwyn Jones' memorandum also outlined a further and completely new objective which was to comprise a turning point in the history of Concorde. In short, the British should secure French consent for the drafting of a completely new agreement over the project. This agreement would fully take into account the developmental history of Concorde and provide for any necessary modifications to the 1962 Treaty.[131]

In essence, the British were finally, firmly broaching the idea of, if not divorce, then at least a legal separation. This separation agreement would state in no uncertain terms that neither party had any financial obligations to the other, beyond the original 16 aircraft. It would explicitly put down on paper the right of either party to refuse to authorise further production – a right that had only been implied in the 1962 Treaty. The memorandum left the door open to further discussions and the possible resumption of production, should new and unforeseen circumstances arise. Again, however, this would require the agreement of both parties.[132]

Wilson and Giscard d'Estaing met on 19th July 1974 in Paris to work out an agreement. Wilson made it clear that Britain would honour its original agreement for 16 aircraft, but no more than that. Chirac, perhaps hoping to tie Britain to a longer-term commitment, again expressed his optimism about the future of Concorde after the oil crisis had subsided. Giscard d'Estaing, however, accepted Wilson's proposal.[133] This signalled the end of British dithering over Concorde, as well as an acceptance from the French that there were strict limits on the partnership between the two countries as outlined in the 1962 Treaty. Nonetheless, it seems likely that both parties came away from this meeting with a certain sense of disappointment that they could not achieve more.

In this way, the much-heralded Concorde project, which was launched to such great fanfare, national pride and hope for the future, came to an end with a slightly pitiful whimper. This revised agreement between the British and the French also signalled the end of the age of SST, as well as over a decade of Anglo–French aerospace collaboration. Moreover, it signalled to Britain the dangers of entering into a binding partnership with Europe in the field of aerospace development.

Conclusion

Concorde was supposed to be a symbol of Anglo–French partnership and of Europe's technological competitiveness with the United States. However, the project quickly became an enormous economic burden to Britain in particular. It gave rise to years of British dithering, whereby the economic futility of continuing with the project was squared off by the essentially political and diplomatic problems posed by withdrawal. Ultimately, the British were able to extricate themselves from the project in a way that did not prove too wounding to French pride. But the costs were considerable.

196 *US–European airliner projects, 1968–82*

Perhaps the most significant upshot of the Concorde affair, at least from the perspective of this book, was the apparent lesson it contained about the dangers of aeronautical collaboration with Europe. Rolls-Royce paid particularly close attention to this lesson. The British aero-engine manufacturer's determination to embark on deeper Anglo–American collaboration in civil aerospace seemed to be vindicated by the Concorde debacle. Rolls subsequently became a key partner of US industry in the production of wide-body aircraft.

Ultimately, though Britain may have spent much of the post-war period riding two horses, it increasingly seemed that one horse was faster than the other. Chapter 9, the final chapter, will expand on this theme. It will focus on the struggles of several British aerospace companies – Rolls-Royce, BAe and BA – as they sought to position themselves between European Airbus and Boeing during the 1980s.

Notes

1 Dawkins and Brockmann (1980).
2 Agger produced the decisive "engine memorandum", which admitted US airlines' purchase of the Rolls-Royce engine. See Chapter 7.
3 *FRUS, 1964–1968, Volume XXXIV*, Document 129.
4 Johnman and Lynch (2002).
5 May (2009, p. 508).
6 May (2009, p. 505).
7 Johnman and Lynch (2002, p. 255).
8 Simons (2012b, p. 19).
9 Lynn ([1995] 1998, p. 62).
10 Owen (1997, p. 19); Simons (2012b, p. 21).
11 TNA CAB128/34, CC (60)44th, 21st July 1960.
12 Simons (2012b, p. 57).
13 Lynn ([1995] 1998, p. 63).
14 Knight (1976, pp. 25–26).
15 May (2009, p. 493).
16 Lynn ([1995] 1998, p. 64).
17 TNA CAB129/150, CP (70)17th, 17th July, 1970.
18 Costello and Hughes (1976, p. 49).
19 Lynn ([1995] 1998, pp. 67–68).
20 Lynn ([1995] 1998, pp. 67–68); *FRUS, 1964–1968, Volume XXXIV*, Document 111; Public Papers of the Presidents of the United States: John F. Kennedy, 1963, p. 441.
21 Bender and Altschul (1982, pp. 500–1).
22 *FRUS, 1964–1968, Volume XXXIV*, Document 111.
23 *FRUS, 1964–1968, Volume XXXIV*, Document 111.
24 Simons (2012b, pp. 70–71).
25 Hayward (1983, p. 125).
26 TNA CAB129/125, C (66)88th, The Concorde Project, 27th June 1966.
27 *FRUS, 1964–1968, Volume XXXIV*, Document 112.
28 *FRUS, 1964–1968, Volume XXXIV*, Document 112.
29 *FRUS, 1964–1968, Volume XXXIV*, Document 112.
30 *FRUS, 1964–1968, Volume XXXIV*, Document 112.
31 Hayward (1983, p. 125).

32 *FRUS, 1964–1968, Volume VIII*, Document 13.
33 *FRUS, 1964–1968, Volume XXXIV*, Document 112, footnote 3.
34 *FRUS, 1964–1968, Volume XXXIV*, Document 114.
35 *FRUS, 1964–1968, Volume XXXIV*, Document 115.
36 Jenkins (1991, p. 163).
37 Jenkins (1991, p. 163).
38 *FRUS, 1964–1968, Volume XXXIV*, Document 115.
39 *FRUS, 1964–1968, Volume XXXIV*, Document 115.
40 705 HC Deb., 20th January 1965, cols. 197–98.
41 *FRUS, 1964–1968, Volume XXXIV*, Document 115, footnote 3.
42 *FRUS, 1964–1968, Volume XXXIV*, Document 115, footnote 3.
43 *FRUS, 1964–1968, Volume XXXIV*, Document 116.
44 *FRUS, 1964–1968, Volume XXXIV*, Document 116.
45 *FRUS, 1964–1968, Volume XXXIV*, Document 117.
46 TNA PREM13/714, Record of a Conversation between the Prime Minister and President de Gaulle at the Élysée Palace at 10 a.m. on Saturday, 3rd April 1965.
47 NARA RG59/E5172/Box 17, Discussion with the Lord Plowden Committee on the Future of the British Aircraft Industry, 15th May 1965.
48 *FRUS, 1964–1968, Volume XXXIV*, Document 121.
49 *FRUS, 1964–1968, Volume XXXIV*, Document 121.
50 *FRUS, 1964–1968, Volume XXXIV*, Document 121, footnote 4.
51 *FRUS, 1964–1968, Volume XXXIV*, Document 121, footnote 4.
52 TNA PREM13/1308, The Concorde Project, Burke Trend to Prime Minister, 29th June 1966.
53 TNA CAB129/125, CP (66)88th, The Concorde Project, 27th June 1966.
54 TNA CAB129/125, CP (68)89th, Concorde, 27th June 1966.
55 TNA CAB125/29, C (66)90th, The Concorde Project, 27th June 1966.
56 TNA CAB128/41, CC (66)33rd, 30th June 1966.
57 TNA CAB128/41, CC (66)39th, 21st July 1966.
58 Lynn ([1995] 1998, p. 69).
59 Lynn ([1995] 1998, p. 71).
60 Benn ([1988] 1989a, p. 2).
61 Benn ([1988] 1989a, pp. 1–2).
62 Dockrill (2002, p. 204); Benn ([1988] 1989a, pp. 3–4).
63 Benn ([1988] 1989a, p. 5).
64 TNA CAB128/43, CC (68)2nd, 5th January 1968.
65 TNA CAB128/43, CC (68)2nd, 5th January 1968.
66 TNA CAB128/43, CC (68)2nd, 5th January 1968; Benn ([1988] 1989a, p. 8).
67 TNA CAB128/43, CC (68)2nd, 5th January 1968.
68 TNA CAB129/139, C (68)109th, The Concorde Criteria: The Next Step, 15th October 1968.
69 TNA CAB129/139, C (68)109th, The Concorde Criteria: The Next Step, 15th October 1968.
70 Benn ([1988] 1989a, p. 103).
71 Benn ([1988] 1989a, p. 103).
72 TNA CAB129/139, C (68)109th, 15th October 1968.
73 TNA CAB128/44, CC (69)13th, 20th March 1969.
74 TNA CAB129/141, C (69)28th, European 250-Seater Aircraft, 17th March 1969.
75 TNA CAB129/141, C (69)31st, The European Project for A Multi-Role Combat Aircraft, 17th July 1969.
76 TNA CAB128/44, CC (69)13th, 20th March 1969; TNA CAB128/44, CC (69) 14th, 25th March 1969.
77 TNA CAB128/44, CC (69)14th, 25th March 1969.
78 TNA CAB128/44, CC (69)14th, 25th March 1969.

US–European airliner projects, 1968–82

79 TNA CAB129/150, CP (70)17th, Concorde: The Legal Position in July 1970, 17th July 1970.
80 *FRUS, 1964–1968, Volume XXXIV*, Document 123.
81 TNA CAB129/150, CP (70)17th, 17th July 1970.
82 TNA CAB128/47, CM (70)9th, 28th July 1970.
83 TNA CAB128/47, CM (70)11th, 30th July 1970; Lynn ([1995] 1998, pp. 72–73); Simons (2012b, p. 140).
84 TNA CAB128/47, CM (70)11th, 30th July 1970.
85 TNA CAB128/47, CM (70)11th, 30th July 1970.
86 TNA CAB129/151, CP (70)40th, Concorde, Note by the Secretary of the Cabinet, 10th September 1970.
87 TNA CAB128/47, CM (70)19th, 17th September 1970.
88 CPRS was an independent think-tank within the Cabinet office that planned long-term economic and political strategies.
89 TNA CAB128/47, CM (70)19th, 17th September 1970.
90 TNA CAB128/47, CM (70)19th, 17th September 1970; TNA CAB128/49, CM (71)15th Conclusions, 18th March 1971.
91 TNA CAB128/49, CM (71)15th, Conclusions, 18th March 1971.
92 TNA CAB129/49, CM (71)15th, Concorde, Memorandum by the Minister of Aviation Supply, 15th March 1971; TNA CAB128/49/15, CM (71)15th, Conclusions, 18th March 1971.
93 TNA CAB129/160, CP (71)144th, 30th November 1971.
94 TNA CAB129/160, CP (71)140th, 29th November 1971.
95 TNA CAB129/160, CP (71)140th, 29th November 1971.
96 TNA CAB129/160, CP (71)140th, 29th November 1971.
97 TNA CAB129/160, CP (71)140th, 29th November 1971.
98 TNA CAB129/160, CP (71)140th, 29th November 1971.
99 TNA CAB129/160, CP (71)144th, 30th November 1971.
100 TNA CAB128/49/61, CM (71)61st, 2nd December 1971.
101 TNA PREM16/2, Concorde.
102 Lynn ([1995] 1998, pp. 72–73); Simons (2012b, p. 91).
103 Simons (2012b, p. 186).
104 Simons (2012b, p. 201).
105 Simons (2012b, pp. 199–202).
106 Bender and Altschul (1982, p. 519).
107 Costello and Hughes (1976, pp. 221–23).
108 TNA FCO33/2451, Concorde, 21st January 1974.
109 TNA FCO33/2451, Concorde, 21st January 1974; TNA FCO33/2451, Future of Concorde – Elements in the French Position, 6th February 1974.
110 Benn ([1988] 1989b, p. 124).
111 TNA CAB128/54, CC (74)5th, 21st March 1974.
112 TNA CAB128/54, CC (74)5th, 21st March 1974.
113 TNA CAB128/54, CC (74)5th, 21st March 1974.
114 TNA CAB130/735, MISC18 (74)22nd, Official Group on Concorde: Aircraft Industry, Final Report of the Group, 24th April 1974.
115 TNA CAB129/176, C (74)48th, 21st May 1974.
116 TNA CAB129/176, Appendix E to C (74)48th, 21st May 1974.
117 TNA CAB129/176, C (74)48th, 21st May 1974.
118 TNA CAB129/176, C (74)48th, 21st May 1974.
119 TNA CAB128/54, CC (74)17th, 23rd May 1974.
120 TNA CAB128/54, CC (74)17th, 23rd May 1974.
121 Benn ([1988] 1989a, p. 160).
122 Adams (1992, p. 348).
123 TNA PREM16/2, R. T. Armstrong to Sir John Hunt.

Trapped in a loveless marriage 199

124 TNA PREM16/2, R. T. Armstrong to Sir John Hunt.
125 TNA PREM16/2, R. T. Armstrong to Sir John Hunt.
126 Benn ([1988] 1989b, p. 185).
127 TNA CAB128/54/21, CC (74)21st, 27th June 1974.
128 TNA CAB128/54/21, CC (74)21st, 27th June 1974.
129 TNA CAB128/54/21, CC (74)21st, 27th June 1974.
130 TNA CAB129/177, C (74)72nd, Concorde, Note by the Lord Chancellor, 12th July 1974.
131 TNA CAB129/177, C (74)72nd, Concorde, Note by the Lord Chancellor, 12th July 1974.
132 TNA CAB129/177, C (74)72nd, Concorde, Note by the Lord Chancellor, 12th July 1974.
133 TNA PREM16/296, Record of a Meeting between the Prime Minister and the President of France held at the Élysée Palace in Paris on 19th July 1974 at 11:45 a.m.

9 Playing a double game

The British aircraft industry in the third jet age

Introduction

A model of the Rolls-Royce Trent 800 aero-engine stands on display at the Imperial War Museum in Duxford, Cambridgeshire. In the accompanying text, this impressive piece of machinery is described as:

> ... a high-bypass turbofan aero-engine (which) was developed to power the Boeing 777 series of aircraft. It is an extremely reliable engine and has achieved significant commercial success. Since 1997, over eighty per cent of 777 aircraft have been fitted with Trent 800 aero-engines.[1]

After 1978, Rolls-Royce focused a huge proportion of its resources on powering Boeing airliners with the RB211. This was to have a considerable impact on the company's commercial success. By the 1980s, Rolls-Royce models were the engines of choice for both American and European airframes.

This book has focused largely on the following question: Was the revitalisation of the post-war British aircraft industry to be achieved primarily through European or Anglo–American collaboration? As late as 1978, Britain was still pursuing both courses. The British airframe manufacturer BAe hoped to co-operate chiefly with European partners.[2] However, aero-engine manufacturer Rolls-Royce and BA preferred to continue their co-operation with the American aircraft manufacturer Boeing.[3]

This book has argued that commercial and geopolitical factors frequently complicated attempts on the part of the British aircraft industry to pursue both the European and American options simultaneously. And, as this chapter shows, this difficulty became particularly acute in the late 1970s. The Labour government under James Callaghan found itself facing a familiar British dilemma. How did it attempt to resolve this dilemma?

The rise of the European Airbus and its fierce competition with Boeing have captured the imagination of business writers such as Matthew Lynn, Stephan Aris and John Newhouse.[4] The absorbing, but somewhat journalistic approach typical of this literature has tended to cast the conflict as "Europe versus America". This has surely contributed to book sales. Nonetheless, it simplifies the confrontation

DOI: 10.4324/9781003127901-12

Playing a double game 201

somewhat, because it overlooks other aero-engine manufacturers whose interests cannot easily be slotted into this dichotomous narrative. Such companies included Rolls-Royce as well as P&W and GE in the United States. Overall, this chapter aims to conceptualise Rolls-Royce's strategy during the Boeing/Airbus confrontation as a bid for survival on the part of the British aviation industry. As we shall see, Callaghan's government was intimately involved in this endeavour.

Britain between Boeing and Airbus

From the 1950s to the 1970s, the Boeing line-up ranged from small 727 and 737 airliners, to the medium-sized 707 airliners, to the much larger 747. By the late 1970s, the American manufacturer dominated 60 per cent of the world airliner market.[5] Their erstwhile domestic rivals, McDD and Lockheed, were exhausted from the fierce competition over wide-bodied airliners, which was the subject of Chapter 7 of this book.

In the early 1970s, the European Airbus suffered from modest sales. Between 1974 and 1976, the company sold only 15 aircraft. This was a period blighted by the 1973 oil crisis, which caused a dramatic slump in airliner business.[6] From 1976, US and European manufactures sought to launch replacement models for the 727 medium jet airliner. The 727 had proven a huge commercial hit upon its release but, at 15 years old, it was beginning to date. These new models would become the so-called "third-generation" airliners of the 1980s. They were more economical, consumed less fuel, and had more efficient engines than their predecessors, including the 727.

With a view to the 1980s, Boeing and McDD busily began to search for partners. US anti-trust laws prohibited collaboration between US manufacturers, whereas partnerships with foreign companies were not subjected to such regulations. Such partnerships also virtually guaranteed financing from the foreign government, as well as orders from the foreign national airline.[7] The American manufacturers thus focused their search for collaborators predominantly on Europe and Japan. Boeing soon locked Italian Aeritalia into a deal that would see the airline purchase its proposed aircraft.[8] McDD, meanwhile, was in discussion with European Airbus over a joint-project – the 200-seater DCX200. McDD also reached an agreement with French Dassault to launch the 175-seater Mercure.[9]

Boeing's dual programme

In this increasingly competitive situation, Boeing was planning to replace the 727 with a dual project – the 757/767. The aircraft companies of Italy and Japan were quickly secured for the 767. The 757, meanwhile, would focus on Britain. Boeing's grand design was that this project would involve the participation of all three British national aviation companies (BAe, Rolls-Royce and BA). BAe would be sub-contracted to provide the wings of the 757; Rolls-Royce would power the aircraft with its newly developed RB211-535 (a smaller version of the RB211); while BA would be the launch customer. Whether or not Boeing deliberately

202 *US–European airliner projects, 1968–82*

intended to draw Britain away from continental Europe and into deeper participation with the United States is difficult to reconstruct from the available sources.
However, the geopolitical implications are unlikely to have escaped the attention
of policymakers in Washington or London, or – indeed – in Paris and Bonn.[10]

At this time, European Airbus was heavily involved in planning the launch of
the new A310. This was smaller than the A300B, and in fact, it represented a
competitor to the 757/767. The possible participation of British companies in
this project was a topic for discussion in the spring of 1976 between Lord
Beswick, Chairman of BAe, and Jacques Mitterrand, chairman of Aérospatiale[11]
(and brother of the future French President François).[12]

At this meeting, it soon became very apparent that Airbus Industrie needed
British money and British wing technology.[13] Britain had left the European
Airbus Consortium in 1969, but Hawker Siddeley had continued to work on the
wings as part of a private venture. Airbus was able to dramatically reduce the
price of the airplane with export financing support from the German and French
governments. This discount, coupled with a surprising "fly-before-you-buy"
scheme, had persuaded American Eastern Air Lines to purchase 23 A300Bs
with nine order options in April 1978.[14] There was a clear message here: that
American airlines were ready to overlook three-engine aircraft and buy economical two-engine models, signalling a rejection of the previous consensus that
two-engine airliners were unacceptably dangerous.

The burgeoning battle between the United States and Europe thus focused
heavily on enticing British airframe and engine builders into the respective folds.
As the British financial journalist Matthew Lynn put it, "the key, as before, was
the British".[15] If Britain were re-integrated into the Airbus project, then it would
not only empower the European Consortium, but it would also signal the effective defeat of Boeing's grand design to enlist British companies as sub-contractors
and launch partners.

The British response to the Boeing 757 offer

For BA and Rolls-Royce, Boeing's 757 offer was attractive. Ever since the
introduction of the 707, BA had been one of the American manufacturer's principal customers. The airline also preferred the narrow body airframe of the 757 to
re-equip its short-haul fleet and ruled out the 767 and the A310.[16] After Rolls-
Royce's rather bitter experience with the Lockheed TriStar, the company
chairman, Sir Kenneth Keith, had high hopes that the company could restore its
reputation by powering Boeing's new aircraft.[17]

BAe, however, was less enamoured by Boeing's offer. The initial proposal would
have involved the company as a mere sub-contractor, responsible for manufacturing the wing box, but with no role to play in development or production. Boeing
would retain overall control of design and programme management. Moreover,
BAe's management were somewhat sceptical about the 757, which they considered a revamped version of the 727. The company had been asked to build a
new wing which required significant investment. Responsibility for the fuselage,

Playing a double game 203

however, lay with Boeing, and this component was virtually identical with the 727. Boeing thus had to invest relatively little in contrast to BAe, which was none-theless treated as a temporary sub-contractor.[18] For these reasons, and in contrast to Rolls-Royce, BAe favoured the more egalitarian terms of European collaboration, and harboured serious reservations about Boeing's offer.

It is here that the crucial detail of the story dealt with in this chapter comes into view. In short, France and Germany insisted that BAe's re-entry into Airbus Industrie was conditional on a BA purchase of the A310. This would necessarily entail BA rejecting a purchase of the Boeing aircraft – and thus scuppering Rolls-Royce's chance of being the launch partner for the American aerospace giant. The role of King Solomon inevitably fell to Callaghan's Cabinet. The British government was effectively confronted by conflicting requirements from BA, BAe and Rolls-Royce – the three key pillars of the British aircraft industry. How did British ministers manage this difficult situation?

Callaghan's first move was to set up the Ministerial Group on Aircraft Policy (GEN130) to discuss commercially and politically sensitive questions in this area. At the first meeting of the committee on 26th April 1978, Callaghan outlined the conflicting interests of the three national companies. The existential problem was that Britain needed to replace its existing fleet of aircraft, with the choice falling between the Boeing 757, the Airbus Industrie A310, and the relative dark horse of the McDD ATMR (advanced technology medium range). At this meeting, several pro-European ministers expressed the fear that Boeing's offer was a "spoiler", intended to undermine BAe's collaboration with Europe.[19]

At a meeting on 16th May 1978, however, it became increasingly clear that some British ministers found the Boeing offer highly attractive. They openly speculated on a possible illustrious future for Rolls-Royce, which would supply major customers, especially in the United States, with the RB211 family. Boeing had made no guarantee that the RB211-535 would be the lead engine. However, Rolls-Royce had an 18-month lead on its main competitors, P&W and GE, which would virtually guarantee a huge share of initial Boeing sales. British ministers also argued that the Boeing plan would even prove beneficial for BAe, because it extended the opportunity of collaboration with Boeing's uniquely successful market organisation. This comprised a 60 per cent share of the civil airliner market. BAe participation in the 757 could open up the prospect of further collaboration over the long term.[20]

Despite this apparent support for the US proposal, however, Callaghan proved reluctant to entirely rule out the European option. He decided to write person-ally to French President Giscard d'Estaing and German Chancellor Schmidt about the possible collaboration between Airbus Industrie and BAe. He would inform his counterparts that this collaboration seemed "commercially uncertain and to offer little for RR".[21] But he also wanted to emphasise to the Europeans that Britain was basing its decisions "in the knowledge that no viable possibilities for European collaboration had been overlooked".[22] Callaghan's reluctance to reject Airbus, then, was rooted predominantly in a diplomatic rather than a commercial logic.[23]

204 *US–European airliner projects, 1968–82*

At this point, Rolls-Royce sent a 12-point memorandum to British Members of Parliament (MPs) lobbying for a BA purchase of the Boeing 757. As this document observed, "the civil aircraft business worldwide is dominated by Boeing".[24] The 757 offered Rolls the chance to be "the launch engine in a new Boeing aircraft for the first time in our history".[25] Without a BA order of the 757, the launch engine would be GE's CF6. The loss of such a prestigious opportunity would be a disaster not only for the company, but also for the British aerospace sector generally.[26]

In this document, Rolls-Royce also called on BAe to join the 757 programme. And yet the proposal was still not advantageous from BAe's point of view. Company officials told *Aviation Week & Space Technology* that the offer was quite simply uneconomical, as well as being highly risky, because it entailed a total concentration of BAe's business into one commercial alliance. For BAe, the question was this: How many airliners would Boeing actually supply with its models? What if the thousands of predicted orders simply failed to materialise?[27] What future aircraft beyond the 757 might BAe participate in the manufacture of?[28] Here at least was one area where the Airbus offer seemed manifestly superior.

Several members of the British Parliament responded with annoyance to Rolls-Royce's lobbying. On 26th May, Terry Walker MP (Kingswood) expressed his preference for establishing a strong European collaborative aircraft industry. Only once this was accomplished should Britain explore the possibility of collaborative projects with North America. Walker argued that prioritising the United States would constitute "an act of folly which would reduce us from the mainstream of aircraft production to the eventual role of sub-contractor for the Americans".[29] Such an outcome, he concluded, "must not be allowed to happen".[30]

On 13th June 1978, a meeting of high-level British officials convened to work out the optimal response to the Boeing and Airbus offers. In attendance were Prime Minister James Callaghan, as well as Eric Varley, Secretary of State for Industry, Sir Kenneth Keith, the chairman of Rolls-Royce, and Sir Kenneth Berrill, head of the CPRS (a think tank under the direct control of the Prime Minister). Callaghan immediately pointed out that the interests of BAe, BA and Rolls-Royce did not coincide. Keith noted that the Boeing offer carried fundamental advantages for Rolls-Royce and identified BAe as "the problem" in this constellation. He very much doubted that the latter's productivity could match Boeing's or McDD's. He also stated that, if Britain vacillated for much longer, then the chance to provide the launch engine for the 757 would pass Rolls by.[31]

The meeting then turned to European questions. Callaghan once again invoked the view of French President Giscard d'Estaing and German Chancellor Schmidt that an independent European aircraft industry was an absolute necessity. He observed that Giscard d'Estaing and Schmidt would have severe misgivings about allowing the American aircraft industry to simply dominate the world. He believed that both would be prepared to subsidise their domestic industries to prevent such an eventuality.[32]

The Prime Minister further expressed his desire for a solution that would prove satisfactory to all three British corporations and not just Rolls-Royce. Keith responded that Rolls-Royce was simply too expansive a company to be restricted to the relatively small European market. If it were to survive in its current form, it must be allowed to operate beyond Europe – which, in effect, meant on the US market.[33]

On 21st June 1978, British ministers met again to consider the Boeing offer and the likely consequences that accepting it would hold for BAe. The latter now openly hoped to join Airbus Industrie, which would allow the company to continue the A300B wing box contract on present terms. The Boeing offer continued to inspire little enthusiasm in BAe officials. There was a 30 per cent price difference between Boeing's offer and BAe's estimated cost of the job, while key figures at the firm were less than enamoured by Boeing's domineering management style. Lastly, BAe believed it had been offered work on a secondary project, with Boeing clearly attaching higher priority to the 767 than the 757.[34]

In June, Varley circulated a memo on aerospace policy to the rest of the Cabinet. He provided a detailed summary of the current state of affairs. Rolls-Royce wanted to power the Boeing 757 with the RB211-535 engine. BA and Eastern Air Lines were ready to order the 757 with this engine. BAe, however, hoped to enter Airbus Industrie as a full partner in the manufacturing of the A300B and the new A310. Varley made the following recommendation: Rolls-Royce should be given authorisation to co-operate with Boeing if the launch orders from BA and Eastern became more concrete; BA should be authorised to purchase the Boeing 757 if it were indeed fitted with a Rolls engine; and BAe should examine the possibility of collaborating with all three of Boeing, McDD and Airbus Industrie.[35]

Varley was hedging his bets. Unfortunately for the Prime Minister, he was coming under increasing pressure from Paris and Bonn to green light the full integration of BAe into the Airbus Consortium. As Callaghan later observed:

> The situation was intensely political. Had we not gone into Airbus, it would have been interpreted as a political act. Giscard would have used it against us and Schmidt would have drawn a similar conclusion. On the one hand, we wanted Anglo–American cooperation. American industry can offer us something. Britain had an important dowry to bestow on a suitor. The question was who would pay the right price for this dowry.[36]

Callaghan in Washington

On 24th June, Callaghan made a personal visit to Washington in an attempt to find a way out of this emerging impasse.[37] One of the key items on the Prime Minister's agenda was lunch with Frank Bohman, President of Eastern Air Lines. During this engagement, Callaghan tried to extract a promise from Bohman that he would order the Boeing 757 if it was fitted with a Rolls-Royce engine. Bohman indicated his willingness to do this. However, he then proceeded to give

206   *US–European airliner projects, 1968–82*

the Prime Minister to a view of the European Airbus which was "slightly different view of Airbus from the line peddled by Callaghan's advisers in London".[38] The European models were, he contended, high quality airplanes, and Eastern would be happy to buy them. This verdict probably did not make Callaghan's job of resolving the British dilemma any easier.

The French knew about the prime ministerial visit to Washington. It was high time for some Parisian shock tactics. French officials formally announced that, if BAe wanted to re-join Airbus Industrie, then Britain had to commit to a purchase of the A310.[39] On the night of this announcement, Callaghan met T.A. Wilson, Chairman of Boeing. The Prime Minister frankly asked Wilson if the Boeing offer was a genuine attempt to enlist British technical knowledge in an exciting project, or if it was merely a tactical manoeuvre to prevent the formation of a united European front. Wilson replied that Boeing was entirely serious about the 757, and that it would proceed with the project whether or not Britain was involved.[40]

The following night, Callaghan met with Sanford McDonnell, President of McDD. The Prime Minister's principal aim at this meeting was to get some feedback on the prospect of a Consortium between BAe, European Airbus and McDD over the development of a medium-range airliner. McDonnell showed himself to be somewhat lukewarm with respect to Callaghan's proposal, for reasons of both time and money.[41]

Callaghan returned from these meetings convinced that "the European commitment offered the best future for BAe".[42] On – ironically enough – 4th July 1978, the Prime Minister gave a less than glowing assessment of the American stance on future British aerospace policy to his ministers. The situation was evidently extremely complicated and fluid. First, if BAe collaborated on the 757, then the McDD ATMR – a rival third-generation plane – would not be built. On the other hand, Eastern Air Lines had more or less committed to buying the 757 with the RB211-535 engine – though its chief executive had also said some positive things about the Airbus.[43]

Callaghan pointed out that both Eastern Air Lines and McDD were convinced of Boeing's intention to prioritise the 767 over the 757. No one at Boeing had said anything to contradict this view. Conversely, it seemed likely that British participation in the 757 would enhance the long-term prospects for extending industrial collaboration between the US giant and BAe. From the Prime Minister's perspective, however, the "strongest cards" in Britain's deck remained Rolls-Royce and BA.[44]

At this point in the proceedings, Berrill pointed out that half of the world airline market was in the United State. That said, US firms would only commit to a manufacturing project when there was a guaranteed market for the product. In contrast, French and German companies could rely on more support from central governments that were not necessarily committed to such projects for purely economic reasons. Consequently, the A310 would be financed and built without any firm orders necessarily being in place. Overall, Berrill seemed convinced that an attempt to reconcile these competing European and American projects would be almost impossible. Britain had to choose.[45]

Playing a double game 207

From Callaghan's perspective, this problem was rendered acutely urgent by looming meetings with Giscard d'Estaing and Schmidt in Bremen and Bonn. The French and Germans would be looking for something tangible. The Cabinet suggested to Callaghan that his emphasis at these meetings should be on finding a substantial role for Rolls-Royce in Europe. They pointed out the folly of France and Germany busily endeavouring to establish a European aerospace industry while relying on an American engine produced by GE, despite the fact that, in Rolls-Royce, they had a world-renowned engine-producer on their doorstep. Why, after all, should British ministers sanction deeper ties with Europe if collaboration with Boeing seemed to offer better long-term prospects?[46]

On 28th July, the CPRS produced a note on aircraft policy for British ministers. In their view, there could be no mistake that the best interests of Rolls-Royce and BA lay in collaboration with Boeing. They stressed the need for a timely and decisive commitment to this project. The CPRS pointed to the danger that, if no firm decision were taken, then Eastern Air Lines, a key launch customer for the 757, might shift its preference from a Rolls-Royce to a GE engine.[47]

BAe continued to be the complicating factor in this decision-making process. Following Varley's visit to Paris and Bonn, the British firm entered into commercial negotiations with Airbus Industrie on the basis that it would join the Consortium as a full risk-sharing partner in the production of the A300B and the new A310. The CPRS report suggested to ministers that the British government should bankroll the project to the tune of £50 million. However, President Giscard d'Estaing was sticking to his demand for a firmer commitment – that if BAe were accepted into Airbus Industrie, then BA would commit to buying the A310. Moreover, BAe still showed no interest in serving as a sub-contractor for the 757 unless it had control over design elements.[48]

BAe's possible re-entry into Airbus Industrie was again the topic of conversation at a Cabinet meeting on 1st August 1978.[49] Varley outlined five conditions that he had put to the French and Germans during the negotiations. These were as follows: (1) a 20 per cent stake for BAe in Airbus Industrie. The French and Germans each had a 47.9 per cent share, while Spain held the remaining 4.2 per cent. It was expected that the two dominant partners would reduce their stake from 47.9 per cent to 37.9 per cent; (2) veto rights for BAe with respect to any future Airbus Industrie projects; (3) price maintenance of the existing A300B wing box sub-contract up to the 150th wing box set; (iv) an exemption for BAe from any liability for past development costs and losses of Airbus Industrie; and (5) a commitment from BAe to *endeavour* (but not to promise) to secure a BA purchase of the Airbus.[50]

The fifth of these conditions was the most problematic. The French and Germans still wanted a guaranteed sale of the A310 to BA as a condition for re-admitting BAe to the Consortium.[51] The immediate issue for Callaghan was whether or not to endorse the prospect of BAe re-joining Airbus Industrie. This decision could not be taken without considering the position of Rolls-Royce, which was as crucial to the UK as BAe, if not more so.

208 US–European airliner projects, 1968–82

BA's stance was also an issue; the company's board of directors made their position clear by formally seeking government approval for an order of 19 Boeing 757s. Combined with the order for 21 Boeing 757s that Eastern Air Lines had already promised, Boeing had enough prospective buyers to justify launching the aircraft. Crucially, these orders were for the 757 with a Rolls-Royce RB211-535 engine. This would hand the British engine manufacturer a significant lead over its American competitors. It would also signal the first instance in several decades that Rolls-Royce possessed such a market advantage. And yet all of this might be jeopardised by any further delay to a BA purchase of the 757, which might turn Eastern in the direction of a GE engine.[52]

The BA order was thus the key factor in this decision-making process. The government could not make a decision that would effectively deprive Rolls-Royce, perhaps the key pillar of the British aerospace industry, of virtually guaranteed sales prospects in the United States. And yet, an announcement that BA would order 19 Boeing 757s would seriously prejudice and perhaps exclude the possibility of BAe entering Airbus Industrie. This would place the future of the company in question and carry potentially serious political penalties. The French and Germans would view it as a clear British rejection of European collaboration, while pro-European MPs, as well as BAe and its affiliated trade unions, would be up in arms.[53]

From Callaghan's point of view, the pressure was intensifying. His goal was to try to keep the two issues as separate as possible. He wanted to ensure that any decision on the 757 and the RB211-535 would not prejudice negotiations with Airbus Industrie, while also guaranteeing that a possible BAe entry into Airbus Industrie would not undermine the prospects for the RB211-535. From a diplomatic point of view, he was also anxious that it would not be possible for – particularly – the French to blame any failure of negotiations on the UK, or to give – particularly – the Germans the impression that the UK was "playing a double game".[54]

Varley elaborated further on the situation at a Cabinet meeting on 2nd August 1978. He first stressed the priority of securing Rolls-Royce's RB211 as the launch engine for the 757. If this were achieved, the company would be virtually guaranteed a substantial windfall. British ministers had seemingly arrived at the consensus that there was no real future for Rolls-Royce in Europe. The principal Airbus customers were seemingly committed to American (GE) engines – indeed, it appeared that "the French had struck an alliance with American aero engine manufactures for producing engines for these planes". Rolls-Royce thus had no real option but to turn to the US market, and Boeing was offering it this chance. According to Varley, Callaghan should be prepared to tell the French and Germans that only the guarantee of "a genuine role for RR in Europe"[55] might persuade British ministers to endorse a BA purchase of the Airbus.[56]

And yet BA's acquiescence to such a purchase seemed far from certain. The airliner clearly considered the 757 to be best suited to its needs, hence the attempt to gain government approval for a purchase of 19 of the aircraft. The French refused to believe that the British government had no control over BA's purchasing policy. This policy, however, was based on financial forecasts, and not on the whims of British ministers.[57]

Boeing continued to provide an option for BAe which, if taken up, would have solved the British dilemma at a stroke. But there remained a gap of £250 million between BAe's and Boeing's estimated costs for the supply of 400 wing sets for the 757. Moreover, BAe manifestly refused to make peace with the fact that its involvement in the Boeing project would only be as a sub-contractor, with no influence over design. By contrast, re-joining Airbus Industrie would entail the renegotiation of a profitable contract for constructing the A300B wing. Collaboration with the French and Germans on civil aircraft would also significantly improve BAe's prospects of future work on military projects. But the French insistence on a guaranteed A310 order for BA as a condition for BAe's entry into the project continued to be the sticking point.[58]

Callaghan ultimately concluded that Rolls-Royce would, indeed, launch the RB211-535, while at the same time, BAe would be authorised to enter negotiations with Airbus Industrie. However, the Prime Minister instructed his ministers not to make any official announcement on either of these developments, so as not to prejudice either set of negotiations. Discretion, it seemed, would the better part of valour, at least for now.[59] Britain was indeed playing a "double game".

BA places its order

In mid-August 1978, the British government authorised BA to purchase the 19 Boeing 757s that company executives had asked for. There was, however, a catch; officials at BA were asked to contact Eastern Air Lines with a view to forming a joint launch order for a Rolls-Royce-powered 757 *without* the French and Germans gaining any knowledge of what was afoot.[60]

On 30th August, a meeting of the GEN130 was held. Varley proposed that ministers should endorse BAe's conclusion of an industrial agreement to join Airbus Industrie and that a grant of £50 million should be pledged by the government to facilitate this arrangement. This grant was opposed by Joel Barnett, Chief Secretary of the Treasury. In Barnett's view, there was no prospect of a return on this investment in either the short or medium term. It would also be wholly inconsistent with Varley's own criteria that BAe should not be involved in commercially questionable projects which were contrary to British industrial strategy.[61]

The discussion then turned to Airbus Industrie's apparent basis in a state-supported "an alternative European bloc".[62] This was a sensitive issue during the Cold War. After all, it could have been argued that such a formation more closely resembled the planned economies of the Soviet zone than the free-wheeling capitalism of the West. If BAe did join the European Consortium, then this could be perceived as endorsing a negation of free market principles in the realm of civil airliners. Boeing, by contrast, was conducting its business in a more identifiably and reassuringly capitalist fashion, fishing for customers internationally and trying to involve as many countries as possible.[63]

210   US–European airliner projects, 1968–82

On the other hand, and as some participants at the meeting pointed out, this concept of a true European "the concept of market blocs"[64] perhaps existed more in theory than in reality. The Germans were anxious to collaborate with the United States, while the French company Snecma already had a close relationship with GE. "The idea of an independent European airframe industry"[65] was perhaps more a rhetorical device than a guide for concrete policy. Nonetheless, it seemed that, in this particular area, the French were more serious about realising their vision of a "European bloc". Paris' stated goal was to ensure that all the national carriers of the countries represented in Airbus Industrie would fly Airbus aircraft. This would naturally include BA, the largest and most profitable of the British aircraft companies.[66]

But it seemed that this would not be acceptable to British ministers. BA's position should in no way be prejudiced; the UK should make this "absolutely clear to the French Government in order that there should be no grounds for misunderstanding".[67] Implementing the previous decision to follow through with the BA purchase of Rolls-Royce-powered 757s should "not be further delayed".[68] As we have already seen in Chapter 3, since the end of the "Fly British" policy, BA's purchasing policy had been determined overwhelmingly by commercial concerns. The company had to make a profit, and British ministers were not about to alter this policy.

From this discussion, Callaghan drew the conclusion that most of his ministers accepted the wider case for a strong European civil airframe industry. There was obviously some support for BAe's becoming a full member of Airbus Industrie. However, the Prime Minister expressed great scepticism about the idea that this would transpire "with a view to establishing an alternative European bloc in a world market at present dominated by American manufacturers".[69] Instead, European collaboration should aim to put European manufacturers "in a position to effectively negotiate future collaboration with their United States counterparts".[70]

The Callaghan government's interest in Airbus was thus underpinned mainly by the desire to strengthen European (and British) bargaining power with respect to a perceivably unassailable United States. On this very limited basis, British ministers were prepared to endorse the terms of the industrial agreement that would see BAe become a full risk-sharing member of Airbus Industrie. As for BA's order for 19 Boeing 757s, this meeting had shown a virtual ministerial consensus that the French insistence on a British purchase of the A310 was not acceptable.[71]

Callaghan thus consented to an early announcement of the decision to approve BA's order for 19 Boeing 757s and the launch of Rolls-Royce's RB211-535. Of course, French Transport Minister Joel le Theule might well stick to his previous position – that BAe joining Airbus Industrie was conditional on a BA order of the Airbus. If this proved to be the case, then Callaghan signalled his intention to write to the French President and the German Chancellor. As he put it to his ministers, "[i]t would then be for the French Government to decide whether they were prepared to drop their condition".[72]

On 1st September, Kenneth Keith wrote a strongly worded letter to the Prime Minister. He was convinced that the BA purchase of the Boeing 757 was "a decision which the country will not regret". He further described the French as "unreasonable and irrational – but that is nothing new". According to the head of Rolls-Royce, "[t]he plain facts are that they [the French] need us [Britain] as much as we need them, and no doubt, in the course of time, they will see it that way, too".[73] Ten days after receiving this letter, Callaghan replied. He congratulated Rolls-Royce on winning Eastern Air Lines' order of the RB211-535 for the 757. He described this as a "great opportunity for Rolls-Royce",[74] and described himself as "very pleased to see that Eastern Airlines have decided to specify this engine for their purchase of Boeing 757s".[75]

Meanwhile, BAe's industrial partners agreed in principle to the company's re-entry into Airbus Industrie. However, the move was stalled by the French government's insistence that BA purchase the Airbus A310. Officials in Paris wanted a letter of intent to this effect. Varley informed French Minister of Transport Joel le Theule that such a letter would not be forthcoming.[76]

The deadlock was broken by an unlikely source. In mid-September, Sir Freddie Laker, Chairman of a small British airline called Laker Airways, placed an order for five McDonnell Douglas DC-10-30s and ten Airbus A300Bs. The French and German governments reluctantly accepted Laker's purchase as constituting the necessary "British purchase" of the Airbus. This was the ticket for BAe's re-entry into the European Consortium.[77]

But the Laker purchase did not induce Paris to give up completely on BA. On 16th October 1978, Varley informed British ministers that French officials were still nominally seeking a BA order for the Airbus. To be sure, France was no longer pressing for this as an essential condition of BAe participation in the project. Nonetheless, the British presumed that Paris would attempt to make political capital out of the issue if negotiations broke down. Indeed, the sole remaining barrier to BAe participation was the French President. Giscard d'Estaing was sensitive to the implications of BA refusing to fly the Airbus, despite the fact that most French officials and industrialists were willing to readmit the British company. Callaghan proved steadfast here, stating that "no further concessions should be conceded to the French beyond those already offered".[78]

On 24th October, the British, French and West German governments announced that an agreement had been reached. London would provide £50 million to BAe, while Paris and Bonn were expected to contribute a further £250 million to the A310 project. BAe would have a 20 per cent stake (£50 million/£250 million), which would entail a reduction in the French and German share from 47.9 per cent to 37.9 per cent each. Spain held the remaining 4.2 per cent. Crucially, the veto hurdle for major decisions was also increased from 75 per cent to 80 per cent. This meant that Britain with Spain would be able to prevent any changes to the project which they found objectionable, even if these changes had the support of France and Germany.[79] BAe, and the Callaghan government, had got what they wanted from Europe.

212 *US–European airliner projects, 1968–82*

The economic case for the RB211-535 was overwhelming. It rested mainly on the commitment of Boeing to use the Rolls-Royce product as a certified engine for the first Boeing 757. This was supported by initial orders for 40 aircraft from BA and Eastern Air Lines. The only competition here came from GE's CF32. However, this would not be certified until at least eight months after the certification of the Rolls-Royce engine. The RB211-535 would be fitted into over 40 per cent of Boeing 757 sales. Over the following 15 years, these would likely total between 1,000 and 1,500.[80]

In fact, the Boeing 757 did not go on to become a commercial success. Rolls-Royce's role in this model, however, proved historic. Peter Pugh, the writer of the official history of Rolls-Royce, has observed that the 757 "would be the first Boeing aircraft to be launched with anything other than a Pratt & Whitney engine".[81] This was the beginning of a close partnership between Rolls-Royce and Boeing in the production of some of the best-selling aircraft in aviation history. Indeed, Rolls constructed an entire engine family, from the medium-size RB211-535 for the 757, to the large RB211-524 for the 747.[82] The RB211 also supplied the blueprint for the Trent, which served as the launch engine for the best-selling Boeing 777. The Trent developed into a family of engines which would go on to power both US-produced and European Airbus airframes in the 1980s and 1990s. By securing a key role in the 757, Rolls-Royce had embarked on a trajectory that would propel it to the very top of the international aviation industry.

Conclusion

As the 1970s drew to a close, a clear division began to emerge in the British aerospace sector. This division was little more than the latest manifestation of a tradition of British vacillating between the United States and Europe which stretched back to the end of the Second World War. On this occasion, the division ranged three British companies into two camps. The pro-American camp comprised Rolls-Royce and BA, whereas the pro-European camp consisted of BAe. The French had made BAe's re-admittance to Airbus Industrie conditional on a BA order for the European Airbus. Rolls-Royce, however, was desperate for this order to go to Boeing, thereby guaranteeing that the American aircraft would be fitted with a Rolls engine. The conflict of interest appeared intractable.

In retrospect, the rise of European Airbus Industrie in the late 1970s created a favourable negotiating environment for British officials. In bargaining with Boeing to power the US company's next-generation airliner with a Rolls-Royce engine, they could point to a viable alternative business partner and thereby strengthen their own position. Indeed, a review of the sources reveals that, at crucial moments, British policymakers did not prioritise the European option. They viewed it more or less from the beginning as a bargaining chip in the more important, and potentially more lucrative, discussions with the Americans.

And yet, in the end, Britain's "double game" in the commercial war between Boeing and Airbus largely paid off. BAe was reaccepted to Airbus Industrie, despite the fact that BA committed to flying American – and Rolls-Royce-powered – aircraft.

Playing a double game 213

This historic success highlighted Rolls-Royce's position as one of the Big Three aero-engine producers along with American P&W and GE. By the 1990s, Rolls was providing the engines for both US and European aircraft.[83] To some extent, the British aircraft industry had successfully learned to ride two horses after all.

Notes

1 As for the Trent family, see Pugh (2002), Chapter 6: The Trent Family.
2 On 29th April 1977, BAC and Hawker Siddeley were merged and nationalised to become BAe, Gardner (1981), p. 287.
3 On 31st March 1974, BOAC and BEA merged into BA, Higham (2013), p. 303.
4 Lynn ([1995] 1998); Aris (2002); Newhouse (1982).
5 TNA, CAB130/1041, GEN 130(8)2nd, 16th May 1978.
6 Aris (2002, p. 85).
7 Newhouse (1982, p.196).
8 Newhouse (1982, pp. 197–98).
9 Aris (2002, p. 92).
10 Newhouse (1982, p. 201); Lynn ([1995] 1998, pp. 137–38); Aris (2002, pp. 105–6).
11 In 1970, French Sud Aviation merged with other French aviation companies and formed Aérospatiale.
12 Lynn ([1995] 1998, p. 137); Aris (2002, pp. 104–5).
13 Aris (2002, p. 95).
14 McGuire (1997, pp. 51–52).
15 Lynn ([1995] 1998, p. 136).
16 Lynn ([1995] 1998, p. 138).
17 TNA CAB130/1123, Rolls-Royce, Presentation to Prime Minister, 16th October 1979.
18 Lynn ([1995] 1998, pp. 139); *AWST*, 24th April 1978, p. 30.
19 TNA CAB130/1041, GEN130 (78)1st, 26th April 1978.
20 TNA CAB130/1041, GEN130 (78)2nd, 16th May 1978.
21 TNA CAB130/1041, GEN130 (78)2nd, 16th May 1978.
22 TNA CAB130/1041, GEN130 (78)2nd, 16th May 1978.
23 TNA CAB130/1041, GEN130 (78)2nd, 16th May 1978.
24 *AWST*, 29th May 1978, p. 31.
25 *AWST*, 29th May 1978, p. 32.
26 *AWST*, 29th May 1978, p. 32.
27 *AWST*, 29th May 1978, p. 32.
28 Lynn ([1995] 1998, p. 139).
29 950 HC Deb., 26th May 1978, col. 1911.
30 950 HC Deb., 26th May 1978, col. 1911.
31 TNA PREM16/1934, Notes of a Meeting Held in the Prime Minister's Study at 10 Downing Street at 10.30 on Tuesday, 13th June 1978.
32 TNA PREM16/1934, Notes of a Meeting Held in the Prime Minister's Study at 10 Downing Street at 10.30 on Tuesday, 13th June 1978.
33 TNA PREM16/1934, Notes of a Meeting Held in the Prime Minister's Study at 10 Downing Street at 10.30 on Tuesday, 13th June 1978.
34 TNA CAB130/1041, GEN130 (78)3rd, 21st June 1978.
35 TNA PREM16/1934, Aerospace Policy (A Note by the Secretary of State for Industry).
36 Newhouse (1982, p. 203).
37 Lynn ([1995] 1998, p. 141).
38 Lynn ([1995] 1998, p. 141).
39 Lynn ([1995] 1998, p. 141); Newhouse (1982, p. 208).
40 Lynn ([1995] 1998, p. 141).

214   *US–European airliner projects, 1968–82*

41 Lynn ([1995] 1998, p. 142).
42 Lynn ([1995] 1998, p. 142); *AWST*, 3rd July 1978, p. 13.
43 TNA CAB130/1041, GEN130 (78)4th, 4th July 1978.
44 TNA CAB130/1041, GEN130 (78)4th, 4th July 1978.
45 TNA CAB130/1041, GEN130 (78)4th, 4th July 1978.
46 TNA CAB130/1041, GEN130 (78)4th, 4th July 1978.
47 TNA CAB130/1041, GEN130 (78)14th, Decisions on Aircraft Policy, Note by the Central Policy Review Staff, 28th July 1978.
48 TNA CAB130/1041, GEN130 (78)14th, Decisions on Aircraft Policy, Note by the Central Policy Review Staff, 28th July 1978.
49 TNA CAB130/1041, GEN130 (78)5th Meeting, 1st August 1978.
50 TNA PREM16/1934, Aerospace: the latest development, Note by the Secretary of State for Industry.
51 TNA CAB130/1041, GEN130 (78)5th, 1st August 1978.
52 TNA CAB130/1041, GEN130 (78)5th, 1st August 1978.
53 TNA CAB130/1041, GEN130 (78)5th, 1st August 1978.
54 TNA CAB130/1041, GEN130 (78)5th, 1st August 1978.
55 TNA CAB128/64, CM (78)29th, 2nd August 1978, Limited Circulation Annex.
56 TNA CAB128/64, CM (78)29th, 2nd August 1978, Limited Circulation Annex.
57 TNA CAB128/64, CM (78)29th, 2nd August 1978, Limited Circulation Annex.
58 TNA CAB128/64, CM (78)29th, 2nd August 1978, Limited Circulation Annex.
59 TNA CAB128/64, CM (78)29th, 2nd August 1978, Limited Circulation Annex.
60 TNA PREM16/1934, Keith to Prime Minister, 1st September 1978; TNA CAB130/1041, GEN130 (78)6th, 30th August 1978.
61 TNA CAB130/1041, GEN130 (78)6th, 30th August 1978.
62 TNA CAB130/1041, GEN130 (78)6th, 30th August 1978.
63 TNA CAB130/1041, GEN130 (78)6th, 30th August 1978.
64 TNA CAB130/1041, GEN130 (78)6th, 30th August 1978.
65 TNA CAB130/1041, GEN130 (78)6th, 30th August 1978.
66 TNA CAB130/1041, GEN130 (78)6th, 30th August 1978.
67 TNA CAB130/1041, GEN130 (78)6th, 30th August 1978.
68 TNA CAB130/1041, GEN130 (78)6th, 30th August 1978.
69 TNA CAB130/1041, GEN130 (78)6th, 30th August 1978.
70 TNA CAB130/1041, GEN130 (78)6th, 30th August 1978.
71 TNA CAB130/1041, GEN130 (78)6th, 30th August 1978.
72 TNA CAB130/1041, GEN130 (78)6th, 30th August 1978.
73 TNA PREM16/1934, Keith to Prime Minister, 1st September 1978.
74 TNA PREM16/1934, Prime Minister to Keith, 11th September 1978.
75 TNA PREM16/1934, Prime Minister to Keith, 11th September 1978.
76 *AWST*, 4th September 1978, p. 20.
77 Aris (2002, pp. 112–13); Newhouse (1982, p. 210); *AWST*, 25th September 1978, pp. 20–21.
78 TNA CAB130/1041, GEN130 (78)7th, 16th October 1978.
79 Aris (2002, p. 115).
80 TNA CAB130/1123, Rolls-Royce, Presentation to Prime Minister, 16th October 1979.
81 Pugh (2001, p. 265).
82 TNA CAB130/1123, Rolls-Royce, Presentation to Prime Minister, 16th October 1979.
83 In 1997, the Trent 500 aero-engine (a variant of the RB211 series) was selected as the sole engine for the European Airbus A340-500/A340-600 (Owen (1999, p. 324)).

Conclusion

The main reason for the British victory in the Falklands War of 1982 was – from the perspective of military hardware – the naval task force's co-operation with Royal Navy Sea Harriers and the RAF's Harrier GR.3 V/STOL fighters. These aircraft won the air battle against Argentina's Mirage III and the Super Étendard. Indeed, at the outbreak of hostilities, 247 Argentine fighters outnumbered the 20 British Sea Harriers by 12–1. The British were required to draw on V/STOL Sea Harriers, the only available aircraft that could take off from the deck of an aircraft carrier far from the mainland.[1] And yet they were victorious.

Some 15 years before the British victory over Argentina, however, the fate of the Harrier had been in the balance. At a meeting of the British Cabinet on 22nd December 1966, a cancellation of the aircraft had been demanded by James Callaghan, Chancellor of Exchequer. Callaghan was concerned about the defence ceiling target of £2,000 million. However, a spirited defence of the Harrier programme was mounted by Fred Mulley, Minister of Aviation, and Denis Healey, Secretary of State for Defence. In the end, Prime Minister Harold Wilson decided to continue with the project, which was licensed for production in the United States.[2] The Wilson government, so notable for scrapping Conservative "prestige" projects, decided to continue with the production of a unique V/STOL. In 1982, this aircraft allowed the British to triumph in the South Atlantic.

On 14th April 1982, Prime Minister Margaret Thatcher stated in a speech to the House of Commons that "the sovereignty of the [Falkland] islands" would not be "affected by the act of invasions".[3] Through its victory over Argentina, Britain projected an image of itself as a world power, capable of exerting military might in the south of the Atlantic. Some half a century after the humiliation of the Suez Crisis, Britain was apparently a force to be reckoned with once again. The war itself became a symbol of a resurgent Britain under Thatcher's leadership, playing into a narrative of phoenix-like re-emergence after the various disasters and indignities of the post-war period.

How do we explain the apparent disparity between these two images – the bankrupt and chastened former-Empire of the Suez Crisis as opposed to the seemingly thrusting world power of the Falklands War? This book has attempted to tell this story from the perspective of the British aircraft industry during these decades. At all times, the aim has been to offer a historical critique of the oft-

DOI: 10.4324/9781003127901-13

216 *Conclusion*

repeated narrative of British "decline", and to show that, despite travails and difficulties, British policymakers were able to negotiate the post-war period with not inconsiderable stealth and skill. By the time that Thatcher gave her speech, Britain had carved out a new role for itself as a key pillar in an American-led process of globalisation.

As Part I of this book showed, things got off to an admittedly inauspicious start. In the immediate post-war period, the priority for British policymakers was to try to maintain Britain's status as a major power in world politics. The implications for the long-haul civil airliner market were clear. Under the "Fly British" policy, the British government promoted British airliners in an ill-fated competition with American models. To be sure, during the initial phase of this contest, the pace was set by British Comet 1 and the VC2 Viscount. Even after the Suez Crisis, a Conservative government under Harald Macmillan continued in its attempt to match up with American aircraft. This entailed a rationalisation of and considerable financial support for the British aircraft industry, particularly in the form of the TSR-2 fighter and VC10 airliners.

By the late 1950s, however, the Boeing 707 and Douglas DC-8 had totally reversed the market situation. This confronted BOAC in particular with chronic financial difficulties. Over time, BOAC withdrew from the "Fly British" policy, and increasingly looked to proven American airliners in the wide-bodied long-haul airliner replacement. Britain's eventual setback in the sectors of long-haul and middle-haul civil airliner market induced its airframe makers to explore their options on the continent, through European projects such as the Airbus and Anglo–French Concorde.

The 1950s thus appear to have been a sobering decade from the perspective of British policymakers. And yet, at the same time as British aircraft manufacturing seemed to be suffering reverses on every front, Britain's aircraft industry was being rationalised and rendered more efficient by a purposeful Conservative government. Moreover, a single British aero-engine maker (Rolls-Royce) was making a case as the principal supplier to American airliners. Indeed, the 707 was powered by a formidable Rolls-Royce engine – the Conway. The green shoots of recovery were hard to detect in the two decades after the war, but they were nonetheless present.

However, and as Part II of this book suggested, Britain's difficult position between Europe and the United States became particularly acute during the 1960s. Once Harold Wilson's government decided to cancel the TSR-2 in 1965, it was clear that Britain had to choose a principal partner for aerospace collaboration. And yet what followed were some contradictory policy decisions and initiatives. On the one hand, the Anglo–French defence package, the Jaguar and the AFVG partially realised a grand European ambition toward Anglo–French collaboration. So, too, did projects such as Concorde and Britain's early championing of the European Airbus, under the moniker of a "European Technological Community".

By the end of the decade, however, the French had discontinued their involvement in the VG project, while London increasingly distanced itself from Paris

Conclusion 217

in the wake of the 1966 NATO Crisis. At the same time, an arrangement between Wilson and Lyndon B. Johnson's administration in Washington centred on the purchase of American F-111s and British exemption from the "Buy American" policy. With these decisions, the British aircraft industry signalled its intention to enter the US military market, as well as the Middle Eastern military market, which had been previously dominated by the United States.

Of course, from the point of view of the British aircraft industry, the choice between Europe and the United States was not either/or. And yet, as Part III showed, Britain's attempt to "ride two horses" was plagued with danger. For a start, aircraft manufacturing was no mere commercial endeavour – it had serious geopolitical implications, which is why de Gaulle's dramatic move in 1966 had such significant ramifications for British aircraft industrial policy. Moreover, in the late 1960s and early 1970s, the commercial competition between Boeing and European Airbus in large jet airliner development became increasingly fraught. This gamut of commercial and geopolitical factors left British companies faced with the choice of either providing the engines for Boeing, or further participating in the European Airbus project.

Ultimately, Britain resolved this dilemma with some skill; Rolls-Royce did, indeed, go on to provide the engines for Boeing, while BAe was permitted to re-enter the European Airbus Consortium. Certainly, this affair showed perhaps more vividly than any other the inherent contradictions of Britain's attempt to keep one foot on either side of the Atlantic. And yet, to some extent, the UK did accomplish this diplomatic and commercial feat, and Rolls-Royce cemented itself as one of the Big Three companies in aero-engine manufacturing.

What all of this amounts to is the basic conclusion of this book, that the rehabilitation of the British aircraft industry was generated *primarily* by participation in a US-led trend towards globalisation. This calls into question the very idea that Britain has been enduring a straightforward process of decline since the nineteenth century. In fact, the UK was able to maintain a healthy share of the global market – with the British aircraft industry an exemplary example of this achievement.

The specific case of Rolls-Royce is highly pertinent here. In his 2001 book, *Rolls-Royce: Collapse of the British Spirit of Ecstasy,* Japanese business historian Akio Okochi took the bankruptcy of Rolls-Royce in 1971 as a symbol of the terminal decline of the British industrial spirit.[4] In fact, the very opposite was the case. Rolls' bankruptcy, and eventual rescue by Nixon and Heath, was in fact a mere historical footnote to the dramatic rise of the company during the 1980s. In this case, the night was indeed darkest before the dawn, and the "spirit of ecstasy" remained largely undiminished as a symbol of British manufacturing until the close of the twentieth century.

This book shows that post-war British manufacturing, engineering and, specifically, the aircraft industry maintained their competitiveness – and, indeed, their indispensability – with respect to the United States and continental Europe. In contrast to the conclusion reached by Geoffrey Owen in *From Empire to Europe,* this successful course lay largely in co-operation with the United States. Britain's

218 *Conclusion*

"struggle for Greatness"[5] was, of course, faltering, at times. The Suez Crisis in 1956, the sterling crisis and the retreat from East of Suez in 1967, and the 1976 International Monetary Fund Crisis could be taken as markers of decline. *The Wall Street Journal* heralded this last development as "Goodbye, Great Britain", while Burke and Cairncross have described it as a prelude to Thatcherism.[6]

Thatcher's neoliberalism may have been dismissed by one journalist as one of the "twin disorders of decline",[7] alongside the statist socialism represented by Tony Benn,[8] and yet, notably, both Thatcher and Benn accorded a high priority to the British aircraft industry. The Foreword to this book relates the anecdotal story of an ardent Labour supporter switching to the Conservatives due to the cancellation of the TSR-2. At key moments, British aircraft manufacturing proved to be a cross-class, cross-parliamentary issue. Might it also be taken as evidence of a basic patriotism which helped to ensure that Britain remained a global power even after losing its Empire?

Notes

1 Ethell and Price ([1983] 1986, pp. 19–20, 213).
2 TNA CAB128/41, CC (66)68th, Conclusions, 22nd December 1966.
3 21 HC Deb., 14th April 1982, col. 1146.
4 Okochi (2001).
5 Holland (1991).
6 Burk and Cairncross (1992, p. 228).
7 Jenkins, Peter (1996, p. 145).
8 Tomlinson ([2000] 2001, p. 96).

Appendix I: Types of jet aircrafts from the 1950s to the 1970s

Table AI.1

Britain and Europe				United States			
Airframe		*Engine*		*Airframe*		*Engine*	
The first jet age (thrust: under 30,000 lbs class)							
Military							
Hawker	Hunter	Rolls-Royce	Avon	Boeing	KC-135	P&W	J57
Handley Page	Victor	Rolls-Royce	Conway	Lockheed	C-130	GM	T56
Vickers	Valiant	Rolls-Royce	Avon	Lockheed	F-104	GE	J79
Vickers	V-1000	Rolls-Royce	Conway	Boeing	B-52	P&W	TF33
Civil							
Vickers	Viscount	Rolls-Royce	Dart	Lockheed	Electra	GM	T56
Bristol	Britannia	Bristol	Proteus	Boeing	707-120	P&W	JT3 (J57)
de Havilland	Comet	de Havilland	Ghost	Boeing	707-320	P&W	JT4 (J75)
Vickers	VC10	Rolls-Royce	Conway	Boeing	707-420	Rolls-Royce	Conway
				Douglas	DC-8	P&W	JT3 (J57)
The second jet age (thrust: 40,000 lbs class)							
Military							
McDD	F-4	Rolls-Royce	Spey	Lockheed	F-104	GE	J79
BAC	TSR-2	BSE	Olympus	McDD	F-4	GE	J79

220 Appendix I: Types of jet aircrafts from the 1950s to the 1970s

Britain and Europe				United States			
Airframe		Engine		Airframe		Engine	
HSA	P.1154	BSE	BS100	Lockheed	C-5A	GE	CF6
HSA	P.1124	Rolls-Royce	Pegasus	GD	F-111	P&W	TF30
				LTV	A-7 Corsair II	Rolls-Royce	Spey
Civil							
BAC	BAC2-11/ BAC3-11	Rolls-Royce	RB211	Boeing	747	P&W	JT9D
Airbus	A300	Rolls-Royce	RB207	McDD	DC-10	GE	CF6
Airbus	A300B	GE	CF6	Lockheed	TriStar	Rolls-Royce	RB211
Supersonic transport							
BAC	Concorde	Rolls-Royce	Olympus	Boeing	2707	GE	4
The third jet age (civil)							
Airbus	A310	GE	CF6	Boeing	757	Rolls-Royce	RB211–535
				Boeing	767	P&W	JT9D

Source: Anglo-American industrial collaboration.
Note: Shaded entries denote a combination of US airframe and UK aero-engine.

Appendix II: UK balance of payments, 1946–1970

Table AII.1

	Vis trd	Invi- sibles	Curr blnc	Sp grnt	Invst- mnt	Blnc itm	tcf	(a)	Tot abv	(b)	Off rsrv
1946	-103	-127	-230		235	50	55	-1	54		-54
1947	-361	-20	-381	30	342	-150	-159	-51	-210	58	152
1948	-151	177	26	138	-128	-100	-64	-6	-70	15	55
1949	-137	136	-1	154	-106	-50	-3		-3		3
1950	-51	358	307	140	128		575		575		-575
1951	-689	320	-369	43	92	-100	-334		-334	10	344
1952	-279	442	163		-404	66	-175		-175		175
1953	-244	389	145		119	32	296		296	-56	-240
1954	-204	321	117		-48	57	126		126	-39	-87
1955	-313	158	-155		-195	121	-229		-229		229
1956	53	155	208		-409	42	-159		-159	201	-42
1957	-29	262	233		-300	80	13		13		-13
1958	29	315	344		-121	67	290		290	-6	-284
1959	-117	269	152		-108	-26	18	-58	-40	-79	119
1960	-406	151	-255		286	294	325	-32	293	-116	-177
1961	-152	158	6		-316	-29	-339		-339	370	-31
1962	-102	224	122		-3	73	192		192	-375	183
1963	-80	204	124		-107	-75	-58		-58	5	53
1964	-519	143	-376		-299	-20	-695		-695	573	122
1965	-237	185	-52		-322	21	-353	-44	-353	599	-246
1966	-73	156	83		-556	-74	-547		-591	625	-34
1967	-552	254	-298		-573	200	-671		-671	556	115
1968	-643	355	-288		-1005	-117	-1410		-1410	1296	114

222   *Appendix II: UK balance of payments, 1946–1970*

	Vis trd	Invi- sibles	Curr blnc	Sp grnt	Invst- mnt	Blnc itm	tcf	(a)	Tot abv	(b)	Off rsrv
1969	-141	581	440		-72	375	743		743	-699	-44
1970	3	576	579		615	93	1287	133	1420	-1295	-125

Source: Central Statistical Office, *United Kingdom Balance of Payments 1971* (London, HMSO, 1971), pp. 5, 7.
Columns: Visible trade, Invisibles, Current balance, Special grants, Investment, Balancing items, Total currency flow, (a) Gold subscription to the International Monetary Fund and Allocation of Special Drawing Rights, Total of above, (b) Net transactions with overseas monetary authority, Official reserves.

Bibliography

Archival sources

United Kingdom (The National Archives, Kew, London)

AIR2 Air Ministry and Ministry of Defence: *Registered Files.*

AIR8 Air Ministry and Ministry of Defence: Department of the Chief of the Air Staff: *Registered Files.*

AVIA63 Ministry of Supply, Air Division, and Ministry of Aviation: *Registered Files.*

AVIA65 Ministry of Supply and successors: *Registered Files.*

AVIA97Ministry of Aviation and Ministry of Technology: Air ADivision, Air A4 Branch and Air CDivision, Air C2 Branch: Committee of Inquiry into the Aircraft Industry (Plowden Committee), *Registered Files (BM Series) 1964–1967.*

BT248 Ministry of Civil Aviation and successors: Safety and General Group: *Papers.*

CAB65 and 66 War Cabinet and Cabinet: *Memoranda.*

CAB87 War Cabinet and Cabinet: Committees on Reconstruction, Supply and other matters: *Minutes and Papers.*

CAB128 and 129 Cabinet Office: *Cabinet Meetings and Memoranda.*

CAB130 Cabinet: Miscellaneous Committees: *Minutes and Papers.*

CAB133 Cabinet Office: Commonwealth and International Conferences and Ministerial Visits to and from the UK: *Minutes and Papers.*

CAB134 Cabinet: Miscellaneous Committees: *Minutes and Papers.*

CAB148 Cabinet Office: Defence and Oversea Policy Committees and Sub-Committees: *Minutes and Papers.*

CAB164 Cabinet Office: *Subject (Theme Series) Files.*

CAB168 Cabinet Office: Chief Scientific Adviser, Solly Zuckerman: *Registered Files.*

FCO33 Foreign Office, Western Department and Foreign and Commonwealth Office, Western European Department: *Registered Files.*

FCO46 Foreign Office and Foreign and Commonwealth Office: Defence Department and successors: *Registered Files.*

FCO70 Foreign and Commonwealth Office: Export Promotions Department: *Registered Files.*

PREM11 Prime Minister's Office: *Correspondence and Papers, 1951–1964.*

PREM13 Prime Minister's Office: *Correspondence and Papers, 1964–1970.*

PREM15 Prime Minister's Office: *Correspondence and Papers, 1970–1974.*

PREM16 Prime Minister's Office: *Correspondence and Papers, 1974–1979.*

T225 Treasury: Defence Policy and Materiel Division: *Registered Files.*

224   *Bibliography*

United States (The National Archives, College Park, Maryland)

Record Group [RG] 56: Department of the Treasury, Office of the Secretary, Office of the Assistant Secretary for International Affairs, Aid Programs, UK9/11, *Mutual Assistance Program*, General (1951–1959).

Record Group [RG] 59: *Department of the State.*

Central Files [CF]

Lot Files

Record Group [RG] 59: Department of the State, subject numeric file, lot files, Entry 1548[E1548] Record of the Mutual Security Program – *West European Country Files, 1952–1956.*

Record Group [RG] 59: Department of the State, subject numeric file, lot files, Entry 5172[E5172] *Subject Files of the Deputy Assistant Secretary for Politico-Military Affairs, 1961–1963.*

Record Group [RG] 59: Department of the State, subject numeric file, lot files, Entry 5178[E5178] Office of Politico-Military Affairs – *Subject Files of the Office of Operations, 1962–1966.*

Record Group [RG] 59: Department of the State, subject numeric file, lot files, Entry 5179[E5178] Office of Politico-Military Affairs – *Subject Files of the Combined Policy Office, 1961–1966.*

Record Group [RG] 59: Department of the State, subject numeric file, lot files, Entry A1 5603[E(A1)5603] *Records Relating to the United Kingdom, 1965–1974.*

Private papers

Edwin Noel Plowden, Baron Plowden: *Papers on Common Market and United States of Europe 1961–73[PLDN]*, Churchill College Archives Centre, Cambridge.

Published official sources

United Kingdom

Central Statistical Office, *United Kingdom Balance of Payments 1971* (London, HMSO, 1971).

Department of Trade and Industry, *Productivity of the national aircraft effort: report of a committee appointed by the Minister of Technology and the President of the Society of British Aerospace Companies, under the chairmanship of St. John Elstub* (London, HMSO, 1969).

Department of Trade and Industry, *Rolls-Royce Limited, Investigation under Section 165 (a)(i) of the Companies Act 1948, Report by R A MacCrindle P Godfrey FCA* (London, HMSO, 1973).

Department of Trade and Industry, *Rolls-Royce Ltd and the RB211 Aero-Engine*, Cmnd. 4860 (London, HMSO, 1972).

Hansard, Debates of the House of Commons.

Minister of Aviation, *Report of the Committee of Inquiry into the Aircraft Industry*, Cmnd. 2853 (London, HMSO, 1965).

Minister of Defence, *Defence: Outline of Future Policy*, Cmnd. 124 (London, HMSO, 1957).

Ministry of Aviation, *The Financial Problems of the British Overseas Airways Corporation*, (London, HMSO, 1963).

Ministry of Civil Aviation, *British Air Services*, Cmd. 6712 (London, HMSO, 1945).

Office of the Minister for Science, *Report of the Committee on the Management and Control of Research and Development* (London, HMSO, 1961).

The Chancellor of Exchequer, *New Policies for Public Spending*, Cmnd. 4515 (London, HMSO, 1970).

The Chancellor of Exchequer, *White Paper on Public Expenditure 1969–70 to 1974–75*, Cmnd. 4578 (London, HMSO, 1975).

United States

Congressional Quarterly Almanac, 92nd Congress, 1st Session, 1971, v. 27 (Washington, Congressional Quarterly Inc., 1972).

Foreign Relations of the United States, 1958–1960, Volume VII, Part 1, Western European Integration and Security, Canada (Washington, USGPO, 1993).

Foreign Relations of the United States, 1958–1960, Volume VII, Part 2, Western European Integration and Security, Canada (Washington, USGPO, 1993).

Foreign Relations of the United States, 1961–1963, Volume XIII, Western Europe and Canada (Washington, USGPO, 1994).

Foreign Relations of the United States, 1964–1968, Volume XII, Western Europe (Washington, USGPO, 2001).

Foreign Relations of the United States, The Conferences at Washington, 1941–1942, and Casablanca, 1943 (Washington, USGPO, 1968).

Public Papers of the Presidents of the United States, John F. Kennedy: containing the public messages, speeches, and statements of the President, January 1 to November 22, 1963 (Washington, USGPO, 1964).

The Commission on International Trade and Investment Policy (1971), *United States international economic policy in an interdependent world: report to the President* (Washington, USGPO).

U.S. Congress, *Military Air Transportation*, 86th Cong., 1st Sess. (Washington, USGPO, 1959).

U.S. Congress, *National Aviation policy: Report of the Congressional Aviation Policy Board of the United States*, 80th Cong., 2d Sess. (Washington, USGPO, 1948).

U.S. Congress, *United States Aid to British Aircraft Program, Report of the Investigations Divisions of Senate Appropriations Committee*, 83rd Cong., 2nd Sess. (Washington, USGPO, 1954).

Newspapers and magazines

Air view (Koku-Joho).
Aviation Week.
Aviation Week & Space Technology.
Business Week.
Flight International.
Fortune.
Interavia.

226 Bibliography

Diaries, memoirs and biographies

Adams, Jad (1992), *Tony Benn: A Biography* (London, Macmillan).

Arnold, Henry H. (1951), *Global Mission* (London, Hutchinson).

Benn, Tony [1988] (1989a), *Office Without Power, Diaries 1968–72* (London, Arrow books Limited).

Benn, Tony [1988] (1989b), *Tony Benn: Against the Tide, Diaries 1973–1976* (London, Hutchinson).

Crossman, Richard [1975] (1978), *The Diaries of a Cabinet Minister*, Volume 1, *Minister of Housing 1964–1966* (London, Hamish Hamilton and Jonathan Cape).

Healey, Denis (1989), *The Time of My Life* (London, Michael Joseph).

Jenkins, Roy (1991), *A Life at the Centre* (London, Macmillan).

McGhee, George C. (1989), *At the Creation of a New Germany from Adenauer to Brandt: An Ambassador's Account* (New Haven; London, Yale University Press).

Pearce, Edward (2002), *Denis Healey: A Life in Our Times* (London, Little, Brown).

Shapley, Deborah (1993), *Promise and Power: The Life and Times of Robert Mcnamara* (Boston, Little, Brown).

Slessor, John (1957), *The Central Blue: The Autobiography of Sir John Slessor, Marshall of the RAF* (New York, Praeger).

Stonehouse, John (1975), *Death of an Idealist* (London, W.H. Allen).

Wilson, Harold (1971), *The Labour Government, 1964–70: A Personal Record* (London, Weidenfeld & Nicolson and Michael Joseph).

Zuckerman, Solly (1988), *Monkeys, Men, and Missiles: An Autobiography, 1946–88* (London, Collins).

Books, articles and book chapters

Aris, Stephen (2002), *Close to the Sun: How Airbus Challenged America's Domination of the Skies* (London, Aurum).

Ashton, Nigel K. (2002), *Kennedy, Mcmillan and the Cold War: The Irony of Interdependence* (London, Palgrave Macmillan).

Badrocke, Mike and Gunston, Bill (1998), *Lockheed Aircraft Cutaways: The History of Lockheed Martin* (London, Osprey Aviation).

Barnett, Correlli (1995), *The Lost Victory: British Dreams, British Realities, 1945–1950* (London, Macmillan).

Baylis, John (1981), *Anglo-American Defence Relations 1939–1980: The Special Relationship* (London, Macmillan).

Baylis, John (1995), *Ambiguity and Deterrence: British Nuclear Strategy, 1945–1964* (Oxford, Clarendon Press).

Bender, Marylin and Altschul, Selig (1982), *The Chosen Instrument: Pan Am, Juan Trippe, the Rise and Fall of an American Entrepreneur* (New York, Simon & Schuster).

Bluth, Christoph (1995), *Britain, Germany and Western Nuclear Strategy* (Oxford, Clarendon Press).

Bozo, Frédéric (2002), *Two Strategies for Europe: De Gaulle, the United States, and the Atlantic Alliance* (Lanham, Md., Rowman & Littlefield).

Brooke, Peter (2018), *Duncan Sandys and the Informal Politics of Britain's Late Decolonisation* (Cham, Palgrave Macmillan).

Buckley, John (1995), 'Atlantic Airpower Co-operation, 1941–1945', Gooch, John (ed,) *Airpower: Theory and Practice* (London, Frank Cass), pp. 175–197.

Bibliography 227

Burk, Kathleen and Cairncross, Alec (1992), *'Goodbye, Great Britain': The 1976 IMF Crisis* (New Haven, Conn.; London, Yale University Press).

Cain, P.J. and Hopkins, A.G. (2002), *British Imperialism, 1688–2000*, 2nd ed. (Harlow, Longman).

Camps, Miriam (1964), *Britain and the European Community 1955–1963* (Princeton, N.J., Princeton University Press).

Churchill, Winston S. (1950), *Europe Unite: Speeches, 1947 and 1948* (London, Cassell).

Cole, Lance (2017), *VC10: Icon of the Skies, BOAC, Boeing and a Jet Age Battle* (Barnsley, South Yorkshire, Pen & Sword Aviation).

Commission on International Trade and Investment Policy (1971), *United States International Economic Policy in an Interdependent World: Report to the President* (Washington, Commission on International Trade and Investment Policy).

Costello, John and Hughes, Terry (1976), *The Concorde Conspiracy: The International Race for the SST* (New York, Scribner).

Darby, Phillip (1973), *British Defence Policy East of Suez, 1947–1968* (London, Oxford University Press for the Royal Institute of International Affairs).

Davies, R.E.G. [1964] (1967), *A History of the World's Airlines* (London, Oxford University Press).

Dawkins, Richard and Brockmann, H. Jane (1980), 'Do digger wasps commit the Concorde fallacy?', *Animal Behaviour*, 28 (3), pp. 892–896.

Dockrill, Saki (2002), *Britain's Retreat from East of Suez: The Choice between Europe and the World?* (Basingstoke; New York, N.Y., Palgrave Macmillan).

Eddy, Paul, Page, Bruce, and Potter, Elaine (1976), *Destination Disaster* (New York, Quadrangle/The New York Times Book Co., Inc.).

Edgar, Alistair (1989), 'The MRCA/Tornado: The Politics and Economics of Collaborative Procurement', Haglund, David G. (ed.), *The Defence Industrial Base and the West* (London, Routledge), pp. 46–85.

Edgerton, David [2006] (2008), *Warfare State: Britain, 1920–1970* (Cambridge, Cambridge University Press).

Ellison, James (2007), *The United States, Britain and the Transatlantic Crisis: Rising to the Gaullist Challenge, 1963–68* (Basingstoke, Palgrave Macmillan).

Endress, Günter (1999), *Airbus A300* (Shrewsbury, Airlife Publishing Ltd.).

Engel, Jeffrey A. (2009), *Cold War at 30,000 Feet: The Anglo-American Fight for Aviation Supremacy* (Cambridge, MA, Harvard University Press).

Ethell, Jeffrey and Price, Alfred [1983] (1986), *Air War South Atlantic* (London, Sidgwick & Jackson).

Gardner, Charles (1981), *British Aircraft Corporation: A History* (London, Batsford).

Garvin, Robert V. (1998), *Starting Something Big: The Commercial Emergence of GE Aircraft Engines* (Reston VA, AIAA).

Gavin, Francis J. (2004), *Gold, Dollars, and Power: The Politics of International Monetary Relations, 1958–1971* (Chapel Hill; London, University of North Carolina Press).

Giffard, Hermione (2016), *Making Jet Engines in World War II: Britain, Germany, and the United States* (Chicago, The University of Chicago Press).

Gold, Bonnie (1995), *Politics, Markets, and Security, European Military and Civil Aircraft Collaboration 1954–1994* (Lanham, Md.; London, University Press of America).

Haftendorn, Helga (1996), *NATO and the Nuclear Revolution: A Crisis of Credibility, 1966–1967* (Oxford, Clarendon Press).

Hartley, Keith (1965), 'The Mergers in the UK Aircraft Industry, 1957–60', *The Aeronautical Journal*, 69 (660), pp. 46–52.

228 Bibliography

Hartley, Keith (1983), *NATO Arms Co-operation: A Study in Economics and Politics* (London, Allen & Unwin).

Hartung, William D. (2011), *Prophets of War: Lockheed Martin and the Making of the Military-Industrial Complex* (New York, Nation Books).

Hastings, Stephen (1966), *The Murder of TSR-2* (London, Macdonald).

Hayward, Keith (1983), *Government and British Civil Aerospace: A Case Study in Post-War Technology Policy* (Manchester, Manchester University Press).

Hayward, Keith (1986), *International Collaboration in Civil Aerospace* (London, Pinter).

Hayward, Keith (1989), *The British Aircraft Industry* (Manchester, Manchester University Press).

Hayward, Keith (2012), 'The Formation of the British Aircraft Corporation (BAC) 1957–1961', *Journal of Aeronautical History*, Paper No. 2012/01.

Higham, Robin (2013), *Speedbird: The Complete History of BOAC* (London, I.B. Tauris).

Hitch, Charles J. and McKean, Roland N. (1960), *The Economics of Defense in the Nuclear Age* (Cambridge, Harvard University Press).

Hogan, Michael J. [1987] (1989), *The Marshall Plan: America, Britain and the Reconstruction of Western Europe, 1947–1952* (Cambridge, Cambridge University Press).

Holland, Robert (1991), *The Pursuit of Greatness: Britain and the World Role, 1900–1970* (London, Fontana Press).

Ichige, Kiyomi (2016), 'From Development to Cancellation of Anglo French Variable Geometry Aircraft (AFVG), 1964–1967', *Journal of Law and Political Studies (Hogaku Seijigaku Ronkyu)*, 110, pp. 1–31.

Ingells, Douglas J. (1973), *L-1011 TriStar and The Lockheed Story* (Fallbrook, Calif, Aero Publishers).

James, D. and Judkins, Phil (2010), 'Chute libre avant le décollage: le programme GVFA d'avion à géométrie variable franco-anglais, 1965–1967', *Dans Histoire, économie & société*, 29, pp. 51–73.

Jenkins, Peter (1996), *Anatomy of Decline: The Political Journalism of Peter Jenkins* (London, Cassell).

Johnman, Lewis and Lynch, Frances (2002), 'A Treaty too Far? Britain, France, and Concorde, 1961–1964', *Twentieth Century British History*, 13 (3), pp. 253–276.

Johnman, Lewis and Lynch, Frances (2006), 'Technological non-cooperation: Britain and Airbus, 1965–1969', *Journal of European Integration History*, 12 (1), pp. 125–140.

Jones, Aubrey (1985), *Britain's Economy: The Roots of Stagnation* (Cambridge, Cambridge University Press).

Kaufman, William W. (1964), *The McNamara Strategy* (New York, Harper & Row).

Kawasaki, Nobuki and Sakade, Takeshi (2001), 'The Marshall Plan and the Formation of the Postwar International System', *Research and Study*, 22, pp. 1–9.

Kennedy, Paul (1987), *The Rise and Fall of the Great Powers: Economic Change and Military Conflict from 1500 to 2000* (New York, Random House).

Kindleberger, Charles P. (1973), *The World in Depression, 1929–1939* (London, Allen Lane).

Knight, Geoffrey (1976), *Concorde: The Inside Story* (New York, Stein and Day).

Kyle, Keith (1991), *Suez: Britain's End of Empire in the Middle East* (London; New York, I.B. Tauris).

Leigh-Phippard, Helen (1995), *Congress and US Military Aid to Britain: Interdependence and Dependence, 1949–56* (Basingstoke, Macmillan, with the Mountbatten Centre for International Studies).

Lichtheim, George (1971), *Imperialism* (New York, Praeger).

Bibliography 229

Lynn, Matthew [1995] (1998), *Birds of Prey: Boeing vs. Airbus: A Battle for the Skies* (New York, Four Walls Eight Windows).

Magaziner, Ira C. and Patinkin, Mark (1989), *Silent War* (New York, Random House).

May, Annabele (2009), 'Concorde – Bird of Harmony or Political Albatross: An Examination in the Context of British Foreign Policy', *International Organization*, 33 (4), pp. 481–508.

McGuire, Steven (1997), *Airbus Industrie* (Basingstoke, Palgrave Macmillan).

Milward, Alan S. [1984] (1992), *The Reconstruction of Western Europe 1945–51* (London, Routledge).

Milward, Alan S. [1992] (2000), *The European Rescue of the Nation State*, 2nd ed. (London, Routledge).

Milward, Alan S. (2002), *The UK and the European Community Vol.1 The rise and fall of a national strategy 1945–1963* (London, Whitehall History Publishing in association with Frank Cass).

Moore, Richard (2010), *Nuclear Illusion, Nuclear Reality: Britain, the United States and Nuclear Weapons, 1958–64* (Basingstoke, Palgrave Macmillan).

Nardi, Philip P. (1995), *Foreign Military Sales Policy of the Kennedy Presidential Administration* (Ohio, Air Force Institute of Technology).

Newhouse, John (1982), *The Sporty Game* (New York, Alfred A. Knopf).

Oberdorfer, Don (2003), *Senator Mansfield: The Extraordinary Life of a Great American Statesman and Diplomat* (Washington, D.C.; London, Smithsonian Books).

O'Brien, Patrick (2002), 'Pax-Britannica and the International Order 1688–1914', Matsuda, Takeshi and Akita, Shigeru (eds.), *Hegemony Nations and World System* (Tokyo, Yamakawa Publishing), pp. 89–134.

Okochi, Akio (2001), *Rolls-Royce: Collapse of the British Spirit of Ecstasy* (Tokyo, University of Tokyo Press).

Onslow, Sue (2008), 'Julian Amery and the Suez Operation', Smith, Simon C. (ed.), *Reassessing Suez 1956: New Perspectives on the Crisis and its Aftermath* (Aldershot, Ashgate), pp. 67–77.

Owen, Geoffrey (1999), *From Empire to Europe: The Decline and Revival of British Industry since the Second World War* (London, HarperCollins).

Owen, Kenneth (1997), *Concorde and the Americans: International Politics of the Supersonic Transport* (Washington; London, Smithsonian Institution Press).

Parr, Helen (2006), *Britain's Policy Towards the European Community: Harold Wilson and Britain's World Role, 1964–1967* (London, Routledge).

Pearce, David W. (1992), *The MIT Dictionary of Modern Economics*, 4th ed. (Cambridge, Mass., The MIT Press).

Peden, George C. (2007), *Arms, Economics and British Strategy: From Dreadnoughts to Hydrogen Bombs* (Cambridge, Cambridge University Press).

Phipp, Mike (2007), *The Brabazon Committee and British Airliners 1945–1960* (Stroud, Tempus).

Phythian, Mark (2000), *The Politics of British Arms Sales since 1964* (Manchester, Manchester University Press).

Pierre, Andrew J. (1972), *Nuclear Politics: The British Experience with an Independent Strategic Force, 1939–1970* (London, Oxford University Press).

Pincher, Chapman (1978), *Inside Story: A Documentary of the Pursuit of Power* (London, Sidgwick & Jackson).

Priest, Andrew (2006), *Kennedy, Johnson and NATO, 1962–68* (London, Routledge).

230 Bibliography

Prouty, L. Fletcher [1996] (2011), *JFK: The CIA, Vietnam, and the Plot to Assassinate John F. Kennedy* (New York, Skyhorse Publishing).

Pugh, Peter (2001), *The Magic of a Name: The Rolls-Royce Story, Part Two: The Power Behind the Jets* (Cambridge, Icon Books).

Pugh, Peter (2002), *The Magic of a Name: The Rolls-Royce Story, Part Three: A Family of Engines* (Cambridge, Icon Books).

Rae, John B. (1968), *Climb to Greatness: The American Aircraft Industry, 1920–1960* (Cambridge, Mass; London, The MIT Press).

Reed, Arthur (1973), *Britain's Aircraft Industry: What Went Right? What Went Wrong?* (London, J.M. Dent & Sons).

Rice, Berkeley (1971), *The C-5A Scandal: An Inside Story of the Military-Industrial Complex* (Boston, Houghton Mifflin).

Rodgers, Eugene (1996), *Flying High: The Story of Boeing and the Rise of the Jetliner Industry* (New York, Atlantic Monthly Press).

Rohde, Joachim (2004), 'The Transfer of American Military Technology to Germany', Junker, Detlef (ed.), *The United States and Germany in the era of the Cold War, 1945–1990. Vol. 2 1968–1990: A Handbook* (New York, Cambridge University Press), pp. 163–170.

Rubinstein, William D. (1993), *Capitalism, Culture, and Decline in Britain, 1750–1990* (London; New York, Routledge).

Sakade, Takeshi (1996), 'NATO Nuclearization and Anglo-American Special Relationship', *Fudai Keizai Ronshu*, 42 (1), pp. 35–52.

Sakai, Akio (1998), *International Political Economy* (Tokyo, Aoki Publishing).

Sampson, Anthony (1977), *The Arms Bazaar* (London, Hodder & Stoughton).

Sampson, Anthony (1992), *The Essential Anatomy of Britain: Democracy in Crisis* (London, Hodder & Stoughton).

Sasaki, Yuta (1997), *The British Empire and the Suez War* (Nagoya, The University of Nagoya Press).

Segell, Glen (1998), *Royal Air Force Procurement: The TSR.2 to the Tornado* (London, G. Segell).

Servan-Schreiber, Jean J. (1968), *The American Challenge* (New York, Atheneum).

Shibazaki, Yusuke (2009), 'Technology Collaboration with Europe and British Policies towards Europe: The European Technological Community in the Late 1960s', *International Relations*, 157, pp. 156–169.

Simons, Graham M. (2012a), *Bristol Brabazon* (Stroud, History Press).

Simons, Graham M. (2012b), *Concorde Conspiracy: The Battle for American Skies 1962–1977* (Stroud, History Press).

Simons, Graham M. (2013), *Comet!: The World's First Jet Airliner* (Barnsley, South Yorkshire, Pen & Sword Aviation).

Straw, Sean and Young, John W. (1997), 'The Wilson government and the demise of TSR-2, October 1964–April 1965', *The Journal of Strategic Studies*, 20 (4), pp. 18–44.

Tomlinson, Jim [2000] (2001), *The Politics of Decline: Understanding Postwar Britain* (London, Pearson Education Limited).

Thayer, George (1969), *The War Business, The International Trade in Armaments* (New York, Simon & Schuster).

Thornton, David W. (1995), *Airbus Industrie: The Politics of International Industrial Collaboration* (Basingstoke, Macmillan).

Trachtenberg, Marc (1999), *A Constructed Peace: The Making of the European Settlement, 1945–1963* (Princeton, N.J., Princeton University Press).

Bibliography 231

Verhovek, Sam Howe (2010), *Jet Age: The Comet, the 707, and the Race to Shrink the World* (London, Penguin Group).

Watanabe, Shouichi (2021), 'The Anglo-American Military Aid negotiations in South Asia', Yokoi, Katsuhiko (ed.), *Indigenous Armaments Production and International Assistance in Cold War Asia* (Tokyo, Nihon Keizai Hyoronsha Ltd.), pp. 199–232.

Wenger, Andreas (2007), 'NATO's transformation in the 1960s and ensuing political order in Europe', Wenger, Andreas, Nuenlist, Christian and Locher, Anna (eds.) *Transforming NATO in the Cold War: Challenges Beyond Deterrence in the 1960s* (London, Routledge), pp. 221–242.

West, James (2001), *The End of an Era: My Story of the L-1011* (United States of America, Xlibris Corporation).

Wiener, Martin J. (1981), *English Culture and the Decline of the Industrial Spirit, 1850–1980* (Cambridge, Cambridge University Press).

Wood, Derek (1986), *Project Cancelled: The Disaster of Britain's Abandoned Aircraft Projects* (London, Jane's Publishing).

Worcester, Richard (1966), *Roots of British Air Policy* (London, Hodder & Stoughton).

Young, John W. (1997), *Britain and the World in the Twentieth Century* (London, Arnold).

Young, John W. (2003), 'Technological Cooperation in Wilson's Strategy for EEC Entry', Daddow, Oliver J. (ed.), *Harold Wilson and European Integration: Britain's Second Application to Join the EEC* (London, Frank Cass), pp. 95–114.

Young, Nancy Beck (2000), *Wright Patman: Populism, Liberalism, and the American Dream* (Dallas, Southern Methodist University Press).

Zimmermann, Hubert (2000), 'Western Europe and the American Challenge: Conflict and Cooperation in Technology and Monetary Policy, 1965–1973', *Journal of European Integration History*, 6 (2), pp. 85–110.

Zimmermann, Hubert (2002), *Money and Security: Troops, Monetary Policy, and West Germany's Relations with the United States and Britain, 1950–1971* (Cambridge, Cambridge University Press).

Index

A300 airliner 138–142, 144, 146–49, 186

A300B airliner 138, 148–57, 185–86, 202, 205, 207, 209, 211

A310 airliner xxxii, 202–03, 205–07, 209, 210–11

Acheson, Dean xxix, 59

ADO12 V/STOL fighter 89–90, 93–94, 97, 115, 126

AFVG fighter (Anglo-French) 76, 87–90, 92–93, 97, 99, 106–07, 113, 115, 119–123, 216

Agger, Donald G. 145, 177

Air Canada 163, 165, 167

Air France xxvii, 11, 15, 17, 35, 41, 140, 147, 151–53, 176, 184, 191, 193

Airco 26, 27, 31

Air Holdings Ltd. 144–45, 155

The American Challenge xxx

American Airlines 142, 144–45, 150, 184

American Embassy in London 16, 181–82

Amery, Julian 24, 39, 42, 44–47, 49, 69, 179–80

Amory, Heathcoat 28, 32–33

ATMR airliner 203, 206

Avro 748 transport 66

Australia 61, 62, 66–68

B-17 bomber 4

B-24 bomber 4

B-47 bomber 12–13

B-52 bomber 12–13

BAC1–11 airliner 33–34, 45

BAC2–11 airliner 138, 143

BAC3–11 airliner 138, 147–148, 150, 154–57, 185–86

BAe xxiv, xxxii, 196, 200–12, 217

Balance of payments (UK) 16, 58, 69–70, 74, 78, 103, 117, 123, 181

Balance of payments (US) 60–61, 63, 124, 143–44, 163

Bank of England 155, 157

Barnett, C. xxiv, xxv, xxix, 3, 4, 9, 19, 51

Belgium 14–16, 41, 61, 64, 115, 120, 126, 151

Benn, Tony Wedgewood 127, 140, 143, 146–49, 177, 183–87, 191–94, 218

Benson, Henry 31, 158

Berber, Anthony 154–56

Beverly transport 35

Béteille, Roger 146–47, 151

Blackburn 33

Blue Streak 25, 59–60

Blue Water 60

Boeing xxiv, xxix, 12, 15, 17–18, 32, 45–46, 50, 138–39, 178–79, 184, 190, 196, 200–09, 212, 217 *see* B-17 bomber, B-47 bomber, B-52 bomber, Boeing 377(Stratocruiser) airliner, Boeing 707 airliner, Boeing 727 airliner, Boeing 737 airliner, Boeing 747 airliner, Boeing 757 airliner, Boeing 767 airliner, Boeing 777 airliner, Boeing 2707 SST airliner, KC-135 tanker

Boeing 2707 SST airliner 184, 188

Boeing 377(Stratocruiser) airliner

Boeing 707 airliner xxvii, 12, 13, 15, 17–19, 29–30, 32, 34–35, 39, 41–47, 49–50, 138, 178–79, 201–02, 216

Boeing 727 airliner 138, 201–03

Boeing 737 airliner 138, 201

Boeing 747 airliner 49–51, 139, 142, 150, 179, 191, 201, 212

Boeing 757 airliner xxxii, 201–12

Boeing 767 airliner 201–02, 205–06

Boeing 777 airliner 200, 212

Brabazon airliner 5–6, 8, 10

Index 233

Brabazon, Lord 5
The Brabazon Committee 5–6, 10
The Brabazon programme xxxi, 4–10, 19
Bretton-Woods system 60, 143
Bristol 5, 13, 26–27, 30, 33, 178 *see*
 Brabazon airliner, Bristol 200 airliner,
 Britannia airliner
Bristol 200 airliner 32
Bristol Siddeley Engine (BSE) 32–33, 35,
 88, 119, 122, 140, 192 *see* Olympus
 engine
Britannia airliner 10–13, 26, 29, 40, 42
British Aircraft Corporation (BAC) 33–35,
 45, 47, 49–50, 58, 67, 69, 88, 96,
 98–99, 102–03, 120, 122, 147–48,
 152, 154, 157, 178, 185–87, 194 *see*
 BAC1–11 airliner, BAC2–11 airliner
BAC3–11 airliner, Concorde SST airliner,
 Super VC10 airliner, Superb airliner,
 MRCA Tornado fighter, TSR-2
 fighter-bomber
British Airways (BA) xxiv, xxxii, 196,
 200–12
British Army of the Rhine (BAOR) 58, 70,
 113, 116–19, 123–25, 152
British Empire xxiii, xxvi, xxix, xxx, xxxi, 3,
 5, 6, 8, 9, 12, 19, 23, 36, 65–66, 81,
 129, 215, 217–18
British European Airways Corporation
 (BEA) 7, 11, 25–27, 30–31, 36, 140,
 143–44, 147–48, 186
British Overseas Airways Corporation
 (BOAC) xxxi, 3, 6–13, 17–19, 25–26,
 29–35, 39–51, 176, 184, 191, 193, 216
Brown, George 69, 74, 128, 184
Brown, Harold 72, 89, 90, 101
Buccaneer fighter 67,
Bundesbank 124
Buy American Act 63, 81, 90, 104, 217

C-130 transport 12, 35, 58, 64, 66, 70,
 72–75, 100, 103
C-54 transport 6
C-5A transport 139, 142, 150, 159
The Cabinet Economic Policy Committee
 xxvii, 10, 28, 42
Callaghan, James 49, 74, 200–01, 203–11,
 216
Capital Airlines 10–11, 13
Canada xxx, 61, 66, 126
Canadair DC-4M 8–9
Canberra light-bomber 10–11, 16, 27,
 60–61, 67, 106
Carrington, Lord Peter 161–67

CF32 engine 212
CF6 engine 139, 142, 147–48, 150–53,
 155, 204
Chamant, Jean 143, 148, 183, 185–87,
 189
the Chequers meeting (November 1964)
 69, 70
Chirac, Jacques 194, 195
Churchill, Winston S. xxvii, xxix, xxxi, 3,
 5, 7, 9, 19, 23–24, 65, 70, 80, 129,
 143
the Citizens' League Against the Sonic
 Boom (CLASB) 188, 190
the City 155–57
Cold War xxvii, 63, 71, 115, 209
Cole, Lord 156–59
Comet airliner xxvii, xxix, 5, 7–12, 17,
 19–20, 26, 29–30, 40–42, 48, 177–79,
 216
Concorde SST airliner (Anglo-French)
 xxxii, 45, 68, 75, 80, 87, 91, 119–20,
 123, 139–40, 154, 169, 176–96, 216
Congress, US 13, 14, 16, 19, 144, 159,
 165–68, 188, 190
Conservative (Anthony Eden) Government
 (1955–57) 8, 9
Conservative (Alec Douglas-Home)
 Government (1963–64) 44, 46–47
Conservative (Edward Heath) Government
 (1970–74) 153–60, 163–64, 166,
 187–90
Conservative (Harold Macmillan) Govern-
 ment (1957–63) xxxi, 5, 25–30, 32–33,
 178
Conservative (Winston S. Churchill)
 Government (1951–55) 10, 25
Conway engine 12–13, 15, 17–18, 42, 49,
 216
Connally, John B. 162–63, 165–67
Constellation airliner 5, 7–9
Cooper Brothers 31, 157–58
Cromer, Lord 162–63, 165–66
CV A01 aircraft carrier 60

Dassault 98, 102–03, 115, 120, 122–23,
 127, 201 *see* Mercure airliner, Mirage
 series fighter
DC-3 airliner 5
DC-4 airliner 5–7
DC-6 airliner 7–8
DC-7 airliner 12
DC-8 airliner xxvii, 12–13, 15, 17, 19, 29,
 32, 39, 42, 47, 49–50, 138, 178–79,
 216

234 *Index*

DC-9 airliner 138
DC-10 airliner 138, 141–42, 144–47, 150–53, 166, 211
DCX200 airliner 201
De Gaulle, Charles xxx, 60, 79–80, 88, 91, 106–07, 113–17, 123, 128–29, 178–79, 182, 217
de Havilland 11, 26–27, 30–33, 36 *see* Comet airliner, Trident airliner
Defence and Overseas Policy Committee (OPD committee) 73, 75–76, 78, 88–89, 96, 105–06, 117, 120–22, 127
Delta airlines 162–63, 165, 167
Department of Defense (DoD), US (Pentagon) 16, 61, 69, 71–72, 76, 89–92, 94, 101–02, 159, 182–83
Department of State (DoS), US 72, 76, 94, 181–82
Director of Defense Research and Engineering (DDR&E) 89–90, 94, 101
Dockrill, S. 35, 57, 74, 86, 114
Douglas xxiv, 12, 15, 17, 50, 138, 141, 178
Douglas-Home, Sir Alexander Frederick 45–46

East of Suez 23, 35, 57–60, 70–73, 77, 79, 99, 114–16, 118, 123, 129, 218
Eastern Airlines 142, 145, 159, 162–63, 165, 167, 186, 202, 205–09, 211–12
Eden, Anthony 16
Edgerton, D. xxvi, 57, 86
Eisenhower Administration (1953–61) 14, 67
Eisenhower, Dwight D. 14, 67
Electra airliner 12
the Empire routes 8, 32, 40
English Electric 27–28, 31–33 *see* Canberra light-bomber
Erhardt, Ludwig 118, 125
European Airbus xxiv, xxxi, xxxii, 86–87, 114, 137–43, 145–57, 168–69, 185–87, 196, 201–12, 216–217 *see* A300 airliner, A300B airliner, A310 airliner
European Economic Community (EEC) 93, 114, 116, 128, 137, 142, 178–79, 184, 187–88, 190
European Technological Community xxxii, 113, 116, 127–29, 168, 216

F-104/F-104G fighter 16, 61, 64, 97, 102–03, 115, 118, 120–21, 125–26
F-111 fighter-bomber 35, 58, 60–61, 66–68, 70–73, 75–80, 86–100, 102–103, 105–07, 114–15, 118, 120, 122–23, 129, 184, 217
F-4 fighter 35, 58, 60, 65–66, 70, 72–75, 100, 103, 119, 121–22
Fairey 26
Falkland War 115, 215
Falklands Islands 215
"Fly British" policy xxxi, 7, 9, 15, 19, 34–35, 39–40, 42, 44–47, 49–51, 210, 216
force de frappe 60, 91, 99, 104, 113, 123
Foreign and Commonwealth Office (FCO) 99
Foreign Office (FO) xxxii, 75, 92, 122, 191

General Agreements on Tariffs and Trade (GATT) 152
General Election (October 1964) 68, 69, 181
General Electric (GE) 90, 94, 100, 135, 137, 139, 142–45, 148–53, 155, 162, 167–68, 186, 201, 203, 207–08, 210, 213 *see* CF6 engine, CF32 engine
Giscard d'Estaing, Valéry 194, 195, 203–04, 207, 211
Guthrie, Sir Giles xxxi, 40, 44–49, 51

Hassel, Kai-Uwe von 98, 125
Hasting transport 35
Haughton, Daniel J. 144, 151, 159–62, 164–65, 167
Hawk missile 103, 106
Hawker 26–27, 33
Hawker Siddeley Aviation (HSA) 30, 32–33, 35, 66, 99, 139, 146, 149, 178, 186, 202 *see* Avro 748 transport, HS.681 (AW681) transport, P.1127 (Harrier) V/STOL fighter, P.1154 V/STOL fighter, Trident airliner
Hayward, K. 4, 19, 58, 146
Healy, Lord Denis 69–79, 87–90, 92, 94–95, 99, 102, 105–06, 119–23, 126–27, 184, 187, 192–93, 215
Heath, Sir Edward 155–63, 165–66, 177, 188–90, 217
Hermes airliner 8
Hitch, Charles J. 61–62
Hitch-McKean theory 62–63, 65, 68

House of Commons 10, 29, 34, 50, 103, 117, 129, 146, 148, 167, 215
HP.97 airliner 32
HS.681 (AW681) transport 35, 57–58, 66, 68–70, 73–75, 79, 86, 90
Hunter fighter 10–11, 61, 75
Hunting 26, 33

India 66–67
International Logistics Negotiations (ILN) 61, 72, 90, 182
Italy 14, 16, 61, 115, 120, 126–27, 151, 201

J57 engine 13, 35
J75 engine 13, 15, 17, 35
Jaguar fighter (Anglo-French) 75–76, 87–89, 92–93, 97, 99, 119–21, 126, 184, 216
Javelin fighter 10, 14, 16
Jenkins, Roy 69, 71, 73, 75–79, 86, 88–89, 92, 94, 96, 99–101, 105, 181–83, 193
Johnson Administration (1963–1969) 70, 90, 118, 145, 217
Johnson, Lyndon B. 70, 75, 117–19, 124, 129, 145, 180–81, 2171
Jones, Aubrey xxxi, 24–27, 29–31, 34, 36, 69, 88, 90, 93, 98, 104–05, 107–08, 182–83
Jones, Elwyn 186, 192–95
JT3D engine 13
JT4D engine 13
JT9D engine 50, 139, 140, 142, 147–48, 150
JTF16 engine 127

KC-135 tanker 13, 15
Keith, Sir Kenneth 161–62, 202, 204–05, 211
Kennedy Administration (1961–63) 59–60, 63
Kennedy, John F. 59–61, 63, 179–180
Kiesinger, Kurt-Georg 118, 124–25
Kissinger, Henry 159
Kuss, Henry J. 61, 72, 76, 90–91, 97, 102–03, 182
Kuwait 59, 60

L-2000 SST airliner 184
Labour (Clement Atlee) Government (1945–51) 8–9
Labour (Harold Wilson) Government (1964–70) 58, 70, 73–75, 78–79, 99, 106, 117, 121, 125, 129, 140, 143–44, 148–49, 183–86, 215
Labour (Harold Wilson) Government (1974–1976) 191–94
Labour (James Callaghan) Government (1976–79) 203, 205, 207–08
Lancaster bomber 6
launch aid 32, 34, 36, 58, 158
Lazard Brothers 144
Lockheed xxix, 12, 16, 66, 102–03, 138–39, 141–55, 158–68, 186–87, 201 see C-130 transport, C-5A transport, Electra airliner, F-104/F-104G fighter, L-2000 SST airliner, *Polaris*, TriStar airliner
Lufthansa xxvii, 17, 41, 50, 140, 147, 151–53, 184

Macmillan, Harold xxxi, 16, 24–26, 30–32, 35–36, 42, 58–60, 66–67, 69, 177–78, 216
Mansfield, Michael 118, 143
Maudling, Reginald 17, 45–46, 66–67
McCloy, John G. 124
McDonnell-Douglas (McDD) 138–39, 141–42, 145, 150, 201, 205–06 see DC-10 airliner, DCX200 airliner, F-4 fighter, Mercure airliner
McNamara, Robert 59–61, 67, 69, 71–73, 76, 90–91, 93–94, 97, 100–03, 180
Mercure airliner 201
Merlin engine 9
Messmer, Pierre 75, 88–89, 92, 119–23
Ministerial Meeting 31–32, 46
Ministry of Aviation (MoA) 31, 34, 36, 42–43, 94, 103, 144
Ministry of Aviation Supply 158
Ministry of Defence (MoD) 16, 65, 70, 94, 101–02
Ministry of Economic Affairs 70
Ministry of Supply (MoS) 12, 15, 26–28, 31
Ministry of Technology (Mintech) 68, 153
Mirage series fighter 60, 88, 96, 98–99, 105–06, 114–15, 120, 123, 127, 215
Moore, William 161–63, 168
Mountbatten, Lord Louis 67
MRCA Tornado fighter (Anglo-German) xvii, xxxii, 113, 115, 123, 126–29, 185–87, 189
MTU 127, 151, 153
Mulley, Fred 47–50, 96, 106, 119–21, 140, 183, 215

236 *Index*

Nassau Conference / Agreement xxiv, 59–60

Netherlands, the (Dutch, Holland) xxvii, 8, 15–16, 61, 64, 115–16, 120, 122, 126–27

North Atlantic Treaty Organization (NATO) xxv, xxx, 10–11, 16, 35, 59–62, 65–66, 70–71, 96–97, 101, 105, 107, 114, 116–19, 124–26, 181, 217

Nixon Administration (1969–74) 159–60, 165, 190

Nixon, Richard 159–60, 165, 167, 190, 217

O'Brien, Leslie 155, 157, 163

offset arrangement (UK-US) 58, 72, 79, 99, 105–07, 118, 123, 129, 144

offset arrangement (UK-West Germany) 116–19, 121, 123–27, 144, 151–52

offset arrangement (US-UK-West Germany) 118, 124–125, 128–29

offset arrangement (US-West Germany) 61, 95, 97, 116, 118, 124

Offshore Procurement Program (OSP) 3, 9–10, 14, 16, 19

Olympus engine 140

Owen, G. xxvi, xxx, 86, 138, 217

P.1127 (Harrier) V/STOL fighter 105, 115, 121, 184, 215

P.1154 V/STOL fighter 35, 57–58, 66, 68–70, 73–75, 79, 86, 90, 121

Packard, David 159, 161, 163

Pan American World Airways (Pan Am) xxvii, 3–4, 11–12, 15, 26, 35, 39–41, 50, 139, 176, 179, 184, 191

Pearson, Denning 15, 17, 66, 76, 95, 120, 140, 144

Perfidious Albion xxiv, 114–15, 130

Plan K 4, 9–10, 14, 16, 19

Plowden, Lord Edwin 10, 69, 86, 88–89, 91, 93–94, 98

The Plowden Committee 69, 86–89, 91–98, 101, 104–05, 107, 182–83

The Plowden Report 64, 86–87, 104, 107–08, 127, 168, 182

Polaris 59–60, 103, 184,

Pompidou, Georges 181, 183, 191

Pound-Sterling xxix, xxx, 10, 23, 58, 66, 70, 117–18, 123, 164, 218

Pratt & Whitney (P&W) 17, 76, 88, 90, 94, 96, 100, 119, 123, 127, 135,

137, 139–42, 149–50, 153, 155, 162, 186, 201, 203, 213 *see* J57 engine, J75 engine, JT3D engine, JT4D engine, JT9D engine, JTF16 engine

Princess Flying Boat airliner 6, 10

Rainbow airliner 8

Rawlinson, Peter 165, 187, 188

Royal Air Force (RAF) 10, 12, 14, 19, 26, 29, 34–35, 46–47, 67, 99 *see* RAF Coastal Command, RAF Germany, RAF Transport Command

RAF Coastal Command 4

RAF Germany 70

RAF Transport Command 25, 26

RB162 V/STOL engine 89

RB178 engine 49, 50, 139

RB189 V/STOL engine 104

RB199 engine 127

RB207 engine 139, 142, 146–48

RB211 engine 137, 139, 142–65, 167–68, 200–01, 203, 212

RB211–524 engine 212

RB211–535 engine 201, 203, 205–06, 208–12

Research and Development (R&D) 23, 28–29, 58, 61, 65, 68, 70–72, 74–76, 79, 87, 89, 92, 94, 96, 98–99, 101, 114, 116, 122, 128, 141, 186

Roberts, Sir Frank 121, 124–28, 184

Rolls-Royce xxiii, xxix, xxii, 1, 12–13, 15, 17–20, 30, 32–33, 35, 50, 64, 66, 74, 76, 81, 88–90, 94–101, 119–20, 122, 127, 135, 137–65, 167–68, 186, 192, 196, 200–13, 216–17 *see* Conway engine, Merlin engine, RB162 V/STOL engine, RB178 engine, RB189 V/STOL engine, RB199 engine, RB207 engine, RB211 engine, RB211–524 engine, RB211–535 engine, Spey engine, Trent engine

Rothschild, Lord Nathaniel Mayer Victor 189

Royal Australian Air Force (RAAF) 67–68

Royal Navy xxvi, xxvii, 67, 215

Rusk, Dean 94, 180

Sampson, Anthony xxiv, 86

Sandys, Duncan xxvii, xxxi, 9–10, 24–25, 27, 31–36, 58, 178

Sandys Defence White Paper 23–25, 28–29, 35–36

Index 237

Saudi Arabia 102–03, 105–07
Schmidt, Helmut 203–05, 207
Schröder, Gerhard 125–26
Second World War xxiii, xxiv, xxv, xxvi,
  xxvii, xxix, 1, 3–4, 11, 19, 40–41, 66,
  212
Singapore 60, 129
Skybolt 59, 60
Snecma 66, 76, 88, 95–96, 119–20, 122,
  140, 151, 153, 210
sonic boom 180, 182–83, 188
South Atlantic 77, 215
Spey engine 30, 34, 71, 96, 98–99,
  105–06, 121
Spey-Mirage affair 98–99, 105–06
Stewart, Michael 76, 105, 117, 183
Stonehouse, John 103, 141, 144
Strauss, Franz Joseph 97, 115, 118, 121,
  125, 148, 149
Sud Aviation 139, 146–47, 178, 186 *see*
  Concorde SST airliner (Anglo-French)
Suez Crisis (1956) 23- 24, 27, 36, 66,
  215–16, 218
Super Étendard fighter 215
Super Sonic Transport (SST) 24, 28, 87,
  176, 178–82, 184, 188, 190–91, 195
Super VC10 airliner 33, 45–50
Superb airliner 49

10 Downing Street 9, 156, 177, 181, 191,
  194
Three circles xxix, 3, 23, 65, 70, 80, 129,
  143
Trans World Airlines (TWA) 35, 41, 142,
  145, 159, 162–63, 165, 167
Treasury xxxii, 50, 65, 69, 70, 209
Trend, Sir Burke St John 70, 89, 125,
  154, 188, 192, 217
Trent engine 200, 212
Trident airliner 26, 27, 30, 34
Trippe, Juan 11, 15, 179, 191
TriStar airliner 137–38, 141–42, 144–55,
  157, 159–68, 202
TSR-2 fighter-bomber xxxi, xxxii, 27,
  31–33, 35–36, 57–61, 65–80, 86–87,
  99, 102–03, 107, 115, 123, 129,
  181–82, 216, 218
Tudor airliner 6–9
Turbomeca 88

UK-France relations 87–89, 92–93, 113,
  119–120, 122–23, 139–40, 143,
  177–81, 183–84 *see* AFVG fighter
  (Anglo-French), Concorde SST airliner

(Anglo-French), European Airbus,
  Jaguar fighter Anglo-French), the
  Spey-Mirage affair
UK-France-West Germany Relations
  114–16, 121–22, 128–30, 146–49,
  155–57, 168–69, 185–87, 203, 207,
  see also European Airbus
UK Relations between US and Europe
  xxiii, xxiv-xxxi, 55, 74–76, 94–95, 135,
  137, 200–01, 212–13, 217–18
UK-US relations xxvi-xxiv, 4–5, 9–10,
  13–14, 16, 19–20, 66–68, 71–73,
  89–92 100–03, 105–08, 129, 144–46,
  159–68, 181–82, 184, 202–06 *see* offset
  arrangement (UK-US)
UK-US-West German Relations 94, *see also*
  offset arrangement (US-UK-West
  Germany)
UK-West German Relations 93, 97–98,
  114, 123–28, 140–41, 151–53
  see BAOR, MRCA Tornado fighter
  (Anglo-German), offset arrangement
  (UK-West Germany)
US aid 3, 9, 10, 14, 16, 24, 29, 36, 61, 66
  see Offshore Procurement Program
  (OSP), Plan K
US Air Force (USAF) 13, 15, 60–62, 77,
  118, 139
US-France Relations 181
US Navy 60–62, 77
US-West German Relations 90 *see* offset
  arrangement (US-West Germany)
United Airlines 142, 145
US Department of Transport 145
US Export-Import Bank 50
US Treasury bill 124

V-1000 transport 11–13, 15, 17–18
Valiant bomber 10, 12, 59
Vanguard airliner 13, 30
Variable Geometry (VG) 75, 78, 80,
  87–90, 93, 113–16, 119–23, 128–29,
  216
Varley, Eric 204–05, 207–09, 211
VC7 airliner 13
VC10 airliner xxxi, 13, 29–36, 42–45,
  47–49, 216
VC11 airliner 33
Vickers 13, 28–34, 42–43, 45, 47–48 *see*
  V-1000 transport, Valiant bomber,
  Vanguard airliner, VC7 airliner,
  VC10 airliner, VC11 airliner,
  Viscount airline
Victor bomber 12–13, 17, 59

238 *Index*

Vietnam War xxx, 61, 71–72, 116, 120

Viscount airliner 5, 8–11, 13, 17, 19–20, 29–31, 216

Vulcan bomber 17, 59

V/STOL (vertical or short take off and landing) aircraft 35, 57, 66, 75, 76, 80, 87, 89–90, 93–97, 99–102, 104–05, 107–08, 113, 115–16, 120–21, 126, 128–29, 215

Wilson, Harold xxxi, xxxii, 47–49, 51, 57–58, 68–71, 73–76, 78–80, 86–89, 101, 106–07, 114–21, 123–25, 127–29, 148, 168, 177, 181–84, 187, 191–95, 215–17

War Cabinet (Winston S. Churchill) (1940–1945) xxxi, 5–7, 19

Zuckerman, Solly 65–67, 72, 76, 87, 95, 99, 101, 119, 120, 144 *see* the Zuckeman system

the Zuckeman system 65, 68

Ziegler, Henri 147–48, 152, 153

Zimmermann, H. 114, 116

Printed in the USA
CPSIA information can be obtained
at www.ICGtesting.com
LVHW011143310724
786976LV00003B/345